The Praeger Handbook on Stress and Coping

The Praeger Handbook on Stress and Coping

Volume 1

EDITED BY ALAN MONAT, RICHARD S. LAZARUS, AND GRETCHEN REEVY

Foreword by Yochi Cohen-Charash

Westport, Connecticut
London

Library of Congress Cataloging-in-Publication Data

The Praeger handbook on stress and coping / edited by Alan Monat,
Richard S. Lazarus, and Gretchen Reevy; foreword by Yochi Cohen-
Charash

  p. cm.
 Includes bibliographical references and index.
 ISBN-13: 978-0-275-99197-5 (set : alk. paper)
 ISBN-10: 0-275-99197-0 (set : alk. paper)
 ISBN-13: 978-0-275-99198-2 (v. 1 : alk. paper)
 ISBN-10: 0-275-99198-9 (v. 1 : alk. paper)
 [etc.]
1. Stress (Psychology) 2. Adjustment (Psychology) I. Monat, Alan, 1945-
II. Lazarus, Richard S. III. Reevy, Gretchen. IV. Title: Handbook on stress
and coping.
 BF575.S75P73 2007
 155.9'042—dc22   2006100437

British Library Cataloguing in Publication Data is available.

Library of Congress Catalog Card Number: 2006100437
ISBN-10: 0-275-99197-0 (set)
   0-275-99198-9 (vol. 1)
   0-275-99199-7 (vol. 2)

ISBN-13: 978-0-275-99197-5 (set)
   978-0-275-99198-2 (vol. 1)
   978-0-275-99199-9 (vol. 2)

First published in 2007

Praeger Publishers, 88 Post Road West, Westport, CT 06881
An imprint of Greenwood Publishing Group, Inc.
www.praeger.com

Printed in the United States of America

∞™

The paper used in this book complies with the
Permanent Paper Standard issued by the National
Information Standards Organization (Z39.48-1984).

10 9 8 7 6 5 4 3 2 1

COPYRIGHTS AND ACKNOWLEDGMENTS

The editors would like to thank the following publishers for permission to reprint materials used in this book.

"Introduction" by Alan Monat and Richard S. Lazarus. Adapted and updated from *Stress and Coping: An Anthology* edited by Alan Monat and Richard S. Lazarus. 1991. New York: Columbia University Press.

"The Twentieth Century: From the 1950s to Richard Lazarus" by Cary L. Cooper and Philip Dewe. From *Stress: A Brief History* by Cary L. Cooper and Philip Dewe. © 2004 Blackwell Publishing Ltd., Oxford. Used with permission.

"Stress and Emotion" by Richard S. Lazarus. From *Stress and Emotion: A New Synthesis* by Richard S. Lazarus. © 1999 Springer Publishing Company, Inc., New York. Used with permission.

"Macro-Level Work Stressors" by Lorne Sulsky and Carlla Smith. From *Work Stress*, 1st edition, by Lorne Sulsky and Carlla Smith. © 2005. Reprinted with permission of Wadsworth, a division of Thomson Learning, www.thomsonrights.com.

"The Wisdom of the Receptors: Neuropeptides, the Emotions, and Body-Mind" by Candace B. Pert. From *Advances*, 3(3), 8–16. © 1986. Reprinted with permission of InnerDoorway Health Media, Inc., Boulder, CO. The chapter was adapted by Harris Dienstfrey from a talk delivered at "Survival and Consciousness," a symposium sponsored by the Institute of Noetic Sciences, in Washington, DC, October 26–27, 1985.

"Allostatic Load: When Protection Gives Way to Damage" by Bruce McEwen and Elizabeth Norton Lasley. Reprinted with permission from *The End of Stress as We Know It* by Bruce McEwen and Elizabeth Norton Lasley. © 2002 by the National Academy of Sciences, courtesy of the National Academies Press, Washington, DC.

From "Dr. Dean Ornish's Program for Reversing Heart Disease" by Dean Ornish. Copyright 1990 by Dean Ornish, M.D. Used by permission of Random House, Inc.

Reprinted from *Patient Education and Counseling*, 56(2), LeChauncy D. Woodard, Marie T. Hernandez, Emily Lees, and Laura A. Petersen, "Racial Differences in Attitudes Regarding Cardiovascular Disease Prevention and Treatment: A Qualitative Study," 225–231. Copyright 2005, with permission from Elsevier. The views expressed are solely of the authors and do not represent those of the VA. Dr. Woodward was supported by a grant from the Health Resources and Services Administration (Grant no. 1 T32 PE 10031-01) at the time this research was conducted. Dr. Petersen was an awardee in the Research Career Development Award Program of the VA HSR&D Service (Grant no. RCD 95-306) at the time this research was conducted and is a Robert Wood Johnson Foundation Generalist Physician Faculty Scholar. This project was made possible through the Excellence Centers to Eliminate Ethnic/Racial Disparities (EXCEED) Initiative and was cofunded by the Agency for Healthcare Research and Quality (AHRQ, grant number POI HS10876) and the Office of Research on Minority Health (ORMH). This material is the result of work supported with resources and the use of facilities at the Houston Center for Quality of Care & Utilization Studies, Houston Veterans Affairs Medical Center.

"Stress: Health and Illness" by Fiona Jones and Jim Bright. From *Stress: Myth, Theory and Research* by Fiona Jones and Jim Bright. Pearson Education Limited. Copyright Pearson Education Limited 2001.

Reprinted with the permission of Scribner, an imprint of Simon & Schuster Adult Publishing Group, from *Noonday Demon* by Andrew Solomon. Copyright 2001 by Andrew Solomon.

"Stress, Metabolism and Liquidating Your Assets" from *Why Zebras Don't Get Ulcers*, 3rd ed. by Robert M. Sapolsky. © 1994, 1998 by W. H. Freeman, © 2004 by Robert M. Sapolsky. Reprinted by permission of Henry Holt and Company, LLC.

"Psychological Factors and Immunity in HIV Infection: Stress, Coping, Social Support, and Intervention Outcomes" by Susan Kennedy. From David I. Mostofsky and David H. Barlow, eds., *The Management of Stress and Anxiety in Medical Disorders*. Published by Allyn and Bacon, Boston, MA. Copyright 2000 by Pearson Education. Reprinted by permission of the publisher.

"Epidemiologic Studies of Trauma, Posttraumatic Stress Disorder, and other Psychiatric Disorders" by Naomi Breslau. From *Canadian Journal of Psychiatry, 47*(10), 923–929. © 2002. Used with permission of the publisher. This review was supported by grant MH 48802 from the National Institute of Mental Health, Bethesda, MD.

"Post-traumatic Stress Disorder and Terrorism" by Alyssa Lee, Mohan Isaac, and Aleksandar Janca. From *Current Opinion in Psychiatry, 15*(6), 633–637. © 2002. Used with permission of the publisher.

Reprinted from *The Psychiatric Clinics of North America, 25*(2), Julia Golier and Rachel Yehuda, "Neuropsychological Processes in Post-traumatic Stress Disorder," 295–315. © 2002, with permission from Elsevier.

"Growing Up under the Gun: Children and Adolescents Coping with Violent Neighborhoods" by David F. Duncan. From *The Journal of Primary Prevention, 16*(4), 1996, 343–356. New York. © Human Sciences Press. Reprinted with kind permission from Springer Science and Business Media.

"What Does It Mean to Cope?" by Chris L. Kleinke. Reprinted by permission of Waveland Press, Inc., from Chris L. Kleinke, *Coping with Life Challenges*, 2nd ed., Long Grove, IL: Waveland Press, Inc., 1998 (reissued 2002). All rights reserved.

"Assessing Coping Strategies: A Theoretically Based Approach" by C. S. Carver, M. F. Scheier, and J. K. Weintraub. From *Journal of Personality and Social Psychology, 56*, 267–283. Copyright 1989 by the American Psychological Association. Adapted with permission.

"Cultivating Optimism in Childhood and Adolescence" by Jane Gillham and Karen Reivich, *Annals of the American Academy of Political & Social Science 591*, 146–163. Copyright 2004 by Sage Publications. Reprinted by Permission of Sage Publications, Inc.

Copyright 2002 by the Educational Publishing Foundation (American Psychological Association) and the Society of Consulting Psychology. Adapted with permission. "The Story of Hardiness: Twenty Years of Theorizing, Research, and Practice" by S. R. Maddi. *Consulting Psychology Journal: Practice and Research, 54*, 3, 175–185.

Forty Studies That Changed Psychology: Explorations into the History of Psychological Research, 5th edition, by Roger R. Hock. © 2005. Reprinted by permission of Pearson Education, Inc.,

Upper Saddle River, NJ, pp. 210–217. Chapter by Hock based on "Racing against Your Heart," Friedman and Rosenman (1959): *JAMA* 169: 1286–1296.

Dr. Richard Lazarus, Dr. Christina Maslach, and Dr. Gerald Mendelsohn, of the University of California, Berkeley, made contributions to the early stages of this project. Dr. Manuel Barrera Jr. of Arizona State University and Dr. Alan Monat of California State University, East Bay, read drafts of the manuscript. These data were presented at the annual convention of the Western Psychological Association in 1993.

"Bad to Worse," "Conversations with Cancer," "Chemo," from *It's Not about the Bike* by Lance Armstrong. Copyright 2000 by Lance Armstrong. Used by permission of G. P. Putnam's Sons, a division of Penguin Group (USA) Inc.

"Experiences in Early Stage Alzheimer's Disease: Understanding the Paradox of Acceptance and Denial" by Colleen R. MacQuarrie. From *Aging and Mental Health,* September, 430–440. Copyright 2005. Reprinted by permission of Taylor & Francis Ltd., http:// www.tandf.co.uk/journals. MacQuarrie expresses her thanks to the Alzheimer's disease participants and their families for their time and candor in making this research possible. The study, funded by a fellowship from the Alzheimer Society of British Columbia, was conducted by MacQuarrie as part of her dissertation research at Simon Fraser University, British Columbia. The University of British Columbia's Clinic for Alzheimer's Disease and Related Disorders was critical as a source for participants and support for the research.

"Coping with Test Situations: Resources, Strategies, and Adaptational Outcomes" by Moshe Zeidner. From *Test Anxiety: The State of the Art* by Moshe Zeidner, pp. 310–321; 326–331. © 1998 Plenum Press, New York, reprinted with kind permission from Springer Science and Business Media.

"*The Black Scholar* Interviews Maya Angelou," by Robert Chrisman (Vol. 8, #4, January–February, 1977, pp. 44–53). Reprinted by permission of *The Black Scholar.*

"What Do We Really Know about Mindfulness-based Stress Reduction?" by Scott R. Bishop. From *Psychosomatic Medicine, 64,* 71–83. Copyright 2002. Used with permission of the publisher.

Copyright © 1998 by the American Psychological Association. Reprinted with permission. Field, T. (1998). Massage therapy effects. *American Psychologist, 53*(12), 1270–1281. This research was supported by a National Institute of Mental Health (NIMH) Research Scientist Award (MH00331), NIMH Research Grant MH46586, and funding from Johnson and Johnson. Field wishes to thank the parents, infants, and children who participated in these studies and the colleagues who collaborated on the research. Melissa G. Warren served as action editor for this chapter.

"Yoga for Stress Reduction and Injury Prevention at Work" by Shira Taylor Gura. From *Work, 19,* 3–7. © 2002 by IOS Press. Reprinted by permission of the publisher.

"Psychotherapy: A Cognitive Perspective" by George S. Everly Jr. and Jeffrey M. Lating. From *A Clinical Guide to the Treatment of the Human Stress Response,* 163–174. © 2002 Kluwer Academic/Plenum Publishers. Reprinted with kind permission from Springer Science and Business Media.

"Stress and Diet." From *Food and Mood: The Complete Guide to Eating Well and Feeling Your Best* by Elizabeth Somer. © 1999 by Elizabeth Somer. Reprinted by permission of Henry Holt and Company, LLC.

"Exercise Treatment for Major Depression: Maintenance of Therapeutic Benefit at 10 Months" by Michael Babyak, James A. Blumenthal, Steve Herman, Parinda Khatri, Murali Doraiswamy, Kathleen Moore, Edward Craighead, Teri Baldewicz, and K. Ranga Krishnan. From *Psychosomatic Medicine, 62,* 633–638. © 2000. Reprinted with permission of the publisher. The study described was supported by Grants MH 49679, HL43028, HL49572, and MO 1-RR-30 from the National Institutes of Health. Babyak and his colleagues thank Julie Opitek, Ph.D., Karen Mallow, M.A., and Denise DeBruycker, B.A., for their assistance in exercise testing and training, and Drs. Robert Waugh and Mohan Chilukuri for performing the medical screening examination on study participants. Pfizer Pharmaceuticals provided the medications for this study.

"Attitudes and Beliefs about 12-step Groups among Addiction Treatment Clients and Clinicians: Identifying Obstacles to Participation" by Alexandre B. Laudet. *Substance Use and Misuse*, *38*(14). Copyright 2003. Reproduced by permission of Taylor & Francis Group, LLC, http://www.taylorandfrances.com. Laudet's work was supported by National Institute on Drug Abuse Grant R03 DA13432.

To Richard S. Lazarus (1922–2002)

Contents

Illustrations

FIGURES

TABLES

BOXES

Abbreviations

AA	Alcoholics Anonymous
ABC	*Activating events, beliefs, emotional consequences* (model) (Albert Ellis)
ACTH	Adreno-corticotropic hormone
AD	Alzheimer's disease
ADHD	Attention deficit hyperactivity disorder
AIDS	Acquired Immune Deficiency Syndrome
ANS	Autonomic nervous system
AVLT	Auditory-Verbal Learning Test
BDI	Beck Depression Inventory
CBT	Cognitive-behavioral therapy
CHD	Coronary heart disease
CNS	Central nervous system
COPE	Coping Orientations to Problems Experienced (scale)
CPT	Continuous Performance Test
CRF	Corticotropin-releasing factor
CRP	C-reactive protein
CVD	Cardiovascular disease
CVLT	California Verbal Learning Test
dB	Decibels
DIS	Diagnostic Interview Schedule
DNA	Deoxyribonucleic acid

DSM	*Diagnostic and Statistical Manual of Mental Disorders* (American Psychiatric Association)
EDRF	Endothelium-derived relaxation factor
EEG	Electroencephalogram
EMG	Electromyography
ENMG	Electroneuromyography
FSIQ	Full-scale intelligence quotient
GAS	General Adaptation Syndrome
GHQ	General Health Questionnaire
HIV	Human immunodeficiency virus
HPA	Hypothalamic-pituitary-adrenal (axis)
H-reflex	Hoffman reflex
HRSD	Hamilton Rating Scale for Depression
IDDM	Insulin-dependent diabetes mellitus
IQ	Intelligence quotient
ISSB	Inventory of Socially Supportive Behaviors
JAS	Jenkins Activity Survey
LEDS	Life Events and Difficulties Schedule
LES	Life Experiences Survey
MBSR	Mindfulness-based stress reduction
MDD	Major depressive disorder
MMSE	Mini-mental state exam
MRI	Magnetic resonance imaging
MSD	Musculoskeletal disorder
NA	Narcotics Anonymous
NDRI	National Development and Research Institutes
NIDA	National Institute on Drug Abuse
NIMH-DIS	National Institute of Mental Health—Diagnostic Interview Schedule
NIOSH	National Institute for Occupational Safety and Health
NK	Natural killer (cells)
NPY	Neuropeptide-Y
OR	Odds ratio
OSHA	Occupational Safety and Health Administration
PET	Positron Emission Tomography
PNS	Peripheral nervous system
POW	Prisoner of war
PRP	Penn Resiliency Program

PSS-Fa	Perceived Social Support from Family (scale)
PSS-Fr	Perceived Social Support from Friends (scale)
PTSD	Posttraumatic stress disorder
RET	Rational Emotive Therapy
SBS	Sick building syndrome
SD	Standard deviation
SHAM TENS	Transcutaneous electrical nerve stimulation without current
SI	Structured interview
SIT	Stress inoculation training
SMILE	Standard Medical Intervention and Long-term Exercise (study)
S-O-R	Stimulus-organism-response (model)
SOS	Secular Organization for Sobriety
S-R	Stimulus-response (model)
SRRS	Social Readjustment Rating Scale
SRT	Selective Reminding Test
TABP	Type A behavior pattern
TENS	Transcutaneous electrical nerve stimulation
TFA	Trans fatty acid
12SG	12-step groups
UCB	University of California, Berkeley
USDA	U.S. Department of Agriculture
VAS	Visual analog scale
WAIS-R	Wechsler Adult Intelligence Scale–Revised
WFS	Women for Sobriety
WHO-CIDI	World Health Organization—Composite International Diagnostic Interview
WMS	Wechsler Memory Scale

Foreword

A brief Google search conducted in early January 2007, for the term "stress" yielded 196 million entries. While this number might be inflated, it still serves as an excellent reminder of the prevalence and importance of stress in our daily lives. As such, the publication of *The Praeger Handbook on Stress and Coping* is as timely as can be. The timeliness and importance of the handbook is further enhanced by the caliber of its authors. One of the leaders of contemporary stress research, the eminent Richard S. Lazarus, collaborated in his last years with co-editors Alan Monat and Gretchen Reevy in compiling this exemplary collection, which is comprised of both academic and nonacademic contributions. The chapters in the handbook deal with various aspects of stress and coping in diverse contexts and are applicable and suitable for a wide audience.

The first part of the handbook deals with the construct of stress and with its psychological and physiological aspects. As such, it provides a basis for the parts to come. The second part of the handbook deals with stress and illness. Here, chapters deal with heart and cardiovascular diseases, depression, ulcers, HIV, and other illnesses. The third part deals with post-traumatic stress as it pertains to war, terror, and violence.

Once stress has been defined and dealt with in particular contexts, the fourth and fifth parts of the handbook turn to coping with stress. The chapters in these sections examine coping and management of stress from both theoretical and applied perspectives. The articles focus on concepts such as optimism, hardiness, and social support, as well as significant and popular coping strategies such as psychotherapy, diet, and yoga. Featured personal accounts of coping include comments by Lance Armstrong and Maya Angelou.

Overall, these two outstanding volumes create a coherent picture and provide valuable and timely knowledge. Without question, there is much here to provide a solid foundation for further study and critical analysis of the issues and controversies in the ever-expanding field of stress and coping.

Yochi Cohen-Charash, Ph.D.
Department of Psychology, Baruch College

Preface

This project is the result of teamwork, and we are grateful for the efforts of all involved. We begin our thanks by acknowledging the contributions of our coeditor, Richard S. Lazarus. In the early stages of the project, Richard Lazarus passed away suddenly and unexpectedly. We have attempted to produce a work that he would be proud of and hope that we have succeeded in our goal. He is deeply missed by many, both professionally and personally. We dedicate this book to him. We also wish to thank Bernice ("Bunny") Lazarus, beloved wife and longtime companion of Richard, for her support and encouragement throughout this project.

We would also like to thank our families and friends for their support. Alan Monat would like to thank Murline and Ian Monat, Harold and Tillie Monat, and Ron, Helene, Jeff and Nicole Monat. In addition, Alan Monat would like to thank his many other relatives, friends, and colleagues for their encouragement throughout the years. Gretchen M. Reevy would like to thank her husband, Todd Manning, parents and siblings, Carole, Bill, Carolyn and Tony, dear friend Kate Harrah, and all other family, friends, and colleagues.

The editorial staff at Praeger was patient and flexible with us. The responses to our many queries were prompt and professional. Thank you Debbie Carvalko, Megan Chalek, and Annie Rehill. We thank the outstanding contributing authors of the chapters in our book. Additionally, we express our appreciation to the library staff at California State University, East Bay, who efficiently and cheerfully granted our hundreds of requests for interlibrary loans. Also, we thank Dr. David Sandberg in the Psychology Department at California State University, East Bay, who supplied references about posttraumatic stress disorder, and Dr. Julia Norton in the statistics department, who commented on some material.

A number of California State University, East Bay, students were involved in this project. Several read through many of the chapters included in these volumes and provided feedback about their educational value and readability. These students were Kerry Becklund, Luba Belova, Cynthia Boykin, Matthew Dailey, Dyese Hunt, Kelly Lencioni, Meghan Meier, and Joel Romero. As we were preparing the manuscript, Chad Kempel helped us to type and verify some references. Diane Williams provided much appreciated encouragement and insight throughout a good portion of the project.

Among those who worked on the project, we are most indebted to California State University, East Bay, graduate student Yvette Malamud Ozer, who toiled for countless hours. She scanned, typed, formatted, checked references, and conducted library research. She provided feedback on writing and is responsible for writing half or more of our glossary terms. Yvette is an outstanding editor and writer and is a pleasure to work with. We are deeply indebted to her.

Introduction

Today, women and men lead complicated lives. We hold multiple roles and face daily pressures in many of them—as parent, as child, as worker, as spouse or partner, as friend. We worry about money and about our health. We struggle to keep up with technology. We create so many goals that it is impossible to meet them all, then may feel inadequate due to our self-defined failures. Given all of these demands, it is not surprising that so many are interested in the field of "stress." At universities, students crowd the waiting lists for courses on the topic. Businesses and all branches of government offer, or even require, stress management courses for employees. Patients suffering from a wide variety of illnesses may enroll in classes through their health insurance companies. Numerous magazine and newspaper articles, books, television shows, websites, and professional journals are devoted to the stress field and related topics.

This anthology presents studies, reviews of research, theoretical chapters, and firsthand accounts to provide the reader with a basic and solid introduction to the history of, and current thought in, the stress and coping field. A summary and discussion of each of the chapters included in this book appear in the introduction to each part.

THE STRESS CONCEPT

Stress is a complex concept. Three general types or levels of stress are usually identified: systemic or physiological, psychological, and sociocultural. *Physiological stress* is the body's potentially harmful reaction to events (as described, for example, by Cannon, 1953, and Selye, 1976). *Psychological stress* is primarily concerned with cognitive and emotional factors that may lead to the appraisal of threat (e.g., Lazarus, 1966), and *sociocultural stress* focuses on disturbance of social systems or social units (e.g., Smelser, 1963). These types of stress are related and may interact.

Historically, the term *stress* has been used in a somewhat ambiguous fashion, and leading researchers in the field are in disagreement as to its precise meaning. "Stress" is sometimes used to refer to the physiological response brought on by an external event (a "stressor"). One of the problems with this definition is that the same or highly similar pattern of responses (increased heart rate, release of stress hormones, mobilization of energy stores, etc.) is caused by very different stimuli, such as nearly being in a car accident, experiencing an argument, or engaging in heavy exercise. One reason this is problematic is because most of us do not think of heavy exercise and a near car accident as stressors in the same sense—they are different types of stressors, or perhaps we may not think of heavy exercise as a stressor at all.

The term *stress* may also be used to refer to the stimulus that produces the response pattern. Again, this definition is incomplete because different individuals interpret situations very differently; one person's source of stress may be another person's source of enjoyment and a third person's source of indifference.

Because of these and other issues, some have proposed an abolition of the term *stress* (e.g., Mason, 1975; Pollock, 1988). Some have suggested using different terms for the stimulus and the response (e.g., McEwen & Lasley, 2002, who suggest using *stress* to refer to "outside events" [stressors] and *allostasis* to refer to a new concept closely related to the stress response concept), while others have argued that use of the term should refer to the whole interactive process of stressors and responses (e.g., Cooper & Dewe, 2004; Lazarus, 1966). Lazarus stated:

> It seems wise to use "stress" as a generic term for the whole area of problems that includes the stimuli producing stress reactions, the reactions themselves, and the various intervening processes. Thus, we can speak of the field of stress, and mean the physiological, sociological, and psychological phenomena and their respective concepts. It could then include research and theory on group or individual disaster, physiological assault on tissues and the effects of this assault, disturbances or facilitation of adaptive functioning produced by conditions of deprivation, thwarting or the prospects of this, and the field of negatively toned emotions such as fear, anger, depression, despair, hopelessness, and guilt. Stress is not any one of these things; nor is it a stimulus, response, or intervening variable, but rather a collective term for an area of study. (1966, p. 27)

Stress researchers, whether they have defined *stress* as stimulus (stressor), as response, or as the broad phenomena to which Lazarus refers, have pursued a fruitful area of study (Cooper & Dewe, 2004). Stress researchers have contributed much to our understanding about the role that stress plays in the cause of disease and psychological discomfort.

THE COPING CONCEPT

Lazarus defined *coping* as "constantly changing cognitive and behavioral efforts to manage specific external and/or internal demands that are appraised as taxing or exceeding the resources of the person" (1998,

p. 201). Several aspects of this definition are noteworthy. First, coping, as Lazarus viewed it, is a process that changes over time and is reactive to the stressful situation. Second, coping does not imply either success or healthy behavior. The process of coping can (and often does) include responses that may have little effect on the stressor itself, responses that may "backfire" (make the stressful situation worse), and responses that may negatively impact one's health or well-being. Some examples of responses that may operate in one or more of these ways include use of drugs, avoidance, and confrontation with a person. Third, coping consists of both behaviors and thoughts. Thus, like stress, coping is a complex concept.

Numerous efforts have been made to categorize or classify coping responses (e.g., Carver, Scheier, & Weintraub, 1989; Cohen, 1987; Cramer, 1998; Folkman & Lazarus, 1980; Haan, 1969, 1977; Lazarus, 1966, 1975; Menninger, 1963). For example, Folkman and Lazarus (1980) have divided coping techniques into two categories: problem-focused and emotion-focused. *Problem-focused coping* approaches are attempts to change the stressful situation itself, for example, by making a plan, by seeking information about how to approach the stressor, or by talking directly to a person with whom one has a problem. *Emotion-focused coping* involves efforts to manage the emotional impact of a stressful situation. Examples include avoidance, using drugs or alcohol, using relaxation techniques such as meditation, or "venting" about the problem with other people.

Another example of an attempt to classify coping responses is Carver et al.'s (1989) COPE questionnaire. It consists of 15 coping styles, which are described in Volume 2 of our book. Some examples include active coping, restraint coping, mental disengagement, acceptance, and turning to religion. Carver et al. argue that measuring a variety of responses, rather than utilizing Folkman and Lazarus's (1980) two-category system (problem- and emotion-focused), is more elucidating and has the potential to produce more applicable results. Supporting part of their claim, research indicates that, in a given stressful situation, people tend to employ a variety of both problem-focused and emotion-focused coping responses (Tennen, Affleck, Armeli, & Carney, 2000).

Coping as a Personality Trait and Coping as Process

Coping can be viewed in terms of personality traits—as "coping styles"—or as a process that occurs in a particular situation, or as both. In studies that focus on coping as a personality trait, researchers generally ask participants about the types of coping responses that they "typically" or "usually" utilize. Consideration of context of stressful situations is generally not the focus in this research. Using this approach or similar approaches, some researchers have found associations between personality traits and coping responses. For example, in a review of research, Hewitt and Flett (1996) concluded that the personality variable neuroticism, which is characterized by negative emotions such as anxiety, depression, and hostility, is generally related to maladaptive coping, including using more destructive strategies and possibly fewer adaptive strategies.

Additionally, Hewitt and Flett's review indicated that the personality variable extroversion tends to be related to more adaptive strategies, including use of restraint and increased rational thinking. In early research on coping, when the personality trait view was dominant, Byrne (1964) identified repression-sensitization as a personality trait associated with coping. Repressors tend to cope with life by avoiding negative emotions, whereas sensitizers cope through attempting to control stressors (for example, by ruminating or by obsessive-compulsive behaviors). Other researchers have identified associations between coping and personality traits (e.g., Goldstein, 1973; Miller, 1980).

An alternative but not necessarily incompatible view is to conceptualize coping as a process and as partly or perhaps largely situation dependent. In studies of this type, researchers make some observation or conduct other monitoring (e.g., asking for self-reports from the participant) of an individual's behaviors as those behaviors occur during a stressful event. The researchers then make inferences about the coping responses that are suggested by the observed behaviors. Folkman and Lazarus (1980, 1985, 1988) conducted early work based on this general model, although they did not study situations *in vivo* but rather asked participants to recall stressful situations and then to report information about their thoughts, emotions, and behaviors in these situations. Since this early work (or contemporaneous with it), other researchers (e.g., Collins, Baum, & Singer, 1983; David & Suls, 1999; Porter & Stone, 1995; Stone & Neale, 1984; Tennen et al., 2000) have studied the process of coping, either retrospectively as Folkman and Lazarus did, or *in vivo*.

Coping Outcomes

A question that sometimes arises regarding coping is whether some coping responses are more healthy or effective than others. In general, as is implied by the discussion regarding coping as a process, it is not accurate to speak of the effectiveness of a coping response devoid of its context. For example, Preece and DeLongis (2005) found that parents should engage in different types of coping responses and problem-solving techniques, depending on whether they are dealing with a child or a stepchild. As a short-term solution to deal with misbehavior of a child and general tension between parent and child, parents are more effective if they engage in compromise with children and withdrawal with stepchildren. A coping mechanism that has traditionally been viewed as maladaptive is denial. Results of some research (e.g., Katz, Weiner, Gallagher, & Hellman, 1970) have indicated that denial can be dangerous, but results of other studies (e.g., Visotsky, Hamburg, Goss, & Lebovits, 1961) have revealed beneficial consequences of denial. Again, context is important. If denial prevents proactive behaviors that could benefit the individual, such as seeking information about cancer in the event of a diagnosis, the results will likely be detrimental. If, on the other hand, denial serves to prevent anxiety in cases where little or no direct action can be taken, denial may serve a useful purpose.

Summary

Coping is an individual's attempt to master threats or life demands and does not necessarily imply a positive outcome. Attempts to categorize types of coping have not yet produced systems about which coping researchers are in agreement, although Folkman and Lazarus's (1980) and Carver et al.'s (1989) models are widely utilized in research. Coping responses can be viewed as dispositional—as coping traits or styles—or as more changeable and reactive to situational demands (the process view of coping). Of late, the focus in coping research has been on process, in which investigators measure coping behaviors as they unfold during a stressful situation. A few years ago, the coping field suffered serious criticism. Coyne and Racioppo (2000) and Somerfield and McCrae (2000) found fault with most coping research to date, arguing that little had been learned that can be applied by those practicing clinical interventions such as psychotherapy and behavioral medicine. Lazarus (2000) characterized this claim as unfair; he responded that the field has gradually discovered the type of research methodology (for example, methodology that involves studying coping as a process) that is necessary to produce applicable findings.

STRESS, COPING, AND ILLNESS

A primary reason for interest in the stress and coping field is because of the view that stress and coping have an impact on both physical and psychological illness. Chapter 8 in our book, by Jones and Bright (2001), reviews much of this research. We would like to point out some issues here that are not covered, or are covered only briefly, in Jones and Bright's chapter.

According to Holroyd and Lazarus (1982), there are three main ways in which stress or coping might lead to illness or dysfunction. First, the stress response itself can directly cause damage to body tissues. The physical stress response is dramatic, causing increased heart rate, increased blood pressure, a flood of very powerful stress hormones, and other responses. Many, perhaps all, of the symptoms of the stress response may cause damage; for example, the stress hormone adrenaline can increase heart rate and blood pressure to dangerous levels. Second, some coping responses are directly damaging to health, especially if used excessively, for example, use of drugs or alcohol, impulsive behavior, overwork, or insufficient rest. Third, some coping responses are indirectly damaging to health—they put one's health at risk—by causing an individual to downplay symptoms or fail to adhere to health care regimens. These coping responses are attitudes that may be individualized (personality traits) or cultural or social values. One such value is a "be tough" attitude in which an individual or a group holds a belief that one should seek medical care only in the event of an extreme emergency. Otherwise, one should be "tough," suffering through pain and discomfort. Another coping response that fits in this category is denial.

The interest in stress and coping and its relationship to illness has led to the development of several professional fields, especially health psychology and psychoneuroimmunology. *Health psychology* is "the branch of psychology that concerns individual behaviors and lifestyles affecting a person's health" (Brannon & Feist, 2004, p. 14). Topics in health psychology textbooks include seeking health care and complying to regimens; stress and disease; pain; behavioral factors in cardiovascular disease and cancer; using tobacco, alcohol, and other drugs; eating to control weight; and exercising.

Psychoneuroimmunology is a professional field concerned with the relationship between psychological factors (such as stress, emotions, and personality) and the immune system. A groundbreaking study in psychoneuroimmunology was published in 1975. Robert Ader and Nicholas Cohen described research on classical conditioning and the immune system in which they showed that behavior, the nervous system, and the immune system can interact. Since then, numerous studies have demonstrated relationships between immune suppression and stress, including school exams (Kiecolt-Glaser, Malarkey, Cacioppo, & Glaser, 1994), relationship conflict (e.g., Miller, Dopp, Myers, Stevens, & Fahey, 1999), and caregiver stress (e.g., Kiecolt-Glaser, 1999). The psychoneuroimmunology concept has been a revolutionary one. A few chapters in our book briefly discuss psychoneuroimmunology.

STRESS MANAGEMENT

Stress management is an attempt to reduce or sometimes help prevent the deleterious effects of stress by practicing a particular technique or collection of techniques. Three general categories of techniques have been identified (Monat & Lazarus, 1991): (1) modification of one's environment and/or lifestyle; (2) modification of personality and/or perception; and (3) modification of the physiological responses to stress. Refer to Table I.1 for some examples representing each of these categories.

Table I.1. Examples of Stress Management Techniques

Environment/Lifestyle	Personality/Perceptions	Physiological Responses
Communication skills	Anger management	Biofeedback
Exercise	Disputing irrational beliefs	Deep breathing
Money management	Personality hardiness	Massage
Proper diet	Spirituality	Meditation
Quitting smoking, alcohol	Utilizing sense of humor	Progressive relaxation

Many stress and coping or stress management textbooks provide discussions of these and other techniques. Examples include Girdano, Dusek, & Everly (2005), Olpin & Hesson (2007), and Seaward (2005).

It is necessary to make some comments about the field of stress management. First, some techniques, such as meditation, some dietary factors, some forms of exercise, and biofeedback, have received considerable empirical investigation into their effectiveness, whereas others have been studied very little. Second, at this point, researchers have not done much to investigate how particular techniques may relate to individual differences in people. Thus, we cannot recommend a particular technique or techniques based upon characteristics of the individual (i.e., personality, cultural background, sex, etc.). Third, utilizing stress management has the potential to cause harm. For example, moderate to high levels of physical activity can be harmful to people with certain medical conditions. Also, research has demonstrated that use of meditation occasionally has its dangers (see for example, Carrington, 1993).

A SAMPLING OF OTHER NEW DEVELOPMENTS IN THE STRESS AND COPING FIELD

The stress and coping field is constantly changing and includes a number of developments from the past several years that we have not yet discussed. One example is the study of the relationship among genes, stress, and behavior. With the mapping of the human genome, a research project that has now spanned a couple of decades, interest in genetic determinants of behavior has been revitalized in most major subfields in psychology, biology, and a number of other disciplines. In the stress and coping field, researchers have been exploring potential genetic differences in response to stressors. For an introduction to this topic, see, for example, Lovallo, 2005.

A second example of an exciting development is the intersection between positive psychology and stress and coping. Positive psychology is a movement in psychology in which the focus is on mental health and the "best" aspects of human nature (for example, creativity, generosity and benevolence, and well-being). Brief discussions of positive psychology appear in Part IV of our book ("The Coping Concept") and in the chapter by Everly and Lating (2002) in Part VI.

A third example is the growing knowledge about posttraumatic stress disorder (PTSD). PTSD is now viewed by many as a very special form of the stress reaction. In the past, it was generally viewed as an extreme, but not qualitatively different, version of the stress response. Now, some research has explored both biological and cognitive factors that make one vulnerable to PTSD. One day we may be able to better predict which individuals are at greater risk for this condition that causes so much suffering. Additionally, much has been learned about potential differences in brain activity and brain anatomy that occur with PTSD patients. Part III of our book is devoted to a discussion of PTSD.

ORGANIZATION OF OUR BOOK

In this book, we have collected chapters that discuss the history of the stress and coping field and that capture many of the current issues in the field. The chapters are arranged into six parts: The Stress Concept, Stress and Illness, Posttraumatic Stress, The Coping Concept, Examples of Coping, and Stress Management. Our goal has been to provide a broad, informative, intellectually challenging, and hopefully enjoyable, introduction to the field.

REFERENCES

Ader, R., & Cohen, N. (1975). Behaviorally conditioned immunosuppression. *Psychosomatic Medicine, 37,* 333–340.

Brannon, L., & Feist, J. (2004). *Health psychology: An introduction to behavior and health.* Belmont, CA: Wadsworth/Thomson Learning.

Byrne, D. (1964). Repression-sensitization as a dimension of personality. In B. A. Maher (Ed.), *Progress in experimental personality research,* (Vol. 1, pp. 169–220). New York: Academic Press.

Cannon, W. B. (1953). *Bodily changes in pain, hunger, fear, and rage.* Boston: C. T. Branford.

Carrington, P. (1993). Modern forms of meditation. In P. M. Lehrer & R. L. Woolfolk (Eds.), *Principles and practice of stress management* (pp. 139–168). New York: Guilford Press.

Carver, C. S., Scheier, M. F., & Weintraub, J. K. (1989). Assessing coping strategies: A theoretically based approach. *Journal of Personality and Social Psychology, 56*(2), 267–283.

Cohen, F. (1987). Measurement of coping. In S. V. Casl & C. L. Cooper (Eds.), *Stress and health: Issues in research methodology* (pp. 238–305). Chichester, England: John Wiley & Sons.

Collins, D. L., Baum, A., & Singer, J. E. (1983). Coping with chronic stress at Three Mile Island: Psychological and biochemical evidence. *Health Psychology, 2,* 149–166.

Cooper, C. L., & Dewe, P. (2004). *Stress: A brief history.* Malden, MA: Blackwell.

Coyne, J. C., & Racioppo, M. W. (2000). Never the twain shall meet? Closing the gap between coping research and clinical intervention research. *American Psychologist, 55*(6), 655–664.

Cramer, P. (1998). Coping and defense mechanisms: What's the difference? *Journal of Personality, 66,* 919–946.

David, J., & Suls, J. (1999). Coping efforts in daily life: Role of Big Five traits and problem appraisals. *Journal of Personality, 67,* 265–294.

Everly, G. S., & Lating, J. M. (2002). *A clinical guide to the treatment of the human stress response.* New York: Kluwer Academic/Plenum.

Folkman, S., & Lazarus, R. S. (1980). An analysis of coping in a middle-aged community sample. *Journal of Health and Social Behavior, 21,* 219–239.

Folkman, S., & Lazarus, R. S. (1985). If it changes it must be a process: Study of emotion and coping during three stages of a college examination. *Journal of Personality and Social Psychology, 48,* 150–170.

Folkman, S., & Lazarus, R. S. (1988). Coping as a mediator of emotion. *Journal of Personality and Social Psychology, 54,* 466–475.

Girdano, D. A., Dusek, D. E., & Everly, G. S. (2005). *Controlling stress and tension.* San Francisco: Pearson/Benjamin Cummings.

Goldstein, M. J. (1973). Individual differences in response to stress. *American Journal of Community Psychology, 1,* 113–137.

Haan, N. (1969). A tripartite model of ego functioning values and clinical and research applications. *Journal of Nervous and Mental Disease, 148,* 14–30.

Haan, N. (1977). Coping and defending: Processes of self-environment organization. New York: Academic Press.

Hewitt, P. L., & Flett, G. L. (1996). Personality traits and the coping process. In M. Zeidner & N. S. Endler (Eds.), *Handbook of coping* (pp. 410–433). New York: John Wiley & Sons.

Holroyd, K. A., & Lazarus, R. S. (1982). Stress, coping, and somatic adaptation. In L. Goldberger & S. Breznitz (Eds.), *Handbook of stress: Theoretical and clinical aspects* (pp. 21–35). New York: Free Press.

Jones, F., & Bright, J. (2001). *Stress: Myth, theory and research*. San Francisco: Pearson/Prentice Hall.

Katz, J. L., Weiner, H., Gallagher, T. G., & Hellman, L. (1970). Stress, distress, and ego defenses: Psychoendocrine response to impending breast tumor biopsy. *Archives of General Psychiatry, 23,* 131–142.

Kiecolt-Glaser, J. K. (1999). Stress, personal relationships, and immune function: Health implications. *Brain, Behavior, and Immunity, 13,* 61–72.

Kiecolt-Glaser, J. K., Malarkey, W. B., Cacioppo, J. T., & Glaser, R. (1994). Stressful personal relationships: Immune and endocrine functions. In R. Glaser and J. K. Kiecolt-Glaser (Eds.), *Handbook of human stress and immunity* (pp. 321–339). San Diego: Academic Press.

Lazarus, R. S. (1966). *Psychological stress and the coping process*. New York: McGraw-Hill.

Lazarus, R. S. (1975). The self-regulation of emotion. In L. Levi (Ed.), *Emotions— Their parameters and measurement* (pp. 47–67). New York: Raven Press.

Lazarus, R. S. (1998). *The life and work of an eminent psychologist: Autobiography of Richard S. Lazarus*. New York: Springer.

Lazarus, R. S. (2000). Toward better research on stress and coping. *American Psychologist, 55*(6), 665–673.

Lovallo, W. R. (2005). *Stress and health: Biological and psychological interactions*. Thousand Oaks, CA: Sage.

Mason, J. W. (1975). A historical view of the stress field. *Journal of Human Stress, 1,* 6–12.

McEwen, B. S., & Lasley, E. N. (2002). *The end of stress as we know it*. Washington, DC: Joseph Henry Press.

Menninger, K. A. (1963). *The vital balance: The life process in mental health and illness*. New York: Viking.

Miller, G. E., Dopp, J. M., Myers, H. F., Stevens, S. Y., & Fahey, J. L. (1999). Psychosocial predictors of natural killer cell mobilization during marital conflict. *Health Psychology, 18,* 262–271.

Miller, S. M. (1980). When is a little information a dangerous thing? Coping with stressful events by monitoring vs. blunting. In S. Levine & H. Ursin (Eds.), *Coping and health*. New York: Plenum.

Monat, A., & Lazarus, R. S. (1991). *Stress and coping: An anthology*. New York: Columbia University Press.

Olpin, M., & Hesson, M. (2007). *Stress management for life*. Belmont, CA: Thomson Brooks/Cole.

Pollock, K. (1988). On the nature of social stress: Production of a modern mythology. *Social Science & Medicine, 26,* 381–392.

Porter, L., & Stone, A. A. (1995). Are there really gender differences in coping? A reconsideration of previous data and results from a daily study. *Journal of Social and Clinical Psychology, 14,* 184–202.

Preece, M., & DeLongis, A. (2005). A contextual examination of stress and coping processes in stepfamilies. In T. A. Revenson, K. Kayser, & G. Bodenmann

(Eds.), *Couples coping with stress: Emerging perspectives on dyadic coping* (pp. 51–69). Washington, DC: American Psychological Association.

Seaward, B. L. (2005). Managing stress: Principles and strategies for health and well-being. Boston: Jones and Bartlett.

Selye, H. (1976). *The stress of life.* New York: McGraw-Hill.

Smelser, N. J. (1963). *Theory of collective behavior.* New York: Free Press.

Somerfield, M. R., & McCrae, R. R. (2000). Stress and coping research: Methodological challenges, theoretical advances, and clinical applications. *American Psychologist, 55*(6), 620–625.

Stone, A. A., & Neale, J. M. (1984). New measure of daily coping: Development and preliminary results. *Journal of Personality and Social Psychology, 46,* 892–906.

Tennen, H., Affleck, G., Armeli, S., & Carney, M. A. (2000). A daily process approach to coping: Linking theory, research, and practice. *American Psychologist, 55,* 626–636.

Visotsky, H. M., Hamburg, D. A., Goss, M. E., & Lebovits, B. Z. (1961). Coping behavior under extreme stress: Observations of patients with severe poliomyelitis. *Archives of General Psychiatry, 5,* 423–448.

Part I

The Stress Concept

Introduction to
"The Stress Concept"

This first part of our book introduces the stress concept. The chapters primarily focus on the history of the stress concept, stressors (causes of stress), and general reactions to stress. We selected writings that discuss stress from different levels of analysis: sociological, psychological, and physiological. The first three chapters look at stress at the psychological and/or sociological level, and the other two emphasize physiological aspects of stress; the last of these discusses some of the damage the stress response causes to the body and is an appropriate transition to the second part of the book, "Stress and Illness."

Chapter 1, from Cooper and Dewe's *Stress: A Brief History* (2004), covers the history of the stress concept from the 1950s to the 1970s, focusing on stress from a psychological perspective. The authors discuss Holmes and Rahe's work on "major life events stress," their development of the Social Readjustment Rating Scale, and the evidence they and their collaborators produced that major life events stress is correlated with vulnerability to illness. Following this discussion is comprehensive coverage of Dohrenwend and Dohrenwend's and Lazarus's criticisms of the major life events stress concept and an introduction to the "minor hassles" or "daily hassles" stress concept associated with Lazarus and his colleagues. Lazarus emphasized that consideration of an individual's cognitive appraisal (perception) of stress is imperative in order to understand the impact of the stress. Cooper and Dewe next describe how, partly due to the appraisal concept, stress researchers developed an interest in the study of individual differences in vulnerability to stress. Several of the individual difference variables to which Cooper and Dewe refer (e.g., Type A Behavior Pattern and hardiness) are discussed at length in Volume 2, Part IV, of our book. The chapter ends with a brief consideration of the history of research on work-related stress in Sweden and the origins of organizational psychology in Sweden, Great Britain, and the United States.

In the second chapter, an excerpt from his book *Stress and Emotion: A New Synthesis*, Lazarus (1999) presents a history of the stress concept that dates back farther than Cooper and Dewe's discussion. As he notes, interest in stress in the United States primarily originated with the extreme stress reactions observed in combat veterans in World Wars I and II. This stress reaction—posttraumatic stress—is discussed comprehensively in Part III of our book. As indicated by the title of his book, Lazarus also makes an argument that the study of stress necessitates a study of emotion for a variety of reasons, including that the presence of one means the presence of the other. Researchers can make use of the broader concept, emotion, to more fully understand stress. This metatheoretical idea of his has survived and developed further since Lazarus's death (e.g., Gross, Richards, & John, 2006).

In the remainder of the chapter, Lazarus, who primarily viewed and researched stress from a psychological perspective, discusses stress from two alternative perspectives: sociocultural and physiological. Societal (e.g., unemployment levels, presence or absence of war) and social structure (e.g., how society is organized into social class, age, gender, etc.) conditions can affect stress levels. From the physiological perspective, Lazarus describes Cannon's classic fight-or-flight response and Selye's classic General Adaptation Syndrome. Lastly, Lazarus describes a "blurring [of] the physiological and psychological levels"; he emphasizes that the physiological stress reaction can be caused by psychological events.

The third chapter is from Sulsky and Smith's 2005 book *Work Stress*. The study of stress in the workplace has been of interest since very early in the history of stress research, as Cooper and Dewe emphasize. Sulsky and Smith begin their chapter by discussing the research on particular high-stress jobs, including police work and firefighting, social work and teaching, and air traffic control work. Next, they consider aspects of the physical work environment as potential causes of stress, including noise and uncomfortable temperatures, followed by discussion of stressful organizational aspects of a job, such as routinized work and shift work. Throughout the chapter, stressors are described as affecting both the performance and the health of workers. The chapter ends with a comparison of the stress involved in "blue collar" and "white collar" jobs. Sulsky and Smith emphasize that the blue collar–white collar distinction can be misleading if we are trying to understand the stressors faced by a worker.

Chapter 4, "The Wisdom of the Receptors: Neuropeptides, the Emotions, and Bodymind," by Pert (1986), is now a classic. In it, Pert describes chemical substances called "neuropeptides" and their receptors, both of which are located throughout the body. She argues that these substances and their activities represent the "biochemistry of emotion." Pert clearly states the purpose of her article (which was originally a talk delivered at a meeting of the Institute of Noetic Sciences in 1985) up front:

I believe that neuropeptides and their receptors are a key to understanding how mind and body are interconnected and how emotions can be manifested throughout the body. Indeed, the more we know about neuropeptides, the harder it is to think in the traditional terms of a mind and a body. It makes more and more sense to speak of a single integrated entity a "bodymind." (p. 9)

Some of the information Pert presents requires updating. First, many more neuropeptides have been discovered since her talk; several hundred are now known to exist, whereas Pert referred to between fifty and sixty. Second, as Pert speculates in her book, recent research has suggested that glial cells in the brain may serve more than a simple nutritive function; some evidence suggests that they may sometimes function in ways similar to the functioning of neurons (Czeh et al., 2001). The impact of Pert's work cannot be overemphasized; her theorizing and research was a springboard for work with far-reaching psychological and medical implications, including research on the effect emotions have on the immune system.

The final chapter in this part presents a relatively new topic in the stress field. "Allostatic Load: When Protection Gives Way to Damage," by McEwen and Lasley (2002), describes a variety of ways that our stress response system can malfunction and make us vulnerable to stress-related illness. *Allostasis* is a mechanism in the body that helps the organism to (1) remain stable even though physical events are changing and (2) maintain enough energy for necessary functioning. The stress response, if all goes well, functions in an allostatic fashion. *Allostatic load* is the damage that occurs to the body when the allostatic response causes a malfunction in body systems.

In this chapter, McEwen and Lasley describe four allostatic load "scenarios." First, an individual may experience chronic, unrelenting stress that can lead to allostatic load. As the authors describe, chronic stress takes its toll on many body systems, including the cardiovascular and immune systems. The second scenario describes circumstances where people are unable to adjust to stress that they should be able to adjust to, thus the person continues to produce the stress response when many or most people would not. For example, if an individual is required to engage in public speaking for several days in a row, most commonly she will experience the greatest amount of stress on the first day, with lower amounts experienced on consecutive days; a failure to adjust to the ongoing stressor of public speaking can lead to stress-related illness. Third, some individuals have stress systems that fail to shut off even after the stressor no longer exists. Like in the other situations, this scenario can cause physical damage; much of the research in this area has been on the destructive effects of the stress hormone cortisol. The fourth and final scenario involves a failure to produce a full stress response, even when one should. As McEwen and Lasley describe, this situation can be damaging also, as the stress system maintains a balance with other body systems. When the release of certain stress hormones that keep the immune system "in check" is very low, an overactivity of the immune system can occur, resulting in asthma, allergies, autoimmune diseases, and other conditions.

The five chapters in this part provide an introduction to different perspectives on stress, including various types of stressors and stress reactions. The next part then turns to a discussion of stress and its relationship to a variety of physical and psychological illnesses.

TERMS

Part I of our book includes a number of technical terms and names of significant persons. Can you define these terms or identify these people? Definitions of terms are included in the glossary in the back of the book.

General Stress and General Psychology Terms

- Allostatic load
- Allostatic response
- Appraisal (also called "psychological appraisal" or "cognitive appraisal")
- Behavorism
- Cognitive mediation
- Fight-or-flight reaction or response
- General Adaptation Syndrome
- Hassles (also called "daily hassles" or "minor hassles")
- Karasek's job strain model
- Major life events stress (also called "life events stress" or "life events")
- Psychoanalytic theory
- Psychosomatic disorder
- Social Readjustment Rating Scale
- Type A Behavior Pattern

Physiological Terms

- Adrenal gland
- Adrenaline
- Adreno-corticotropic hormone
- Amino acid
- Amygdala
- Atherosclerosis
- Autonomic nervous system
- Cortisol
- Glial cell
- Hippocampus
- HPA axis
- Hypothalamus
- Limbic system
- Neuropeptide
- Parasympathetic nervous system
- Pituitary gland
- Sympathetic nervous system

Statistical or Research Methods Terms

- Correlational research design
- Experimental research design
- Mediation
- Moderation

Stress Researchers and Theorists

- Walter Cannon
- Richard Lazarus
- Hans Selye

REFERENCES

Cooper, C. L., & Dewe, P. (2004). *Stress: A brief history.* Malden, MA: Blackwell.
Czeh, B., Michaelis, T., Watanabe, T., Frahm, J., de Biurrun, G., Van Kampen, M., Bartolumucci, A., & Fuchs, E. (2001). Stress-induced changes in cerebral

metabolites, hippocampal volume, and cell proliferation are prevented by anti-depressant treatment with tianeptine. *Proceedings of the National Academy of Sciences of the United States of America, 98(22),* 12796–12801.

Gross, J. J., Richards, J. M., & John, O. P. (2006). Emotion regulation in every-day life. In D. K. Snyder, J. A. Simpson, & J. N. Hughes (Eds.), *Emotion regulation in couples and families: Pathways to dysfunction and health* (pp. 13–35). Washington, DC: American Psychological Association.

Lazarus, R. S. (1999). *Stress and emotion: A new synthesis.* New York: Springer.

McEwen, B., & Lasley, E. N. (2002). *The end of stress as we know it.* Washington, DC: Joseph Henry Press.

Pert, C. (1986). The wisdom of the receptors: Neuropeptides, the emotions, and bodymind. *Advances, 3*(3), 8–16.

Sulsky, L., & Smith, C. (2005). *Work stress.* Belmont, CA: Thomson Wadsworth.

CHAPTER 1

Stress: A Brief History from the 1950s to Richard Lazarus

Cary L. Cooper and Philip Dewe

STRESS IN THE 1950s AND 1960s

By the end of the 1950s, "stress as a legitimate subject area of study had arrived" (Newton, 1995, p. 31). By this time the concept had also become established within the discipline of psychology. But, even at this stage, as a relative newcomer to psychology, concerns were being voiced as to whether stress was just another fad, like other fads bringing with it "an enthusiasm not altogether commensurate with their value to our science as a whole" and with emotional overtones "sometimes apt to blind protagonists to the deficiencies which exist in most new ideas" (Haward, 1960, p. 185). Giving rise to this early speculation as to whether stress was just a fad was an even more fundamental concern that was, and is, still being played out. Then, as now, this concern found expression in "stress, the term," rather than "stress, the concept," and the ostensibly careless approach to defining it, coupled with the inconsistent ways in which the term was being used. The history of stress in the second half of the twentieth century is no less controversial than the fifty years of debate and discussion that preceded it.

"However vacuous or not," the term *stress* "has taken a tenacious hold on our society and is likely to be around for some time to come" (Jones & Bright, 2001, p. 12). The elasticity in its meaning provided an opportunity to consider stress from a number of perspectives. Developments throughout this period meant that attempts to provide any coherent theoretical framework required that different perspectives be identified, tested, reviewed, integrated, or even discarded. As researchers gained confidence in researching the concept, identifying the strengths and weaknesses of

different perspectives and searching for common features that would provide an organizing context, the history of stress spills out into a history of
traditions and themes, of distinctive approaches, of paradigm shifts, and of
practical concerns and appropriate methods.

> What is a "popular" area of research, at any given time is not at all a random
> matter. There is often a theoretic and methodological history leading up to
> the point at which a research topic blossoms; and there is usually a contem-
> poraneous *zeitgeist* containing forces conducive to that blossoming.
> (McGrath, 1970, p. 2)

The blossoming of stress research is captured in the history that follows.

If the history of stress is a history of distinctive approaches, then the
history of stress is also, to a very large measure, a history of psychosomatic
medicine. In the 1960s and 1970s psychosomatic theories took as a goal
the exploration of those psychosocial variables that increase vulnerability to
illness as well as those that support adaptive coping with it (Lipowski,
1977). This goal provided the fertile ground for much of the early work
on life events, life changes, and stressors. But psychosomatic medicine had
already left its mark on the concept of stress, inspired by the force of psychoanalytic theory. Although by the 1950s the influence of these theories
"suffered a sharp drop in popularity and credibility and seemed to be
heading for the annals of medical history" (Lipowski, 1977, p. 235), they
are part of the history of stress and are mentioned here to give a sense of
completion. Perhaps the most influential representative of this psychody-
namic approach was Alexander.

Alexander's "specificity theory" linked unresolved unconscious conflicts
that "engendered chronic emotional tensions" with "specific somatic disorders" (Lipowski, 1977, p. 235). Alexander applied his theory to several
"chronic diseases of unknown etiology" such as, for example, hypertension
and peptic ulcer (Lipowski, 1986a, p. 3). These diseases soon became
known as "psychosomatic disorders." His theory came to dominate psychosomatic medicine for around twenty-five years until the mid-1950s.
However, his "specificity hypothesis" proved extremely difficult to validate,
simplified what were complex causal links, and failed to bring about the
hoped-for "treatment results." This approach simply "ground to a halt,"
leaving behind a feeling of "widespread disenchantment" (1977, p. 235).
The field survived this crisis with a change in emphasis from the increasingly
narrow preoccupation with psychodynamics to a much broader approach,
both in scope and method, concerned with the bio-psycho-social determinants of health and disease.

It is difficult to give an overview of a field like psychosomatic medicine
"that is so broad, diversified and vigorously evolving" (Lipowski, 1977,
p. 233). The field is much more than a scientific discipline (1977, 1986b). It
sees individuals as "ceaselessly interacting with the social and physical environment in which they are embedded" and it sees its role as a reformist movement that advocates a more complex, holistic, and systems view of the
individual that straddles "interdisciplinary boundaries" (1977, pp. 235–236).

It asks a number of "deceptively simple questions" that center on the kinds of social situations, the characteristics of individuals, the coping strategies they adopt, and those pathways and mechanisms that help to explain "why a person responds to particular social situations and specific life events with a given pattern of psychological and physiological changes" (1977, p. 236). The revival of the field in the 1960s posed a number of challenges for researchers that focused on two main issues. The first was the causal relationship between life events and illness, while the second concerned the role of individual difference and personality variables in illness (Lipowski, 1986c). These issues are part and parcel of the history of stress and reflect the new phase into which stress research was to enter (Lipowski, 1986b).

STRESSFUL LIFE EVENTS

Almost all introductions to stressful life events begin by acknowledging the work of Selye. "Recognition of the generality of the stress process as suggested by Selye," notes Cassidy, "led a number of psychiatrists in the psychosomatic tradition to look at the relationship between life events and psychiatric disorders" (1999, p. 38). Dohrenwend described the importance of stressful life event research by first making the point that "life events are eminently researchable," followed it up with the view that "they are important to the people we study, things that they are interested in and can tell us about," and concluded that "if environmentally induced stress is an important factor in psychopathology in the general population, then life events are strategic phenomena on which to focus as major sources of such stress" (1979, p. 11). Systematic research on stressful life events grew mainly from the seminal work of Cannon, Wolff, and Meyer. It was "Cannon's experimental work" that "provided a necessary link in the argument that stressful life events can be harmful. That is, he showed that stimuli associated with emotional arousal cause changes in basic physiological processes" (Dohrenwend & Dohrenwend, 1974a, p. 3).

Wolff (1950) also provided a stimulus for more systematic research into stressful life events, following his review of the proceedings of the Association for Research in Nervous and Mental Disease Conference in 1949 on "Life Stress and Bodily Disease." The extent of the research that had accumulated by then on the effects of stressful life events and the range of diseases covered (Wolff, Wolf, & Hare, 1950) led Wolff to conclude: "The common denominator in psychosomatic illness is the interpretation of an event as threatening. This implies anxiety, conscious or unconscious and the need to formulate a protective reaction pattern" (1950, p. 1090). "These threats and conflicts," Wolff noted, "are omnipresent, and constitute a large section of stress to which man [sic] is exposed" (p. 1059). These threats are reacted to by the mobilization of an individual's defenses. Wolff, in trying to explain the impact of life stress that had, by then, become evident, identified three propositions aimed at taking life event research forward (Dohrenwend & Dohrenwend, 1974b). All three propositions "have proved controversial" (Dohrenwend & Dohrenwend, 1974a, p. 4), but it was the first, more generic statement—indicating that, irrespective of its scale, the potential of a given event to evoke a protective reaction is dependent on its significance to that person (Wolff, 1950)—that was to become "central to subsequent research on stressful life events" (Dohrenwend & Dohrenwend, 1974a, p. 4).

If Selye, Cannon, and Wolff were to provide the links between stressful life events and disease, then much of life event research "evolved from the chrysalis of psychobiology generated by Adolf Meyer through his invention and use of the 'life chart'" (Holmes & Masuda, 1974, p. 45). Meyer's philosophy is captured in the foreword to Lief's 1948 biographical narrative *The Common-sense Psychiatry of Dr. Adolf Meyer*. Meyer argued, "Psychiatry has to be found in the function and the life of the people" (Lief, 1948, p. viii). "A patient," he added, "was not a mere summing-up of cells and organs, but a human being in need of readjustment to the demands of life.... The physician must now add to the disturbances of part-functions those of person-functions and the story of life.... It is 'the story' that counts in a person" (p. x).

In his paper on the life chart, Meyer wrote, "Medical psychology consists largely in the determination of the actual life history and experiences and concrete reactions of the patient" (1948, p. 418). To capture "the story," Meyer used "a device which, I hope, illustrates not only our practice, but also the entire philosophy involved in it" (1919, p. 1129). Onto the life chart, after entering date and year of birth, "we next enter the periods of disorders of the various organs, and after this the data concerning the situations and reactions of the patients." Meyer goes on to indicate that "we may note the change of habitat ... the various 'jobs'; the dates of possibly important births and deaths in the family, and other fundamentally important environmental incidents" (1919, p. 1132).

Meyer's teaching illustrated the important part that life events play in the onset of disease, and his suggestion that even the most usual and ordinary life events are potential contributors to the development of illness provided, for a number of researchers, the way forward (Dohrenwend & Dohrenwend, 1974b). Meyer's life-charting technique, and many of the life events he identified, provided for Holmes and Rahe a framework and context from which they developed the Social Readjustment Rating Scale (SRRS) (Holmes & Rahe, 1967). This was one of two paths that life event research was to follow: to explore the accumulated effect of a series of major life events. The other focused on the effect of single events or classes of events.

THE SOCIAL READJUSTMENT RATING SCALE

By the time Holmes and Rahe came to publish their Social Readjustment Rating Scale in 1967, the "life chart device had been used systematically with over 5,000 patients to study the quality and quantity of life events empirically observed to cluster at the time of disease onset" (1967, p. 215). From this pool of events, forty-three were identified as reflecting these experiences. The life events used in the SRRS were originally used to construct a Schedule of Recent Experience (SRE). The work using the SRE (Rahe, Meyer, Smith, Kjaer, & Holmes, 1964) "had been used to adduce data that the life events cluster significantly in the 2-year period preceding onset of tuberculosis, heart disease, skin disease, hernia and pregnancy" (Holmes & Masuda, 1974, p. 57). The development of the SRRS took the SRE a stage further by developing a scale reflecting the magnitude for each life event and so "provided a unique method for validation of the findings of the retrospective studies and for a quantitative definition of a life crisis" (Holmes & Masuda, 1974, p. 57).

The forty-three events fell into two categories: "those indicative of the *life style* of the individual, and those indicative of *occurrences* involving the individual" (Holmes & Rahe, 1967, p. 216, emphasis added). These included, for example, death of a spouse, marriage, change in financial state, change to a different line of work, revision of personal habits, and vacation. Interviews during the development phase of the SRRS to capture the meanings individuals gave to events identified one theme common to the life events. The occurrence of each was, for the individual involved, associated with, or required some form of, coping behavior (Holmes & Rahe, 1967). Holmes and Rahe were to add that, for each event in the SRRS, the "emphasis is on change from the existing steady state and not on psychological meaning, emotion, or social desirability" (p. 217).

The next step in the development of the SRRS was to determine the *magnitude* of the different events. In this stage of the research, it was explained to participants that social readjustment referred to "the amount and duration of change in one's accustomed pattern of life resulting from various life events" (Holmes & Masuda, 1974, p. 49). Each participant was then asked to rate the events "as to their relative degrees of necessary adjustment" (p. 49). To give respondents some referent point, marriage was given an arbitrary value of 500. Each event was then considered in relation to whether it required more or less adjustment than marriage. The mean score for each event was then divided by 10 to produce a life change unit (LCU) score. A life crisis was defined "as any clustering of life-change events whose individual values summed to 150 LCU or more in any one year" (p. 59). Research using the SRRS was to show that the magnitude of life changes was significantly related to the timing of disease onset and to the seriousness of the illness experienced. This life events approach has, over the last thirty years, generated a huge amount of research and a considerable number of publications. The SRRS or one of its adaptations is frequently found in popular health magazines and self-help books. It "represented a significant leap forward in researchers' ability to measure life events and assess their impacts. However, inevitably the approach has generated a great deal of criticism" (Jones & Kinman, 2001, p. 23).

In 1973, Dohrenwend and Dohrenwend decided, because of the interest in and importance of stressful life events, to hold a conference entitled "Stressful Life Events: Their Nature and Effects." Their motivation for holding the conference was that they felt "the time was ripe for stock-taking and that a careful and thorough job of it could be not only an immediate help to those working on the problem but also a platform from which major new advances could be launched" (1974b, p. vi). Their book, published in 1974, resulted directly from this conference, and the trends, problems, and prospects identified in the presentations and discussions covered a number of the criticisms leveled at this approach. The debate that accompanied research into stressful life events ranged over fifteen years, and in 1990 the lead article (Lazarus, 1990b) and the commentaries that followed in the first edition of *Psychological Inquiry* (an international journal of peer commentary and review) continued to discuss methodological and conceptual issues surrounding the measurement of stressful life events. The criticism has been wide-ranging and well covered within the literature (see Jones & Kinman, 2001, pp. 23–24), for example, that the measures failed to discriminate between positive and negative events, ignored chronic or recurrent events, or failed to take into account individual differences. Other criticisms questioned the reliability and validity of reporting of events over the space of a year, and asked whether there were moderating variables that influenced the relationship.

The criticism that attracted the most attention, however, surrounded "whether it is the objective presence of life events that should be the focus of interest or the person's appraisal of them as being stressful" (Jones & Kinman, 2001, p. 24). This objective–subjective debate reached such a level that, at its peak, one commentator (Deutsch, 1986) called for a "freeze" on what she described as "these stress wars." The debate stemmed from Lazarus and his colleagues' (Lazarus, DeLongis, Folkman, & Gruen, 1985) plea to account for the appraisal of events, which would provide an understanding of the process through which stressful life events may influence health, and from Dohrenwend and Shrout (1985), who "urged researchers to measure pure environmental events, uncontaminated by perceptions, appraisals or reactions" (p. 782). This debate was somewhat fueled by arguments that it was "daily hassles and uplifts" (Kanner, Coyne, Schaefer, & Lazarus, 1981, p. 1) that were a more useful measure than stressful life events, because of their "conceptual closeness to the person's experience" (Jones & Kinman, 2001, p. 25) and because they were more closely related to illness.

DAILY HASSLES AND UPLIFTS AND THE DEBATE THAT FOLLOWED

Efforts to measure "daily hassles and uplifts" arose out of a concern about the measurement difficulties associated with the SRRS. The debate that was to follow the development of the Hassles Scale may well have had its roots in the fact that the scale's authors made it clear that the critical life events approach left almost completely unexamined, and offered nothing by way of an explanation, as to the *processes* through which life events might influence quite different aspects of health. As a result, the life event approach to stress failed to give any attention to more complex issues, such as the influence of the meaning of the event and the impact of different coping behaviors. Despite "the essential reasonableness of the assumption that the accumulation of life events should be relevant to health status," such "indexes tell us nothing about what actually happens in day-to-day living" (Kanner et al., 1981, p. 2). It is these day-to-day events "that ultimately should have proximal significance for health outcomes and whose accumulative impact therefore, should also be assessed" (p. 3).

The primary objective in constructing the Daily Hassles Scale portion of the Hassles and Uplifts Scale was to capture a broad range of everyday life difficulties as perceived by the individual, rather than to attempt to generate purely objective environmental events (Lazarus, 1984a). "Daily hassles" were defined as "experiences and conditions of daily living that have been appraised as salient and harmful to the endorser's well-being" (Lazarus, 1984b, p. 376). This definition places hassles firmly as a subjective experience, with the meanings associated with them leading them to be remembered. Scale events (Kanner et al., 1981) generated by the researchers and colleagues included, for example, misplacing and losing things, concerns about getting credit, smoking too much, nonfamily members living in one's house, not enough money for food, not getting enough sleep, and having too many things to do. "Daily uplifts" were defined as "experiences and conditions of daily living that have been appraised as salient and positive or favorable to the endorser's well-being" (Lazarus, 1984b, p. 376). Scale events (Kanner et al., 1981) included, for example, being lucky, feeling healthy, being efficient, making a friend, and relaxing. The scale was made up of 117 hassles and 135 uplifts. It was possible, using the scale's scoring procedures, to calculate the frequency, cumulated severity, and intensity of the events. The testing of the scale led the authors to conclude that the pattern of results offer "a surprisingly robust case" that "daily hassles provide a more direct and broader estimate of stress than major life events" and are "more strongly associated with adaptational outcomes than are life events" (Kanner et al., 1981, p. 20).

THE DEBATE: CRITICAL LIFE EVENTS VERSUS HASSLES AND UPLIFTS

The lines had been drawn between those favoring a critical life event approach (objective presence of an event) and those arguing for the focus to shift to daily hassles and uplifts (personal appraisal of an event). One issue separating the two groups was that of confounding or overlap between measures. *Confounding* occurs when an event is expressed in such a way that it may, more likely, be measuring symptoms of illness (e.g., not enough personal energy, concerns about inner conflicts) and so overlap with the measures of illness themselves, thus confusing the measurement of events with the measurement of health outcomes.

The debate developed along two lines. The first was to approach the confounding problem by identifying events that had symptom-like properties. For example, Monroe points to a number of hassles that he describes as "being more directly related to psychological problems or symptoms" (1983, p. 191). These he identified as trouble relaxing, trouble making decisions, not getting enough sleep, and too many responsibilities. The debate began in earnest in 1985 with Dohrenwend, Dohrenwend, Dodson, and Shrout attempting to examine more systematically the issue of confounding. Their findings suggested that, while there was a level of confounding in most scales, critical life events and hassles alike, the issue was more apparent in the Hassles Scale. These authors did, however, temper their results with the view that "more care needs to be paid to how they [events] are conceptualized, measured, and employed in the design of research" (Dohrenwend et al., 1984, p. 228).

The debate then shifted to the pages of the *American Psychologist*. The response by Lazarus and his colleagues (1985) was quick, robust, and clear. In their view, the appraisal process simply cannot and should not be separated from the measurement of psychological stress and, therefore, some degree of confounding is unavoidable. It is not possible, they argued, because of the fundamental role of appraisal in the stress process, to simply focus on the environmental aspects of the event, as Dohrenwend et al. (1984) suggested, and make it independent of the stress process. The rejoinder by Dohrenwend and Shrout was just as clear, with their plea to researchers to "measure pure environmental events uncontaminated by perceptions, appraisals or reaction" (1985, p. 782). To Dohrenwend and Shrout, the Hassles Scale was, in terms of their examination, even more confounded than they had originally thought, although they recognized that the impact of life events would vary depending on individual differences, personal agenda, and available resources. To investigate these issues was, they argued, an important next step. But their advice to Lazarus and his colleagues was unequivocal. "We think, however, that Lazarus and his colleagues would do well to first change their approach to measuring hassles" (Dohrenwend & Shrout, 1985, p. 785).

In 1988, DeLongis, Folkman, and Lazarus presented findings from a thoroughly revised version of the Hassles Scale. In the revised version, redundant items and words that could be confused with symptoms were all eliminated. The format was also changed so that respondents could rate each item on how much of a hassle or uplift it was for them that day. The revised scale consisted of fifty-three items. In summarizing the main findings, the authors indicated that an increase in daily hassles tended to be associated with a decline in health (DeLongis, Folkman, & Lazarus, 1988). Referring to the debate on confounding, DeLongis and colleagues reported that, because those items that appear to be confounded with psychological well-being were removed from the present analysis, the suggestion that it was confounding that accounted for the relationship between hassles and health status was indefensible.

The debate was not yet ready to disappear. In his target article in *Psychological Inquiry* in 1990, Lazarus once again made clear that if you adopt the position, as he had, that stress is always a product of appraisal, then inevitably there is going to be some confounding between measures of stress and illness. Again he set out the argument that it was the appraisal process that linked the person and the environment, and so it was just not possible to return to objective environmental events or purifying an event of some contaminating subjective influence.

Those commenting on Lazarus's arguments were to suggest otherwise. This time the question of confounding took a different direction. Rather than focusing on item overlap, commentators argued that confounding arose because the Hassles Scale was not so much a measure of "proximal stressors, but an indirect measure of personality" (Costa & McCrae, 1990, p. 23), in this case neuroticism. Watson (1990) was also to assert that the Hassles Scale "can be most parsimoniously viewed as a measure of dissatisfaction and emotional distress" (p. 34). Furthermore, Costa and McCrae added, "It is perfectly reasonable to analyze the impact of objective-environmental events, because some events may be presumed to be stressful for most individuals" (1990, p. 23).

To the notion that the source of confounding in the Hassles Scale is because it is a surrogate measure of some undisclosed personality trait, Lazarus (1990a) responded that this criticism may in part be correct, but was somewhat overstated. Turning the question back on his critics, Lazarus asked why must it be some personality trait; why not the other way around, where it is simply the appraisal process that is the appropriate causal link. As to the issue of objective measurement, Lazarus's view was that it is never quite as easy as one thinks and once more reiterated that, while objective measures are "widely venerated," they are not that easy to develop, because one is faced with the difficulty of showing that what is being measured is actually the person's objective reality (1990a, p. 45). Later, in his autobiography, Lazarus (1998) was to conclude that there were no real underlying problems between life events and daily hassles as measures of stress. Both, he suggested, were concerned with different but associated events in a person's life. Nevertheless, he went on to add, it was their proximal qualities that led him to favor a daily hassles approach, and it was these qualities that made them, in his mind, a more useful tool for investigating the impact of typical stress on well-being.

The debate did produce some middle ground. Brown (1990, pp. 19–22), for example, argued that his Life Events and Difficulties Schedule (LEDS) "represents a position midway between that of Lazarus et al. (1985) and their critics Dohrenwend et al. (1984)." The LEDS (Brown & Harris, 1986) involves semistructured interviews in order to "obtain a full account of any reported event and its personal significance for the respondent" (Lipowski, 1986c, p. 17). Each event is then rated using normative ratings, capturing the "likely appraisal of a typical person rather then the actual appraisal of that particular individual" (Brown, 1990, p. 20). The idea behind this approach is that the comprehensive collection of biographical and contextual material through a structured interview and the rating of this in a normative way "can go a long way to provide us with an 'objective' assessment of such appraisals" (Brown, 1990, p. 20). In this way it recognizes, on the one hand, the importance of appraisal, while meeting the competing view that events should not be "contaminated" by the person's subjective response, on the other.

The importance of this approach, argues Brown (1990), lies in the way the interview data can be processed. The use of intense semistructured interviews "is likely to bring the kind of sensitivity, accuracy, and control of potential bias in reporting of life events that is required" (p. 20). Lazarus was to comment that he found the crux of Brown's views compatible with his own. On the use of interviews versus questionnaires to collect life event–hassles data, Lazarus (1990a), foreshadowing perhaps the debate that was yet to come, essentially suggested that, if researchers are going to come to terms with what may be good or not so good in terms of methodology, then when it comes to stress research both approaches are necessary. However, he added that, from his point of view, the use of in-depth, holistic-style approaches, well thought out and planned, are given less recognition than they deserve by stress researchers, and so their potential as an explanatory tool is consistently being underplayed.

The debate about confounding and objective–subjective stressor measurement was something more than a debate about critical life events versus daily hassles and uplifts, although it was, to begin with, argued out in that context. It was much more fundamental than that, because it was a debate aimed at the very nature of stress and those psychological processes that link the individual to the environment. It was a debate about theory, a new-look psychology (Lazarus, 1999), which saw a transition to cognitive mediation and a rebellion against methodological preciousness. It is a debate that occurs time and time again in the history of stress, because it has at its heart how we conceptualize stress, how we measure it, and how we explain our results. It is for stress the never-ending story, because it reflects where we have been, where we are now, and where we are going. We will keep returning to it, just as we will return to the work of Lazarus and the pioneering and lasting contribution he made to the field of stress research.

But what happened to stressful life events research? The enthusiasm for this sort of research has waned considerably. The reasons for this, Lazarus (1999) argued, lay partly in the failure to take into account individual meanings and coping and partly in that the list of events did not keep up-to-date or comprehensive enough. Lists of events "do pose methodological problems, however, so students of stress outcomes are probably better advised to focus on a single fateful event, such as bereavement or technological disaster" (Costa & McCrae, 1990, p. 23). Changing social and economic conditions may also have been responsible for researchers accepting that certain major events such as unemployment, for example, have widespread effects, and so singled them out for investigation rather than continuing the more traditional approach of focusing on the accumulated effect of different stressful life events.

PERSONALITY AND TYPE A BEHAVIOR PATTERNS

Continuing for a time in the footsteps of psychosomatic theory, one of the core questions identified by this field of research asked which personality variables increase susceptibility to or resistance to illness. Stressful life events may be predictive of the onset of illness, but to better understand the pathways through which this occurs, "we still need to study personality variables and enduring behavior patterns as well as chronic life situations and social conditions for clues to etiology" (Lipowski, 1977, p. 240). The study of personality variables and behavior patterns must "help identify who is at risk, from what disease, and when" (p. 240).

We begin by exploring Type A behavior patterns. The idea of "coronary-prone personality" (Friedman & Booth-Kewley, 1987, p. 540) has a long history. Chesney and Rosenman (1980), for example, refer to the 1892 writings of the Canadian physician William Osler, who described the coronary-prone individual as "a keen and ambitious man, the indicator of whose engines are set at full speed ahead" (Chesney & Rosenman, 1980, p. 188). It was in the 1950s that Friedman and Rosenman (1959), building on their earlier work, "observed that their coronary heart disease patients shared a characteristic pattern of behaviors and emotional reactions they labeled as Type A behaviors" (Ganster, 1987, p. 67). This behavior, described by Friedman and Rosenman as an "emotional complex" pattern, was primarily characterized by "intense ambition, competitive 'drive,' constant preoccupation with occupational 'deadlines,' and a sense of time urgency" (1959, p. 1295). The absence of this behavior pattern was termed Type B. In reviewing their data, Friedman and Rosenman indicated that it was significant that, among patients "with clinical coronary disease, many of them already have been found to exhibit many of the qualities making up the [Type A] behavior pattern" (p. 1294). They concluded that whatever was responsible for this behavior pattern was not confined to "any echelon of corporate or industrial life," that it seemed to be a ubiquitous and status-transcending phenomenon, and that it needed to be emphasized "that the stresses of this same society are of a variety never previously witnessed in any age of society" (p. 1294).

To investigate the relationship between coronary heart disease (CHD) and Type A behavior further, Rosenman, with his colleague Friedman and others, followed 3,500 males in an eight-and-a-half-year study known as the Western Collaborative Group Study (Rosenman et al., 1964; Rosenman et al., 1975). The results of this prospective study "confirmed the behaviour pattern as a precursor of *CHD,* independent of the standard risk factors" (Chesney & Rosenman, 1980, p. 189). Rosenman and his colleagues were to conclude that their findings "would appear to have important clinical implications for the primary prevention of CHD. Moreover, evaluating patients with CHD for presence of the coronary-prone behavior pattern may well improve the prognostic prediction of the course of the disease" (Rosenman et al., 1975, p. 877).

For forty years, the Type A behavior pattern has maintained a central position in research into personality and coronary heart disease. However, studies have challenged the role of Type A behavior in the development of coronary heart disease "with results varying considerably depending upon the method of measuring Type A behavior patterns" (Edwards, 1991, p. 151). The two primary methods of assessing Type A behavior patterns are the Structured Interview (SI) and the Jenkins Activity Survey (JAS) (see Booth-Kewley & Friedman, 1987; Edwards, 1991). While, from these reviews, there was some cautious support for the SI as a tool for assessing Type A behavior patterns, a second finding from these reviews was to raise even more questions in the minds of researchers. The finding suggested that the traditional practice of measuring Type A by collapsing the constellation of behaviors into a single index should be abandoned in favor of measures that focus on the distinct behaviors themselves. "Separating existing global measures into their constituent components may reveal previously undetected relationships" (Edwards & Baglioni, 1991, p. 287).

The evidence pointed in favor of this conclusion as well. "The hard-driving and competitive aspects of the Type A personality may be somewhat related to CHD but the speed and job-involvement aspects are probably not" (Booth-Kewley & Friedman, 1987, pp. 357–358). Similarly the anger/hostility aspect of Type A behavior may be a more powerful predictor of risk than other Type A components (Cooper & Bright, 2001; Ganster, Schaubroeck, Sime, & Mayes, 1991), although the mechanisms through which anger and hostility might have an impact remain unclear. An approach that has gained some support among researchers (see Barling, Kelloway, & Cheung, 1996; Jex, 1998) is to assess Type A behavior in terms of two components, "achievement strivings" (working harder) and "impatience-irritability" (showing annoyance with others). In this way, "researchers have essentially captured the positive aspects of Type A in achievement strivings and the negative aspects in impatience-irritability" (Jex, 1998, p. 80). The general feeling seems to be that by developing these separate component measures "using appropriate validation procedures and explicitly modelling their interactions and relationships, our understanding of the determinants, nature, and consequences of Type A behavior patterns will be considerably enhanced" (Edwards, 1991, p. 173).

With "Type A behavior documented as a CHD risk factor, it was logical to examine the prevalence of Type A behavior in the occupational environment and to examine its relationship to correlates of occupational success and stress" (Chesney & Rosenman, 1980, p. 191). The picture that was to emerge led to a number of cautious conclusions (Chesney & Rosenman, 1980; Ganster, 1987; Jex, 1998). While there was evidence that Type A's may impose demands on themselves and describe their jobs as having more responsibility and greater workloads, "there is no convincing evidence from the organizational studies that objective job demands facing Type A's are really higher than B's" (Ganster 1987, p. 73) nor, it seems, do Type A's generally "report more job dissatisfaction, anxiety or depression than do Type B's" (Chesney & Rosenman, 1980, p. 195). However, in terms of how Type A's respond to work situations involving, for example, stress, it would be possible to speculate based on laboratory findings that

the Type A person may be more likely than the Type B person to respond physiologically to the challenges that are ubiquitous in our modern social and work environments. Thus Type A workers, alert to these challenges, may find themselves frequently engaging in specific Type A behaviors, such as hostile competitiveness, that are linked with arousal and risk of CHD. (Chesney & Rosenman, 1980, p. 202)

Nevertheless, the evidence associating Type A behavior with stress still remains equivocal. One reason for this is that, although the Type A behavior pattern may have health implications, it "is a complex constellation of cognitive, behavioral, and physiological responses" (Ganster, 1987, p. 81) requiring more focused measurement practices (Edwards, 1991; Edwards & Baglioni, 1991). A second reason may be that more attention should be given to conceptualizing the role of Type A behavior in the stress process (Cooper & Payne, 1991).

In summary, the general consensus seems to be that "Type A is worth keeping and pursuing further but also that Type A should be regarded as only one part of the coronary-prone personality" (Booth-Kewley & Friedman, 1987, p. 355). Booth-Kewley and Friedman go on to suggest:

> Overall, the picture of the coronary-prone personality emerging from this review does not appear to be that of the workaholic, hurried, impatient individual, which is probably the image most frequently associated with coronary proneness. Rather the true picture seems to be one of a person with one or more negative emotions. (1987, p. 358)

The future it seems is for research to focus on identifying the relevant aspects of Type A behavior in conjunction with refining assessment and measurement practices. The message is clear: "Personality and disease should be vigorously investigated" (Friedman & Booth-Kewley, 1987, p. 552).

TOWARD THE STUDY OF INDIVIDUAL DIFFERENCES

Because of a research tradition that places considerable emphasis on understanding differences between people in their perception of and reaction to stress, it is not surprising that the curiosity of researchers led them inevitably to turn their attention to exploring the role of a range of individual differences.

> [The] question of individual differences in relation to the experience and effects of stress and in relation to coping is virtually a defining characteristic of the more psychological approaches. As a result, much research effort has been expended in exploring their nature and role, and in trying to establish the natural "laws" which govern their behavior. (Cox & Ferguson, 1991, p. 7)

This research was to result in a plethora of individual differences being studied (Cooper & Bright, 2001). These have included "genetic and biological differences, differences in skills or cognitive capabilities and differences in the goals and motivations which propel people into different kind of situations" (Bartlett, 1998, p. 65), but they are often classified according to

Payne's (1988) three categories: genetic, acquired, and dispositional. While, as Payne makes clear, there are obviously complex influences among the three categories, he does identify a number of questions that, in many ways, sum up the different approaches that have been taken when individual differences have been researched. These questions identified such issues as, for example, "how do individual differences relate to the development of symptoms of psychological strain ... how do individual differences relate to perceptions of stress in the environment ... do they act as moderators of the stress-strain relationship," and "do they affect the way people cope with stress?" (Payne, 1988, p. 210).

Individual differences have been hypothesized as influencing the stressor–strain relationship in one of three ways: either directly or by operating as a moderator or mediator of the relationship. A *direct* effect is where the individual difference variable directly impacts the level of strain. When individual difference variables operate as *moderators*, they "alter the strength or direction of the stress–strain relationship" (Cooper & Bright, 2001, p. 114). In this case, it is possible to hypothesize, for example, that the relationship between stressor and strain would be much stronger for those individuals displaying Type A behavior. That is, Type A moderates the stressor–strain relationship. When individual differences operate as *mediators*, they become "responsible for the transmission of an effect" (Cox & Ferguson, 1991, p. 12). In this case, the individual difference variable operates as a pathway through which the stressor travels to affect strain. As Cox and Ferguson point out, the mediating role of individual differences "offers some explanation of *how* external physical events take on psychological meaning" (p. 12). Examining individual differences as mediators provides researchers with a mechanism for understanding more about the role they play in the stress process. Moderator research using different individual differences tends to support them more in a predictor role (Cox & Ferguson, 1991).

The list of individual difference variables studies is long and, using Payne's (1988, p. 209) classification, would include under the heading of *genetic* gender, constitution, intelligence, and reactivity. Under the heading of *acquired* would be social class, education, and age, while *dispositional* variables would cover, for example, trait anxiety/neuroticism, Type A, locus of control, self-esteem, and extroversion–introversion. Despite the "common sense argument that people differ in their responses to stress, researchers have only just begun to unravel the complexity of these relationships" (Cooper & Bright, 2001, p. 130). There is now as much written (e.g., Bartlett, 1988; Cooper & Bright, 2001; Cooper, Dewe, & O'Driscoll, 2001; Cox & Ferguson, 1991; Parkes, 1994) about, for example, *negative affectivity* (a disposition to focus negatively on issues and be introspective, with a greater tendency to report more stress and dissatisfaction), *hardiness* (a "hardy" personality encompasses a number of resistance resources, including commitment, perceived control over events, and a tendency to view demands in terms of challenges), and *locus of control* (an expectation of control over event—internal locus of control—versus the expectation that much is up to fate—external locus of control) as there has been about the hostility dimension of Type A behavior patterns.

All reviewers of individual difference variables agree that there is much work still to be done both in terms of measurement strategies, identifying appropriate methodological approaches, and developing frameworks that integrate individual differences into the stress process. One individual difference that has not yet been discussed is coping. "For most of its history, the study of coping and adaptation has been divorced from the study of individual differences" (Suls, David, & Harvey, 1996, p. 711). We will follow this history when we turn our attention to the concept of coping.

A RETURN TO THE 1950s AND 1960s AND A CHANGE IN FOCUS

While the psychosomatic tradition continued to influence stress research by propagating "a holistic and biopsychosomatic approach" (Lipowski, 1986c, p. 20) to illness, other forces were also stirring. The early years of the twentieth century saw the rise in popularity of *behaviorism*. Although "its initial reception within psychology was cool or even grudging" (Viney, 1993, p. 289), it was to have a profound influence on psychological thought and practice and very quickly came to dominate. Behaviorism in its most radical form claimed, "All forms of behavior are to be found outside the organism and therefore explanations of behavior in terms of physiological or mental events should be avoided" (p. 368). However, the 1950s and 1960s saw a growing consensus that the vision offered by behaviorists "was too narrow, and that methodologically and substantively, they had closed too many doors" (p. 345). A new broader approach to understanding behavior was called for, and "one of the most conspicuous trends in psychology in the 1950s [was] the renewed interest in cognition" (p. 439).

The transition was not without controversy, fierce debate, or the taking of sides that demanded intense loyalty. The influence of behaviorism did not, of course, just disappear, nor did the "dogma of positivism" (Lazarus, 1999), to which it so rigidly subscribed. Psychologists were, however, interested in a "new-look psychology" that would open the door to the study of the mind by offering a wide variety of phenomena for investigation that simply were just not seen as necessary by radical behaviorism (Lazarus, 1999, p. 7). But even during the period of radical behaviorism, the beliefs of cognitive psychology were always present and "did not disappear far from it" (Hergenhahn, 1992, p. 542), but for many psychologists what they now wanted was a discipline that emphasized cognitive experience and a context that would allow that emphasis to flourish.

By the 1960s and 1970s, the *stimulus-response* (S-R) model of psychology, which was the heir of behaviorism, was slowly being put to one side (Lazarus, 1999). Described as "reductionist" (Aldwin, 2000) and conveying a "rather pinched outlook" (Lazarus, 1999), the S-R model was transformed into a much more forward-looking *stimulus-organism-response* (S-O-R) model (Lazarus, 1999, p. 7). Now the S-O-R model freed researchers to explore, with renewed enthusiasm, the nature of those mental processes that might be found in the "black box" of the mind and that helped to explain the way people behave (Lazarus, 1999). As Lazarus (1991) makes clear, while the "O" stands for organism, it more commonly came to refer to those thoughts that mediate between the environment and the behavioral response, and it was these thoughts that became identified as having a causal influence. The inclusion of some sort of *cognitive mediation* (Lazarus, 1991; 1999) process in psychological models led many to see this period as some sort of cognitive revolution, but given the long history of cognitive psychology, as Lazarus (1999) explained, the only time it could really be described as a revolution was when it was placed hard up against the views of radical behaviorism.

The S-R and S-O-R models represented two forces or intellectual traditions in psychology: the outer-objective (exogenic) and the inner-subjective (endogenic). Psychology has always had a strong exogenic character "committed as it been to rendering an account of objective knowledge of the world" (Gergen, 1985, p. 269). This approach is illustrated by research on critical life events and the view that life events are external occurrences uncontaminated by personal meanings. Yet the 1960s and 1970s saw a "full force" return to the "endogenic perspective in the guise of cognitive psychology," where behavior is critically dependent on the "cognitive processing of information, that is, on the world as cognized rather than the world as is" (p. 269). Crucial aspects of knowledge are lost if the objective is emphasized at the expense of the subjective, and the challenge "has been to transcend the traditional object-subject dualism and all its attendant problems and to develop a framework of analysis" (p. 270). If we carry this reasoning into the domain of stress research then, as Lazarus (1991) suggests, since *both* person (subjective) and environment (objective) are key players in stress and coping, the swing between one and the other could simply be ended as soon as researchers accept the relational nature of each to the other, and that both are part of the same transaction. All we need, Lazarus adds, is to find a suitable language that lets us describe the nature of this relational-transactional approach. The idea of applying a cognitive-relational framework to stress research was to have a profound impact on the field.

The shift in the 1950s and 1960s to a relational framework for investigating stress had "enormous implications, not only for the manner in which science is conducted, but for much of everyday life" (Aldwin, 2000, p. 6). The work that flowed from this period was as pioneering and inspiring as the work of those from earlier decades. Paradigm changes sent ripples in all sorts of directions, and the decades of stress research that were to follow are as much a debate about methods and approaches as they are about advancing our understanding of stress. Never far from the center of any debate on stress are questions asking where current methodologies are taking us and what alternative methodologies can offer. The question, as Lazarus puts it, is whether we have become "too smug" (1990a, p. 47) in our acceptance and use of traditional methods and procedures to even begin to think about, or look at, whether they are providing relevant answers to the questions we are asking, and whether the answers we are coming up with are as good as we can get. The debate surrounding methods is deeply engrained and pervades the whole history of stress—a part of its history that we will be returning to time and time again.

THE HISTORY OF STRESS IN SWEDEN

The foundation for stress research in Sweden was laid in the 1960s by Ulf von Euler, professor of physiology at the Karolinska Institute in Stockholm. Professor von Euler had developed methods for the measurement of the stress hormones adrenaline and noradrenaline in the urine. He was later to be awarded the Nobel Prize in Physiology and Medicine (1970) for this work. The development of such new methods would become a key factor in future research programs aimed at studying the experience of stress in different situations, including at work. Early stress research in Sweden focused on hospitalized patients or was laboratory based using healthy subjects. It was now possible, building on the earlier work of von Euler, for researchers to measure stress hormone levels using measures that could be obtained outside the laboratory. Researchers were now able to follow people going about their everyday routines and still take exact measures of stress hormone levels (Frankenhaeuser, 1993).

Several researchers were inspired by the work of von Euler. One of the most well known was Lennart Levi. In 1959, he founded the now-famous Stress Research Laboratory at Karolinska Institute, which was designated a World Health Organization collaborating center for research and training in psychosocial factors and health. As a result of Levi's and his coworkers' research on the significance of the relationship between psychosocial factors and health, the National Institute for Psychosocial Factors and Health was founded in 1980, with Levi as its director (Theorell, 1997). The influence of the work carried out at the Stress Research Laboratory was soon to be reflected in the Swedish work environment law (SOU, 1976, p. 1), particularly in relation to piecework and night shift work.

A selection of Levi's most well-known publications can be found in "Four Decades of Lennart Levi's Research—A Selection," published (in English) by the Department of Stress Research, Karolinska Institute, and the National Institute for Psychosocial Factors and Health in celebration of his sixtieth birthday in 1990 (Levi, 1990). Papers in this collection range from early studies on fundamental aspects of stress to studies on piecework and nightwork and research on unemployment and population health (Theorell, 1997).

Issues relating to work-related stress and its impact on individual health and well-being had been discussed in Sweden for many decades. Bertil Gardell, professor of work psychology at Stockholm University, was the first researcher to make associations between control/decision latitude at work, and stress and psychosocial work problems (Gardell, 1971). These ideas inspired other researchers (Frese, 1977; Karasek, 1979; Karasek &

Theorell, 1990). It is interesting to note that Robert Karasek (of the University of Southern California) did some of his work leading to the formulation of the demand-control model at the Stress Research Laboratory of the Karolinska Institute in Stockholm in close cooperation mainly with Töres Theorell. Further work in Sweden saw the Karasek model expanded to include social support (Johnson, 1986). The demand-control model was to inspire stress research across the world. However, the model is not without controversy, with research yielding conflicting results.

Marianne Frankenhaeuser, professor of psychology at the Karolinska Institute and a colleague of Levi, was instrumental in including theories and methods from psychophysiological stress research into traditional working life research. One of her many theses was that our biological "equipment" has undergone a much slower development than technology and society. This ever-increasing discrepancy puts high demands on our ability to adjust (Frankenhaeuser, 1981; Frankenhaeuser & Ödman, 1983). Her research aimed at understanding the causes of stress, defining contributing work and organizational factors, and identifying factors protecting people from harmful stress. The results can then be used as a basis for prevention and intervention (Frankenhaeuser & Johansson, 1986). Another important aspect of Frankenhaeuser's research was the studies on gender-related differences in stress levels and stress perception (Frankenhaeuser, 1991; 1993; Lundberg, Mårdberg, & Frankenhaeuser, 1994). One of the most striking differences between men and women that are shown in this research is the ability to relax when coming home from work. At about five o'clock in the afternoon, stress hormones and blood pressure go down in men, while they go up in the women. This is particularly true for female professionals.

In a recent contribution to a textbook on stress, Levi (2002) concluded that although researchers today study stress reactions and their causes multifactorially, they presuppose a linear relationship. Levi advocates a nonlinear, interactionistic, and systems analytic approach at several levels from molecular to organizational to societal. Another important direction for future stress research has been discussed by Arnetz (2002), who emphasized the importance of addressing work-related stress at the organizational level, the critical role of management to address such stress, and the ability of management to optimize the competitiveness of the organization by also considering biological aspects of work.

THE ORIGINS OF ORGANIZATIONAL PSYCHOLOGY

The 1950s and 1960s saw other developments that were also to enrich the history of stress. One of these was the growth and maturity of organizational psychology, along with the application of psychological techniques and methods to work settings. Work stress research was to generate volumes of research and create an enthusiasm for stress that has continued unabated to the present day. Not without its own controversies and debates, occupational psychology has a history spanning much of the twentieth century. The nature and scope of organizational psychology was profoundly influenced by the two world wars, where demand for increased productivity brought with it a need to understand how factors like fatigue, for example, affected the health and efficiency of workers. "Even the enlightened few who were aware of what psychology had to offer on the industrial front could not have foreseen its pervasive impact on the conduct of war" (Shimmin & Wallis, 1994, p. 18). The tremendous contribution psychologists made in terms of selection and assessment during the war years, coupled with the work on leadership, added new depth to the growing field of industrial psychology, with the discipline that we now know as organizational or occupational psychology beginning to take shape.

Other initiatives were also nudging the emerging field of industrial psychology toward a focus on work stress. One of these was the launch, in the late 1950s, of a program of research to understand the impact of the organization on the individual, at the University of Michigan as a joint effort by the Survey Research Center and the Research Center for Group Dynamics. The research aim of this program was "concerned with developing research methods, theory, and substantive findings which treat fully the influences of the contemporary environment on mental health" (Kahn, Wolfe, Quinn, Snoek, & Rosenthal, 1964, p. vii). The focus of much of this work was on "the mental health of the adult, with special attention to social psychological factors in large scale organizations" (French & Kahn, 1962, p. 1). A review of the work carried out by this program in 1962 concluded that "the findings may best be viewed as evidence that social psychological research on the origins and consequences of behavior relevant to mental health is under way and that future research can confidently be expected to expand upon and integrate results such as those described" (Zander & Quinn, 1962, p. 63).

In Britain, "interest on the part of government officials and industrialists in this topic [occupational stress] was aroused in the late 1960s by high levels of sickness absence among industrial workers. These levels appeared to be associated with symptoms of illness and psychological disorder thought to be 'stress-related'" (Shimmin & Wallis, 1994, p. 98). Accordingly, "a programme of research into occupational stress was initiated by the Medical Research Council, supported by the Department of Employment and the Trade Union Congress" (p. 98). Even at this early stage, there were concerns as to whether adequate field research would prove possible or would make a difference to work practices, but "research into stress soon got under way at a number of locations and the late seventies saw the flowering of many studies by occupational psychologists and other specialists, directed at all manner of jobs and occupations" (p. 99).

There was, in Britain as in the United States, a strong social emphasis in examining work behavior, and the work of the Tavistock Institute in the late 1940s and early 1950s into the behavior of groups in work settings captured the "imagination of social scientists from a number of disciplines concerned with social and technological changes in the workplace" (Shimmin & Wallis, 1994, p. 87). This early work of the Tavistock Institute provided one of the most "enduring multi-level frameworks for considering individuals, groups and organizations in relation to their environments" (p. 87). Interestingly, the Survey Research Center at the University of Michigan and the Tavistock Institute in London, because of their similar aims based around a "focus on human relations within organizations" (Newton, 1995, p. 32), maintained close links with each other, with both providing instructive directions for research into health and well-being in the workplace. So began, in both countries, what French and Kahn referred to as a "programmatic approach to studying the industrial environment and mental health" (1962, p. 1).

THE RISE OF ERGONOMIC/HUMAN FACTORS

The world wars were also the catalyst that saw the "initial rise of interest in the relationship between man and the working environment" (Oborne, 1987, p. 4) and then the transformation of this interest into the field of *ergonomics* or *human factors*. July 1949 is pinpointed as the time when, in Britain, "an interdisciplinary group was formed (the Human Research Group) for those interested in human work problems and by February 1950 the term *ergonomics* was adopted and the discipline could finally said to be born" (p. 4). Ergonomics arose out of need to consider how individuals cope with their environment and reflects a multidisciplinary field of study where a range of disciplines come together "to maximize safety, efficiency and comfort by shaping the 'machine' to the operator's capabilities" (p. 6).

A similar history can be found in the United States, where following World War II, the Department of Defense continued to recognize the value of what was then called *human engineering* or *engineering psychology* (Howell, 1991, p. 211). By the late 1950s, after some trouble agreeing on a name, the discipline emerged as "human factors," with a focus on what was then, and still remains today, its analytic cornerstone: the "attempt to improve the fit between humans and technology. What has changed is our understanding of human performance and the factors that control it" (p. 212). What has not changed is that "psychology is still the best (though certainly not the only) source of theories on human performance" (p. 212).

This discipline has made a substantial contribution to our understanding of stress. Not surprisingly, there are clear similarities between an engineering model of stress and the approach adopted by ergonomics/human factors. In general, most ergonomists approach stress by first suggesting that there are optimal conditions for performance and reasonable levels of work intensity. It is when performance is required under environmental conditions that depart from, or are outside of, reasonable limits that some form of stress is imposed. Returning to the engineering analogy, individuals, like physical systems, may be able to tolerate certain levels of stress, "but when it becomes intolerable permanent damage, physiological and psychological, may result" (Cox, 1978, p. 13). Stress, from this point of view, is frequently discussed in terms of the relationship between levels of performance and concepts such as arousal, signal detection theory, and different environmental demands. While the underlying theme from this work emphasizes that it is those situations that tax individual capabilities that cause stress, there is also the recognition that the "interaction between an operator and the environment is a very complex event," and "it is now important to question how this complexity can interfere with work performance" (Oborne, 1987, pp. 8–9)—a hint, perhaps, that to try to understand this complexity requires researchers to consider those psychological processes that link the individual and the environment.

SUMMARY

The 1950s and 1960s provided fertile ground for stress researchers. Change was in the wind, and there was a real sense of urgency as researchers strove to take advantage of new opportunities, new ideas, and new frameworks for doing research. Different developments each have their own history and at the same time contribute to the sum that makes up a history of stress. At times, researchers appear to accept the need for change at the conceptual level, but continue to research, unaware or unable to accept that established practices and methods might need to be rethought. The greatest danger that emerged from this period, and one which continues to haunt stress research, "lies not in the abundance of ideas and creative opportunities but that many researchers will simply nod wisely but continue with their own work believing that such opportunities are best left to others" (Dewe, 2001, p. 92). The 1950s and 1960s provided the opportunity for a period of quiet reconstruction in stress research.

REFERENCES

Aldwin, C. M. (2000). *Stress, coping, and development: An integrative perspective.* New York: Guilford Press.

Arnetz, B. (2002). Organizational stress. In R. Ekman & B. Arnetz (Eds.), *Stress: Molekylerna, individen, organisationen, samhället* [Stress: Molecules, individuals, organization, society]. Stockholm: Liber.

Barling, J., Kelloway, E. K., & Cheung, D. (1996). Time management and achievement striving interact to predict car sales performance. *Journal of Applied Psychology, 81,* 821–826.

Bartlett, D. (1998). *Stress: Perspectives and processes.* Buckingham, England: Open University Press.

Booth-Kewley, S., & Friedman, H. S. (1987). Psychological predictors of heart disease: A quantitative review. *Psychological Bulletin, 101,* 343–362.

Brown, G. W. (1990). What about the real world? Hassles and Richard Lazarus. *Psychological Inquiry, 1,* 19–22.

Brown, G. W., & Harris, T. O. (1986). Establishing causal links: The Bedford College studies of depression. In H. Katsching (Ed.), *Life events and psychiatric disorders* (pp. 107–187). Cambridge: Cambridge University Press.

Cassidy, T. (1999). *Stress, cognition and health.* London: Routledge.

Chesney, M. A., & Rosenman, R. H. (1980). Type A behaviour in the work setting. In C. L. Cooper & R. Payne (Eds.), *Current concerns in occupational stress* (pp. 187–212). Chichester, England: John Wiley & Sons.

Cooper, C. L., Dewe, P., & O'Driscoll, M. (2001). *Organizational stress: A review and critique of theory, research and applications.* Thousand Oaks, CA: Sage.

Cooper, C. L., & Payne, R. (1991). Introduction. In C. L. Cooper & R. Payne (Eds.), *Personality and stress: Individual differences in the stress process* (pp. 1–4). Chichester, England: John Wiley & Sons.

Cooper, L., & Bright, J. (2001). Individual differences in reactions to stress. In Jones & Bright 2001, pp. 111–132.

Costa, P. T., & McCrae, R. R. (1990). Personality: Another "hidden factor" in stress research. *Psychological Inquiry, 1,* 22–24.

Cox, T. (1978). *Stress.* London: Macmillan.

Cox, T., & Ferguson, E. (1991). Individual differences, stress and coping. In C. L. Cooper & R. Payne (Eds.), *Personality and stress: Individual differences in the stress process* (pp. 7–30). Chichester, England: John Wiley & Sons.

DeLongis, A., Folkman, S., & Lazarus, R. S. (1988). The impact of daily stress on health and mood: Psychological social resources as mediators. *Journal of Personality and Social Psychology, 54,* 486–495.

Deutsch, F. (1986). Calling a freeze on "stress wars": There is hope for adaptational outcomes. *American Psychologist, 41,* 713.

Dewe, P. (2001). Work stress, coping and well-being: Implementing strategies to better understand the relationship. In P. L. Perrewe & D. Ganster (Eds.), *Exploring theoretical mechanisms and perspectives,* vol. 1 (pp. 63–96). Amsterdam: JAI-Elsevier Science.

Dohrenwend, B. P. (1979). Stressful life events and psychopathology: Some issues of theory and method. In J. E. Barrett, R. M. Rose, & G. L. Klerman (Eds.), *Stress and mental disorder* (pp. 1–15). New York: Raven Press.

Dohrenwend, B. S., & Dohrenwend, B. P. (1974a). A brief introduction to research on stressful life events. In Dohrenwend & Dohrenwend 1974b, pp. 1–6.

Dohrenwend, B. S., & Dohrenwend, B. P. (1974b). *Stressful life events: Their nature and effects.* New York: John Wiley & Sons.

Dohrenwend, B. S., Dohrenwend, B. P., Dodson, M., & Shrout, P. E. (1984). Symptoms, hassles, social support and life events: Problem of confounded measures. *Journal of Abnormal Psychology, 93*(2), 222–230.

Dohrenwend, B. P., & Shrout, P. E. (1985). "Hassles" in the conceptualization and measurement of life stress variables. *American Psychologist, 40,* 780–785.

Edwards, J. R. (1991). The measurement of type A behaviour pattern: An assessment of criterion-oriented validity, content validity, and construct. In C. L. Cooper & R. Payne (Eds.), *Personality and stress: Individual differences in the stress process* (pp. 151–180). Chichester, England: John Wiley & Sons.

Edwards, J. R., & Baglioni, A. J. (1991). Relationship between type A behavior pattern and mental and physical symptoms: A comparison of global and component measures. *Journal of Applied Psychology, 76,* 276–290.

Frankenhaeuser, M. (1981). Coping with stress at work. *International Journal of Health Services, 11*(4), 491–510.

Frankenhaeuser, M. (1991). The psychophysiology of workload, stress and health: Comparison between the sexes. *Annals of Behavioral Medicine, 4,* 197–204.

Frankenhaeuser, M. (1993). *Women, men and stress.* Höganäs, Sweden: Bra Böcker/Wiken.

Frankenhaeuser, M., & Johansson, G. (1986). Stress at work: Psychobiological and psychosocial aspects. *International Review of Applied Psychology, 35,* 287–299.

Frankenhaeuser, M., & Ödman, M. (1983). *Stress: A part of life.* Stockholm: Brombergs.

French, J. P. R., & Kahn, R. (1962). A programmatic approach to studying the industrial environment and mental health. *Journal of Social Issues, 18,* 1–47.

Frese, M. (1977). *Psychische Störungen bei Arbeitern: Zum Einfluss von Gesellschaftlicher Stellung und Arbeitsplatzmerkmalen* [Workers' psychological disturbances: The influence of social position and job characteristics]. Salzburg, Austria: Müller.

Friedman, H. S., & Booth-Kewley, S. (1987). The "disease-prone personality": A meta-analytic view of the construct. *American Psychologist, 42,* 539–555.

Friedman, M., & Rosenman, R. H. (1959). Association of specific overt behavior pattern with blood and cardiovascular findings. *Journal of the American Medical Association, 169,* 1286–1296.

Ganster, D. C. (1987). Type A behavior and occupational stress. In J. M. Ivancevich & D. C. Ganster (Eds.), *Job stress: From theory to suggestion* (pp. 61–84). New York: Haworth Press.

Ganster, D. C., Schaubroeck, J., Sime, W., & Mayes, B. (1991). The nomological validity of the type A personality among employed adults. *Journal of Applied Psychology, 76,* 143–168.

Gardell, B. (1971). *Production technology and work satisfaction: A social psychological study of industrial world.* Stockholm: PA-Rådet.

Gergen, K. J. (1985). The social constructionist movement in modern psychology. *American Psychologist, 40,* 266–275.

Haward, L. R. C. (1960). The subjective meaning of stress. *British Journal of Psychology, 33,* 185–194.

Hergenhahn, B. R. (1992). *An introduction to the history of psychology.* Belmont, CA: Wadsworth.

Holmes, T. H., & Masuda, M. (1974). Life change and illness susceptibility. In Dohrenwend & Dohrenwend 1974b (pp. 45–72).

Holmes, T. H., & Rahe, R. H. (1967). The social readjustment scale. *Journal of Psychosomatic Research, 11,* 213–218.

Howell, W. C. (1991). Human factors in the workplace. In M. D. Dunnette & L. M. Hough (Eds.), *Handbook of industrial and organizational psychology,* vol. 2 (2nd ed., pp. 209–269). Palo Alto, CA: Consulting Psychologists Press.

Jex, S. M. (1998). *Stress and job performance: Theory, research, and implications for managerial practice.* London: Sage.

Johnson, J. V. (1986). The impact of the workplace social support, job demands, and work control under cardiovascular disease in Sweden. Doctoral dissertation Johns Hopkins University. Distributed by Department of Psychology, University of Stockholm, Report no. 1-86.

Jones, F., & Bright, J. (2001). *Stress: Myth, theory and research.* Harlow, England: Prentice-Hall.

Jones, F., & Kinman, G. (2001). Approaches to studying stress. In Jones & Bright 2001 (pp. 17–45).

Kahn, R. L., Wolfe, D. M., Quinn, R. P., Snoek, J. D., & Rosenthal, R. A. (1964). *Organizational stress: Studies in role conflict and ambiguity.* New York: John Wiley & Sons.

Kanner, A. D., Coyne, J. C., Schaefer, C., & Lazarus, R. S. (1981). Comparison of two modes of stress measurement: Daily hassles and uplifts versus major life events. *Journal of Behavioral Medicine, 4,* 1–39.

Karasek, R. (1979). Job demands, job decision latitude and mental strain: Implications for job redesign. *Administrative Science Quarterly, 24,* 285–308.

Karasek, R., & Theorell, T. (1990). *Healthy work: Stress, productivity and the reconstruction of working life.* New York: Basic Books.

Lazarus, R. S. (1984a). On the primacy of cognition. *American Psychologist, 39,* 124–129.

Lazarus, R. S. (1984b). Puzzles in the study of daily hassles. *Journal of Behavioral Medicine, 7*, 375–389.

Lazarus, R. S. (1990a). Author's response. *Psychological Inquiry, 1*, 41–51.

Lazarus, R. S. (1990b). Theory based stress measurement. *Psychological Inquiry, 1*, 3–12.

Lazarus, R. S. (1991). *Emotion and adaptation*. New York: Oxford University Press.

Lazarus, R. S. (1998). *The life and work of an eminent psychologist: Autobiography of Richard S. Lazarus*. New York: Springer.

Lazarus, R. S. (1999). *Stress and emotion: A new synthesis*. London: Free Association Books.

Lazarus, R. S., DeLongis, A., Folkman, S., & Gruen, R. (1985). Stress and adaptational outcomes: The problem of confounded measures. *American Psychologist, 40*, 770–779.

Levi, L. (1990). *Four decades of Lennat Levi's research—A selection*. Stockholm: Karolinska Institute.

Levi, L. (2002). Stress—an overview: International and public health perspective. In R. Ekman, & B. Arnetz (Eds.), *Stress: Molekylerna, individen, organisationen, samhället* [Stress: Molecules, individuals, organization, society]. Stockholm: Liber.

Lief, A. (1948). *The common-sense psychiatry of Dr Adolf Meyer: Fifty-two selected papers edited, with biographical narrative*. New York: McGraw-Hill.

Lipowski, Z. J. (1977). Psychosomatic medicine in the seventies: An overview. *American Journal of Psychiatry, 134*, 233–244.

Lipowski, Z. J. (1986a). Psychosomatic medicine: Past and present; Part I: Historical background. *Canadian Journal of Psychiatry, 31*, 2–7.

Lipowski, Z. J. (1986b). Psychosomatic medicine: Past and present; Part II: Current state. *Canadian Journal of Psychiatry, 31*, 8–13.

Lipowski, Z. J. (1986c). Psychosomatic medicine: Past and present; Part III: Current research. *Canadian Journal of Psychiatry, 31*, 14–21.

Lundberg, U., Mårdberg, B., & Frankenhaeuser, M. (1994). The total workload of male and female white-collar workers as related to age, occupational level, and number of children. *Scandinavian Journal of Psychology, 35*, 315–327.

McGrath, J. E. (Ed.). (1970). *Social and psychological factors in stress*. New York: Holt, Rinehart & Winston.

Meyer, A. (1919). The life chart and the obligation of specifying positive data in psychopathological diagnosis. In *Contributions to medical biological research dedicated to Sir William Osler in honour of his seventieth birthday July 12 1919: By his pupils and co-workers* (pp. 1128–1133). New York: Paul B. Hoeber.

Meyer, A. (1948). The life chart. In Lief 1948 (pp. 418–422).

Monroe, S. M. (1983). Major and minor life events as predictors of psychological distress: Further issues and findings. *Journal of Behavioral Medicine, 6*, 189–205.

Newton, T. (1995). *"Managing" stress: Emotional and power at work*. London: Sage.

Oborne, D. J. (1987). *Ergonomics at work*. Chichester, England: John Wiley & Sons.

Parkes, K. R. (1994). Personality and coping as moderators of work stress processes: Models, methods and measures. *Work & Stress, 8*, 110–129.

Payne, R. (1988). Individual differences in the study of occupational stress. In C. L. Cooper & R. Payne (Eds.), *Causes, coping and consequences of stress at work* (pp. 209–232). Chichester, England: John Wiley & Sons.

Rahe, R. H., Meyer, M., Smith, M., Kjaer, G., & Holmes, T. H. (1964). Social stress and illness onset. *Journal of Psychosomatic Research, 15,* 33–39.

Rosenman, R. H., Brand, R. J., Jenkins, D., Friedman, M., Straus, R., & Wurm, M. (1975). Coronary heart disease in the Western Collaborative Group Study. *Journal of the American Management Association, 233,* 872–877.

Rosenman, R. H., Friedman, M., Straus, R., Wurm, M., Kositchek, R., Huhn, W., et al. (1964). A predictive study of coronary heart disease. *Journal of the American Medical Association, 189,* 103–110.

Shimmin, S., & Wallis, D. (1994). *Fifty years of occupational psychology in Britain.* Leicester, England: British Psychological Society.

SOU (1976). *Work environment law.* Stockholm: Statens Offentliga Utredningar.

Suls, J., David, J. P., & Harvey, J. H. (1996). Personality and coping: Three generations of research. *Journal of Personality, 64,* 711–735.

Theorell, T. (Ed.). (1997). Future worklife: Special issue in honour of Lennart Levi. *Scandinavian Journal of Work, Environment, and Health 23*(Suppl. 4).

Viney, W. (1993). *A history of psychology: Ideas and context.* Boston: Allyn & Bacon.

Watson, D. (1990). On the dispositional nature of stress measures: Stable and non-specific influences on self-reported hassles. *Psychological Inquiry, 1,* 34–37.

Wolff, H. G. (1950). Life stress and bodily disease—A formulation. In Wolff, Wolf, & Hare 1950, pp. 1059–1094.

Wolff, H. G., Wolf, S. G., & Hare, C. C. (Eds.). (1950). *Life stress and bodily disease.* New York: Hafner.

Zander, A., & Quinn, R. (1962). The social environment and mental health: A review of past research at the Institute for Social Research. *Journal of Social Issues, 18,* 48–66.

CHAPTER 2

Stress and Emotion:
A New Synthesis

Richard S. Lazarus

Never before has there been so much interest in stress, worldwide, among social and biological scientists, and on the part of the general public. This interest extends to diverse clinical practitioners who apply scientific knowledge to help ameliorate emotional distress, dysfunction, physical diseases, and social ills generated by stress. Stress has become a household word, and we are flooded with messages about how it can be prevented, eliminated, managed, or just lived with. A major reason for the currently high profile that stress research and theory has acquired is abundant evidence that it is important for our social, physiological, and psychological health.

HOW STRESS BECAME A MAJOR INTERDISCIPLINARY CONCEPT

It was not always this way. When I did my graduate work in psychology in the late 1940s and took my first academic job, there was virtually no public or scientific interest in stress. In the United States, the first professional stirrings arose in connection with World Wars I and II, especially the latter. It can legitimately be said that war is a likely impetus for the exploration of stress, especially how it affects the well-being and performance of soldiers.

Every country that maintains a fighting force needs to be concerned with the fact that a substantial proportion of its soldiers develop symptoms of stress, ranging from mild anxiety to severe and debilitating emotional distress and major mental disorder. Although some are more vulnerable than others, the longer soldiers are exposed to battle conditions, and the higher the casualties, the greater is the statistical probability of emotional disorders. Thus, the relative incidence of such disorders in combat airplane flight crews during night bombing, when flying casualties occur after only 160 hours, is 12.0, but is only 3.3 for coastal reconnaissance, when they occur after 360 hours of flying. This incidence is only 1.1 in training, when it takes 1,960 hours of flying to result in a casualty (Tomkins, 1989). These disorders not only impair or destroy the ability to fight but also make soldiers miserable and sometimes unable to function at all.

During World War I, when Americans in France were experiencing very high casualties in trench warfare, "shell shock," which is what battle-induced emotional breakdown was called in those days, was erroneously attributed to the effects on the brain of the terrible noise of exploding shells. In World War II, a psychological cause was recognized, which was a dramatic and important advance in our thinking, and combat-induced emotional disorders came to be called "war neurosis" or "battle fatigue." A more recent expression for these and other stress-induced ailments is *posttraumatic stress disorder*, a term that originated following the Vietnam War.

Notice that the terms *battle fatigue* and *posttraumatic stress disorder* imply an external cause for the symptoms. Unlike *war neurosis*, these terms are less onerous to the victim, because they do not connote personal responsibility for the trouble, with its implication of inadequacy and, therefore, blame. Regardless of terminology and related to the role of individual vulnerability, however, the bottom line is that the emotional problems are presumed to be the result of stress.

During and following World War II, it was mainly the military brass who were concerned about stress, and they hoped research would provide two kinds of practical information: First, how should men be selected for combat and what kind of person would be resistant to the stresses it inevitably creates? Second, how should people be trained to cope effectively with combat stress and its deleterious effects?

These important questions, and the thinking behind them, continued to be features of military psychology in the United States during the Korean and Vietnam wars. Like previous wars, they were major research laboratories for the study of stress and coping and helped fuel the growth of the stress industry. The answers required a basic knowledge about how stress works, which we did not yet have.

Simple answers were not forthcoming because of the complexities that result from individual differences in the conditions that arouse stress. A different approach was needed, and it became necessary to examine personality factors that influence individual vulnerability and to study how diverse people cope with stress. As we shall see later, psychological stress is neither solely in the environment itself nor just the result of personality characteristics, but depends on a particular kind of person–environment relationship.

In the aftermath of World War II, something else also became evident. Stress became the province of everyone, not just soldiers. No one could escape stress, and all of us had to learn how to deal with it. Two reasons can be given for the expansion of interest from the military aspects of stress to its role in our routine daily existence.

First, modern war had become what is referred to as total war. Leaders of nations at war came to realize that the way to win was to make it impossible for the enemy to continue to fight, and the civilian population was just as important in this as the military. Civilians maintained the industrial machine needed to wage war. They were as much the enemy as the soldiers who were fighting.

Technologically advanced weapons carried by airplanes could also rain down terror on a population from the skies and made large-scale destruction and killing possible. This realization led to the sustained bombing of London by Nazi Germany for the purpose of destroying factories and commerce and to kill or demoralize civilians who kept the Allied war machine going. The besieged Allies, the United States and Great Britain, quickly followed suit (most of Europe and quite a bit of Asia had already been overrun by the main Axis powers, Germany and Japan). As we gained air superiority, we did the same to German and Japanese cities. Everyone had now become potential victims of war, and combat stress was no longer restricted to soldiers. The face of major war had changed forever.

Second, and even more important, it slowly dawned on us that stress was a problem in peacetime as well as wartime, and this awareness was the primary impetus for the extraordinary growth in the stress industry in the 1960s, 1970s, and beyond. Stress takes place at one's job, in one's home, and in school—in effect, anywhere people work with each other or have close relationships as, for example, coworkers, family members, lovers, friends, students, or teachers. Stress became a topic of major importance in the social and biological sciences. Knowledge about it filtered down to the lay public via the media, though not always accurately, and interest was widespread.

What happened to the terminology designating the diverse phenomena of stress is also an interesting story in its own right. Even before the struggle to adapt to life was given the name "stress," its importance had been implicitly recognized by scholars and professional workers, if not the public at large. Sociologists, anthropologists, physiologists, psychologists, and social workers had previously used several divergent yet overlapping terms for the subject matter—for example, conflict, frustration, trauma, anomie, alienation, anxiety, depression, and emotional distress.

These concepts, which reflected the adaptational problems imposed by difficult conditions of life, were brought together under the rubric of stress. Stress became the dominant concept uniting them. As Cofer and Appley put it in a scholarly treatment of motivation, "It is as though, when the word stress came into vogue, each investigator, who had been working with a concept he felt was closely related, substituted the word stress and continued in his same line of investigation" (1964, p. 449). Stress became the dominant term for uniting these concepts and for identifying the causes and emotional consequences of the struggle to manage the pressures of daily living.

In a review of major self-help books on stress management, Roskies presents an amusing and somewhat sardonic comment about the overkill involved in the public discovery of stress, as manifested in self-help books. She was not impressed with these books or the evidence about what they accomplished, writing:

> In recent years our traditional understanding of the causes of disease has been transformed by a powerful new concept: stress. From its humble origins as a laboratory term in the 1950s, stress has now become a short-hand symbol for explaining much of what ails us in the contemporary world, invoked to explain conditions as diverse as nail biting, smoking, homicide, suicide, cancer, and heart disease. From an anthropological perspective, stress serves the same purpose in modern society as ghosts and evil spirits did in former times, making sense of various misfortunes and illnesses that otherwise might remain simply random games of chance. . . .
>
> It would be un-American to accept a new cause for disease without seeking to cure or control it. Thus, it is not surprising that the ranks of self-help manuals have recently been joined by books devoted to teaching us how to manage stress. Among the array of do-it-yourself guides to increasing sexual pleasure, building the body beautiful, and unlocking hidden mental and emotional capacities is a new crop of manuals devoted to taming the killer stress. (1983, p. 542)

As always in the field of psychology, in which we constantly seem to rediscover the wheel, ideas and the language used to express them can usually be traced to an earlier time. For example, Plato and Aristotle in Ancient Greece more than two thousand years ago had important and provocative things to say about internal conflicts among thoughts, desires, and the emotions, which seem quite modern, but the word "stress" had not yet been invented.

The basic trilogy of mind began with Plato who, to oversimplify a bit, divided the mind—he called it the "soul"—into reason, appetite, and spirit. Today we label them cognition (thinking), motivation, and emotion. These *mental faculties*, as they are sometimes called—or better still, *mental functions*, with reason regarded as the highest—are often in conflict.

Aristotle followed in this tradition but added a very important idea in his book *Rhetoric*—namely, that how one construes an event causes our emotional reaction to it. He wrote, for example, that anger is the result of the subjective interpretation that we have been slighted by another, and this causes our desire for revenge. Thus, Aristotle treated cognition as being in the service of emotion as well as its regulator. This treatment is, to my knowledge, the earliest version of what today we call *cognitive mediation*.

The Ancient Greek tradition of conflict between reason and emotion ("passion," in those days) was borrowed and further amplified by a Roman scholar, teacher, and writer named Seneca, whose main interests centered on the control of anger and violence. Later, the social and personal need for rational control of our emotions became a centerpiece of the Roman Catholic Church in the Middle Ages, which wanted its flock to make moral choices in which animal instincts or passions—as emotions were called until modern times—were subordinated to reason and controlled by human will. In effect, the classicists saw reason and will as processes that could keep destructive emotions in check, making psychological conflict inevitable.

ORIGINS OF THE STRESS CONCEPT

As nearly as anyone can tell, the word *stress* was first used in a nontechnical sense in the fourteenth century to refer to hardship, straits, adversity, or affliction (Lumsden, 1981). In the late seventeenth century, a prominent physicist-biologist, Robert Hooke (Hinkle, 1973), made a lasting contribution by formulating an engineering analysis of stress. He addressed the practical question of how man-made structures, such as bridges, should be designed to carry heavy loads without collapsing. They must resist buffeting by winds, earthquakes, and other natural forces capable of destroying them.

Hooke's analysis of the problem drew on three basic concepts: load, stress, and strain. *Load* refers to external forces, such as weight; *stress* is the area of the bridge's structure over which the load was applied; and *strain* is the deformation of the structure, produced by the interplay of load and stress. This analysis greatly influenced twentieth-century models of stress, which drew on the idea of load as an external force exerted on a social, physiological, or psychological system. Load is analogous to an external stress stimulus, and strain is analogous to the stress response or reaction.

When these engineering ideas were applied to society, the body, and the mind of an individual, the basic concepts were relabeled and often used differently. *Stress* and *strain* were the main terms to survive. We now speak of a *stress stimulus* or stressor as the external input, and *stress response* or reaction as the output.

Strain is still used by physiologists to represent the stress-produced change in or deformation of the body. Sociologists, who focus on the social system, reverse the order of the terms, speaking instead of a strain in the social system, and stress reactions in the people who are part of that system. Whatever the terms used, however, in stress analysis there is almost always a stimulus—that is, an external event or stressor—and a response or reaction. As you will soon see, however, much more than input and output is needed to understand the stress process fully.

WHY IT IS USEFUL TO STUDY EMOTION IN ADDITION TO STRESS

In the past, stress was viewed as a unidimensional concept—that is, as a continuum ranging from low to high, a concept superficially analogous to arousal or activation (Duffy, 1962). For a while, there was considerable interest in the concept of activation, which united a psychological dimension, ranging from sleepiness to alert excitement, with a dimension of activity and inactivity in portions of the nervous system—specifically the brain stem and the autonomic nervous system.

However, there were two early attempts to divide stress into types, both of which have remained influential. In one, the distinguished physiologist Hans Selye (1974) suggested two types: distress and eustress. *Distress* is the destructive type, illustrated by anger and aggression, and it is said to damage health. *Eustress* is the constructive type, illustrated by emotions associated with empathic concerns for others and positive striving that would benefit the community, and it is said to be compatible with or protective of good health. This important hypothesis remains vague and controversial and, despite its widespread appeal, has still not been adequately supported or refuted by empirical research.

In a second attempt, I drew a distinction among three types of psychological stress—harm/loss, threat, and challenge—and argued that the appraisals associated with each are different (Lazarus, 1966). *Harm/loss* deals with damage or loss that has already taken place. *Threat* has to do with harm or loss that has not yet occurred, but is possible or likely in the near future. *Challenge* consists of the sensibility that, although difficulties stand in the way of gain, they can be overcome with verve, persistence, and self-confidence. Each is coped with differently and has different psychophysiological and performance outcomes.

Despite these subdivisions of stress types, the typical idea of stress is much simpler than that of the emotions. Either as a single dimension or with only a few functional categories, stress tells us relatively little about the details of a person's struggle to adapt. Emotion, conversely, includes at least fifteen different varieties, greatly increasing the richness of what can be said about a person's adaptational struggle.

My list of fifteen emotions includes anger, envy, jealousy, anxiety, fright, guilt, shame, relief, hope, sadness, happiness, pride, love, gratitude, and compassion and is at present one of the longest lists in the field. Each emotion tells us something different about how a person has appraised (evaluated) what is happening in an adaptational transaction and how that person is coping with it. In effect, each emotion has a different scenario or story about an ongoing relationship with the environment.

So, if we know what it means to experience each emotion—that is, the dramatic plot for each—then knowing the emotion being experienced provides a ready understanding of how it was brought about. This provides the advantage of substantial clinical insight about the dynamics of that person's adaptational life. We should not allow this potential gain to be forgotten in our research on stress by failing to consider the emotions involved in stress and adaptation.

To offer a few brief examples, anger is about being demeaned or slighted. Guilt is about a moral lapse. Hope is about a threat or a promise whose outcome is uncertain but could possibly be realized. Happiness is about attaining a goal one has been seeking or making significant progress in that direction. Compassion is about having empathy for someone else's plight—and so forth for the other emotions.

There is another potential gain from knowing the emotion being experienced and the story it reveals about the person–environment relationship. If someone typically responds in many encounters with the same emotion—say, anger, anxiety, sadness, or happiness—we have captured a stable feature of this person's emotional life. That is, he or she is evidently disposed to be an angry, anxious, sad, or happy person, or perhaps more accurately, the person–environment relationship is a stable one. The emotional response in some degree can be said to transcend the situational context; we have discovered a personality trait and have learned something structurally important about how this person relates to the world.

THE UNITY OF STRESS AND EMOTION

One of the dilemmas of writing about stress is that this topic is interdependent with the field of emotion. When there is stress, there are also emotions—perhaps we could call them stress emotions—and the reverse, although not always the case, often applies. That is, when there are emotions, even positively toned ones, there is often stress, too, but by no means always.

During the 1950s and 1960s, several pioneers in stress theory and research published important and forward-looking treatises on psychological stress and emotion. The interdisciplinary quality of the stress concept is illustrated by the fields represented by these scientists. The only important fields not represented in the examples cited in the next paragraph are anthropology and social work, the latter being more akin to psychiatry as an applied field, though professionals in both these fields have made important contributions to what we know about stress and emotion.

Two research-oriented psychiatrists, Grinker and Spiegel (1945), studied the stresses of military combat; a social psychologist, Irving Janis (1958), studied how a patient he was treating psychoanalytically dealt with the stress of major surgery; a sociologist, David Mechanic (1962), carefully documented the stresses and coping processes provoked in graduate students facing a career-threatening examination; a personality psychologist, Magda Arnold (1960), formulated the first programmatic statement of appraisal theory; and several clinical psychologists formulated approaches to treatment and prevention designed to help patients cope with stress more effectively.

My first monograph on stress and coping (Lazarus, 1966) reviewed research and formulated a theory of psychological stress, which was based on the construct of *appraisal.* This theory drew frankly on a subjective approach, which relied on the idea that stress and emotion depend on how an individual evaluates (appraises) transactions with the environment.

In the process of formulating this theory, I also began to see that stress was an aspect of a larger set of issues that included the emotions. So I subsequently set about transforming the construct of appraisal to fit the emotions, too (Lazarus, 1966, 1968; Lazarus & Averill, 1972; Lazarus, Averill, & Opton, 1970, 1974; Lazarus, Coyne, & Folkman, 1982; Lazarus, Kanner, & Folkman, 1980).

Stress and emotion are interdependent; we cannot sensibly treat stress and emotion as if they were separate fields without doing a great disservice to both. There are more commonalities than divergences in the way these embodied states of mind are aroused and coped with and how they affect psychological well-being, functioning, and somatic health.

It should be obvious that certain emotions—for example, anger, envy, jealousy, anxiety, fright, guilt, shame, and sadness—could be called *stress emotions*, because they usually arise from stressful, which refers to harmful, threatening, or challenging, conditions. Although we think of many emotions as positively toned, because they arise from circumstances favorable to the attainment of important goals, they are often closely linked to harm or threat. For example, relief results from a harmful or threatening situation that has abated or disappeared; hope, more often than not, stems from a situation in which we must prepare for the worst while hoping for better.

Even happiness, pride, love, and gratitude, which are usually considered to be positive in tone, are frequently associated with stress. For example, though happy about something good that has happened, we may fear that the favorable conditions provoking our happiness will end, so we engage in coping efforts to prevent this from happening. Or we fear that when conditions of our life are very favorable, others will resent our good fortune and try to undermine it. And when pride is viewed by others as the result of having taken too much credit, say, for our success or that of our child or someone we are identified with, or as a competitive putdown, we must either reject the social pressure or soft-peddle our pride. Our biblical language expresses this in the aphorisms: "Pride goeth before a fall," and "overweening pride."

Love, which is so often treated as a highly desirable emotional state, can be exceedingly stressful when it is unrequited or if we think our lover is losing interest. When gratitude is grudging or violates one's values, the social necessity of showing it may be stressful. And compassion can be aversive when we fail to control our emotional reaction to the suffering of others. All this makes a strong case that stress applies not only to the so-called stress emotions but also to those that are positively toned and the relational conditions that surround them.

THE UNITY OF STRESS, EMOTION, AND COPING

Usually coping has been linked to stress rather than the emotions, and emotion theorists have either ignored it or treated it as separate from the emotion process. Coping is said, incorrectly, to come into focus after an emotion has been aroused to regulate it or deal with the conditions provoking it.

This is unfortunate, because coping is an integral part of the process of emotional arousal. Judging the significance of what is happening always entails evaluating what might be done about it, which determines whether we react with, say, anxiety or anger. For example, when demeaned, viewing oneself as helpless favors anxiety and withdrawal, whereas having a sense of power over the outcome favors anger and aggression. Separating emotion from coping does a disservice to the integrity and complexity of the emotion process, which at every turn considers how we might cope.

We should view stress, emotion, and coping as existing in a part–whole relationship. Separating them is justified only for convenience of analysis because the separation distorts the phenomena as they appear in nature. The three concepts—stress, emotion, and coping—belong together and form a conceptual unit, with emotion being the superordinate concept because it includes stress and coping.

LEVELS OF STRESS ANALYSIS

Returning now to the stress process itself, to remain clear-minded we must distinguish between the way different scientific disciplines treat it, thereby reflecting different levels of scientific analysis. Physiology is concerned with the body, especially the brain and its hormonal neurotransmitters. Two other disciplines—sociology and its cousin cultural anthropology—deal primarily with the society or sociocultural system. A fourth discipline, psychology, is concerned with individual mind and behavior.

In the following sections, I take up two of these levels of stress analysis, the sociocultural and the physiological levels, examine how they relate to each other, and review the distinctive variables essential to each.

Sociocultural Level

The social structure has to do with the way society is organized—for example, into social classes, age, and gender—and how objective and subjective membership in these subgroups influences social meanings, values, social beliefs, attitudes, and actions, which are the major aspects of culture. Sociology and cultural anthropology are the main disciplines concerned with this level.

What connects the social structure and culture to stress is that certain conditions, including sociocultural change, immigration, war, racism, natural disasters, and social crises such as economic depressions, unemployment, poverty, social isolation, privation, and social anarchy, all breed stress reactions in individual persons and social groups, depending on their respective positions in the society. As I noted earlier, these sources of turmoil in the society are often referred to by sociologists as *social strains*, which produce *psychological stress* in individuals and collectivities or groups (Smelser, 1963).

In addition, social scientists of diverse interests, as well as clinical psychologists, psychiatrists, and social workers who draw on social science concepts in their efforts to help troubled individuals, also study natural and industrial disasters (Baker & Chapman, 1962; Lucas, 1969), common social sources of stress such as school examinations (Mechanic, 1962), family problems (Hetherington & Blechman, 1996), and organizational or job stress (Cooper & Payne, 1980; French, Caplan & Van Harrison, 1982; Kahn, Wolfe, Quinn, Snoek, & Rosenthal, 1964; Perrewé, 1991).

In the nineteenth century, several seminal social thinkers, such as Max Weber, Emil Durkheim, and Karl Marx, who could be considered among the founding fathers of modern sociology, were concerned about social injustices and their role in producing alienation from society in large segments of the population. Durkheim (1893) wrote about the experience of *anomie*, which overlaps with alienation but refers specifically to the loss or lack of acceptable norms on which to predicate one's life in a troubled society. This is also a concern of anthropologists and psychologists, as in the problems presented by dislocation and immigration (Berry, 1997) and change within a culture (Shore, 1996).

All three founding fathers of sociology wrote about alienation from work and from society as a result of the Industrial Revolution and technological change. They observed that factory workers no longer could take responsibility for their product from start to finish, as once was true of artisans and guild workers in preindustrial society. Instead, they saw themselves as contributing only a small part to the total production process. Their only reward was economic, so they lost a sense of efficacy, pride, and commitment to their work.

Anomie and alienation, regardless of the way they are brought about, are not only antithetical to the maintenance of a rule-based society but also play an important negative role in morale, personal motivation, identity, and social commitment. Other words for these states of mind are "powerlessness," "meaninglessness," "normlessness," "isolation," and "estrangement from the self," all of which have negative emotional consequences.

Sociological research has shown that when a community is undergoing strain, the incidence of social deviance and mental illness increases (as observed, for example, in a classic study by Hollingshead and Redlich, 1958). The connection is so strong that alcoholism, suicide, crime, and mental illness are widely regarded as symptoms of social decay, but these symptoms are most prevalent in people who are excluded from or have a marginal position in the social structure. This brings sociological concepts closer to psychology. An important difference between the concepts of stress as found in sociology and psychology is that sociology focuses more on the social structure, whereas psychology attends more to the state of mind of individual persons and subgroups that the social system comprises.

Cultural anthropology, in many respects, mixes these two outlooks, but all the social sciences touch on both levels of analysis, even when it is centered mainly on a single level. Cultural anthropologists focus attention on diverse cultural values and meanings. Presumably, values and meanings are strongly influenced in childhood. The resultant values, goal commitments, and beliefs about self and world are perpetuated—though they can also change—when these children grow up. These variables influence what is stressful and how stress emotions are coped with and expressed publicly.

The important point about levels of analysis is that sociological concerns with panic, riot, and fads and fashions (Smelser, 1963), and anthropological concerns with social meanings and cultural values, direct our attention to *collectivities*—that is, subgroups within the society—though attention must also be paid to the *individuals* whom these collectivities comprise, which is the major domain of psychology. Similarly, suicide, crime, and mental illness can be viewed as both social and psychological phenomena, but the way they are understood at these different levels is not exactly the same.

Before proceeding, I should also offer a mild disclaimer about field differences and territoriality, which stereotype sociologists, anthropologists, and psychologists, often distorting what as individuals they are concerned with. When it comes to stress and emotion, it should be clear that considerable overlap exists among the several social science disciplines. The distinctions in levels of analysis between sociology, psychology, and cultural anthropology, therefore, get blurred because of the interdependence of social structure, culture, and individual lives.

This is illustrated by the fact that many cultural anthropologists today refer to themselves as cultural psychologists or psychological anthropologists and, along with sociologists, often sound much like psychologists and vice versa (White & Lutz, 1986). Blurring also occurs with certain metatheoretical outlooks within disciplines—for example, symbolic interactionism in sociology, and appraisal theory and social constructionism in psychology—all of which are frankly subjective in their approach to social behavior and psychological processes.

We must not, however, allow these overlaps among social science disciplines to fool us about the main differences between the two levels of analysis—that is, that of the *society* and the *individual mind*, regardless of the discipline that deals with them. Concepts of stress and emotion are handled differently at these two levels of analysis. This difference applies also within psychology, within sociology, and within cultural anthropology and helps account for many of the standard arguments within and between representatives of each field.

To concretize the level-of-analysis problem, consider two families and the individuals living within them. Imagine that one family is living in comparative harmony; the parents generally present a common front in dealings with their children. Another family, in contrast, suffers from much social strain in the form of marital conflict, anarchy, and resentment. Other social characteristics of these families also can converge or diverge—for example, how they make decisions, as in the contrast between authoritarian or democratic styles of parenting.

Social scientists need to recognize that descriptions of the two families as social systems do not necessarily characterize the states of mind of the individual children living within them, which points up the importance of paying attention to the problem of levels of analysis. We are likely to find some of the children of the authoritarian family secure, sociable, and accepting of others, and others who reject parental authority and are hostile and in trouble with the law. In the democratic family, too, we are apt to find some children who reject parental authority or authority in general—as represented, for example, by teachers and police—and other children who are respectful of authority and comfortable with themselves.

The point is that social system differences between the two family environments apply to some extent to their individual children, but only in a probabilistic sense. Each individual child grows up with a distinctive temperament, unique values and goals, and particular styles of thinking.

Although parents have an important influence on their children, the effect on any individual child is usually complex and variable both in kind and degree. Often we grossly overstate this influence. And often, too, the effects of parenting can even work in a direction opposite to the parental pressure, as when the parents drink or smoke, but none of the children do, perhaps because they have become conscious of the bad example set by their parents or are strongly influenced in this by the community, peers, and the media.

The important point is that children do not come out as carbon copies of their parents, and it is open to question whether parents should always be held responsible for their children's vices or receive credit for their virtues. The child's emotional pattern, which is affected by a combination of family, environmental, and individual personal variables—some of them genetic, some experiential, or both—cannot be explained by reference to the social structure in which they are living. Nor can we explain the social structure of the families by referring to the characteristics of the individual children. Any determinism imposed by family environments is a soft (i.e., loose) one.

This is also true of the coping process. The way a family as a whole copes with stress—that is, as a family culture—say, by denial and avoidance or by vigilance, does not allow us to predict how any given individual within the family copes. And vice versa, we cannot identify the family coping pattern by reference to the coping of its individual members.

To make this statement more general, as in the issue of the different levels of analysis of mind and brain, the makeup and behavior of any given individual cannot be adequately explained by reference to the culture of a social system any more than the social system is explainable by reference to the individuals living within it. It is valuable to look at the interplay of both levels, but one cannot be reduced to the other. This epistemological point is constantly missed by many researchers who regularly fail to distinguish between what is happening at the social and individual levels.

The Physiological Level

Physical stressors have to do with the body's reaction to noxious physical conditions; the term *noxious* means harmful to living tissues. Major classes of noxious agents include injuries resulting from accidents; ingestion of harmful substances, such as alcohol, drugs, or medicines; invasion by microorganisms, such as bacteria and viruses; and abnormal growths, such as cancers or malignancies that spread unchecked and, if not successfully treated, ultimately produce death by destroying vital organs. There are also special systemic failures we barely understand, examples being allergies and autoimmune diseases in which the immune system fails to distinguish between a foreign protein and one's own tissues and attacks its own organs as if they were alien.

The nineteenth-century scientist who made a major contribution to the physiology of stress was the French physiologist Claude Bernard, who discovered that one of the liver's functions was to store sugar, which is essential to all biological and psychological functions. A pancreatic hormone, insulin, regulates how much sugar is stored in the liver and how much is sent into the bloodstream to provide energy for the cells of the body. If the pancreas is unable to make and secrete insulin, diabetes occurs, which is fatal unless the right amount of the hormone is supplied from the outside. If too much insulin is secreted (sometimes as a result of a tumor of the eyelet cells of the pancreas), the opposite of diabetes occurs, leading to insufficient sugar in the blood and brain, attacks of mental confusion, and ultimately coma and death.

This discovery directed the attention of biological and social scientists to the concept of *homeostasis*, whereby a stable internal equilibrium of the body is maintained that is essential to survival. Just as the right amount of sugar must be available in the bloodstream and in the cells of the brain despite a lack of food, other bodily equilibria must also be maintained. For example, the body temperature must be kept within a narrow range regardless of the outside temperature—on the average, roughly around 98.6°F. Sufficient oxygen must also be provided to the cells of the brain for them to function, even when it is not in good supply in the environment, say, on very high mountains where the oxygen level of the atmosphere is low.

Bernard did not contribute directly to the field of stress and emotion, but his research and ideas paved the way for a complex and sophisticated, modern view of adaptive processes that facilitate evolution-based survival. The danger from these processes, however, arises when we engage in adaptive actions, such as obtaining food, seeking shelter, putting on clothing against the cold, seeking shade to protect against the heat, and dealing with predators, that disrupt the homeostatic steady state.

Concretely, the danger is that the very struggle to adapt and survive, especially the last mentioned one, can severely impair the homeostatic steady state on which our lives depend. This became the central theme of the research and ideas of another distinguished physiologist, Walter Cannon. Cannon (1932) focused his attention on dealing with predators, or what he called the "fight-or-flight" reaction, which is associated with the emotions of anger and fear. Bodily resources must be mobilized to sustain an attack or to flee from danger. This places considerable strain on the body's ability to maintain a stable internal environment. In effect, if prolonged and intense, anger and fear are physiologically stressful and carry the potential for bodily harm.

Following from both Bernard's and Cannon's work, the most important modern theory of physiological stress was formulated by Hans Selye (1976). For the purpose of understanding physiological stress, grasping its connection with the psychology of stress, and making sense of the role of stress emotions in health, it should help the reader to know at least the main outlines of Selye's most important ideas. His research and theoretical formulations provide chapter and verse about how the body responds when it must mobilize to cope with harms and threats to its integrity. He described an orchestrated neurochemical set of bodily defenses—referred to as the General Adaptation Syndrome (GAS)—which is brought to bear against noxious conditions or physical stressors.

The GAS consists of three stages. The first stage is the *alarm reaction*. A noxious agent initiates this elaborate neurohumoral process in defense of the living body. If the stress continues, the second stage, *resistance*, comes into play as the body is mobilized to defend itself. The injured tissues become inflamed, which helps isolate them from the rest of the body so the damage can be contained and dealt with without further harm. When the initial swelling has been relieved by anti-inflammatory adrenocortical hormones, healing is facilitated. The stage of resistance is catabolic in action—that is, it draws on and uses up bodily resources rather than building or restoring them anabolically.

The third stage is that of *exhaustion*. If the stress is severe enough or continues long enough, bodily resources begin to fail. Although the GAS helps us survive in the face of noxious environments, depletion of resources is the potential physiological cost of the defense, which is usually controlled because the syndrome does not often go beyond the second stage. However, if the struggle so weakens the organism that it can no longer sustain itself, it results in death.

Though initiated by a noxious agent, the GAS is actually set in motion by action of the pituitary gland, which is closely linked to the hypothalamus. The pituitary is a part of the brain that also serves as an endocrine gland. It manufactures and secretes a master hormone, ACTH, which, when released, stimulates the adrenal glands to pour their hormones into the bloodstream. ACTH stands for *adreno-corticotropic hormone; adreno-* refers to the adrenal glands, *cortico-* to the cortex or outer rind of the glands, and *tropic*, originating with the word *tropism*, to the stimulating agent.

One set of adrenal hormones released by ACTH consists of corticosteroids, which are produced by the outer rind of each adrenal gland. The other set, influenced more by the autonomic nervous system, consists of two closely related catecholamines, adrenaline and noradrenaline, which are produced by the medulla or inner portion of each gland. In recent years, biochemists have discovered another group of hypothalamic hormones, the endorphins, which act on the mind and body like morphine and the opiates, producing euphoria and reducing pain. It might not be amiss to think of ACTH as the main biochemical initiator of the GAS defense against stress, and the endorphins as having the opposing effect of dampening the awareness of pain and stress and the defense against them.

The antagonistic action between hormones, as noted previously, is a property of many other physiological systems of the body, most notably, the nervous system. Stimulating one portion of the system increases arousal, whereas stimulating the other dampens it, making it possible for the internal environment to return to its preprogrammed equilibrial state. To see how this works, we need to know something about the human nervous system.

The nervous system is divided into two major parts: the central nervous system (CNS) or brain, and the peripheral nervous system (PNS). The brain exerts substantial control over the striate muscles of the body that control voluntary or intentional action, as well as over the PNS, which, in turn, is also divided into two subsystems: The voluntary nervous system, or somatic system, is controlled volitionally (by our will or intention), and the autonomic nervous system (ANS), which is sometimes called the involuntary nervous system, is not under volitional control. However, the ANS influences the action of hormones and has a profound effect on all the tissues of the body.

The ANS also has two branches. One consists of sympathetic nerves that arouse us, as when we react with a stress emotion. Its action on the body is largely catabolic—that is, it uses up bodily resources for energy and emergencies. The other, consisting of parasympathetic nerves, dampens this arousal and facilitates relaxation and anabolic processes—that is, the reconstruction of bodily resources and the restoration of energy. As in the case of hormonal systems, here too we see the antagonism between different subsystems of the body—one that arouses and the other that dampens arousal—only, in this case, it is the primary result of neural rather than biochemical action. Hormones and nerves control the body and mind in concert, overlapping greatly in their effects.

Blurring the Physiological and Psychological Levels

Selye proposed that the initiator of the GAS may be psychological as well as physical. In other words, this complex defense process can be brought about by *psychological harms and threats* as well as by physically noxious agents. The idea that what is going on in the mind can do bodily harm is in no sense new. This was assumed by ancient philosophers and is also by modern medicine. One version is the proposal of Sir William Osler, a famous physician writing in the first decade of the twentieth century, that a life of intense work and pleasure exposes people to chronic stress and strain and predisposes them to heart disease—an obvious forerunner of a related hypothesis about the Type A personality (Hinkle, 1977).

The principle that physiological stress reactions may have psychological origins tends to obscure the distinction that needs to be drawn between physiological and psychological stressors. As in the contrast between social and psychological stress, physiological and psychological stress also operate at distinctly different levels of analysis, each of which draws on separate concepts and observations. When the cause of the physiological defense is psychological, the process leading to the GAS is indirect, because a mind rather than some body process initiates or sustains it.

This proposal that psychological and physiological events are separate and distinct—albeit two versions of the same process—points us toward some of the difficulties of distinguishing between physiologically and psychologically noxious agents. For example, exercise, a change in temperature and humidity, and other physical demands on the body will produce many of the same bodily changes that psychological stress and emotion will produce, such as elevated heart rate, blood pressure, respiration rate, and so forth.

If one wishes to attribute the physiological reaction to psychological causes, one must rule out physical causes, which is why, when psychological stress is studied in the laboratory, the physical conditions must be kept constant and the research subject relaxed and prevented from moving too much. These experimental controls eliminate or greatly reduce bodily changes that have a physical cause. The same potential confounding complicates the effort to attribute bodily diseases to psychological causation.

The confounding of physical and psychological causes imposes a tricky problem for Selye's concept of the GAS. If the environment is noxious, the animal or person usually senses the presence of a harm or threat. But it is possible that the two kinds of stress, physiological and psychological, have different consequences for the body, a possibility not foreseen by Selye.

Experimental monkeys that are being starved in a research study normally get very upset when it is feeding time and they see control monkeys being fed. If the temperature in their cage is rapidly increased, they perceive a clear danger to their well-being and become emotional even before the heat begins to cause significant physiological change. And if a human male is placed on a treadmill, in addition to being physiologically changed, he is apt to become ego-involved in how he is doing and, therefore, threatened psychologically, especially if a female friend is present or there is an attractive female nurse monitoring the test. All this illustrates the confounding of physical and psychological stressors.

Mason et al. (1976) reported a fascinating study designed to eliminate the confounding between the two levels of analysis. Primates were exposed to physical harms, such as heat, fasting, and physical exertion, without being allowed to realize that there was any danger. The starved experimental monkeys were given nonnutritive placebos, which calmed them while the control monkeys were being fed. When the temperature was increased in their cage, it was done so gradually that they would not be alarmed. And a human male subject who was placed on the treadmill was never permitted to attain a treadmill speed at which his competitive ego would be engaged. In this way, the physical stressors were kept separate from the psychological stressors so that their effects could be studied without the contaminating psychological effects.

These researchers found that corticosteroid secretion is minimal or absent in the case of physical harms, but is strongly activated when an animal recognizes a harm or threat, resulting in a confounding of the two levels of causation. We need to realize that a threat is purely psychological because it is a potential harm that has not yet materialized, though it too can affect the body via the emotions, such as anxiety, it produces. The physical stressors in these experiments did not, by and large, produce major corticosteroid secretion as Selye would have predicted, whereas the psychological stressors did. This suggests, ironically, that the corticosteroid response of the GAS could be a special product of psychological threat.

Consistent with this interpretation, there is also an old study by Symington, Currie, Curran, and Davidson (1955), which suggests that unconsciousness eliminates the adrenal effects of physical stressors. As long as patients remained unconscious while they were dying of injury or disease, they showed a normal adrenal cortical level—that is, as assessed during autopsy, their corticosteroids were not elevated. In contrast, those who were conscious during the death process, and were presumably aware of what was happening, showed elevated adrenal cortical changes. It would seem, therefore, that some psychological awareness—akin to a conscious perception or appraisal—of the psychological significance of what is happening may be necessary to produce the adrenal cortical changes of the GAS.

In 1955, Selye was invited to speak to the American Psychological Association, and he gave a lecture that helped communicate knowledge of and an interest in his theories among psychologists and stimulated added interest in psychological as well as physiological stress. The result of the increased interest generated for psychological stress has been quite remarkable. In a literature search, Hobfoll, Schwarzer, and Chon (1996) found that more than 29,000 research papers had been published on psychological stress and coping between 1984 and 1996, not even including relevant publications that did not include the keywords "stress" or "coping."

However, Selye did not help us understand the way psychological stressors work, only how they affected the body. The most difficult problem for psychological stress theory is to specify what is psychologically noxious— that is, to identify the rules that make a psychological event stressful, thereby producing a stress reaction.

REFERENCES

Arnold, M. B. (1960). *Emotion and personality.* Vols. 1–2. New York: Columbia University Press.

Baker, G. W., & Chapman, D. W. (Eds.). (1962). *Man and society in disaster.* New York: Basic Books.

Berry, J. W., & commentators (1997). Immigration, acculturation, and adaptation. *Applied Psychology, 46,* 5–68.

Cannon, W. B. (1932). *The wisdom of the body* (2nd ed.). New York: Norton.

Cofer, C. N., & Appley, M. H. (1964). *Motivation: Theory and research.* New York: John Wiley & Sons.

Cooper, C. L., & Payne, R. (1980). *Current concerns in occupational stress.* Chichester, England: John Wiley & Sons.

Duffy, E. (1962). *Activation and behavior.* New York: John Wiley & Sons.

Durkheim, E. (1893). *De la division du travail social* [The social division of labor]. Paris: F. Alcan.

French, J. R. P., Jr., Caplan, R. B., & Van Harrison, R. (1982). *The mechanisms of job stress and strain.* Chichester, England: John Wiley & Sons.

Grinker, R. R., & Spiegel, J. P. (1945). *Men under stress.* New York: McGraw-Hill.

Hetherington, E. M., & Blechman, E. A. (1996). *Stress, coping, and resiliency in children and families.* Mahwah, NJ: Erlbaum.

Hinkle, L. E., Jr. (1973). The concept of "stress" in the biological and social sciences. *Science, Medicine & Man, 1,* 31–48.

Hinkle, L. E., Jr. (1977). The concept of "stress" in the biological and social sciences. In Z. J. Lipowski, D. R. Lipsitt, & P. C. Whybrow (Eds.), *Psychosomatic medicine: Current trends and clinical implications* (pp. 27–49). New York: Oxford University Press.

Hobfoll, S. E., Schwarzer, R., & Chon, K. K. (1996). Disentangling the stress labyrinth: Interpreting the meaning of the term stress as it is studied. *Japanese Health Psychology, 4,* 1–22.

Hollingshead, A. B., & Redlich, F. C. (1958). *Social class and mental illness.* New York: John Wiley & Sons.

Janis, I. L. (1958). *Psychological stress: Psychoanalytic and behavioral studies of surgical patients.* New York: John Wiley & Sons.

Kahn, R. L., Wolfe, D. M., Quinn, R. P., Snoek, J. D., & Rosenthal, R. A. (1964). *Organizational stress: Studies in role conflict and ambiguity.* New York: John Wiley & Sons.

Lazarus, R. S. (1966). *Psychological stress and the coping process.* New York: McGraw-Hill.

Lazarus, R. S. (1968). Emotions and adaptation: Conceptual and empirical relations. In W. J. Arnold (Ed.), *Nebraska symposium on motivation* (pp. 175–266). Lincoln: University of Nebraska Press.

Lazarus, R. S., & Averill, J. R. (1972). Emotion and cognition: with special reference to anxiety. In C. D. Spielberger (Ed.), *Anxiety and behavior* (2nd ed., pp. 242–283). New York: Academic Press.

Lazarus, R. S., Averill, J. R., & Opton, E. M., Jr. (1970). Toward a cognitive theory of emotions. In M. Arnold (Ed.), *Feelings and emotions* (pp. 207–232). New York: Academic Press.

Lazarus, R. S., Averill, J. R., & Opton, E. M., Jr. (1974). The psychology of coping: Issues of research and assessment. In G. V. Coelho, D. A. Hamburg, & J. F. Adams (Eds.), *Coping and adaptation* (pp. 249–315). New York: Basic Books.

Lazarus, R. S., Coyne, J. C., & Folkman, S. (1982). Cognition, emotion and motivation: The doctoring of Humpty-Dumpty. In R. W. J. Neufeld (Ed.), *Psychological stress and psychopathology* (pp. 218–239). New York: McGraw-Hill.

Lazarus, R. S., Kanner, A., & Folkman, S. (1980). Emotions: A cognitive-phenomenological analysis. In R. Plutchik & H. Kellerman (Eds.), *Theories of emotion* (pp. 189–217). New York: Academic Press.

Lucas, R. S. (1969). *Men in crisis.* New York: Basic Books.

Lumsden, D. P. (1981). Is the concept of "stress" of any use, anymore? In D. Randall (Ed.), *Contributions to primary prevention in mental health: Working papers.* Toronto: Toronto National Office of the Canadian Mental Health Association.

Mason, J. W., Maher, J. T., Hartley, L. H., Mougey, E., Perlow, M. J., & Jones, L. G. (1976). Selectivity of corticosteroid and catecholamine response to various natural stimuli. In G. Serban (Ed.), *Psychopathology of human adaptation* (pp. 147–171). New York: Plenum Press.

Mechanic, D. (1962). *Students under stress: A study in the social psychology of adaptation.* New York: Free Press (Reprinted 1978, Madison: University of Wisconsin Press).

Perrewé, P. L. (1991). *Job stress.* Corte Madera, CA: Select Press.

Roskies, E. (1983). Stress management: Averting the evil eye. *Contemporary Psychology, 28,* 542–544.

Selye, H. (1974). *Stress without distress.* Philadelphia: Lippincott.

Selye, H. (1976). *The stress of life.* Rev. ed. New York: McGraw-Hill (Original work published 1956).

Shore, B. (1996). *Culture in mind: Cognition, culture, and the problem of meaning.* New York: Oxford University Press.

Smelser, N. J. (1963). *Theory of collective behavior.* New York: Free Press.

Symington, T., Currie, A. R., Curran, R. C., & Davidson, J. N. (1955). The reaction of the adrenal cortex in conditions of stress. In *Ciba Foundation*

Colloquia on Endocrinology, vol. 8, *The human adrenal cortex* (pp. 70–91). Boston: Little, Brown.

Tomkins, J. (1989). Fighting words. *Harpers Magazine*, March, 33–35.

White, G. M., & Lutz, C. (1986). The anthropology of emotions. *Annual review of anthropology, 15,* 405–436.

CHAPTER 3

Work Stress: Macro-Level Work Stressors

Lorne Sulsky and Carlla Smith

THE JOB OR OCCUPATION

Most people are guided by the implicit assumption that some jobs are more stressful than others. For example, you probably agree that the job of a demolitions expert is more stressful than that of a janitor. If pressed to give a reason for your answer, you would undoubtedly say that the demolitions expert faces the threat of injury or death in the performance of his or her job, whereas the janitor typically does not. However, jobs are often considered to be stressful for a variety of reasons other than threat to life or limb.

From a study of the health records of 22,000 workers in 130 occupations, the National Institute for Occupational Safety and Health (NIOSH) compiled data on stress-related disease incidence by occupation (M. J. Smith, Colligan, & Hurrell, 1977). Twelve occupations out of a top-40 list with a very high incidence of health care admissions and mortality were identified: laborers, secretaries, inspectors, clinical laboratory technicians, office managers, managers/administrators, foremen, waitresses/waiters, machine operatives, farm owners, mine operatives, and painters (see Table 3.1). Some other occupations that showed a higher than average incidence of health care admissions and mortality were health care itself (e.g., registered nurses, nurses aides, dental assistants), skilled blue-collar work (e.g., machinists, electricians), public services (e.g., social workers, police), and sales (e.g., sales managers and representatives).

In another NIOSH-sponsored study, Murphy (1991) examined the association between job types and disability from cardiovascular disease in a 1978 U.S. health interview survey of almost 10,000 workers. Across

Table 3.1. Occupations with High Incidence of Stress-Related Diseases

Occupation	Rank	Mean z-scores for death certificates*	Mean z-scores for mental health admissions*	Mean z-scores for general hospital admissions
Laborers	1	216.84	97.97	44.85
Secretary	2	−2.40	42.64	25.95
Inspector	3	5.76	10.71	17.80
Clinical Laboratory Technician	3	0.57	5.87	17.46
Office Manager	3	0.57	0.16	14.48
Foreman	4	0.84	−9.50	12.07
Manager/ Administrator	4	4.26	−13.76	20.03
Waitress/Waiter	5	0.13	26.15	−1.13
Operatives	5	−13.74	16.52	0.25
Farm Owner	6	35.30	−3.60	−8.50
Mine Operative	6	21.97	0.33	−2.16
Painter (not artist)	6	15.09	−0.38	−2.71

*Note: High positive scores indicate high (above average) levels; scores close to 0 indicate average or normal levels; high negative scores indicate low (below average) levels.

2,485 occupations, he found that the job dimensions associated with cardiovascular disability were hazardous situations, responsibility for others, exchanging information, and attention to devices (equipment, machinery). Occupations with high scores on these dimensions included transportation jobs (air traffic controllers, truck drivers, airline pilots/attendants, bus drivers, and locomotive engineers), teachers (preschool and adult education), and craftsmen/foremen (machinists, carpenters, and foremen).

According to the NIOSH-sponsored research that has investigated stress-related occupational differences across thousands of American workers in several hundred different jobs, many of the jobs at the bottom of the organizational ladder (e.g., laborers, secretaries, and machine operators) are among the most stressful. The NIOSH studies identified a few common stressors across many of these jobs, for example, a fast work pace, long working hours, repetitive and boring job tasks, physical hazards, and dealing with equipment or machinery.

Despite the common themes across occupations identified by NIOSH researchers, they and others have noted distinct occupational differences, both in the amount and type of stress experienced (Sparks & Cooper, 1999). For example, French, Caplan, and Harrison (1982) reported that the administrators in their sample identified very different job-related stressors than the scientists or engineers.

In addition, Grosch and Murphy (1998) examined more than 8,000 employees across diverse jobs and discovered that workers whose occupations involved the use of machines or transportation equipment reported higher levels of depression and lower levels of health compared to managerial and professional occupations. These results suggest that there may be systematic differences across occupations in terms of both the quality and quantity of work stressors.

The identification of occupationally specific stressors has been particularly important in targeting areas for change or intervention. If stressors unique to a particular job or class of jobs can be identified, interventions can be developed that potentially attenuate or even eliminate the stressors in question. This is akin to "curing the disease" rather than treating the symptoms through individual-level stress management techniques like meditation or structured relaxation exercises. We now examine some specific occupations and consider what is known about the stressors that are frequently associated with these occupations.

Police and Firefighters

The law enforcement profession has long been universally recognized as stressful. Hans Selye even stated, "Unlike most professions, it [police work] ranks as one of the most hazardous, even exceeding the formidable stresses and strains of air traffic control" (1978, p. 7). Research on the stress of police work has proliferated in recent years, a testimony to the increasing awareness that police work is inherently stressful (e.g., Beehr, Johnson, & Nieva, 1995; Hart, Wearing, & Headey, 1995; Stephens & Long, 2000). Increased job stress, unfortunately, has been linked to increased police violence (Kop, Euwema, & Schaufeli, 1999).

Besides the obvious physical dangers often associated with this profession, police officers have identified excess paperwork, red tape, dealing with the court system, coworker and supervisor conflict, shift work, and lack of support from the public as job-related stressors (Greller, Parsons, & Mitchell, 1992). Because of the erratic nature of police work, officers often report both work overload (too much to do) and work underload (too little to do).

A study of occupational stress in a group of police officers in the Midwestern United States found that the stressors of (1) underutilization of skills, (2) quantitative work (over)load, and (3) job future ambiguity were related to individual psychological strain (Kaufmann & Beehr, 1989). These police officers not only were stressed by having too much to do that was too easy or routine but also feared for their future employment. The stressor of job future ambiguity (i.e., uncertainty about one's continued or future employment prospects) is unfortunately an increasingly common occupational stressor, particularly in corporate America.

Many occupational stressors associated with police work, especially shift work, exposure to physical dangers (Beaton & Murphy, 1993), and psychological trauma (Corneil, Beaton, Murphy, Johnson, & Pike, 1999), are shared with firefighters. In fact, firefighters' 1990–1991 rates of occupational injury and illness were the highest of any group of U.S. workers (U.S. Bureau of Labor Statistics, 1990). Police work, as well as fire fighting, has frequently been glamorized in the media, so it is indeed surprising to people that many facets of both professions are considered to be boring and unstimulating (Davidson & Veno, 1980; Mitchell & Bray, 1990). Added to these stressors, firefighters must rely heavily on teamwork and spend many hours at the station, both of which can aggravate administrative and coworker conflicts (Beaton & Murphy, 1993). High rates of divorce (Hurrell, 1977) and alcoholism (Heiman, 1975), common strains among police officers and firefighters, underscore the potentially devastating effects of these job-related stressors.

Before we leave this discussion, we thought we might share an observation from our applied work with firefighters. Specifically, one common theme that emerges is that triggering the fire alarm appears to set in motion another type of alarm—Selye's alarm reaction—as firefighters undergo the beginnings of the General Adaptation Syndrome, or GAS (see also Beaton, Murphy, Pike, & Jarrett, 1995). What many of them report as very stressful, however, is the uncertainty and the related feeling of no control over what awaits them at the scene. Often, this surge of adrenaline proves to be of no use, because the problem turns out to be either a false alarm or relatively minor. The uncertainty about whether a serious fire or hazard awaits is often reported as a salient stressor for many firefighters. We expect that a similar type of uncertainty likely leads to perceived stress in police officers, as well.

Social Workers and Teachers

Some people-oriented service professions, such as social work and teaching, have job stressors in common with both the police and health care professions. Social service workers report little positive feedback from their jobs or the public, unsafe work environments, frustration in dealing with bureaucracy and excessive paperwork, a sense of personal responsibility for clients, and work overload (Eaton, 1980; Ross, 1993).

Teachers indicate that excessive paperwork, lack of adequate supplies/ facilities, work overload, and a lack of positive feedback are salient stressors (Kyriacou & Sutcliffe, 1978; Phillips & Lee, 1980; Starnaman & Miller, 1992). Urban teachers have also complained of the stress of dealing with vandalism and physical violence from students (Dworkin, Haney, & Telschow, 1988; Phillips & Lee, 1980). Burnout, a special type of stress response often associated with the human service professions, appears to occur all too frequently in the teaching profession as well (e.g., Bakker & Schaufeli, 2000; Friedman, 2000).

Data obtained from a recent study of teacher stress utilizing the Teacher Stress Inventory (Fimian & Fastenau, 1990) indicate that professional investment is a particularly salient issue for teachers. Professional investment refers to a number of specific stressors, including a lack of opportunities for promotion, lack of control over job-related decisions, and a lack of emotional/ intellectual stimulation. Clearly, we applaud attempts to develop surveys specific to particular occupations or jobs. Such specialized surveys allow stressors unique to the job or occupation in question to be uncovered.

Finally, Richard and Krieshok (1989) were interested in the possibility that coping moderates the relationship between stress and strain in university faculty. Moreover, they were interested in examining whether gender and academic rank (e.g., assistant vs. associate professor) are important variables to consider when investigating the associations among stress, strain, and coping. Eighty-three faculty members from a large university completed a number of questionnaires assessing levels of stress, strain, and coping activities. Although coping, gender, and rank did not function as hypothesized in their data, they reasoned that academic rank might be an important variable for understanding the stress process in university faculty. Specifically, in terms of reported strains, men tended to suffer less from the effects of perceived stress as they moved up in academic rank, while the opposite was true for women.

Health Care Workers

Medical personnel, particularly nurses, have been studied in much contemporary stress research, although research has also considered other workers in the health care professions (e.g., Arsenault, Dolan, & Van Ameringen, 1991; Landsbergis, 1988). Nurses have reported that work overload, heavy physical work, shift work, patient concerns (dealing with death and medical treatment), and interpersonal problems with other medical staff, particularly physicians, are common stressors (Hipwell, Tyler, & Wilson, 1989; Lee, 1986; Marshall, 1978). A study of 171 nurses across five hospitals also found that some of these identified stressors—work overload, little support from supervisors, and negligent or incompetent coworkers—were sources of stress related to depression and decreased work performance (Motowidlo, Packard, & Manning, 1986).

In a sample of 252 nurses, Hemingway and Smith (1999) found that characteristics of the organization predicted the onset of stressors, which, in turn, predicted outcomes such as absenteeism. These results suggested that researchers need to more closely examine organizational characteristics (e.g., the amount of support; the nature of formal/informal relationships) as antecedents of stressors and perhaps attempt to alter characteristics deemed to be detrimental to employees. Another implication of their study is that context-driven or organizationally specific theory may prove to be superior to the more general approaches in guiding research and practice.

Many of the job-related stressors reported by nurses are experienced to an even greater degree by medical doctors, who also suffer from high rates of depression and alcoholism (Firth-Cozens, 2001). For example, early research (Caplan, Cobb, French, Van Harrison, & Pinneau, 1975) found that physicians encountered the highest levels of workload, job complexity, and responsibility for people. Revicki and May (1985) reported that dealing with suffering, fear, death, and difficult patients were very salient stressors for medical doctors. Kirkcaldy, Trimpop, and Cooper (1997) also found that German physicians working more than 48 hours per week experienced a greater number of driving accidents and higher job-related stress.

Revicki and Whitley (1995) investigated the occupational stress of emergency medicine residents. They reasoned that emergency medicine residency should be a particularly stressful position because of the unpredictable and often extreme nature of the job itself and the relative inexperience of many workers. Over a three-year period, the researchers followed a large sample of emergency medicine residents comprising 20 to 37 percent of that job category in the United States. Their results confirmed previous cross-sectional research (e.g., Revicki, Whitley, Gallery, & Allison, 1993) in demonstrating the importance of task and role clarity in defusing the effects of job-related stress: Emergency medicine residents who reported a great deal of ambiguity regarding their roles and responsibilities and little task clarity also reported more depression than their peers who reported less ambiguity and more clarity.

One medical professional who has attracted the attention of stress researchers is the dentist. C. L. Cooper (1980) attempted to identify dentists' job-related stressors by interviewing a group of American dentists gathered for a professional meeting. He found that coping with difficult patients, building a practice, administrative duties, and public opinion of the dentist as an inflictor of pain were identified as salient stressors. Cooper also found that the dentists most bothered by these stressors showed increased blood pressure and abnormal heart rhythms (electrocardiograms). Cooper and his colleagues (Cooper, Watts, Baglioni, & Kelly, 1988) replicated many of these findings several years later with a sample of dentists in Great Britain. In addition, lack of respect for practicing dentistry and having too little professional and personal time were identified as occupational stressors in a longitudinal study of 108 American dentists (DiMatteo, Shugars, & Hays, 1993). One common theme cutting across these studies is that dentists are distressed by their poor public image, at least relative to other medical professionals. Perhaps the media could help out by televising programs that portray dentists in a positive light!

A common theme linking occupational stressors across different types of medical professions is difficulty with interpersonal interactions and/or interdependency on others (coworkers or patients). Medical professionals are trained to be skilled scientists and clinicians, but are often woefully unprepared to deal with people-oriented issues. These types of issues are also quite frequently beyond individual control; for example, some patients are dissatisfied regardless of the quality of care they receive. Lack of control over the work environment also undoubtedly contributes to the stress experienced by these professionals.

Another area of concern is workplace violence, which has increasingly caught the attention of the media, as well as organizational researchers and practitioners (Braverman, 1999). This violence has often resulted in assaults on health care workers (Schat & Kelloway, 2000). Much of the documented violence has been against nurses (Arnetz, Arnetz, & Petterson, 1996) and, more specifically, psychiatric workers in hospitals (Carmel & Hunter, 1991). Although few statistics exist on the incidence of violence against health care workers in outpatient settings, the meager evidence does suggest that assaults are underreported (Bloom, 1989). In an exploratory survey of 108 psychologists, Fong (1995) found that 17 percent of her sample had experienced some type of assaultive incident by a client or patient. These incidents ranged from threats to actual attacks against person or property.

Air Traffic Controllers

In addition to the occupational stressors common to many jobs, behavioral scientists believe that the reported stressfulness of contemporary jobs is due, in large measure, to the small amount of control that workers perceive they have over their daily work activities and working conditions (Fisher, 1985; Sauter, Hurrell, & Cooper, 1989). A perceived lack of control is reported to be one of the most potent stressors for air traffic controllers, a profession that is legendary for its stressfulness. Air traffic controllers, who monitor air traffic through electronic devices in airport facilities, often have little control over potential crisis situations and workload (Zeier, 1994).

One study compared occupational stressors reported by Canadian and New Zealand air traffic controllers and found high agreement regarding the top job-related stressors: equipment limitations, peak traffic situations, general work environment, and fear of causing an accident (Shouksmith & Burrough, 1988).

More recently, Zeier (1994) found a positive relationship between subjective and objective workload and saliva cortisol levels in a sample of air traffic controllers in Switzerland. For each controller, subjective workload was measured through questionnaire responses; objective workload was measured with a composite index of the average number of aircraft controlled, number of radio communications, and duration of radio communications during successive ten-minute intervals. These results are consistent with previous research that has shown a link between work (traffic) load and health problems in air traffic controllers (Cobb & Rose, 1973; Laurig, Becker-Biskaborn, & Reiche, 1971). Although Zeier estimated that only 10 to 15 percent of his sample was at risk for serious stress-related problems, he claimed that complaints from controllers about excessive work stress should be taken seriously.

Office and Managerial Workers

Another surprisingly high-stress occupation is clerical and secretarial work. A national study that examined the relationship between coronary heart disease and employment (Haynes, Feinlieb, & Kannel, 1980) found that the incidence of heart disease was much higher in female clerical workers than in any other group of women studied. The women at highest health risk reported they had little control over their job mobility and nonsupportive supervisors. Additionally, Narayanan, Menon, and Spector (1999) found that compared to select other occupations, clerical workers suffered from higher levels of work overload and a perceived lack of control.

An occupation that has been identified as quite stressful but that is typically characterized by considerable control and discretion is managerial work (Cavanaugh, Boswell, Roehling, & Boudreau, 2000). Some important stressors for managers are work overload, conflict and ambiguity in defining the managerial role, and difficult work relationships (Burke,

1988; Glowinkowski & Cooper, 1986). Managers who experience these stressors have also reported increased anxiety and depression (Cooper & Roden, 1985), alcohol consumption (Margolis, Kroes, & Quinn, 1974), and propensity to leave their organizations (Bedeian & Armenakis, 1981).

Gender differences may be important when considering stress and managerial work. Research conducted in Sweden, for example, suggests that male managers' catecholamine output dropped at the end of the workday, although this was not true for female managers; for females, norepinephrine levels actually *increased* after work (Frankenhaeuser et al., 1989). These results suggest that, for females, the work–home spillover of managerial stress to their personal life is a potentially serious problem. Compared to males, female managers appear to have greater difficultly leaving their problems at the office when they go home.

Interestingly, some occupations are considered stressful not because they require too much in work quantity from workers but because they require too much in quality. This aspect of work overload is called *qualitative overload*, as opposed to the *quantitative overload* typically reported by managers. Qualitative overload has been identified as an occupational stressor for workers in highly technical jobs such as science and engineering (French & Caplan, 1973).

This short exploration of stressful occupations has revealed that stressful jobs span the organizational hierarchy. We focused on the diversity of stressors across occupations because such information is useful in designing stress management interventions or employee development programs for different types of workers. However, many of these high-stress jobs share some common stressors. Some of these stressors (e.g., exposure to physical hazards and use of machinery and equipment) are frequently associated with industrial or blue-collar occupations, a topic to which we now turn our attention.

THE PHYSICAL WORK ENVIRONMENT

The stressors faced by workers in industrial settings, such as foundries or factories, are often qualitatively quite different from stressors faced by office workers or managers. In a sense, all stressors emanate from the physical environment (unless, of course, they are simply figments of one's imagination!). However, white-collar workers rarely must endure excessive noise or temperature extremes as part of their daily job-related activities. Environmental stressors are also quite unique in that they can result in direct physical trauma regardless of workers' perceptions. The perception of elements of the physical environment as stressful or harmful may even compound the trauma induced by the environment. For these reasons, the effects of such stressors can be particularly devastating. We now examine some specific physical stressors.

Noise

Foundry and factory workers are often exposed to noise created by the operation of equipment or machinery, such as jackhammers or drill presses. The most obvious concern with such noise in work environments is the potential for hearing loss. After initial exposure to high-intensity noise, some temporary hearing loss occurs, which is recovered a few hours or days following exposure. However, after repeated exposure to high-intensity noise, recovery decreases over time, resulting in permanent hearing loss. This type of deafness is particularly insidious because it is caused by damage to the auditory receptors in the inner ear, and, consequently, nerve impulses cannot be transmitted to the brain. Hearing loss caused from nerve damage to the inner ear is usually not correctable surgically or with a hearing aid. Some nerve deafness also naturally occurs with the deterioration associated with the aging process, so the effects of occupational deafness may be compounded in older workers.

Because of the serious health implications of noise exposure, the Occupational Safety and Health Administration (OSHA) has set standards for exposure times of workers at different noise intensities (see Table 3.2). A permissible exposure for a sound (noise) intensity level of 110 decibels (dB), which is equivalent to being 6 feet from an amplifier at a rock concert, is only thirty minutes—a duration routinely exceeded by many young concertgoers. However, workers with ear protection can lengthen their permissible exposure times.

Besides hearing loss, it seems logical that occupational noise may also affect work performance, as anyone who has tried to concentrate on a task in a noisy environment can attest. However, the effects of noise on performance are not clear-cut. In general, task performance is impaired only at very high noise intensities (over 95 dB). Performance on simple or well-learned tasks may even show performance improvements in slightly noisy settings. This enhancement probably occurs because the noise acts to focus a person's attention on the task at hand or because the noise acts as a stressor, raising the person's arousal level and therefore overcoming the boredom associated with the task (Broadbent, 1976; Poulton, 1978).

An exception to the enhancement effect seems to be the performance of verbal tasks, particularly the comprehension of written material, in a noisy environment (A. Smith, 1989). Such performance decrements are presumed to occur because the noise masks the "inner" speech associated with reading and/or contributes to overarousal (Broadbent, 1976, 1978; Poulton, 1977, 1978). Performance deterioration under noisy conditions has also been noted when tasks are performed continuously without rest pauses (Davies & Jones, 1982) and when tasks are very difficult, especially in terms of information-processing requirements (Eschenbrenner, 1971). There is even some evidence that changing or intermittent noise levels affect task performance to a greater extent than constant noise levels. Intermittent noise seems to act as a distractor, preventing any adaptation to the noise (Teichner, Arees, & Reilly, 1963).

Recently, Evans and Johnson (2000) performed an interesting experiment, designed to simulate open-office noise levels. They randomly assigned forty female clerical workers to either a low-intensity noise exposure condition or to a control condition. Compared to the control group, subjects in the noise condition experienced elevated urinary epinephrine

Table 3.2. Descriptions of Noise Levels and Exposure Limits According to OSHA

Sound Level (dB)	Specific Noise Examples	Permissible Time (hours)
80		32
85		16
90	Subway train (20 feet)	8
95		4
100		2
105		1
110	Riveting machine (operator)	0.5
115		0.25
120*	Rock concert with amplifier (6 feet)	0.125*
125*		0.063*
130*		0.031*

*Exposures above 115 dB are not permitted regardless of duration, but should they exist, they are to be included in computations of the noise dose.

(adrenaline) levels, made fewer attempts to solve difficult tasks (puzzles) after exposure, and were less likely to make necessary postural adjustments in their computer workstation (a risk factor for musculoskeletal disorders). Given the deficits that were found after only three hours of noise exposure, the researchers emphasized the potential health effects of chronic exposure to low-intensity noise in the workplace.

Unfortunately, most of the evidence about task performance in noisy conditions comes from laboratory experiments. The tasks in such experiments are typically simple or short in duration (e.g., arithmetic and reaction-time tasks), and the subjects are students (cf. Persinger, Tiller, & Koren, 1999) or military personnel. The conclusions from these studies may not be very generalizable to older workers who perform a variety of tasks and who have been subjected to noisy work environments for years (Sanders & McCormick, 1993).

Temperature

Heat

As anyone who has worked near a blast furnace in a steel or glass mill can confirm, exposure to extreme temperature conditions can be very stressful. Under conditions of extreme heat stress, the body absorbs more heat than it can expel, body temperature rises, and illness or death can eventually result. Some industries are notorious for heat-related illness, for example, construction (Jensen, 1983) and the iron and steel industry (Dinman, Stephenson, Horvath, & Colwell, 1974). NIOSH has estimated that between five million and ten million workers in the United States may be exposed to levels of heat at work that represent both a safety and health hazard (Hancock & Vasmatzidis, 1998).

Because of the potentially serious health effects of extreme heat exposure, various professional and government agencies have proposed heat exposure limits in workplaces. These recommended limits are multidimensional, simultaneously considering several factors that can influence heat tolerance. For example, NIOSH's guidelines (1986) consider energy expenditure (workload), degree of heat acclimatization, and work–rest cycle (frequency of work breaks). Other obvious heat-reduction strategies can also be implemented, such as the use of air conditioners, fans, and protective clothing (Wasterlund, 1998). Under extremely hot conditions, medical supervision and protective clothing are mandatory.

Similar to the effects of noise, the effects of heat on task performance are complex, varying with the type of task. Performance on simple or routine tasks, such as reaction time, short-term memory, and arithmetic laboratory tasks, shows little or no deterioration under physical tolerance limits (Ramsey & Kwon, 1988). In fact, brief exposure to heat stress may even improve performance on these simple tasks. An arousal mechanism is again believed to account for this effect: The physical arousal produced by the heat compensates for the boredom created by the task, thus enhancing performance.

Performance on complex tasks, (e.g., vigilance and dual or multiple tasks) begins to deteriorate at about 86°F. Although various explanations have been proposed for this decrement, one interesting perspective is that complex task performance is affected by brain temperature, which is extremely sensitive to heat stress (Ramsey & Kwon, 1988). Similar to the noise data, the research on heat stress is largely composed of short-term laboratory experiments with young subjects. The generalizability of these findings to older adults who chronically endure heat stress at work is unknown.

Cold

Although job-related cold exposure is less common than heat exposure, some workers must endure exposure in winter weather and refrigerated chambers. The industry that leads in cold injuries is oil and gas extraction (particularly in Arctic climates), followed by transportation, warehousing, and protective services (Sinks, Mathias, Halpern, Timbrook, & Newman, 1987). Cold stress, unlike heat stress, is usually not severe and rarely results in death. This is fortunate, because human beings are not able to cold-acclimatize in the same way they can heat-acclimatize (Astrand & Rodahl, 1986). The use of heaters and insulated clothing, particularly gloves, seems to be quite effective in protecting against cold stress.

Apart from the health risks associated with cold exposure (e.g., frostbite), little is known about performance under frigid conditions. The effects of cold stress on performance are influenced by several factors, such as air temperature, humidity, air flow, type of task, and length of cold exposure.

Manual performance is most affected by cold exposure: Finger dexterity decreases at temperatures below 55°F, with much greater decreases at lower temperatures (Riley & Cochran, 1984). Performance data on complex cognitive tasks under cold conditions are limited and inconclusive. Cold exposure seems to be associated with apathy and motivational decrements (Payne, 1959), which could definitely affect task performance. Again, the scanty data on performance under cold stress are mostly limited to laboratory experiments, which may have only limited generalizability to actual work settings.

Interaction Effects of Environmental Stressors

Our discussion has previously focused only on the effects of different single types of environmental stressors, although we alluded to more complex effects when we mentioned that noise or heat can raise a person's arousal level sufficiently to overcome the boredom associated with the task. Indeed, coping with multiple stressors is the norm for many contemporary workers, so it makes little sense to examine stressors in isolation (Danna & Griffin, 1999). One of the most well-known interactive effects deals with noise and sleep loss. Wilkinson (1963) examined the effects of noise and sleep deprivation on performance in a laboratory reaction-time task. He found that both noise and sleep loss individually resulted in task performance errors. However, for those subjects who were sleep deprived, task performance actually improved under the noise condition relative to the quiet condition. The two stressors, noise and sleep loss, canceled each other out because the noise increased arousal sufficiently to overcome the lethargy associated with sleepiness.

Stressors can also produce effects that linger after the stressors are no longer present. Glass and Singer (1972) provided evidence of the aftereffects of an environmental stressor in their classic experiment on the effects of intermittent and unpredictable noise on laboratory task performance (solving puzzles). They found that subjects exposed to unpredictable noise (i.e., noise presented at seemingly random time intervals) performed worse, after the noise was removed, relative to subjects exposed to predictable noise. Further, those who had experienced the unpredictable noise tended to show motivational, as well as performance, deficits by making fewer attempts to solve the experimental tasks (see also the experiment discussed earlier that examined task performance under low-intensity noise; Evans & Johnson, 2000).

A recent longitudinal field study by Melamed, Fried, and Froom (2001) also illustrates the potent interactive effects of chronic stressors. The researchers followed 1,831 industrial employees in Israel over a two- to four-year interval. They found that, among workers exposed to high noise levels, those with complex jobs (i.e., high task complexity and variety) showed twofold increases in blood pressure levels relative to those with simple jobs. Workers in complex jobs also reported lower job satisfaction under high, compared to low, noise exposure. Overall, under low noise conditions, job complexity appeared to have beneficial effects. The researchers concluded that those workers who perform complex jobs under high noise exposure (common scenarios in many modern industrial facilities) are at considerable risk.

The Wilkinson (1963), Glass and Singer (1972), and Melamed et al. (2001) studies illustrate the complexity by which environmental stressors undoubtedly operate in real life. Not only are workers simultaneously exposed to multiple stressors (e.g., noise, heat, cold) that may have both individual and interactive effects among themselves (e.g., noise and heat), attributes of the person (e.g., sleep loss), and the job (e.g., job complexity), but these effects may also linger long after the stressors have disappeared. Small wonder that researchers have frequently been frustrated in their attempts to document the individual impact of specific job-related stressors in both work and nonwork domains!

One very real problem in modern workplaces that is undoubtedly influenced by the interaction of multiple stressors is "sick building syndrome," or SBS (Danna & Griffin, 1999; Frazer, 1998). SBS is a collection of symptoms of general malaise associated with the habitation of some work environments. These symptoms include irritation of the skin, eyes, nose, and throat, neurotoxic complaints (e.g., headache, nausea, drowsiness, fatigue), congested eyes and nose, and reports of unpleasant or unusual odors or tastes (Molhave, 1989). SBS is frequently associated with air-conditioned working environments and poor indoor air quality (Bourbeau, Brisson, & Allaire, 1996; Hedge, 1984; Mendell & Smith, 1990). However, many studies have failed to find specific environmental stressors associated with reports of SBS.

Hedge, Erickson, and Rubin (1992) investigated a possible relationship between SBS and personal and occupational factors. Of the eighteen office buildings they surveyed, all met acceptable standards for indoor air quality, although more than 70 percent of the workers reported at least one symptom of SBS. Those workers who reported the greatest number of symptoms were also women who reported high job stress, low job satisfaction, and video display terminal use. The researchers concluded that the mystery of SBS will be solved only by considering a complex pattern of environmental, occupational, and personal factors, some of which have yet to be determined.

Recent studies have reconfirmed the impact of multiple personal and occupational factors, as well as the obvious environmental ones, on SBS. For example, stress and lack of social support (Mendelson, Catano, & Kelloway, 2000), along with problems in organizational structure and communication patterns (Thoern, 2000), have all been implicated in the development of sick building syndrome.

THE ORGANIZATIONAL ENVIRONMENT

Routinized Work

In addition to the effects of noise and extreme temperature stress, other environmental characteristics of industrial work are considered stressful, such as the repetitive, routinized tasks associated with many assembly-line jobs in factories. This type of work is commonly experienced as boring and monotonous. In fact, behavioral scientists have long known that boredom is associated both with decreased physiological arousal and negative attitudes toward work, which lead to perceptions of repetitiveness, unpleasantness, and constraint (Barmack, 1937; Kivimaeki, & Kalimo, 1996; Melamed, Ben-Avi, Luz, & Green, 1995).

Workers report that job-related boredom often results from quantitative and qualitative underload (i.e., not having enough work and having work that is too easy, respectively; Fisher, 1993). However, because industrial work is largely defined by technology and therefore not easily amenable to change, researchers have concentrated their efforts on identifying particular types of workers who are more or less suitable for machine-paced work. In general, more intelligent and extroverted individuals become easily bored (Fisher, 1993), and many probably self-select out of such jobs.

The jobs that are totally machine-paced, such that a machine completely controls the work flow, are considered to be the most stressful. In these jobs, workers have no control over their tasks and often have difficulty consistently pacing themselves properly with the machine. Workers in these types of machine-paced jobs have shown high levels of physiological stress (adrenaline), anxiety, depression, somatic (physical body) complaints, and job dissatisfaction (M. J. Smith, 1985).

A weakness of most research on job-related monotony is that the existence of routinized work has simply been inferred from incumbents' job titles. Few studies have obtained objective assessments of routinized work and both subjective (perceived) and objective measures of work monotony. Melamed et al. (1995) asked blue-collar workers in twenty-one manufacturing plants in Israel to respond to self-report measures of subjective monotony (i.e., the job descriptors "routine," "monotonous," and "varied enough"), job satisfaction, and psychological distress. Sickness and absence data were collected from personnel records. From job analysis data, worker's jobs were classified as having a work cycle—that is, the work activities that must be performed repetitively during the course of a workday—that was short (less than one minute), medium (one to thirty minutes), long (thirty minutes to one hour), or varied (no predetermined order of activities).

The researchers found that workers in short-cycle repetitive jobs perceived the highest levels of subjective monotony. Repetitive work was also related to job dissatisfaction and psychological distress, particularly for workers in short-cycle jobs, who reported lower job satisfaction and higher psychological distress compared to workers engaged in varied work. Satisfaction and distress were mainly related to subjective monotony, whereas the absence data were related to both subjective and objective monotony. Interestingly, the subjective and objective measures of monotony were only moderately related; Melamed and his colleagues speculated that the indirect manner in which the job analysis data were collected could have influenced this relationship. These results confirm that repetitive work, measured both from the worker's perspective and from independent assessments of the work environment, are directly related to important personal and organizational outcomes. The results also make a case for collecting different types of repetitive work variables, given the lack of convergence between them.

Of course, some routinized work may suffer from the opposite of boredom: namely, a high requirement for constant attention. The need for constant attention is a feature of many blue-collar jobs where attention to detail in the manufacturing process is critical (e.g., assembling circuit boards). For example, Martin and Wall (1989) conducted two studies with alternative methodologies to investigate the effects of attentional demand and cost responsibility on psychological strains. Specifically, they investigated the hypothesis that psychological strain is the end result of an interaction between attentional demand and high-cost responsibility. In the first study, a field experiment, operators of computer-based equipment experienced each of four different job conditions that varied in attentional demand and cost responsibility. As predicted, the job condition that was highest on both dimensions was associated with the highest level of strain. However, because their design did not include a low-demand, high-cost responsibility condition, it was not possible to rule out the possibility that cost responsibility alone was responsible for the results.

The second study was conducted in the same electronics plant. However, this study used survey methodology to assess the variables of interest in the first study across a wide variety of shopfloor jobs. Overall, the survey results suggested that high attentional demands, combined with the knowledge that errors will be costly, predict both health and job attitudes. Thus, support for the interactional hypothesis was obtained, although the nonexperimental design of the second study did not permit causal inferences about the effects of demands and responsibility on strains. The authors echoed a point we emphasized earlier: the need to consider how stressors interact to produce various outcomes.

Recent studies on repetitive work have examined the impact of stress and psychosocial factors on worker health, especially musculoskeletal disorders (Lundberg, 1999). For example, Rissen, Melin, Sandsjo, Dohns, and Lundberg (2000) found that supermarket employees who reported high stress levels also had elevated muscle activity (sEMG). Increased muscle activity is often implicated in the development of musculoskeletal disorders.

In sum, routinized work is inherently stressful. Not only do workers often find these types of jobs boring, but the nature of the work, which usually requires some type of pacing with machine output, can be quite demanding. Unfortunately, technological advances can exacerbate the demands and therefore further increase the stressfulness of these jobs. New technology not only has increased the requirements of many jobs but also enables management to continuously monitor workers' activities.

In discussing job-related noise, temperature extremes, and repetitive or routinized tasks, we have by no means exhausted the list of macro-level stressors. Poorly designed equipment, machinery, and workstations (e.g., an uncomfortable chair or work surface) can create considerable joint and muscle pain, not to mention the possible accompanying perceived stress; all of these stressors will eventually have implications for worker health, performance, and attitudes. However, the study of such stressors usually falls under the domain of engineering or human factors psychology and will not be directly addressed here.

Another macro-level stressor that has been historically associated with certain types of work (e.g., nursing, policing), but can have pervasive effects throughout the organization, is shift work (Parkes, 1999; C. S. Smith et al., 1999), which is discussed next.

Shift Work

If you have ever pulled an all-nighter—whether cramming for an exam, tending a sick child, or making the rounds of New Year's parties—you probably remember how you felt the next day. Do you think your performance at work or school the next day was below average? If you took a nap in the afternoon or evening, were you groggy and unable to function well afterward? Did you sleep poorly throughout the night after napping earlier? The answer to all of these questions is probably yes. The lost night's sleep both deprived you of a night's sleep and disturbed your body's normal sleep–wake cycle.

Circadian Rhythms and Stress

Human beings, unlike some other mammals such as bats, are day-oriented creatures. Our society and our personal lives are typically geared toward daytime activity and nighttime inactivity (mostly sleep). It is therefore not surprising that many other human functions are oriented toward this type of cycle. The most well known are physiological variables such as body temperature, heart rate, and blood pressure, although non-physiological variables, notably self-rated alertness and some types of task performance, also follow this trend. Concentrations of many of these substances in the body usually reach a peak during the day and a trough, or low level, during the night. This cyclic activity repeats every twenty-four hours; such twenty-four-hour cycles are called *circadian cycles* or *circadian rhythms.* Theoretically, these twenty-four-hour cycles will change if the sleep–wake period is altered for ten to fourteen days. For example, if you decided to consistently alter your waking hours to include 1 A.M. to 6 A.M. and your sleeping hours to include 9 A.M. to 3 P.M., the peaks and troughs of your twenty-four-hour temperature cycle would change accordingly.

This information about circadian rhythms should clarify why people generally do not function well at night: Many bodily processes are at their lowest ebb at night, much like an idling automobile. So it is not surprising that people who try to work at night and sleep during the day often report that they cannot do either very well. Shift workers, who comprise approximately 20 to 25 percent of the workforce, must chronically cope with changing work and sleep schedules. Shift work is defined broadly here, referring to any regular employment outside the 7 A.M. to 6 P.M. interval (Monk, 1989). The costs of adjusting to shift work can be high, affecting every aspect of a person's life from personal relationships to work performance. The extreme importance of this facet of organizational life has even been recognized by the federal government in a recent publication by the Office of Technology Assessment (1991).

As a job-related stressor, shift work has been conceived to function similarly to other stressors. In fact, shift work researchers have argued that stress theory has conceptually guided the development of much shift work theory (Taylor, Briner, & Folkard, 1997). For example, Colquhoun and Rutenfranz (1980) proposed a "stress and strain" model to describe the process whereby the detrimental effects of shift work arise. However, some researchers believe that shift work functions quite differently from other types of job-related stressors (Cervinka, 1993). In their model, stress develops from the disruption of the shift worker's circadian rhythms created by modifying working and sleeping hours. The shift work strains, such as performance and health problems, are shaped by intervening variables (or moderators, e.g., personality characteristics and organizational policies).

Monk (1988) also proposed a model to explain how strain arises from shift work. As well as the disruption of circadian cycles just discussed, his model emphasizes the influence of sleep interruption and deficit, and social and domestic problems.

More recently, C. S. Smith et al. (1999) extended prior research to propose a process model of shift work and health. This model attempts to explain how personal and situational factors (e.g., age and workload, respectively) influence the development of sleep and social and domestic disturbances in shift workers. In turn, active and passive coping responses affect the manner in which these disturbances negatively or positively affect the progression of both proximal and distal strains (e.g., anxiety, gastrointestinal symptoms). They found preliminary support for the model across three samples of shift workers. However, because Smith and colleagues used cross-sectional, self-report data to test their model, their results should be viewed with caution.

Performance

Task performance has been widely investigated by shift work researchers, although most studies have been conducted in the laboratory. Compelling real-world evidence for the influence of circadian factors on work performance draws from some widely publicized nuclear power plant accidents, such as those at Three Mile Island and Chernobyl. The Three Mile Island mishap occurred at 4 A.M., when the nuclear power plant operators were halfway through their night shift. The shift workers who committed the almost fatal errors were on a weekly rotating shift schedule (a shift schedule that changed every seven days). Knowing that shift work disrupts cyclic physiological functions and sleeping patterns, it is obvious why shift workers often perform worse than comparable permanent day workers. However, the impact of shift work, particularly night work, is not simply to adversely affect all task performance. The nature of the performance differences is complex and seems to depend on the type of work or task being performed.

Scientists have long known that levels of arousal in the body parallel the twenty-four-hour temperature cycle. The performance trends (over twenty-four hours) of many simple tasks (e.g., simple reaction time and visual search) also parallel the body temperature and arousal cycles. Therefore, performance on simple tasks, such as monitoring and inspection in assembly-line work, would be expected to reach their lowest levels during the late night and early morning hours (Folkard, 1990; Monk, 1989). These performance decrements, of course, would be further exaggerated by sleep loss.

Paradoxically, some complex mental tasks involving short-term memory may be performed fairly well at night, assuming they are not accompanied by severe sleep deficits. Monk and Embrey (1981) studied workers who operated a process control refinery in a large automated chemical plant and were on a rapidly rotating shift schedule (three days on rotating shifts followed by two rest days). Because the shift cycle changed so rapidly, these workers retained their day orientation. Their job activities were relatively complex cognitively, requiring the aggregation of information about plant operations. Because these tasks were performed on the computer, performance could be objectively monitored. The researchers measured the shift workers' actual work performance over a one-month interval. As predicted, job performance was better on the night shift than on the day shift. However, the researchers concurrently measured the shift workers' performance on a simple visual search task, which required the identification of a specific target (a certain number or letter). Also as predicted, simple task performance was worse on the night shift relative to the day shift.

Although it is widely accepted that simple task performance is tied to the body's temperature and arousal cycle, the process underlying complex task performance is unknown at this time. To further complicate this issue, some studies have not shown the night superiority in complex task performance found by Monk and Embrey (1981). Researchers currently believe that the complex task performance cycle is itself very complex, varying widely with the *type* of complex task. Evidence also exists suggesting that the biological clock underlying complex performance adjusts more readily (less than ten to fourteen days) to changes in sleep schedules than the clock underlying simple task performance (Folkard, 1990).

The implications of these task-based performance differences for scheduling shift work in industry are enormous. For example, routine, highly learned, or monotonous work should be automated or closely monitored at night. Slowly rotating or fixed shifts would also aid simple task performance, assuming workers adjusted their sleeping hours accordingly. Complex tasks, requiring judgment and decision making, might be more effectively performed at night and on rapidly rotating (every two or three days) shift systems, assuming workers retained their day orientation and were not sleep deprived. Unfortunately, industry has largely neglected to consider these issues when designing shift systems (Monk, 1989; C. S. Smith et al., 1999).

Health

A paradoxical finding in shift work research is that shift workers often report fewer health complaints than comparable day workers. Workers who are the most distressed frequently leave shift work, and thus those who remain in shift work undoubtedly comprise a select group (Angersbach et al., 1980). Frese and Okonek (1984) maintained that published statistics are probably biased because they do not distinguish among the reasons workers left shift work and therefore underestimate the number of workers who left specifically for health reasons. "Reminiscence" data from former shift workers (retired police officers) even indicated that, in retrospect, they perceived their health and well-being as being worse than they realized at the time (Spelten, Barton, & Folkard, 1993).

Gastrointestinal disorders are the most prevalent health problems associated with shift and night work (Angersbach et al., 1980; Koller, 1983; Vener, Szabo, & Moore, 1989). Rutenfranz, Knauth, and Angersbach's (1981) review of health statistics for over 30,000 workers reported the incidence of gastric ulcers to be 0.3 to 7 percent for day workers, 5 percent for shift workers with no night work, 2.5 to 15 percent for shift workers on the night shift, and 10 to 30 percent for shift workers who left shift work. More recently, Costa, Folkard, and Harrington (2000) estimated that 20 to 75 percent of shift and night workers, compared to 10 to 25 percent of day workers, complain of irregular bowel movements and constipation, heartburn, gas, and appetite disturbances. In many cases, these complaints eventually develop into chronic diseases, such as chronic gastritis and peptic ulcers (Costa, 1996).

Night work, not just shift work, appears to be the critical factor in the development of gastrointestinal disease (Angersbach et al., 1980). A review of thirty-six studies covering fifty years of data and 98,000 workers indicated that disorders of the digestive tract were two to five times more common among shift workers who experienced night work than among day workers or shift workers who did not work at night (Costa, 1996).

Tucker, Smith, Macdonald, and Folkard (1998) also found that the length of shifts and the timing of the changeover from night to morning shifts predicted self-reports of physical health. Specifically, they found that shift workers' reported health was poorer (e.g., digestive problems) for relatively longer shifts (i.e., twelve hours vs. eight hours) and relatively early changeovers (i.e., 6 A.M. vs. 7 A.M.).

Shift work researchers have often speculated that gastrointestinal problems may be greater for shift workers because they have less access to healthy food than day workers (i.e., restaurants and stores are often closed at night), and their irregular hours encourage inconsistent dietary habits. Although no confirming studies have been reported (e.g., Tepas 1990), Lennernäs, Hambræus, and Åkerstedt (1994) investigated a large number of nutritional variables across both shift workers and day workers and found no differences in nutritional intake between the groups. Other factors, such as circadian disruption or sleep deficits, may be the culprit in this case (Vener et al., 1989).

Despite years of debate, most researchers now acknowledge that a relationship between shift work and cardiovascular disease exists (e.g., Tucker, Barton, & Folkard, 1996). In a controlled study, Koller (1983) found that 19.9 percent of shift workers suffered from some form of cardiovascular disease, compared to 7.4 percent of day workers. Using data from a longitudinal study spanning fifteen years, Knutsson, Åkerstedt, Jonsson, and Orth-Gomer (1986) also reported an increased risk of cardiovascular disease in shift workers. In a recent review of the epidemiological literature on cardiovascular disease and shift work, Boggild and Knutsson (1999) calculated that shift workers have a 40 percent increase in risk in cardiovascular mortality or morbidity over day workers.

Similar to our discussion on the origin of gastrointestinal disorders in shift workers, the etiology of cardiovascular disorders is unknown (Åkerstedt & Knutsson, 1997). The risk factors for cardiovascular disease are consistent with many of the problems associated with shift work, such as gastrointestinal symptoms, sleeping dysfunction, and smoking. Shift work can also function as a stressor, thus exacerbating the stress response over time and resulting in increased blood pressure, heart rate, and cholesterol (Costa, 1996).

Attitudes and Social Factors

Shift workers' job-related attitudes have not been widely researched, but existing data suggest that shift workers are more disgruntled than their day-working counterparts. In general, shift workers report lower job satisfaction (Agervold, 1976; Furnham & Hughes, 1999; Herbert, 1983), need fulfillment, and emotional well-being (Frost & Jamal, 1979) than day workers. These negative attitudes can probably be attributed, at least in part, to the personal problems that seem to be associated with shift work.

The negative effects of shift work are most pronounced in shift workers' nonwork lives. The most frequent complaint voiced by shift workers is that shift work interferes with their personal lives, particularly their marital and parental roles (Jackson, Zedeck, & Summers, 1985; Staines & Pleck, 1984). The interference is most strongly felt when shift work schedules require night and weekend work that conflicts with family activities. In a rare study of the views and feeling of shift workers' partners, L. Smith and Folkard (1993) reported that shift workers' spouses were unhappy with their partners' shift work and felt that their lives were substantially disrupted by it. This sentiment was echoed in a survey of more than 1,400 hourly workers, in which divorces and separations were reported to be 50 percent more frequent in night workers than in other groups of workers (Tepas, Armstrong, Carlson, & Duchon, 1985).

In addition to the disruption associated with unusual or changing schedules, shift work can impose excessive domestic load: Shift workers, and particularly women, frequently work at night and tend to domestic and child-rearing duties during the day. This type of schedule does not allow sufficient time for sleep and leisure activities. As evidence, female night workers with two children sleep on the average nine hours less per week than unmarried female day workers (Gadbois, 1981). Men who work the night shift sleep approximately eight hours less per week than their day-working counterparts.

Whether married or unmarried, shift workers often complain that they are unable to become involved in social, community, and religious activities because of their work schedules (Folkard, Minors, & Waterhouse, 1985; Monk, 1989). A survey of British shift workers in the steel industry found that their major complaint was their work schedule's effect on their social life. This social isolation undoubtedly contributes to the fewer friends and more leisure time spent in solitary pursuits reported by shift workers compared to day workers (Herbert, 1983; Walker, 1985). Similarly, Bohle and Tilley (1998) found that night shift workers expressed negative attitudes toward shift work, and a primary explanation given was the social isolation resulting from sleep during the daytime.

Shift workers' relationships and life outside of work appear to be almost universally negatively affected by their hours of work. However, their employing organizations and the shift workers themselves can accomplish much toward alleviating these effects, which is a topic we turn to next.

Shift Work Coping Strategies

The preceding discussion has presented a bleak picture indeed: Shift workers suffer greater health problems, more negative attitudes, decreased job performance, and increased personal problems relative to comparable day workers. In addition, roughly 20 percent of all workers who attempt shift work are unable to successfully adapt to its demands (Monk, 1988). These problems will not diminish in the future as the percentage of shift workers grows with increased automation and computerization, continuous manufacturing operations, and twenty-four-hour service facilities. Fortunately, there are a number of personal and organizational strategies to aid adaptation to unusual and changing work schedules (see Table 3.3).

From an organizational perspective, shift systems should be designed with some regard for human circadian functioning. A fixed shift allows workers to adapt fully to their specific schedules and is therefore potentially the best type of shift schedule. However, on days off, shift workers often revert back to a day schedule and must readapt to their shift schedule when they return to work. This situation is equivalent to a self-imposed rotating shift system. Because rotating shift systems do not restrict shift workers to evening or night work, such schedules are becoming increasingly popular in America, and they are already common in some European countries.

Due to the popularity of rotating shift systems, shift work researchers have debated which variation of the rotating shift is optimal. All experts agree that the weekly rotating system, which is very common in the United States, most likely has negative effects on worker health and performance because the body only partially adapts to the new schedule within the seven-day interval (Czeisler, Moore-Ede, & Coleman, 1982; Monk, 1989). Beyond the agreed admonition against weekly rotating schedules, shift work researchers are divided on the best type of rotating system, with some advocating a rapidly rotating system (Åkerstedt, 1985) and some a slowly rotating system (Czeisler et al., 1982). Regardless of type, however, every shift system should be implemented only after a detailed analysis of the specific situation, which may consider such factors as the type of worker and job tasks (Monk, 1989).

Table 3.3. Summary of Recommendations for Shift Workers

1. Keep a set or routine sleeping schedule as much as possible. Sleep the same number of hours each day or night. While on one shift, go to sleep the same time each day or night.
2. Eat meals at the same or similar times of the day and night. While on one shift, adopt an eating schedule and stick to it.
3. If you're hungry, eat a light snack before going to sleep.
4. Exercise regularly, but not within two or three hours before sleeping.
5. Limit use of caffeine and alcohol. Don't take caffeine within four or five hours of bedtime.
6. While sleeping during the day: (1) Pick the quietest room, and reduce light and noise as much as possible. (2) Encourage family members to recognize "quiet times."
7. Relax before going to bed, and regard the bedroom as only a place to relax and sleep.
8. Focus on *adaptation*. Shift work can be difficult, but it can also be an acceptable, alternative way to schedule work.

At the individual level, two factors—circadian type (C. S. Smith, Reilly, & Midkiff, 1989) and age—seem to influence adjustment to shift work. You are undoubtedly familiar with people who feel best in the early morning hours and prefer to arise and retire early: They are often called "larks" or morning people. Conversely, other people feel best in the evening or night hours and prefer to arise and retire late: They are called "owls" or evening types. Extreme morning types especially seem to experience difficulty coping with night work and changing shifts (Hildebrandt & Stratmann, 1979; Moog, 1993). Age also affects adaptation to shift work because, as people age, their circadian rhythms become more morning oriented and less flexible; shift workers in their forties and fifties often experience sleeping difficulties and decreased well-being (Foret, Bensimon, Benoit, & Vieux, 1981; Monk & Folkard, 1985). Consequently, organizations should counsel both morning types and older shift workers about the potentially negative effects of night work for them.

In addition to designing shift systems to be consistent with human circadian functioning and monitoring certain types of high-risk shift workers, organizations can generally improve adaptation to shift work by providing education and counseling. Information about the effects of changing sleep–wake cycles and coping with such lifestyles should be incorporated into existing employee orientation and development programs (e.g., Monk, 1988; Monk & Folkard, 1992; C. S. Smith, Reilly, Moore-Hirschl, Olsen, & Schmieder, 1989; see also Table 3.3).

Blue-Collar versus White-Collar Work

Based on the stressors just discussed, it might be tempting to draw a simple distinction between blue-collar and white-collar work, such that the macro-level stressors we examined pertain more to blue-collar occupations.

After all, stressors like excessive noise and shift work are often (although not always) associated with industrial work or trade occupations. Thus, from an organizational standpoint, should stressors be classified as either "blue-collar stressors" or "white-collar stressors"? In this section, we would like to point out that such a simple distinction is misleading.

Wallace, Levens, and Singer (1988) offered some thoughts about the concept of blue-collar work. Wallace noted that researchers have not been able to agree on exactly what constitutes "blue-collar" work. The term historically implied unskilled, manual work performed for an hourly wage, but it has been widely applied to many types of service work, such as the jobs of janitors, waiters (food servers), and beauticians (hairstylists). Other definitions have included both skilled and unskilled work in service or production jobs, or any work that is not professional or managerial.

One of the problems in classifying blue-collar work is that occupation is closely related to social class, which is itself related to housing options, leisure pursuits, diet, access to medical care, and educational attainment, among other things. Of course, all of these factors individually and collectively greatly affect individual lifestyle (Sorensen et al., 1985). For example, smoking, alcohol consumption, and unhealthy eating appear to be more prevalent among blue-collar workers than white-collar (especially professional and managerial) workers (Badura, 1984; McMichael & Hartshorne, 1980; Wallace et al., 1988). The link between lifestyle (especially the health risk factors just mentioned) and medical or health outcomes has long been acknowledged. Therefore, not only are blue-collar workers exposed to environmental risk factors at work (e.g., extreme heat, loud noise) but their lifestyle exposes them to additional risk factors.

The lower echelons of white-collar work and the upper echelons of blue-collar work are also often indistinguishable. The classification of certain service occupations, (e.g., police, firefighters, and nurses) has been particularly perplexing; these jobs have even been labeled "nonprofessional white-collar." One of the reasons for the definitional confusion between white- and blue-collar work is that the traditional boundaries are disappearing in contemporary organizations. Advances in automation and technology, particularly computer technology, have eased the physical demands of many blue-collar jobs and elevated their status (Briner & Hockey, 1988; Howell, 1991). Computerized production workers, for example, operate keyboards and read technical material from computer screens. They often have computer access to information, such as equipment costs and specifications, formerly available only to management.

Conversely, computer technology has resulted in the de-skilling of many white-collar jobs (Charmot, 1987). Office workers seated in front of a computer screen for eight hours every day often find that computerization has resulted in work tasks that are simpler, fractionated, and more boring than before. White-collar work, in this case, has assumed many aspects of assembly-line or production work, including specialization and higher speed and accuracy requirements. Added to the "routinization" of their job tasks, many workers at all levels are having to adapt to some form of computer monitoring of work performance.

These new white-collar jobs may benefit from the broader view of job-related boredom provided by C. D. Fisher (1993). Fisher extended prior conceptualizations of boredom, which focused primarily on a limited number of task- and person-specific issues (see previous discussion), to include attributes of the task, environment, person, and person–environment fit. For example, she hypothesized that strengthening perceptions of internal control of worker behavior (e.g., greater autonomy through relaxation of rules and work procedures) and implementing goal-setting programs may alleviate job-related boredom. In both cases, workers should perceive greater personal investment, and consequently increased involvement, in their work activities.

S. Fisher (1985) claimed that, even though the gap between white- and blue-collar work may be narrowing, the blue-collar worker still endures greater industrial (environmental) hazards and less comfortable physical working conditions than the typical white-collar worker. Blue-collar work also frequently commands less pay and status than white-collar work. All of these factors add up to the blue-collar worker perceiving high demands (stressors) and reduced control at work. According to Karasek's job demands–control theory of work stress, individuals who work in high-demand, low-control jobs are more likely to experience job-related stress and stress-related illnesses. Thus, we expect that the blue-collar worker would incur higher work distress, with the resulting consequences.

Nevertheless, Wallace and her colleagues asserted that "a division into blue and white-collar groupings is no longer a meaningful exercise" (1988, p. 56). Indeed, their in-depth assessment of blue- and white-collar differences collected from 919 workers randomly drawn from a large data bank found surprisingly few differences between the two groups. In the years ahead, blue- and white-collar workers may share the same job stressors, or they may develop entirely new sets of stressors. For example, a production worker who formerly enjoyed physically active work may find sitting at a computer screen highly stressful. Regardless of the outcome, future discussions specifically of blue-collar stress may be meaningless or, at the very least, quite different from the current ones.

CONCLUSIONS

In this chapter, we adopted a macro-perspective by examining occupations or job types and the work environment (physical and organizational characteristics) as sources of stress. We reported that, although many stressors are specific to certain occupations, many jobs share a common set of stressors. Numerous lower-level or industrial jobs also require workers to adapt to environmental stressors, routinized work, and night and shift work. Researchers have discovered a great deal about the parameters of human functioning under noise and temperature stress in the laboratory. However, the generalizability of their findings to workers who are chronically exposed to several of these environmental stressors over years is unknown. Conversely, from both laboratory and field studies, researchers have amassed considerable knowledge about routinized work and shift work, although little of that information has been directly applied to organizations.

To conclude this chapter, we would like to pose a series of questions arising from the material presented in this chapter and offer our responses accordingly.

1. From a practical standpoint, should individuals be assessed on a common set of stressors, or should stress assessments be tailored to particular occupations or jobs?

On the one hand, some commonalities in stressors across occupations do seem to exist. On the other hand, however, specific occupations are associated with stressors that do not generalize across occupations. Perhaps the solution is to consolidate stress assessment measures by including both generic items as well as items tailored to specific occupations.

2. Should one assume that physical stressors, such as noise or heat, have equal effects across individuals, thus directly leading to unwanted outcomes?

There is no question that excessive noise or heat can directly lead to unwanted and potentially dangerous physiological outcomes, such as hearing damage or heatstroke, respectively. However, the role of cognitive appraisal should not be discounted, even if the stressor is physical and can lead to strains.

The key point is that the process of cognitive appraisal will directly influence the outcomes of the stress process. For example, a loud air conditioner may be perceived by some individuals as an extreme nuisance and stressor, affecting their concentration, making them anxious, and raising their blood pressure. Other individuals exposed to the same sound may not be bothered by it nearly as much (or at all). Similarly with heat, individuals vary in terms of their subjective appraisals of how hot it actually is. In sum, cognitive appraisal is an important component of the stress process for both physical and nonphysical stressors; and the appraisal process has direct implications for psychological, behavioral, and physiological outcomes.

3. Should job enrichment programs be uniformly applied to reduce or alter jobs commonly viewed as monotonous or boring?

Clearly, technological constraints may limit the ability to reconceptualize some jobs to render them less routine and boring. Nonetheless, for at least some work commonly perceived as monotonous, it is possible to reconfigure the work to make it more challenging and interesting. One example is the use of autonomous work groups in a manufacturing setting (Wall, Kemp, Jackson, & Clegg, 1986).

Although it might seem logical to equate the enrichment of a job with job improvement, improvement is in the eye of the beholder. Indeed, a recent review of job-redesign studies provided by Briner and Reynolds (1999) suggests that generally these interventions lead to somewhat mixed reviews: Some improvements are realized (e.g., job satisfaction), while some negative consequences result as well (e.g., increased absenteeism). An implicit assumption underlying these interventions is that all employees would like a job with more challenge and responsibility. However, there are individual differences across employees in terms of their receptivity to an enriched job (Hackman & Oldham, 1980). Some employees would rather have a routine, boring job and would see an increase in responsibility as a serious stressor. This point underscores the challenge organizational psychologists face when introducing an organizational-level intervention: How does one accommodate the almost inevitable variability across employees exposed to any intervention? At a minimum, any intervention such as job enrichment must be carefully considered and the implications—both positive and negative—anticipated before actually enacting the intervention.

4. When selecting applicants for hire in a job involving shift work, should screening tests be developed, such that adaptability to shift work is considered as a selection criterion?

Clearly, one may be able to determine that some applicants are more likely to be stressed by shift work than others. One may even be able to determine that some applicants will more likely be effective on day shifts compared to night shifts. However, no evidence exists suggesting that adaptability to shift work (as we currently measure it) will predict job performance beyond other more traditional selection predictors, such as selection interviews and cognitive ability tests. For a shift work predictor to be useful, and perhaps legally defensible, the predictor must forecast job performance beyond other predictors already in use. The idea is arguably a provocative one and worthy of future research. Of course, as we discussed previously, these predictors have been successfully used in shift worker counseling and development programs for some time.

REFERENCES

Agervold, M. (1976). Shiftwork: A critical review. *Scandinavian Journal of Psychology, 17*, 181–188.

Åkerstedt, T. (1985). Adjustment of physiological circadian rhythms and the sleep–wake cycle to shiftwork. In Folkard & Monk 1985 (pp. 185–197).

Åkerstedt, T., & Knutsson, A. (1997). Cardiovascular disease and shift work. *Scandinavian Journal of Work, Environment & Health, 23*(4), 257–265.

Angersbach, D., Knauth, P., Loskant, H., Karvonen, M. J., Undeutsch, K., & Rutenfranz, J. (1980). A retrospective cohort study comparing complaints and diseases in day and shift workers. *International Archives of Occupational and Environmental Health, 45*, 127–140.

Arnetz, J. E., Arnetz, B. B., & Petterson, I. (1996). Violence in the nursing profession: Occupational and lifestyle risk factors in Swedish nurses. *Work and Stress, 10*, 119–127.

Arsenault, A., Dolan, S. L., & Van Ameringen, M. R. (1991). Stress and mental strain in hospital work: Exploring the relationship beyond personality. *Journal of Organizational Behavior, 12*, 483–493.

Astrand, P., & Rodahl, K. (1986). *Textbook of work physiology* (3rd ed.). New York: McGraw-Hill.

Badura, B. (1984). Life-style and health: Some remarks on different viewpoints. *Social Science and Medicine, 19*, 341–347.

Bakker, A. B., & Schaufeli, W. B. (2000). Burnout contagion processes among teachers. *Journal of Applied Social Psychology, 30*, 2289–2308.

Barmack, J. E. (1937). Boredom and other factors in the physiology of mental effort: An exploratory study. *Archives of Psychology, 218*, 1–83.

Beaton, R. D., & Murphy, S. A. (1993). Sources of occupational stress among fire fighters and paramedics and correlations with job-related outcomes. *Prehospital and Emergency Medicine, 8*, 140–150.

Beaton, R. D., Murphy, S. A., Pike, K., & Jarrett, M. (1995). Stress symptom factors in firefighters and paramedics. In Sauter & Murphy 1995 (pp. 227–245).

Bedeian, A. G., & Armenakis, A. A. (1981). A path-analytic study of the consequences of role conflict and ambiguity. *Academy of Management Journal, 24*, 417–424.

Beehr, T., Johnson, L., & Nieva, R. (1995). Occupational stress: Coping of police and their spouses. *Journal of Organizational Behavior, 16*, 3–25.

Bloom, J. D. (1989). The character of danger in psychiatric practice: Are the mentally ill dangerous? *Bulletin of the American Academy of Psychiatry and the Law, 17*, 241–255.

Boggild, H., & Knutsson, A. (1999). Shift work, risk factors and cardiovascular disease. *Scandinavian Journal of Work, Environment & Health, 25*(2), 85–99.

Bohle, P., & Tilley, A. J. (1998). Early experience of shiftwork: Influences on attitudes. *Journal of Occupational and Organizational Psychology, 71*, 91–79.

Bourbeau, J., Brisson, C., & Allaire, S. (1996). Prevalence of the sick building syndrome symptoms in office workers before and after being exposed to a building with an improved ventilation system. *Occupational and Environmental Medicine, 53*, 204–210.

Braverman, M. (1999). *Preventing workplace violence: A guide for employers and practitioners.* Thousand Oaks, CA: Sage.

Briner, R., & Hockey, R. J. (1988). Operator stress and computer-based work. In C. L. Cooper & R. Payne (Eds.), *Causes, coping, and consequences of stress at work* (pp. 115–140). New York: John Wiley & Sons.

Briner, R. B., & Reynolds, S. (1999). The costs, benefits, and limitations of organizational level stress interventions. *Journal of Organizational Behavior, 20*, 647–664.

Broadbent, D. (1976). Noise and the details of experiments: A reply to Poulton. *Applied Ergonomics, 7*, 231–235.

Broadbent, D. (1978). The current state of noise research: Reply to Poulton. *Psychological Bulletin, 85*, 1052–1067.

Burke, R. J. (1988). Some antecedents and consequences for work–family conflict. *Journal of Social Behavior and Personality, 3*, 287–302.

Caplan, R. D., Cobb, S., French, J. R. P., Jr., Van Harrison, R., & Pinneau, S. R. (1975). *Job demands and worker health* (NIOSH Research Report, #75-160). Washington, DC: National Institute for Occupational Safety and Health.

Carmel, H., & Hunter, M. (1991). Psychiatrists injured by patient attack. *Bulletin of the American Academy of Psychiatry and the Law, 19*, 309–316.

Cavanaugh, M. A., Boswell, W. R., Roehling, M. V., & Boudreau, J. W. (2000). An empirical examination of self-reported work stress among U.S. managers. *Journal of Applied Psychology, 85*, 65–74.

Cervinka, R. (1993). Night shift dose and stress at work. *Ergonomics, 36*, 155–160.

Charmot, D. (1987). Electronic work and the white-collar employee. In R. E. Kraut (Ed.), *Technology and the transformation of white-collar work* (pp. 23–34). Hillsdale, NJ: Erlbaum.

Cobb, S., & Rose, R. M. (1973). Hypertension, peptide ulcer, and diabetes in air traffic controllers. *Journal of the American Medical Association, 224*, 489–492.

Colquhoun, W. P., & Rutenfranz, J. (1980). *Studies of shiftwork.* London: Taylor & Francis.

Cooper, C. L. (1980). Dentists under pressure: A social psychological study. In Cooper & Marshall 1980 (pp. 3–17).

Cooper, C. L., & Marshall, J. (Eds.). (1980). *White collar and professional stress.* New York: John Wiley & Sons.

Cooper, C. L., & Roden, J. (1985). Mental health and satisfaction among tax officers. *Social Science and Medicine, 21,* 747–751.

Cooper, C. L., Watts, J., Baglioni, A. J., Jr., & Kelly, M. (1988). Occupational stress amongst general practice dentists. *Journal of Occupational Psychology, 61,* 163–174.

Corneil, W., Beaton, R., Murphy, S., Johnson, C., & Pike, K. (1999). Exposure to traumatic incidents and prevalence of posttraumatic stress symptomatology in urban firefighters in two countries. *Journal of Occupational Health Psychology, 4,* 131–141.

Costa, G. (1996). The impact of shift and night work on health. *Applied Ergonomics, 27*(1), 9–16.

Costa, G., Folkard, S., & Harrington, J. M. (2000). Shiftwork and extended hours of work. In P. J. Baxter, P. H. Adams, T. C. Aw, A. Cockcroft, & J. M. Harrington (Eds.), *Hunter's diseases of occupations* (pp. 581–589). London: Edward Arnold.

Czeisler, C. A., Moore-Ede, M. C., & Coleman, R. M. (1982). Rotating shift work schedules that disrupt sleep are improved by applying circadian principles. *Science, 217,* 460–463.

Danna, K., & Griffin, R. W. (1999). Health and well-being in the workplace. *Journal of Management, 25,* 357–384.

Davidson, M. J., & Veno, A. (1980). Stress and the policeman. In Cooper & Marshall 1980 (pp. 131–166).

Davies, D., & Jones, D. (1982). Hearing and noise. In W. T. Singleton (Ed.), *The body at work* (pp. 365–413). New York: Cambridge University Press.

DiMatteo, M. R., Shugars, D. A., & Hays, R. D. (1993). Occupational stress, life stress and mental health among dentists. *Journal of Occupational and Organizational Psychology, 66,* 153–162.

Dinman, B. D., Stephenson, R. R., Horvath, S. M., & Colwell, M. O. (1974). Work in hot environments. I. Field studies of work load, thermal stress and physiologic response. *Journal of Occupational Medicine, 16,* 785–791.

Dworkin, A. G., Haney, C. A., & Telschow, R. L. (1988). Fear, victimization, and stress among urban public school teachers. *Journal of Organizational Behavior, 9,* 159–171.

Eaton, J. W. (1980). Stress in social work practice. In Cooper & Marshall 1980 (pp. 167–185).

Eschenbrenner, A. J. (1971). Effects of intermittent noise on the performance of a complex psychomotor task. *Human Factors, 13*(1), 59–63.

Evans, G. W., & Johnson, D. (2000). Stress and open-office noise. *Journal of Applied Psychology, 85,* 779–783.

Fimian, M. J., & Fastenau, P. S. (1990). The validity and reliability of the Teacher Stress Inventory: A re-analysis of aggregate data. *Journal of Organizational Behavior, 11,* 151–157.

Firth-Cozens, J. (2001). Interventions to improve physicians' well-being and patient care. *Social Science and Medicine, 52,* 215–222.

Fisher, C. D. (1993). Boredom at work: A neglected concept. *Human Relations, 45*(3), 395–417.

Fisher, S. (1985). Control and blue collar work. In C. L. Cooper & M. J. Smith (Eds.), *Job stress and blue collar work* (pp. 19–48). New York: John Wiley & Sons.

Folkard, S. (1990). Circadian performance rhythms: Some practical and theoretical implications. *Philosophical Transactions of the Royal Society of London: Biological Sciences, 327*, 543–553.

Folkard, S., Minors, D., & Waterhouse, J. (1985). Chronobiology and shift work: Current issues and trends. *Chronobiologica, 12*, 31–54.

Folkard, S., & Monk, T. (Eds.). (1985). *Hours of work: Temporal factors in work-scheduling.* Chichester, England: John Wiley & Sons.

Fong, J. Y. (1995). Patient assaults on psychologists: An unrecognized occupational hazard. In Sauter & Murphy 1995 (pp. 273–281).

Foret, J., Bensimon, G., Benoit, O., & Vieux, N. (1981). Quality of sleep as a function of age and shift work. In Reinberg, Vieux, & Andlauer 1981 (pp. 149–154).

Frankenhaeuser, M., Lundberg, U., Fredrikson, M., Melin, B., Tuomisto, M., & Myrsten, A. (1989). Stress on and off the job as related to sex and occupational status in white-collar workers. *Journal of Organizational Behavior, 10*, 321–346.

Frazer, H. T. (1998). RMs can curb indoor air-pollution. *National Underwriter Property & Casualty-Risk Benefits Management, 102*, 23, 78.

French, J. R. P., & Caplan, R. D. (1973). Organizational stress and individual strain. In A. J. Marrow (Ed.), *The failure of success* (pp. 8–19). New York: AMACOM.

French, J. R. P., Caplan, R. D., & Harrison, R. V. (1982). *The mechanisms of job stress and strain.* London: John Wiley & Sons.

Frese, M., & Okonek, K. (1984). Reasons to leave shiftwork and psychological and psychosomatic complaints of former shiftworkers. *Journal of Applied Psychology, 69*, 509–514.

Friedman, I. (2000). Burnout in teachers: Shattered dreams of impeccable professional performance. *Journal of Clinical Psychology, 56*, 595–606.

Frost, P. J., & Jamal, M. (1979). Shift work, attitudes, and reported behavior: Some associations between individual characteristics and hours of work and leisure. *Journal of Applied Psychology, 64*, 77–81.

Furnham, A., & Hughes, K. (1999). Individual difference correlates of nightwork and shift-work rotation. *Personality & Individual Differences, 26*, 941–959.

Gadbois, C. (1981). Women on night shift: Interdependence of sleep and off-the-job activities. In Reinberg, Vieux, & Andlauer 1981 (pp. 223–227).

Glass, C. G., & Singer, J. E. (1972). Behavioral after effects of unpredictable and uncontrollable aversive events. *American Scientist, 60*, 457–465.

Glowinkowski, S. P., & Cooper, C. L. (1986). Managers and professionals in business/industrial settings: The research evidence. In J. M. Ivancevich & D. C. Ganster (Eds.), *Job stress: From theory to suggestions* (pp. 177–193). New York: Hawthorne Press.

Greller, M. M., Parsons, C. K., & Mitchell, D. R. D. (1992). Additive effects and beyond: Occupational stressors and social buffers in a police organization. In J. C. Quick, L. R. Murphy, & J. J. Hurrel, Jr. (Eds.), *Stress and well-being at work* (pp. 33–47). Washington, DC: American Psychological Association.

Grosch, J. W., & Murphy, L. (1998). Occupational difference in depression and global health: Results from a national sample of U.S. workers. *Journal of Occupational and Environmental Medicine, 40*, 153–164.

Hackman, J. R., & Oldham, G. R. (1980). *Work redesign.* Reading, MA: Addison-Wesley.

Hancock, P. A., & Vasmatzidis, I. (1998). Human occupational and performance limits under stress: The thermal environment as a prototypical example. *Ergonomics, 41,* 1169–1191.

Hart, P. M., Wearing, A. J., & Headey, B. (1995). Police stress and well-being: Integrating personality, coping, and daily work experiences. *Journal of Occupational and Organizational Psychology, 68,* 133–156.

Haynes, S. G., Feinleib, M., & Kannel, W. B. (1980). The relationship of psychosocial factors to coronary heart disease in the Framingham study: Eight-year incidences of coronary heart disease. *American Journal of Epidemiology, 37–58.*

Hedge, A. (1984). Suggestive evidence for a relationship between office design and self-reports of ill-health among office workers in the United Kingdom. *Journal of Architectural Planning and Research, 1,* 163–174.

Hedge, A., Erickson, W. A., & Rubin, G. (1992). Effects of personal and occupational factors on sick building syndrome reports in air-conditioned offices. In J. C. Quick, L. R. Murphy, & J. J. Hurrell, Jr. (Eds.), *Stress and well-being at work* (pp. 286–298). Washington, DC: American Psychological Association.

Heiman, M. F. (1975). The police suicide. *Journal of Police Science and Administration, 3,* 267–273.

Hemingway, M. A., & Smith, C. S. (1999). Organizational climate and occupational stressors as predictors of withdrawal behaviors and injuries in nurses. *Journal of Occupational and Organizational Psychology, 72,* 285–299.

Herbert, A. (1983). The influence of shift work on leisure activities: A study with repeated measures. *Ergonomics, 26,* 565–574.

Hildebrandt, G. & Stratmann, I. (1979). Circadian system response to night work in relation to the individual circadian phase position. *International Archives for Occupational and Environmental Health, 3,* 73–83.

Hipwell, A. E., Tyler, P. A., & Wilson, C. M. (1989). Sources of stress and dissatisfaction among nurses in four hospital environments. *British Journal of Medical Psychology, 62*(1), 71–79.

Howell, W. C. (1991). Human factors in the workplace. In M. D. Dunnette & L. M. Hough (Eds.), *Handbook of industrial and organizational psychology* (2nd ed., Vol. 2, pp. 209–269). Palo Alto, CA: Consulting Psychologist Press.

Hurrell, J. J. (1977). *Job stress among police officers: A preliminary analysis* (NIOSH Publication No. 7604228, U.S. Department of Health, Education, and Welfare). Cincinnati, OH: U.S. Government Printing Office.

Jackson, S. E., Zedeck, S., & Summers, E. (1985). Family life disruptions: Effects of job-induced structural and emotional interference. *Academy of Management Journal, 28,* 574–586.

Jensen, R. (1983). Workers' compensation claims attributed to heat and cold exposure. *Professional Safety,* September, 19–24.

Kaufmann, G. M., & Beehr, T. A. (1989). Occupational stressors, individual strains, and social supports among police officers. *Human Relations, 42*(2), 185–197.

Kirkcaldy, B. D., Trimpop, R., & Cooper, G. L. (1997). Working hours, job stress, work satisfaction, and accident rates among medical practitioners and allied personnel. *International Journal of Stress Management, 4,* 79–88.

Kivimaeki, M., & Kalimo, R. (1996). Self-esteem and the occupational stress process: Testing two alternative models in a sample of blue-collar workers. *Journal of Occupational Health Psychology, 1,* 187–196.

Knutsson, A., Åkerstedt, T., Jonsson, B., & Orth-Gomer, K. (1986). Increased risk of ischaemic heart disease in ship workers. *Lancet*, Vol. 328, Issue 8498, July 12, 89–92.

Koller, M. (1983). Health risks related to shift work: An example of time-contingent effects of long-term stress. *International Archives of Occupational and Environmental Health*, *53*, 59–75.

Kop, N., Euwema, M., & Schaufeli, W. (1999). Burnout, job stress and violent behaviour among Dutch police. *Work and Stress*, *13*, 326–340.

Kyriacou, C., & Sutcliffe, J. (1978). Teacher stress: Prevalence, sources and symptoms. *British Journal of Educational Psychology*, *48*, 159–167.

Landsbergis, P. A. (1988). Occupational stress among health care workers: A test of the job demands-control model. *Journal of Organizational Behavior*, *9*, 217–239.

Laurig, W., Becker-Biskaborn, G. U., & Reiche, D. (1971). Software problems in analyzing physiological and work study data. *Ergonomics*, *14*, 625–631.

Lee, C. L. (1986). Professional in medical settings: The research evidence in the 1980s. *Journal of Organizational Behavior Management*, *8*, 195–213.

Lennernäs, M. A., Hambræus, L., & Åkerstedt, T. (1994). Nutrient intake in day workers and shift workers. *Work and Stress*, *8*, 332–342.

Lundberg, U. (1999). Stress responses in low-status jobs and their relationship to health risks: Musculoskeletal disorders. *Annals of the New York Academy of Sciences*, *896*, 162–172.

Margolis, B. L., Kroes, W. H., & Quinn, R. P. (1974). Job stress: An unlisted occupational hazard. *Journal of Occupational Medicine*, *16*, 654–661.

Marshall, J. (1978). Stress amongst nurses. In Cooper & Marshall 1980, 19–59.

Martin, R., & Wall, T. D. (1989). Attentional demand and cost responsibility as stressors in shopfloor jobs. *Academy of Management Journal*, *32*, 69–86.

McMichael, A. J., & Hartshorne, J. M. (1980). Cardiovascular disease and cancer mortality in Australia, by occupation, in relation to drinking, smoking, and eating. *Community Health Studies*, *4*, 76–80.

Melamed, S., Ben-Avi, I., Luz, J., & Green, M. S. (1995). Objective and subjective work monotony: Effects on job satisfaction, psychological distress, and absenteeism in blue-collar workers. *Journal of Applied Psychology*, *80*, 29–42.

Melamed, S., Fried, Y., & Froom, P. (2001). The interactive effect of chronic exposure to noise and job complexity on changes in blood pressure and job satisfaction: A longitudinal study of industrial employees. *Journal of Occupational Health Psychology*, *6*, 182–195.

Mendell, M., & Smith, A. (1990). Consistent pattern of elevated symptoms in air-conditioned office buildings: A reanalysis of epidemiological studies. *American Journal of Public Health*, *80*, 1193–1199.

Mendelson, M. B., Catano, V. M., & Kelloway, K. (2000). The role of stress and social support in sick building syndrome. *Work and Stress*, *14*, 137–155.

Mitchell, J., & Bray, G. (1990). *Emergency service stress*. Englewood Cliffs, NJ: Prentice Hall.

Molhave, L. (1989). The sick building and other buildings with indoor climate problems. *Environment International*, *15*, 65–74.

Monk, T. H. (1988). Coping with the stress of shiftwork. *Work and Stress*, *2*, 169–172.

Monk, T. H. (1989). Human factors implications of shiftwork. *International Review of Ergonomics*, *2*, 111–128.

Monk, T. H., & Embrey, D. E. (1981). A field study of circadian rhythms in actual and interpolated task performance. In Reinberg, Vieux, & Andlauer 1981 (pp. 473–480).

Monk, T. H., & Folkard, S. (1985). Shiftwork and performance. In Folkard & Monk 1985 (pp. 239–252).

Monk, T. H., & Folkard, S. (1992). *Making shiftwork tolerable.* London: Taylor & Francis.

Moog, R. (1993). Optimization of shift work: Physiological contributions. *Ergonomics, 36,* 1249–1259.

Motowidlo, S. J., Packard, J. S., & Manning, M. R. (1986). Occupational stress: Its causes and consequences for job performance. *Journal of Applied Psychology, 71,* 618–629.

Murphy, L. (1991). Job dimensions associated with severe disability due to cardiovascular disease. *Journal of Clinical Epidemiology, 44*(2), 155–166.

Narayanan, L., Menon, S., & Spector, P. E. (1999). Stress in the workplace: A comparison of gender and occupations. *Journal of Organizational Behavior, 20,* 63–73.

NIOSH (National Institute for Occupational Safety and Health). (1986). *Occupational exposure to hot environments, revised criteria.* Washington, DC: U.S. Department of Health and Human Services.

Office of Technology Assessment, U.S. Congress. (1991). *Biological rhythms: Implications for the worker* (OTA-BA-463, September). Washington, DC: U.S. Government Printing Office.

Parkes, K. R. (1999). Shiftwork, job type, and the work environment as joint predictors of health-related outcomes. *Journal of Occupational Health Psychology, 4,* 256–268.

Payne, R. L. (1959). Tracking performance as a function of thermal balance. *Journal of Applied Physiology, 14,* 387–389.

Persinger, M. A., Tiller, S. G., & Koren, S. A. (1999). Background sound pressure fluctuations (5 dB) from overhead ventilation systems increase subjective fatigue of university students during three-hour lectures. *Perceptual & Motor Skills, 88,* 451–456.

Phillips, B. N., & Lee, M. (1980). The changing role of the American teacher: Current and future sources of stress. In Cooper & Marshall 1980, 93–111.

Poulton, E. C. (1977). Continuous intense noise masks auditory feedback and inner speech. *Psychological Bulletin, 84,* 977–1001.

Poulton, E. C. (1978). Blue collar stressors. In C. L. Cooper & R. Payne (Eds.), *Stress at work,* 51–79. New York: John Wiley & Sons.

Ramsey, J., & Kwon, Y. (1988). Simplified decision rules for predicting performance loss in the heat. In *Proceedings on heat stress indices.* Luxembourg: Commission of the European Communities.

Reinberg, A., Vieux, N., & Andlauer P. (Eds.). (1981). *Night and shift work: Biological and social aspects.* Oxford, England: Pergamon Press.

Revicki, D. A., & May, H. J. (1985). Occupational stress, social support, and depression. *Health Psychology, 4,* 61–77.

Revicki, D. A., & Whitley, T. W. (1995). Work-related stress and depression in emergency medicine residents. In Sauter & Murphy 1995 (pp. 247–258).

Revicki, D. A., Whitley, T. W., Gallery, M. E., & Allison, A. J. (1993). Organizational characteristics, occupational stress, and depression in rural emergency medicine technicians. *Journal of Rural Health, 4,* 73–83.

Richard, G. V., & Krieshok, T. S. (1989). Occupational stress, strain, and coping in university faculty. *Journal of Vocational Behavior, 34,* 117–132.

Riley, M. W., & Cochran, D. J. (1984). Dexterity performance and reduced ambient temperature. *Human Factors, 26,* 207–214.

Rissen, D., Melin, B., Sandsjo, L., Dohns, I., & Lundberg, U. (2000). Surface EMG and psychophysiological stress reactions in women during repetitive work. *European Journal of Applied Physiology, 83*, 215–222.

Ross, E. (1993). Preventing burnout among social workers employed in the field of AIDS/HIV. *Social Work in Health Care, 18*, 91–108.

Rutenfranz, J., Knauth, P., & Angersbach, D. (1981). Shiftwork research issues. In L. C. Johnson, D. I. Tepas, W. P. Colquhoun, & M. J. Colligan (Eds.), *Advances in sleep research*, vol. 7, *Biological rhythms, sleep and shift work* (pp. 165–196). New York: Spectrum.

Sanders, M. S., & McCormick, E. J. (1993). *Human factors in engineering and design* (7th ed.). New York: McGraw-Hill.

Sauter, S. L., Hurrell, J. J., Jr., & Cooper, C. L. (1989). *Job control and worker health*. New York: John Wiley & Sons.

Sauter, S. L., & Murphy, L. R. (Eds.). (1995). *Organizational risk factors for job stress*. Washington, DC: American Psychological Association.

Schat, A. C. H., & Kelloway, K. (2000). Effects of perceived control on the outcomes of workplace aggression and violence. *Journal of Occupational Health Psychology, 5*, 386–402.

Selye, H. (1978). The stress of police work. *Police Stress, 1*(1), 7–8.

Shouksmith, G., & Burrough, S. (1988). Job stress factors for New Zealand and Canadian air traffic controllers. *Applied Psychology, 37*(3), 263–270.

Sinks, T., Mathias, C., Halpern, W., Timbrook, C., & Newman, S. (1987). Surveillance of work-related cold injuries using workers' compensation claims. *Journal of Occupational Medicine, 29*(6), 504–509.

Smith, A. (1989). A review of the effects of noise on human performance. *Scandinavian Journal of Psychology, 30*, 185–206.

Smith, C. S., Reilly, C., & Midkiff, K. (1989). Evaluation of three circadian rhythm questionnaires with suggestions for an improved measure of morningness. *Journal of Applied Psychology, 74*(5), 728–738.

Smith, C. S., Reilly, C., Moore-Hirschl, S., Olsen, H., & Schmieder, R. (1989). *The shiftworker's guide to a good night's sleep*. Bowling Green, OH: Bowling Green State University Press.

Smith, C. S., Robie, C., Folkard, S., Barton, J., Macdonald, I., Smith, L., et al. (1999). A process model of shiftwork and health. *Journal of Occupational Health Psychology, 4*, 207–218.

Smith, L., & Folkard, S. (1993). The perceptions and feelings of shiftworkers' partners. *Ergonomics, 36*, 299–305.

Smith, M. J. (1985). Machine-paced work and stress. In C. L. Cooper & M. J. Smith (Eds.), *Job stress and blue collar work* (pp. 51–64). New York: John Wiley & Sons.

Smith, M. J., Colligan, M. J., & Hurrell, J. J., Jr. (1977). A review of NIOSH psychological stress research. Paper presented at the UCLA Conference on Job Stress, Los Angeles, November.

Sorensen, G., Pirie, P., Folsom, A., Luepker, R., Jacobs, D., & Gillum, R. (1985). Sex differences in the relationship between work and health: The Minnesota Heart Survey. *Journal of Health and Social Behavior, 26*, 379–394.

Sparks, K., & Cooper, C. L. (1999). Occupational differences in the work–strain relationship: Towards the use of situation-specific models. *Journal of Occupational and Organizational Psychology, 72*, 219–229.

Spelten, E., Barton, J., & Folkard, S. (1993). Have we underestimated shiftworkers' problems? Evidence from a "reminiscence" study. *Ergonomics, 36*, 307–312.

Staines, G. L., & Pleck, J. (1984). Nonstandard work schedules and family life. *Journal of Applied Psychology, 69*, 515–523.

Starnaman, S. M., & Miller, K. I. (1992). A test of a causal model of communication and burnout in the teaching profession. *Communication Education, 41*, 40–53.

Stephens, C., & Long, N. (2000). Communication with police supervisors and peers as a buffer of work-related traumatic stress. *Journal of Organizational Behavior, 21*, 407–424.

Taylor, E., Briner, R. B., & Folkard, S. (1997). Models of shiftwork and health: An examination of the influence of stress on shiftwork theory. *Human Factors, 39*, 67–82.

Teichner, W. H., Arees, E., & Reilly, R. (1963). Noise and human performance: A psychophysiological approach. *Ergonomics, 6*, 83–97.

Tepas, D. I. (1990). Do eating and drinking habits interact with work schedule variables? *Work & Stress, 4*(3), 203–211.

Tepas, D. I., Armstrong, D. R., Carlson, M. L., & Duchon, J. C. (1985). Changing industry to continuous operations: Different strokes for different plants. *Behavior Research Methods, Instruments, & Computers, 17*(6), 670–676.

Thoern, A. (2000). Emergence and preservation of a chronically sick building. *Journal of Epidemiology and Community Health, 54*, 552–556.

Tucker, P., Barton, J., & Folkard, S. (1996). A comparison of 8 and 12 hour shifts: Impacts on health, well-being and on shift alertness. *Occupational and Environment Medicine, 53*, 767–772.

Tucker, P., Smith, L., Macdonald, I., & Folkard, S. (1998). The impact of early and late shift changeovers on sleep, health, and well-being in 8- and 12-hour shift systems. *Journal of Occupational Health Psychology, 3*, 265–275.

U.S. Bureau of Labor Statistics. (1990). *Occupational injuries and illnesses in the United States by industry.* Bulletin 2399. Washington, DC: U.S. Government Printing Office.

Vener, K. J., Szabo, S., & Moore, J. G. (1989). The effect of shift work on gastrointestinal (GI) function: A review. *Chronobiologica, 16*, 421–439.

Walker, J. (1985). Social problems of shiftwork. In Folkard & Monk 1985 (pp. 211–225).

Wall, T. D., Kemp, N. J., Jackson, P. R., & Clegg, C. W. (1986). Outcomes of autonomous workgroups: A long-term field experiment. *Academy of Management Journal, 29*, 280–304.

Wallace, M., Levens, M., & Singer, G. (1988). Blue collar stress. In C. L. Cooper & R. Payne (Eds.), *Causes, coping, and consequences of stress at work* (pp. 53–76). Chichester, England: John Wiley & Sons.

Wasterlund, D. S. (1998). A review of heat stress research with application to forestry. *Applied Ergonomics, 29*(3), 179–183.

Wilkinson, R. T. (1963). Interaction of noise with knowledge of results and sleep deprivation. *Journal of Experimental Psychology, 66*, 332–337.

Zeier, H. (1994). Workload and psychophysiological stress reactions in air traffic controllers. *Ergonomics, 37*(3), 525–539.

CHAPTER 4

The Wisdom of the Receptors: Neuropeptides, the Emotions, and Bodymind

Candace B. Pert

In this chapter, I am going to describe an array of fascinating, mostly new findings about the chemical substances in the body called neuropeptides. Based on these findings, I am going to suggest that neuropeptides and their receptors form an information network within the body. Perhaps this suggestion sounds fairly innocuous, but its implications are far reaching. I believe that neuropeptides and their receptors are a key to understanding how mind and body are interconnected and how emotions can be manifested throughout the body. Indeed, the more we know about neuropeptides, the harder it is to think in the traditional terms of a mind and a body. It makes more and more sense to speak of a single integrated entity, a "bodymind."

Most of what I will describe are laboratory findings, hard science. But it is important to recall that the scientific study of psychology traditionally focuses on animal learning and cognition. This means that if you look in the index of recent textbooks on psychology, you are not likely to find "consciousness," "mind," or even "emotions." These subjects are basically not in the realm of traditional experimental psychology, which primarily studies behavior because it can be seen and measured. What goes on in the so-called black box of the brain/mind, B. F. Skinner has maintained, is not something to be speculated about. It cannot be observed, and so its study is not hard science.

One of the things I can report today is that the realm of laboratory research has widened enormously. My findings come from the domain of hard science, and I believe they are directly relevant to the comprehension of emotions and even open a window into the black box of the mind.

THE SPECIFICITY OF RECEPTORS

Now, there is one area where mind—at least consciousness—has been objectively studied for perhaps twenty years as a part of psychology, and that is the area of psychopharmacology. People have thought of highly rigorous ways to measure the effects of drugs and altered states of consciousness.

Pharmacology evolved talking about how no drug acts unless it is fixed—that is, somehow gets attached to the brain—and people imagined hypothetical tissue constituents that they called *receptors*. In this way, the notion of specific receptors became a central theory in pharmacology. It is a very old idea. In the past several years, the critical development for the study of receptors has been the invention of new technologies for actually binding drugs to these molecules and for studying both their distribution in the brain and body and their actual molecular structure.

My initial work in this area was in the laboratory of Solomon Snyder at Johns Hopkins University, and we focused our attention on opium, a drug that obviously alters consciousness and that also is used medicinally, to alleviate pain. I worked long and hard, over many months of failure, to develop a technical system for measuring the material in the brain with which opium interacts to produce its effects. To make a long (and technical) story short, we used radioactive drug molecules, and with this technology were able to identify the receptor element in the brain. You can imagine a molecule of opium attaching itself to a receptor much as a key fits into a lock—and then from this small connection, large changes follow.

It next turned out that the whole class of drugs to which opium belongs—they are called opiates, as you probably know, and they include morphine, codeine, and heroin as well as opium—attach to the *same* receptors. Further, we discovered that the receptors were scattered throughout not only the brain but also the body.

I might mention that each opiate is slightly different in its shape and binds more or less tightly to the receptor molecules. For instance, the reason a person does not get the tremendous rush from codeine that comes with heroin is that heroin has blobs of molecular matter that allow it to course into the brain while codeine first has to be transformed into morphine in the liver. Morphine, for its part, penetrates the brain, where euphoria receptors are located, very poorly.

After finding the receptor for the external opiates, our thinking took another step. If the brain and the other parts of the body have a receptor for something taken into the body—called an *exogenous ligand*—it makes sense to suppose that something produced inside the body—an *endogenous ligand*—also fits the receptor. Otherwise, why would the receptor be there? This perspective ultimately led to the identification of the brain's own form of opiates—or, rather, one of them. This is a chemical substance called *beta endorphin*. With beta endorphin, we come to the first of the neuropeptides—which are simply peptide structures produced by nerve cells in the brain. Beta endorphin is created in nerve cells and chemically consists of peptides, so it is a neuropeptide.

Perhaps I should explain that peptides are strings of amino acids. As you know, there are sixteen amino acids, and everything in the body is made out of these sixteen amino acids strung out and arranged in different sequences. You can think of the amino acids as sixteen different colored beads, and they provide an almost infinite number of sequences. Different sequences produce different chemicals, some of which are neuropeptides.

In the case of beta endorphin, we now know its precise sequence of amino acids. I want to mention in passing that beta endorphin is found in very large quantities in the human pituitary gland, which, of course, is part of the brain, and recently it has been shown to be in the gonads as well. Brain and body. We will come back to this point later.

Now, it is quite exciting that the endogenous ligands for the opiate receptors turn out to be peptides, because peptides come directly from the DNA. There is no enzyme in between. They grow directly off the DNA, which stores the information to make our brains and bodies.

If you picture an ordinary nerve cell, you can visualize the general mechanism. In the center (as in any cell) is the DNA, and a direct printout of the DNA leads to the production of a neuropeptide, which then traverses down the axons of the nerve cell to be stored in little balls at the end, waiting for the right electrophysical events that will release it. The DNA also has the information that codes for the receptors, which are made out of the same peptide material but are much bigger. Beta endorphin has thirty amino acids, but the opiate receptor for it turns out to have about twenty thousand amino acids.

What has to be added to this picture is the fact that fifty to sixty neuropeptides have been identified, each of them as specific as the beta endorphin neuropeptide. In other words, the DNA produces all these neuropeptides, which all traverse down axons and all wait for the right electrophysical events. We have here an enormously complex system, which is kept straight by the high specificity of the neuropeptides and their receptors.

Until quite recently, it had been thought that the information in the nervous system was distributed across the gap between two nerve cells, called *synapses.* We all learned about synapses in high school biology. The notion was that one nerve cell communicated to another across a synapse, which meant that the proximity of the nerve cells determined what could be communicated. Now we realize that synapses are not as important as we thought. They help control some kinds of information flow, particularly muscle contraction. But the largest portion of information coming from the brain is kept straight not by the close physical juxtaposition of nerve cells, but by the specificity of the receptors. What was thought of as a highly rigid linear system appears to be one with far more complex patterns of distribution.

When a nerve cell squirts out opiate peptides, the peptides can act "miles" away at other nerve cells. The same is true of all neuropeptides. At any given moment, many neuropeptides may be floating along within the body, and what enables them to attach to the correct receptor molecules is, to repeat, the specificity of the receptors. Thus, the receptors serve as the mechanism that sorts out the information exchange in the body.

THE BIOCHEMISTRY OF THE EMOTIONS

What is this leading up to? To something very intriguing: the notion that the receptors for the neuropeptides are in fact the keys to the biochemistry of emotion. In the last two years, the workers in my lab have formalized this idea in a number of theoretical papers (Pert, Ruff, Weber, & Herkenham, 1985; Pert, 1985; Schmitt, 1984), and I am going to review briefly the evidence to support it.

I should say that some scientists might describe this idea as outrageous. It is not, in other words, part of the established wisdom. Indeed, coming from a tradition where the textbooks do not even contain the word *emotions* in the index, it was not without a little trepidation that we dared to start talking about the biochemical substrate of emotions.

I will begin by noting a fact that neuroscientists have agreed on for a long time: that emotions are mediated by the limbic system of the brain. The *limbic system* refers to a section of neuroanatomical parts of the brain that includes the hypothalamus (which controls the homeostatic mechanisms of the body and is sometimes called the "brain" of the brain), the pituitary gland (which regulates the hormones in the body), and the amygdala. We will be talking mostly about the hypothalamus and the amygdala.

The experiments showing the connection between emotions and the limbic system were first done by Wilder Penfield and other neurologists who worked with conscious, awake individuals. The neurologists found that when they used electrodes to stimulate the cortex over the amygdala, they could evoke a whole gamut of emotional displays—powerful reactions of grief, of pain, or of pleasure associated with profound memories, and also the total somatic accompaniment of emotional states. The limbic system was first identified, then, by psychological experiments.

Now, when we began to map the location of opiate receptors in the brain—by a method involving radioactive molecules, whose density, as they accumulate in the opiate receptors in different spots of the brain, can be transformed into a quantitative color scale—we found that the limbic system was highly enriched with opiate receptors (and with other receptors, too, we eventually learned). The amygdala and the hypothalamus, both classically considered to be the main components of the limbic system (the great physiologist Walter B. Cannon singled out the hypothalamus as the foremost area for emotions to hook up to the brain), are in fact blazing with opiate receptors—fortyfold higher than in other areas in the brain. These hot spots correspond to very specific nuclei or cellular groups that physiological psychologists have identified as mediating such processes as sexual behavior, appetite, and water balance in the body. The main point is that our receptor mapping confirmed and expanded in important ways the psychological experiments that defined the limbic system.

Let me backtrack a moment and bring in some other neuropeptides. I have already noted that fifty to sixty substances are now considered to be neuropeptides. Where do they come from? Many of them are the natural analogs of psychoactive drugs. But another major source—very unexpectedly—is hormones. Hormones historically have been conceived of as being produced by glands—in other words, not by nerve cells. A hormone presumably was stored in one place in the body, then traveled over to its receptors in other parts of the body. The prime hormone is insulin, which is secreted in the pancreas. But, now, it turns out that insulin is not just a hormone. In fact, insulin is a neuropeptide, made and stored in the brain, and there are insulin receptors in the brain. When we map insulin, we again find hot spots in the amygdala and hypothalamus. In short, it has become increasingly clear that the limbic system, the seat of emotions in the brain, is also the focal point of receptors for neuropeptides.

Another critical point. As we have studied the distribution of these receptors, we have found that the limbic system is not just in the forebrain, in the classical locations of the amygdala and the hypothalamus. It appears that the body has other places in which many different neuropeptide receptors are located—places where there is a lot of chemical action. We call these spots *nodal points*, and they are anatomically located at places that receive a lot of emotional modulation. One nodal point is the dorsal (back) horn of the spinal cord, which is the spot where sensory information comes in. This is the first synapse within the brain where touch-sensory information is processed. We have found that for virtually all the senses for which we know the entry area, the spot is always a nodal point for neuropeptide receptors.

I believe these findings have amazing implications for understanding and appreciating what emotions do and what they are about. Consider the chemical substance *angiotensin*, another classical hormone that is also a peptide and now shown to be a neuropeptide. When we map for angiotensin receptors in the brain, we again find little hot spots in the amygdala. It has long been known that angiotensin mediates thirst, so if one implants a tube in the area of a rat's brain that is rich with angiotensin receptors and drops a little angiotensin down the tube, within ten seconds, the rat will start to drink water, even if it is totally sated with water. Chemically speaking, angiotensin translates as an altered state of consciousness—a state that makes animals (and humans) say, "I want water." In other words, neuropeptides bring us to states of consciousness and to alterations in those states.

For another example, we have in the laboratory mapped the receptors for PCP (commonly referred to as "angel dust"), a drug of abuse that induces an altered state of consciousness. Using radioactive PCP, we have shown that the receptors tend to be in the brain cortex, and with rats as our subjects, we have been able to determine (using the technique of operant animal behavior) that we are in fact measuring the peptide molecules of PCP that are responsible for an altered state of consciousness.

Equally important is the fact that neuropeptide receptors are not just in the brain, they are also in the body. We have mapped and shown biochemically that there are angiotensin receptors in the kidney identical to those in the brain, and in a way that is not yet quite understood, the kidney-located receptors conserve water. We know that they play with the ion fluxes so that water is conserved. The point is that the release of the neuropeptide angiotensin leads both to the behavior of drinking and to the internal conservation of water. Here is an example of how a neuropeptide—which perhaps corresponds to a mood state—can integrate what happens in the body with what happens in the brain. (A further important point that I only mention here is that overall integration of behavior seems designed to be consistent with survival.)

My basic speculation here is that neuropeptides provide the physiological basis for the emotions. As my colleagues and I argued in a recent paper in the *Journal of Immunology* (Pert et al., 1985), the striking pattern of neuropeptide receptor distribution in mood-regulating areas of brain, as well as their role in mediating communication throughout the whole organism, makes neuropeptides the obvious candidates for the biochemical mediation of emotion. It may be, too, that each neuropeptide biases information processing uniquely when occupying receptors at nodal points with the brain and body. If so, then each neuropeptide may evoke a unique "tone" that is equivalent to a mood state.

In the beginning of my work, I matter-of-factly presumed that emotions were in the head or the brain. Now, I would say they are really in the body as well. They are expressed in the body and are part of the body. I can no longer make a strong distinction between the brain and the body.

COMMUNICATING WITH THE IMMUNE SYSTEM

I now want to bring the immune system into this picture. I have already explained that the hormone system, which historically has been studied as being separate from the brain, is conceptually the same thing as the nervous system. Pockets of juices are released and diffuse very far away, acting via the specificity of receptors at sites far from where the juices are stored. So, endocrinology and neuroscience are two aspects of the same process. Now I am going to maintain that immunology is also part of this conceptual system and should not be considered a separate discipline.

A key property of the immune system is that its cells move. The brain, of course, is stable. It stays in one place. The cells of the immune system—although they are identical to the cells of the brain with their little nuclei, their cell membranes, and all of their receptors—move around. Monocytes, for example, which ingest foreign organisms, start life in your bone marrow, and they then diffuse out and travel through your veins and arteries, and decide where to go by following chemical cues. A monocyte travels along in the blood and at some point comes within "scenting" distance of a neuropeptide, and because the monocyte has receptors for that neuropeptide on its cell surface, it begins literally to chemotax, or crawl, toward that chemical. This is very well documented, and there are excellent ways of studying it in the laboratory.

Now, monocytes are responsible not just for recognizing and digesting foreign bodies but also for wound-healing and tissue-repair mechanisms. For example, they have enzymes that produce and degrade collagen, an important structural material out of which the body is made. What we are talking about, then, are cells with vital, health-sustaining functions.

The new discovery I want to emphasize here is that *every* neuropeptide receptor that we have looked for (using an elegant and precise system developed by my colleague, Michael Ruff) is also on human monocytes. Human monocytes have receptors for opiates, for PCP, for another peptide called bombasin, and so on. These emotion-affecting biochemicals actually appear to control the routing and migration of monocytes, which are so pivotal in the immune system. They communicate with B-cells and T-cells and interact in the whole system to fight disease and to distinguish between self and non-self, deciding, say, which part of the body is a tumor cell to be killed by natural killer cells and which parts need to be restored. I hope the picture is clear to you. A monocyte is circulating—this health-sustaining element of the immune system is traveling in the blood—and then the presence of an opiate pulls it over. It can connect with the neuropeptide because it has the receptor to do so—it has, in fact, many different receptors for different neuropeptides.

It turns out, moreover, that the cells of the immune system not only have receptors for these various neuropeptides, as is becoming clear, but also make the neuropeptides themselves. There are subsets of immune cells that make beta endorphins, for example, and the other opiate peptides. In other words, they are making the same chemicals that we conceive of as controlling mood in the brain. They control the tissue integrity of the body, and they also make chemicals that control mood. Once again, brain and body.

I want to emphasize the point that the same receptors are in the brain and in the immune system. CCK, another neuropeptide, was first sequenced and discovered by its action on the gut. In the pharmacological beginnings of the search for receptors, people would string up gut muscles in organ baths and study their contractions. Since the gut contained functional receptors, it was used to isolate and determine the chemical structures of the bioactivity in tissue extracts. It turns out that CCK is highly involved with food satiety. Doses of CCK make you not want to eat any more. We have recently shown that the brain and the spleen—which can be described as the "brain" of the immune system—contain receptors for CCK. So brain, gut, and immune system can all be affected by CCK.

What do these kinds of connections between brain and body mean? Ordinarily they are referred to as "the power of the mind over the body." As far as I am concerned, that phrase does not describe what we are talking about here. The body in these experiments is the outward manifestation of the mind. I would go further. When we document the key role that the emotions, expressed through neuropeptide molecules, play in affecting the body, it will become clear how emotions can be a key to the understanding of disease.

I want to expand on this speculation by returning to the example of the gut. The entire lining of the intestine, from the esophagus through the large intestine, is lined with cells—nerve cells and other kinds of cells—that contain neuropeptides and neuropeptide receptors. It seems entirely possible to me that the richness of the receptors may be why a lot of people feel their emotions in their gut—why they have a "gut feeling."

We are all aware of the bias built into the Western idea that consciousness is totally in the head. I believe the research findings I have described indicate that we need to start thinking about how consciousness can be projected into various parts of the body. Unfortunately, people who think about these things do not usually work in a government laboratory.

Let me summarize the basic idea I have been developing. My argument is that the three classic areas of neuroscience, endocrinology, and immunology, with their various organs—the brain (which is the key organ that the neuroscientists study), the glands, and the immune system (consisting of the spleen, the bone marrow, the lymph nodes, and of course the cells circulating through the body)—are actually joined to each other in a bidirectional network of communication and that the information "carriers" are the neuropeptides. There are well-studied physiological substrates showing that communication exists in both directions for every single one of these areas and their organs. Some of the research is old, some of it is new. We now know, for example, that peptide-producing neurons come from the brain and actually enervate the bone marrow.

The word I would stress in regard to this integrated system is *network*, which comes from information theory. What we have been talking about all along is information. In thinking about these matters, then, it might make more sense to emphasize the perspective of psychology rather than of neuroscience, for the term *psycho-* clearly conveys the study of mind, and perhaps "mind" is the information flowing among all of these bodily parts. That may be what "mind" is: A mind is composed of information, and it has a physical substrate, which is the body and the brain, and it also has another immaterial substrate that has to do with information flowing around. Maybe "mind" is what holds the network together.

THE UNITY OF THE VARIETY

The last point I am going to make about the neuropeptides is an astounding one, I think.

As we have seen, neuropeptides are signaling molecules. They send messages all over the body (including the brain). Of course, to have such a communications network, you need components that can talk to each other and listen to each other. In the situation we are discussing here, the components that "talk" are the neuropeptides, and the components that "hear" are the neuropeptide receptors. How can this be? How can fifty to sixty neuropeptides be produced, float around, and talk to fifty or sixty types of listening receptors that are on a variety of cells? Why does order rather than chaos reign?

The finding I am going to discuss is not totally accepted, but our experiments show that it is true. I have not published it yet, but I think that it is only a matter of time before everybody can confirm these observations.

There are thousands of scientists studying the opiate receptors and the opiate peptides, and they see great heterogeneity in the receptors. They have given a series of Greek names to the apparent heterogeneity. However, all the evidence from our lab suggests that in fact *there is actually only one type of molecule in the opiate receptors—one long polypeptide chain whose formula you can write.* This molecule is quite capable of changing its conformation within its membrane so that it can assume a number of shapes.

I note in passing that this interconversion can occur at a very rapid pace—so rapid that it is hard to tell whether it is one state or another at a given moment in time. In other words, receptors have both a wave-like and a particulate character, and it is important to note that information can be stored in the form of time spent in different states.

As I said, the molecular unity of the receptors is quite amazing. Consider the tetrahymena, a protozoan that is one of the simplest organisms. Despite its simplicity, the tetrahymena can do almost everything we can do—it can eat, have sex, and, of course, make the same neuropeptide components that I have been talking about. The tetrahymena makes insulin. It makes beta endorphins. We have taken tetrahymena membranes and, in particular, studied the opiate receptor molecules on them, and we have studied the opiate receptor in rat brains and on human monocytes. Receptors, as you know, are proteins consisting of a long sequence of amino acids, but the chain is all twisted up because of electric and physical forces that cause it to assume a shape. It is possible to take receptors out of the membrane and put them in detergent, which takes away their tertiary structure—that is, makes them a straight line—and then you can determine their molecular weight and characteristics (by running them in an electrical field). Having done this for opiate receptors, we believe that we have shown that the molecular substance of *all* opiate receptors is the same. The actual molecule of the rat-brain opiate receptor is identical to the human-brain opiate receptor and is also identical to the opiate receptor components in that simplest of animals, the tetrahymena. I hope the force of this is clear. The opiate receptor in my brain and in your brains is, at root, made of the same molecular substance as the tetrahymena.

This finding gets to the simplicity and the unity of life. It is comparable to the four DNA-based pairs that code for the production of all the proteins, which are the physical substrates of life. We now know that in this physical substrate there are only sixty or so signal molecules, the neuropeptides, that account for the physiological manifestation of emotions—for enlivening emotions, if you will, or perhaps better yet, for flowing energy. The protozoa form of the tetrahymena indicates that the receptor molecules do not become more complex as an organism becomes more complex. The identical molecular components for information flow are conserved throughout evolution. The whole system is simple, elegant, and may very well be complete.

IS THE MIND IN THE BRAIN?

We have been talking about the mind, and the question arises: Where is it? In our own work, consciousness has come up in the context of studying pain and the role of opiate receptors and endorphins in modulating pain.

A lot of labs are measuring pain, and we would all agree that the area called *periaqueductal gray*, located around the third ventricle of the brain, is filled with opiate receptors, making it a kind of control area for pain. We have found that the periaqueductal gray is also loaded with receptors for virtually all the neuropeptides that have been studied.

Now, everyone knows that there are yogis who can train themselves so that they do or do not perceive pain, depending on how they structure their experience. There are other people, called mothers, who have done the same thing. What seems to be going on is that these sort of people are able to plug into their periaqueductal gray. Somehow they gain access to it—with their consciousness, I believe—and set pain thresholds. Note what is going on here. In these situations, a person has an experience that brings with it pain, but a part of the person consciously does something so that the pain is not felt. Where is this consciousness coming from—this conscious "I"—that somehow plugs into the periaqueductal gray so that he or she does not feel a thing?

I want to go back to the idea of a network. A network is different from a hierarchical structure that has one top place. You theoretically can plug into a network at any point and get to any other point. A concept like this seems to me valuable in thinking about the processes by which a consciousness can manage to reach the periaqueductal gray and use it to control pain.

The yogi and the laboring woman both use a similar technique to control pain: breathing. Athletes use it, too. Breathing is extremely powerful. I suggest that there is a physical substrate for these phenomena: the brain stem nuclei. I would say that we now must include the brain stem nuclei in the limbic system because they are nodal points, thickly encrusted with neuropeptide receptors and neuropeptides. The idea, then, goes like this: breathing has a physical substrate, which is also a nodal point; this nodal point is part of an information network in which each part leads to all the other parts; and so, from the nodal points of the brain stem nuclei, the consciousness can, among other things, plug into the periaqueductal gray.

I think it is possible now to conceive of mind and consciousness as an emanation of emotional information processing, and as such, mind and consciousness would appear to be independent of brain and body. One little hint about how the mind might send its information through the brain and body is suggested by another astounding fact. It is well established in experimental work that some of the monocytes, which rise in the bone marrow and circulate around, actually enter the brain and are transformed and become glial cells. What are glial cells? They have been generally ignored by neuroscientists. They are ten times more plentiful in the brain than nerve cells. People say, "They're nutritive," or "They clean up." They have not been studied much because they do not have measurable electric properties. (A lot of neuroscience has been based on the ability to measure electrical epiphenomena.) It is possible that glial cells have the potential to be programmed in the brain and under the appropriate cues to leave the brain and go out into the body. Also, there is a precedent for monocyte-like cells, which contain information about the state of the body, to take up residence in—and talk directly to—the brain. Perhaps that is one mechanism of action by which the mind and body intercommunicate.

One last speculation, an outrageous one perhaps: Can the mind survive the death of the physical brain? Perhaps here we have to recall how mathematics suggests that physical entities can suddenly collapse or infinitely expand. I think it is important to realize that information is stored in the brain, and it is conceivable to me that this information could transform itself into some other realm. The DNA molecules surely have the information that makes the brain and body, and the bodymind seems to share the information molecules that enliven the organism. Where does the information go after the destruction of the molecules (the mass) that compose it? Matter can neither be created nor destroyed, and perhaps biological information flow cannot just disappear at death and can be transformed into another realm. Who can rationally say "impossible"? No one has yet mathematically unified gravitational field theory with matter and energy. The mathematics of consciousness have not even been approached. The nature of the hypothetical "other realm" is currently in the religious or mystical dimension, where Western science is clearly forbidden to tread.

REFERENCES

Pert, C. B. (1985). Neuropeptides, receptors, and emotions. *Cybernetics, 1*(4), 33–34.

Pert, C. B., Ruff, M. R., Weber, R. J., & Herkenham, M. (1985). Neuropeptides and their receptors: A psychosomatic network. *Journal of Immunology, 135*(2), 820s–826s.

Schmitt, F. O. (1984). Molecular regulation of brain function: A new view. *Neuroscience, 13*(4), 991–1001.

CHAPTER 5

Allostatic Load: When Protection Gives Way to Damage

Bruce McEwen and Elizabeth Norton Lasley

In the late 1980s, the U.S. Department of Agriculture (USDA), under pressure from animal rights activists, suggested a change to the guidelines for the care of laboratory animals, which the USDA oversees. The department proposed that research monkeys housed individually (to meet the requirements of whatever study they were in) would henceforth be given an hour or so a week in a large enclosure with other monkeys. It was thought this would be a good way for the animals to relax, socialize, and enjoy themselves.

Actually, this is a good way to give a monkey a heart attack, says Robert Sapolsky at Stanford University. When unacquainted monkeys first meet, they need time to squabble and test each other, eventually establishing who's who. A few hours a week would not be enough: the animals would be returned to their individual cages before coming to an understanding. So the social hour would become a weekly brawl never to be resolved, beginning anew every time the monkeys got together—a setup likely to generate the very stress-related problems it was designed to prevent.

Sapolsky, a pioneer in the field of stress research, had previously studied wild monkeys that had been thrust into a cage together for shipment to the United States. Many arrived dead, not from any noticeable injury but from the trauma of being trapped in a hostile environment. He and several other scientists convinced the USDA not to carry out the proposed change, and the stressor of social disruption never became a federally mandated animal-handling guideline.

This story illustrates the first of four ways in which the allostatic response can turn coat and become allostatic load: being activated too frequently when a person or animal is subjected to repeated, unrelieved, or unremitting stress. This does not involve a malfunction per se; even the most finely tuned stress response in the healthiest of individuals can begin to cause damage if activated again and again over a long period. In other words, chronic stress can cause illness, putting a strain on the heart, undermining the power of the immune system, and triggering processes that may lead to diabetes and other chronic illnesses. And as Sapolsky says in the preface to his book, under conditions of extreme and unusual stress (in some zoos, for example), zebras can sometimes get ulcers.

ALLOSTATIC LOAD SCENARIO 1: UNREMITTING STRESS

Chronic stress takes its toll most immediately on the heart. When the fight-or-flight response swings into action, one of the most important things the animal (or person) must do is to move quickly. So the first of the stress hormones, adrenaline, courses through the sympathetic nervous system to step up the heart rate, increasing blood pressure to drive more oxygen to the large muscles of the arms and legs. But these sudden surges, when activated too often, cause damage to the blood vessels in the coronary arteries. The sites of damage are places where the arteries become clogged with the sticky buildup that sets the stage for atherosclerosis.

In humans, too many sudden escalations in blood pressure can trigger myocardial infarctions (heart attacks) in blood vessels that have become clogged (Muller, Tofler, & Stone, 1989). Studies with primates show that stress can aggravate the clogging-up process. Jay Kaplan of Bowman Gray University made the social disruption the USDA had proposed for laboratory monkeys into an experiment. After weeks and months of shuffling the groups around, forcing the monkeys repeatedly to scramble for position, the resulting elevations in blood pressure sped up the process of atherosclerosis and increased the risk of heart attacks (Kaplan, Pettersson, Manuck, & Olsson, 1991). (Sapolsky and other scientists cited Kaplan's work when protesting the USDA's suggestion.)

Studies of social disruption in monkeys have parallels in the world of humans. A striking example was observed in the British Civil Service (a fount of information about stress-related diseases) during the years of privatization under Prime Minister Margaret Thatcher. In a classic series called the Whitehall Studies, blood pressure was found to be lowest among the highest grade of employees and highest among the rank and file (Marmot, Davey, & Stansfield, 1991) (food for thought for those who believe that stress plagues only fast-track yuppies). One study that focused on a department that was undergoing privatization during the Thatcher years, found increases in body mass index, need for sleep, incidence of stroke, and cholesterol (Ferris, Shipley, Marmot, Stansfield, & Smith, 1998).

The British privatization effort was more radical than anything that has happened here in the United States. Thatcher took some big entities that had been parts of the government, including the telephone company and the electric utilities, and turned them into private companies, selling stock to investors and severing all ties to the government. Before, these groups were run as bureaucracies with a public mission, with civil service types of incentives and penalties—basically, a job for life if you did your work and kept your head down. Afterward, they were private companies run for the benefit of their shareholders, with private-sector incentives and penalties—make more money and do things cheaper and better or you'll be fired. Privatization had essentially propelled the civil service employees into a situation very much like the one that confronted the monkeys in the social disruption studies. The known social order, in which people knew their place and each person's place was secure, went up in smoke. Suddenly employees had to compete and produce, often for the first time in their professional lives.

Something similar occurred in Russia and Eastern Europe following the collapse of Communism in 1989. A study that examined morbidity and mortality rates (that is, illness and death) showed a dramatic increase in both rates in virtually all Eastern European countries. Cardiovascular disease and hypertension were to blame for many deaths, but, interestingly, suicide and homicide also increased. In the former Soviet Union, the change was most dramatic: the life expectancy for men dropped from sixty-four to fifty-nine years (Bobak & Marmot, 1996; Notzon et al., 1998). Once again, the status quo had been hopelessly jumbled, and people were no longer sure of their jobs, their homes, their government, or their place in society.

Of course, the situation in Eastern Europe and Russia is unlike that in the United Kingdom in many ways, making it difficult to pinpoint exact causes. In Britain, all civil service employees had jobs and access to health care, something that was not the case in Russia and Eastern Europe. Moreover, when the causes of mortality were examined in the Eastern European studies, cardiovascular disease and alcoholism ranked very high. But, interestingly, so did deaths from accidents and violence in the form of murder and suicide. One could still argue that, in the wreckage of the former Soviet Union, health care and emergency services were in disarray, making death from such causes more likely than in a stable country like the United Kingdom (Margaret Thatcher notwithstanding). But the fact remains that instability takes a heavy toll on life and health.

LOWERING RESISTANCE TO ILLNESS

The immune system also suffers from unremitting stress. Most people can probably think of a time when they were under stress and always seemed to be getting a cold, and it's not their imagination. The connection between chronic stress and susceptibility to upper respiratory infection has been well explored by scientists. In times of sudden acute stress, the immune system's activity is stepped up to prepare to deal with injury. But under conditions of chronic stress, the immune system is temporarily squelched.

This effect is not always temporary, though, depending on just how chronic the stress is. Sheldon Cohen of Carnegie Mellon University asked some three hundred volunteers to complete a questionnaire about stressful events in their lives and then inoculated them with common cold viruses and watched to see who would begin to show symptoms. The ones who fell sick were the ones who had reported stress that lasted for a month or longer, usually in the form of unemployment or ongoing difficulty with family or friends. This type of chronic stress carried an increased risk of catching a cold compared to subjects who reported stress of less than a month's duration (Cohen et al., 1998).

Working with Kaplan, Cohen studied the same connection in primates. Male cynomolgus monkeys were randomly assigned to stable or unstable social conditions and, at the end of fifteen months, were exposed to an adenovirus, one of the common cold viruses. Unlike the results of Kaplan's experiments with social disruption and cardiovascular disease, this time colds were not a direct response to upheaval; the animals in the unstable groups were not more likely to become infected. But the ones with lower social status in both groups were (Cohen et al., 1997).

Clearly, then, frequent overactivation of the stress response can overwhelm the body's ability to manage it properly. People who have had excessive stress in their lives, as measured by multiple episodes of living at the poverty level, show earlier aging, more depression, and an earlier decline of both physical and mental functioning (Lynch, Kaplan, & Shema, 1997). And individuals who were abused as children suffer an increased risk of depression, suicide, substance abuse, and earlier illness and death from a wide range of diseases (Felitti et al., 1998).

ALLOSTATIC LOAD SCENARIO 2: INABILITY TO ADJUST

There are also situations in which, though the stress itself is not lengthy or severe, the body responds in a way that is inappropriate. Often we perceive a situation as stressful not because it imperils our survival but because it is unfamiliar and a bit challenging—a new job, perhaps, or a newly assumed position of leadership in the community. Once the alarming becomes commonplace, we cease to activate the fight-or-flight sequences. In some people, though, when an initially threatening experience becomes business as usual, the stress response doesn't get the message.

Clemens Kirschbaum and colleagues at the University of Trier subjected a group of twenty male volunteers to some of the most threatening events imaginable—public speaking and mental arithmetic in front of an audience—for five consecutive days. The investigators measured the stress hormone cortisol in saliva samples taken from the subjects on each day. Most of the subjects became comfortable on stage by the second day, and their cortisol levels diminished accordingly. But seven of them showed no discernible difference in their reported discomfort or in their cortisol levels between days 1 and 2 and only a very slight decrease by day 5. Perhaps not coincidentally, a personality questionnaire revealed that the still-stressed men had low self-confidence and self-esteem (Kirschbaum et al., 1995). In short, the men were not able to habituate to an experience that was no longer novel. Although no particular diseases or symptoms were matched up to this group (which Kirschbaum dubbed "high responders"), it's likely they were overexposing their bodies to stress hormones under many circumstances in daily life that other people might not consider stressful. And we know, for example, that frequent jumps in blood pressure are a risk for cardiovascular disease.

One study turned up a closer correlation between people's stress levels in the lab and in their day-to-day lives. Karen Matthews and colleagues at the University of Pittsburgh studied a group of employed middle-aged men and women. Again, volunteers were put through the torture of public speaking in a laboratory while plugged into equipment that monitored their vital signs. In the ensuing 24 hours, the participants wore a cuff that recorded their blood pressure every half hour: at the same time, they reported how they felt. Those whose blood pressure shot up during the public-speaking test showed the same elevation when they reported feelings of stress throughout the day. But on other days when they weren't feeling stressed, the same people did not show elevations in blood pressure during the test. Thus, our reactions to situations depend very much on our current emotional status and what other things we are experiencing (Matthews, Owens, Allen, & Stoney, 1992).

ALLOSTATIC LOAD SCENARIO 3: NOT HEARING THE ALL CLEAR

Most of us can probably remember repeatedly rehashing some argument or other stressful scene, getting worked up over and over again until our friends grew tired of hearing about it. For some people, this condition is chronic; they continue to mount an allostatic response long after the stressful event has ended, and here there is evidence that genes may play a role.

Bill Gerin and Tom Pickering of the Hypertension Center at Cornell University gave an arithmetic test to more than five hundred undergraduate volunteers, measuring heart rate and blood pressure before, during, and after the test. They were interested in seeing whether differences in cardiovascular response could be attributed to the students' race, sex, or parental history of hypertension. It turned out that none of these factors had anything to do with cardiovascular response while the test was going on. But afterward, a certain percentage of the students still showed elevated blood pressure. Even though the stress was over, their systems were not able to recover and return to baseline. Most of these subjects had two parents with hypertension, suggesting they were genetically ill disposed to let go of a stressful situation (Gerin & Pickering, 1995).

Failure to shut off the sympathetic nervous system and the hypothalamic-pituitary-adrenal (HPA) axis when appropriate may also be a function of aging, as animal studies show, although there is less evidence for this in humans. In some aging laboratory animals, stress-induced secretions of both cortisol and adrenaline return to baseline more slowly than in normal animals (McCarty, 1985). In humans, the negative feedback effects of cortisol (by which it tells the brain to ease off on some aspects of the stress response) don't work as well in the elderly (Wilkinson, Peskind, & Raskind, 1997).

STRESS HORMONE OVERDOSE

All of the above three scenarios involve long-term overexposure to adrenaline and cortisol, whether it's because the stress itself goes on too long, because the system cannot accommodate the fact that the situation should no longer be stressful, or because the shutoff processes are not functioning. Stress hormones do more than raise blood pressure and stifle the immune system. For example, cortisol is often chronically elevated in depression, and some women with a history of depressive illness have decreased bone mineral density (Michelson, Stratakis, & Hill, 1996). This is because bone formation is one of those long-term luxuries that get played down as part of the fight-or-flight response; cortisol actually interferes with the processes by which bone is formed. Prolonged exposure to cortisol has been shown to create allostatic load in women undergoing intense athletic training; though exercise may not seem stressful to the athlete, when carried to an abusive extreme it elevates both the sympathetic nervous system and the HPA axis. Results can include weight loss, lack of menstruation, and anorexia, a condition often related to exercise extremism (Boyar et al., 1977; Loucks, Mortola, Girton, & Yen, 1989).

Chronically elevated cortisol can also dampen the effects of insulin, and indeed chronic stress—defined as feelings of fatigue, lack of energy, irritability, demoralization, and hostility—has been linked to the development of insulin resistance, a risk factor for type 2 or non–insulin-dependent diabetes (Raikkonen, Keltikangas-Javinen, Adlercreutz, & Hautenen, 1996).

It's also possible that overactivation of the stress response over a lifetime may undermine the whole process of allostasis itself, causing the systems to wear out and become exhausted. One particularly vulnerable link is the hippocampus, which helps turn off the HPA axis after stress and is also a nexus of memory and cognition. Because the hippocampus is rich in receptors for cortisol, using levels of this hormone to play its checks-and-balances role in the stress response, it is one of the first targets when levels of cortisol get too high. According to the so-called glucocorticoid cascade hypothesis, when the hippocampal region of the brain is flooded with cortisol, the resulting wear and tear leads to both an improperly functioning HPA axis and cognitive impairment (Sapolsky, 1992; Sapolsky, Krey, & McEwen, 1986).

The hippocampus's major role in episodic and declarative memories means that it is involved in remembering daily events and information, such as shopping lists and names of people, places, and things. The hippocampus is also important for the memory of context—the time and place of events, particularly those that have a strong emotional significance (LeDoux, 1995). Excessive levels of stress hormones interfere with the formation and retrieval of these memories, including those associated with context (Lupien et al., 1994). This may add even more stress by blocking the informational input needed to decide that a situation is not a threat

(Sapolsky, 1990). For example, suppose someone averse to office politics finds himself in the deep end of a dicey negotiation. High levels of cortisol may leave him unable to remember who's likely to be in his camp and who isn't and which names go with which faces. (Cortisol works in another part of the brain, too: the amygdala, which plays a prominent role in forming long-term memories associated with fearful or traumatic events. The amygdala is also involved in what we might call "anticipatory angst," the fears and anxieties that we harbor regardless of whether there is legitimate reason to worry [Schulkin, McEwen, & Gold, 1994]. So, increased stress hormone levels in the amygdala can make us fret even more, augmenting the stress we are already under.) Finally, the hippocampus is involved in the shutoff of the stress response (Jacobson & Sapolsky, 1991). In sum, damage to this brain structure can both weaken our ability to perceive that something is not genuinely stressful and prevent the stress response from being shut off, thereby ratcheting up stress levels even higher.

ALLOSTATIC LOAD SCENARIO 4: TOO LITTLE IS AS BAD AS TOO MUCH

The idea of checks and balances in the stress response brings us to the final way in which the protective systems of allostasis can trigger the damage of allostatic load: When the stress response is insufficient, resulting in underproduction of the stress hormones, particularly cortisol, wear and tear can also result (see Table 5.1). How can this be? Surely, if there are no stress hormones, there must be no stress and consequently no stress-related illness. But like most of human physiology, it isn't quite that simple. Cortisol acts somewhat like a thermostat; in fact, it clamps down on its own production. It slows the production of the two hormones that touch off the HPA axis: corticotrophin-releasing factor (CRF) in the hypothalamus and adrenocorticotropic hormone in the pituitary. Cortisol also reins in the immune system and reduces inflammation and swelling from tissue damage.

When one of the participants in a checks-and-balances arrangement isn't doing its job, the others may go overboard in doing theirs. In some people, allostatic load takes the form of a sluggish response by the adrenals and a subsequent lack of sufficient cortisol. The most immediate result is that the immune system, without cortisol's steadying hand, runs wild and reacts to things that do not really pose a threat to the body. Allergies are one example of this process. In most people, the immune system does not put things like dust and cat dander on a par with pathogenic (disease-causing) bacteria. But in people prone to allergies, the immune system goes on red alert in the presence of such usually innocuous substances, throwing everything it's got at the irritants: uncontrollable sneezing to expel the invaders, mucous secretion to entrap them, and swelling caused by the influx of white blood cells to the infected area, leading to pain, redness, and general misery. All of these symptoms are reduced by the action of cortisol.

Table 5.1. Disorders Linked to Overproduction and Underproduction of Cortisol

Overproduction	Underproduction
Cushing's syndrome	Atypical/seasonal depression
Melancholic depression	Chronic fatigue syndrome
Diabetes	Fibromyalgia
Sleep deprivation	Hypothyroidism
Anorexia nervosa	Nicotine withdrawal
Excessive exercise	Rheumatoid arthritis
Malnutrition	Allergies
Obsessive-compulsive disorder	Asthma
Panic disorder	
Chronic active alcoholism	
Childhood physical and sexual abuse	
Functional gastrointestinal disease	
Hyperthyroidism	

Asthma is another example in which the small tubes in the lungs called *bronchioles* swell and constrict. Once again, the oversensitized system is trying to ward off things that are not actually harmful (such as dust, cold, and exercise), in this case by barring the portals of access to the lungs. Allergies and asthma are both considered inflammatory diseases, and they are classic signs of the type of allostatic load signaled by the underproduction of cortisol. People who suffer from these conditions notice that their symptoms worsen when they are under stress.

Other kinds of inflammatory disorders are the so-called autoimmune diseases, in which the immune system fails in its prime directive—distinguishing self from non-self—and goes after the person's own body tissue. These conditions, too, are normally prevented by cortisol (and often treated with cortisol by doctors). Rashes are a prime example of the immune system attacking healthy skin: one type, atopic dermatitis, in children is a sign of both stress and an underresponsive HPA axis (Buske-Kirschbaum et al., 1997). Other autoimmune disorders, often exacerbated by stress, are rheumatoid arthritis, in which the joints are chronically inflamed, and multiple sclerosis, a degenerative disease in which the immune system destroys a part of the nervous system known as the myelin sheath.

A feeble HPA response can often manifest itself in conditions not always immediately associated with the immune system. Fibromyalgia, for example, is a condition of chronic pain that most doctors consider psychosomatic (and some consider imaginary, though the patients certainly don't) (Crofford, Pillemer, & Kalogeras, 1994; Heim, Ehlert, Hanker, & Hellhammer, 1998). The connection with the immune system and cortisol becomes clear when we consider that pain is a part of the inflammatory response; pain warns us that there's a problem and encourages us to leave the affected area alone until the problem is resolved. But in many chronic pain states, as with other inflammatory disorders, there is no apparent threat. Rather, the system is responding in a maladaptive way, which the available supply of cortisol is too low to prevent.

INFLUENCING THE COURSE OF ALLOSTASIS— FOR GOOD OR EVIL

It's important to remember that allostatic load is more than the experience of being under stress. It also reflects our lifestyle and ways of coping with daily life. What we eat, if we smoke, how well we sleep, and whether we exercise, all feed into the final common path that is the production of cortisol, adrenaline, and other cast members in the allostatic scenario.

To a certain degree, we ourselves can determine whether allostasis will slide into allostatic load by the ways in which we cope with stress. If we make poor choices, we can tilt the scales in favor of stress-related illness. For example, smoking (a frontline defense for many) elevates blood pressure and accelerates clogging of the coronary arteries, thereby raising the risk of both heart attack and stroke (Verdecchia et al., 1995). Finding solace in high-fat snacks, such as doughnuts or potato chips, can also lead to health problems. A high-fat diet accelerates atherosclerosis and increases cortisol secretion. Increased cortisol, in turn, steps up the accumulation of body fat, which is a risk factor for cardiovascular disease, stroke, and diabetes (Bernadet, 1995).

On the other hand, if we counteract stress with a brisk walk or a visit to the health club, we can increase the odds in our favor. Exercise prevents the buildup of body fat, protects against cardiovascular disease, and reduces chronic pain and depression. We can also protect ourselves by seeking company and support. Sheldon Cohen (2005), who studies the relationship between stress and upper respiratory disease, has reported that people with many social connections get fewer colds. Ronald Glaser and Janice Kiecolt-Glaser (Kiecolt-Glaser et al., 1984) of Ohio State University have shown that isolation can undermine the activity of the immune system.

With so many ways of going wrong, it may sound as if the fight-or-flight response is a fragile thing, but actually it's quite resilient. In the past ten years, research into the effects of stress on the cardiovascular, immune, and nervous systems has shown in detail what can happen when allostasis gets out of kilter, while at the same time indicating just how resilient these systems really are.

REFERENCES

Bernadet, P. (1995). Benefits of physical activity in the prevention of cardiovascular diseases. *Journal of Cardiovascular Pharmacology, 25*(Suppl. 1), s3–s8.

Bobak, M., & Marmot, M. (1996). East–West mortality divide and its potential explanations: Proposed research agenda. *British Medical Journal, 312*, 421–425.

Boyar, R. M., Hellman, L. D., Roffwarg, H., Katz, J., Zumoff, B., O'Connor, J., et al. (1977). Cortisol secretion and metabolism in anorexia nervosa. *New England Journal of Medicine, 296*, 190–193.

Buske-Kirschbaum, A., Jobst, S., Wustmans, A., Kirshbaum, C., Rauth, W., & Hellhammer, D. H. (1997). Attenuated free cortisol response to psychosocial stress in children with atopic dermatitis. *Psychosomatic Medicine, 59*, 419–426.

Cohen, S. (2005). The Pittsburg common cold studies: Psychosocial predictors of susceptibility to respiratory infectious illness. *International Journal of Behavioral Medicine, 12* (3), 123–131.

Cohen, S., Frank., E., Doyle, W. J., Sconer, D. P., Rabin, B. S., & Gwaltney, J. M., Jr. (1998). Types of stressors that increase susceptibility to the common cold in healthy adults. *Health Psychology, 17*, 211–213.

Cohen, S., Line, S., Manuck, S. B., Rabin, B. S., Heise, I. R., & Kaplan, J. R. (1997). Chronic social stress, social status, and susceptibility to upper respiratory infections in nonhuman primates. *Psychosomatic Medicine, 59*, 213–221.

Crofford L. J., Pillemer, S. R., & Kalogeras, K. T. (1994). Hypothalamic-pituitary-adrenal axis perturbation in patients with fibromyalgia. *Arthritis & Rheumatism, 37*, 1583–1592.

Felitti, V. J., Anda, R. E., Nordenberg, D., Williamson, D. F., Spitz, A. M., Edwards, V., et al. (1998). Relationship of childhood abuse and household dysfunction to many of the leading causes of death in adults: The Adverse Childhood Experiences (ACE) study. *American Journal of Preventative Medicine, 14*, 245–258.

Ferris, J. E., Shipley, C. M. J., Marmot, M. G., Stansfield, S. A., & Smith, G. D. (1998). An uncertain future: The health effects of threats to employment security in white collar men and women. *American Journal of Public Health, 88*, 1030–1036.

Gerin, W., & Pickering, T. G. (1995). Association between delayed recovery of blood pressure after acute mental stress and parental history of hypertension. *Journal of Hypertension, 13*, 603–610.

Heim, C., Ehlert, U., Hanker, J. P., & Hellhammer, D. H. (1998). Abuse-related posttraumatic stress disorder and alterations of the hypothalamic-pituitary-adrenal axis in women with chronic pelvic pain. *Psychosomatic Medicine, 60*, 309–318.

Jacobson, L., & Sapolsky, R. M. (1991). The role of the hippocampus in feedback regulation of the hypothalamic-pituitary-adrenal axis. *Endocrine Reviews, 12*, 118–134.

Kaplan, J. R., Pettersson, M. K., Manuck, S. B., & Olsson, G. (1991). Role of sympatho-adrenal medullary activation in the initiation and progression of atherosclerosis. *Circulation, 84*(Suppl. 6), VI23–VI32.

Keicolt-Glaser, J. K., Garner, W., Speicher, C., Penn, G. M., Holliday, J. E., & Glaser, R. (1984). Psychosocial modifiers of immunocompetence in medical students. *Psychosomatic Medicine, 46*, 7–14.

Kirschbaum, C., Prussner, J. C., Stone, A. A., Federenko, I., Gaab, J., Lintz, D., et al. (1995). Persistent high cortisol responses to repeated psychological stress in a subpopulation of healthy men. *Psychosomatic Medicine, 57*, 468–474.

LeDoux, J. E. (1995). In search of an emotional system in the brain: Leaping from fear to emotion and consciousness. In M. Gazzaniga (Ed.), *The cognitive neurosciences* (pp. 1049–1061). Cambridge, MA: MIT Press.

Loucks, A. B., Mortola, J. F., Girton, L., & Yen, S. S. C. (1989). Alterations in the hypothalamic-pituitary-ovarian and the hypothalamic-pituitary-adrenal axes in athletic women. *Journal of Clinical Endocrinology and Metabolism, 26*, 402–411.

Lupien, S., Lecours, A. R., Lussier, I., Schwartz, G., Nair, N. P., & Meany, M. J. (1994). Basal cortisol levels and cognitive deficits in human aging. *Journal of Neuroscience, 14*, 2893–2903.

Lynch, J. W., Kaplan, G. A., & Shema, S. J. (1997). Cumulative impact of sustained economic hardship on physical, cognitive, psychological, and social functioning. *New England Journal of Medicine, 337*, 1889–1895.

Marmot, M. G., Davey, S. G., & Stansfield, S. (1991). Health inequalities among British civil servants: The Whitehall II Study, *Lancet, 337*, 1387–1393.

Matthews, K. A., Owens, J. F., Allen, M. T., & Stoney, C. M. (1992). Do cardiovascular responses to laboratory stress relate to ambulatory blood pressure levels? Yes, in some of the people some of the time. *Psychosomatic Medicine, 54*, 686–697.

McCarty, B. (1985). Sympathetic-adrenal medullary and cardiovascular responses to acute cold stress in adults and aged rats. *Journal of the Autonomic Nervous System, 12*, 15–22.

Michelson, D., Stratakis, C., & Hill, L. (1996). Bone mineral density in women with depression. *New England Journal of Medicine, 335*, 1176–1181.

Muller, J. E., Tofler, G. H., & Stone, P. H., (1989). Circadian variations and triggers of onset of acute cardiovascular disease. *Circulation, 79*, 733–743.

Notzon, F. C., Komarov, Y. M., Ermakov, S. P., Sempos, C. T., Marks, J. S., & Sempos, E. V. (1998). Causes of declining life expectancy in Russia. *Journal of the American Medical Association, 279*, 793–800.

Raikkonen, K., Keltikangas-Javinen, L., Adlercreutz, H., & Hautenen, A. (1996). Psychosocial stress and the insulin resistance syndrome. *Metabolism, 45*, 1533–1538.

Sapolsky, R. M. (1990). Stress in the wild. *Scientific American, 262*(1), 116–123.

Sapolsky, R. M. (1992). *Stress, the aging brain and the mechanisms of neuron death.* Cambridge, MA: MIT Press.

Sapolsky, R. M., Krey, L. C., & McEwen, B. S. (1986). The neuroendocrinology of stress and aging: The glucocorticoid cascade hypothesis. *Endocrine Reviews, 7*, 284–301.

Schulkin, J., McEwen, B. S., & Gold, P. W. (1994). Allostasis, amygdala, and anticipatory angst. *Neuroscience & Biobehavioral Reviews, 18*, 385–396.

Verdecchia, P., Schillaci, G., Borgioni, C., Zampi, I., Battistelli, M., Gattobigio, R., et al. (1995). Cigarette smoking, ambulatory blood pressure and cardiac hypertrophy in essential hypertension. *Hypertension, 13*, 1209–1215.

Wilkinson, C. W., Peskind, E. R., & Raskind, M. A. (1997). Decreased hypothalamic-pituitary-adrenal axis sensitivity to cortisol feedback in human aging. *Neuroendocrinology, 65*, 79–90.

Part II

Stress and Illness

Introduction to "Stress and Illness"

This second part of our book examines the relationship between psychosocial factors, especially stress, and illness or symptoms. Following a number of significant research findings in the 1940s and 1950s, including Selye's (1956) identification of the General Adaptation Syndrome, as described in Part I of this book, and work by Wolff (e.g., 1953), researchers have been interested in this issue of potential harmfulness of the stress response (see Cooper & Dewe, 2004, for a historical discussion). At present, there is an explosion of research on this area. For example, a search of biology's chief primary-source database, Biological Abstracts, turned up 5,757 articles and book chapters that include the terms *stress* and *heart disease* in default fields for the ten years prior to July 2006, and 6,221 that include *stress* and *immune system*. The stress response can clearly harm the body; this part of the book is devoted to current research in this area.

The first chapter in this part is from *Dr. Dean Ornish's Program for Reversing Heart Disease* (1990). Ornish, in his engaging and accessible writing style, describes the effect that chronic stress has on the cardiovascular system. He argues that the stress response is clearly advantageous for our survival in many circumstances, but the chronicity of our stressors and our inability to shut off the stress response often produce blood vessel and/or heart damage. His emphasis in this chapter is on both stress and a high fat diet as contributing to heart disease. He also repeats a theme present in other parts of this book, individual differences in vulnerability to damage caused by stress, citing Kaplan et al.'s (1982) research on dominant and submissive monkeys as an example.

Two of his claims require updates. First, as Ornish claimed, his diet continues to have some effectiveness for weight loss and improvement of cardiovascular health. However, a recent randomized trial comparing the Ornish, Atkins, Weight Watchers, and Zone diets for reduction of heart disease risk and weight loss indicated that all four diets produced some modest degree of weight reduction and reduced some heart disease risk factors. No diet was clearly superior to any other diet (Dansinger, Gleason, Griffith, Selker, & Schaefer, 2005). Second, heart disease still kills many people who were not aware that they suffered from this disease. For example, Goraya et al. (2003) found that 49 percent of sudden cardiac deaths occurred in people who were not diagnosed with heart disease.

The second chapter, "Racial Differences in Attitudes Regarding Cardiovascular Disease Prevention and Treatment" (Woodard, Hernandez, Lees, & Petersen, 2005), compares African American and Caucasian male Veterans Administration patients' experiences with and beliefs about their coronary heart disease health care. The data in this study were collected during the men's participation in focus groups. The researchers drew a number of conclusions from their study, including that African American participants experienced racism as a stress in their health care situation, were less assertive than Caucasians in the physician–patient relationship, and appeared to possess less specific knowledge than Caucasian participants about the particulars of risk for coronary heart disease. This study fits into at least two larger bodies of research: the field of multicultural health psychology (see, for example, Lewis, 2002), and research on racism as a source of stress (see Clark, Anderson, Clark, & Williams, 1999, for a review).

Chapter 8 is drawn from Jones and Bright's book *Stress: Myth, Theory and Research* (2001). The chapter is a review of the literature on a variety of specific topics under the umbrella of the relationship between stress and disease. The authors begin by describing the difficulties inherent in research that explores the stress–disease link. They follow with a review of research on stress and a number of health conditions: breast cancer, cardiovascular disease, the common cold, immune suppression, and psychiatric conditions, focusing on depression. Jones and Bright's summary discusses research involving many of the concepts in other parts of our book, such as stress conceptualized as both life events and hassles, the appraisal concept, and statistical mediation. Also, research related to Karasek's demand–control model, touched on in Smith and Sulsky's chapter in Part I, is discussed in some detail here. Jones and Bright do an excellent job of conveying the complexities of the research on stress and illness. They conclude that evidence generally supports a stress–illness/symptom link for some outcomes, such as depression, but that research results have been conflicting for other outcomes, such as breast cancer.

The fourth chapter is an excerpt from Andrew Solomon's book *The Noonday Demon: An Atlas of Depression* (2001), which won the National Book Award in 2001. Solomon describes depression as he experienced it; for a technical description of depression, the reader should refer to the American Psychiatric Association's *Diagnostic and Statistical Manual*, fourth edition (1994). In the second part of this selection, Solomon provides a brief description of the relationship between stress and depression, focusing largely on the relationship between the stress hormone cortisol and the neurotransmitter (chemical brain messenger) serotonin, which appears to be often indicated in depression. For a more detailed, and also highly readable discussion of the stress–depression relationship, refer to Sapolsky (2004).

Chapter 10 comes from Sapolsky's book *Why Zebras Don't Get Ulcers* (2004) and describes the energy storage and energy mobilization systems of the body. This leads to a discussion of a disease that is now epidemic in the United States and is on the rise in many other societies as well, diabetes. Sapolsky covers both type 1 and type 2 diabetes, focusing on the impact that stress has on these diseases. He ends with a brief description of Metabolic syndrome (Syndrome X).

The final chapter of Part II is Kennedy's chapter from *The Management of Stress and Anxiety in Medical Disorders* (2000) entitled "Psychological Factors and Immunity in HIV Infection: Stress, Coping, Social Support, and Intervention Outcomes." Kennedy provides a review of research on the relationship between psychosocial factors and HIV. The psychosocial factors discussed are stress, coping styles (for example, denial, optimism about AIDS, realistic acceptance), and social support. She also looks at research on two potentially important interventions for AIDS patients: cognitive-behavioral stress management and aerobic exercise training. Kennedy concludes that, in general, evidence indicates that psychosocial factors may be related to HIV progression. She conveys the excitement inherent in AIDS research as research results that appear to conflict create opportunities for researchers to work toward a greater understanding of the relationship between psychosocial factors and HIV.

The readings in this part of the book address a variety of illnesses that are or may be related to stress. The subsequent part of the book will then focus on a psychological condition that appears to have a unique and dramatic connection to stress: posttraumatic stress disorder.

TERMS

The readings in Part II of our book include a number of technical terms. Can you define these terms? Definitions are included in the glossary in the back of the book.

General Stress and General Psychology Terms

- Affect
- Allostatic load
- Allostatic response
- Appraisal (also called "psychological appraisal" or "cognitive appraisal")
- Attributional style
- Bipolar disorder
- Cognitive-behavioral therapy (CBT)
- *Diagnostic and Statistical Manual of Mental Disorders (DSM)*
- Diathesis-stress approach
- Fight-or-flight reaction or response
- Hassles (also called "daily hassles" or "minor hassles")
- Karasek's job strain model
- Major life events stress (also called "life events stress" or "life events")
- Psychoneuroimmunology
- Social support
- Unipolar (major) depression

Physiological Terms

- Adrenal gland
- Adrenaline (epinephrine)
- Amino acid
- Amygdala

- Atherosclerosis
- Catecholamine
- Contraction band necrosis
- Corticotropin-releasing factor (CRF)
- Cortisol
- C-reactive protein
- Endocrine system
- Free fatty acid
- Glucocorticoid
- Glucose
- Glycerol
- Glycogen
- Hippocampus
- Insulin
- Ischemia
- Lymphocyte
- Mitogen
- Neurotransmitter
- Noradrenaline (norepinephrine)
- Parasympathetic nervous system
- Serotonin
- Sympathetic nervous system
- Triglyceride
- Ventricular fibrillation

Statistical or Research Methods Terms

- Confounding factor
- Correlational research design
- Cross-sectional study
- Experimental research design
- Longitudinal study
- Mediation
- Meta-analysis
- Operationalization
- Prospective study
- Retrospective study

REFERENCES

American Psychiatric Association (1994). *Diagnostic and statistical manual of mental disorders* (4th ed.). Washington, DC: American Psychiatric Association.

Clark, R., Anderson, N. B., Clark, V. R., & Williams, D. R. (1999). Racism as a stressor for African Americans: A biopsychosocial model. *American Psychologist, 54*(10), 805–816.

Cooper, C. L., & Dewe, P. (2004). *Stress: A brief history.* Malden, MA: Blackwell.

Dansinger, M. L., Gleason, J. A., Griffith, J. L., Selker, H. P., & Schaefer, E. J. (2005). Comparison of the Atkins, Ornish, Weight Watchers, and Zone diets for weight loss and heart disease risk reduction—A randomized trial. *Journal of the American Medical Association, 293*(1), 43–53.

Goraya, T. Y., Jacobsen, S. J., Kottke, T. E., Frye, R. L., Weston, S. A., & Roger, V. L. (2003). Coronary heart disease death and sudden cardiac death: A 20-year population-based study. *American Journal of Epidemiology, 157*(9), 763–770.

Jones, F., & Bright, J. (2001). *Stress: Myth, theory and research.* New York: Prentice Hall.

Kaplan, J. R., Manuck, S. B., Clarkson, T. B., Lusso, F. M., & Taub, D. M. (1982). Social status, environment, and atherosclerosis in cynomolgus monkeys. *Arteriosclerosis, 2*(5), 359–368.

Kennedy, S. (2000). Psychological factors and immunity in HIV infection: Stress, coping, social support, and intervention outcomes. In D. I. Mostofsky & D. H. Barlow (Eds.), *The management of stress and anxiety in medical disorders* (pp. 194–205). Needham Heights, MA: Allyn & Bacon.

Lewis, M. K. (2002). *Multicultural health psychology: Special topics acknowledging diversity.* Boston: Allyn & Bacon.

Ornish, D. (1990). *Dr. Dean Ornish's program for reversing heart disease.* New York: Random House.

Sapolsky, R. (2004). *Why zebras don't get ulcers.* New York: Henry Holt.

Selye, H. (1956). *The stress of life.* New York: McGraw-Hill.

Solomon, A. (2001). *The noonday demon: An atlas of depression.* New York: Scribner.

Wolff, H. G. (1953). *Stress and disease.* Springfield, IL: Charles G. Thomas.

Woodard, L. D., Hernandez, M. T., Lees, E., & Petersen, L. A. (2005). Racial differences in attitudes regarding cardiovascular disease prevention and treatment: A qualitative study. *Patient Education and Counseling, 57*(2), 225–231.

CHAPTER 6

Dr. Dean Ornish's Program for Reversing Heart Disease

Dean Ornish

Emotional stress comes in two basic categories: acute and chronic. We are designed to cope with acute stress much better than with chronic stress.

The body responds to stress—whether emotional stress (perceived danger) or physical stress (extreme temperature changes or exertion)—by activating a series of mechanisms collectively known as the fight-or-flight response, which prepares us either to fight or to run. The body does this in two ways.

First, there are direct connections between your brain and your heart. These nerves, called the *sympathetic nervous system*, stimulate receptors in the heart that make it beat faster and harder and can cause the coronary arteries to constrict. Second, the brain causes other organs, such as your adrenal glands, to secrete stress hormones such as *adrenaline* and steroids such as *cortisol*, which circulate in the blood until they reach the heart. Acute stress tends to cause rises in production of adrenaline and its relative, *noradrenaline*, whereas chronic stress causes increases in cortisol production.

As a result of signals from these hormones, a series of physiological reactions occur:

- Our muscles begin to contract, thereby fortifying our "body armor." We are more protected from bodily injury.
- Our metabolism speeds up, providing more strength and energy with which to fight or run. Both our heart rate and the amount of blood pumped with each beat increase.

- Our rate of breathing begins to increase, providing more oxygen to do battle or to run from danger.
- Our digestive system begins to shut down, diverting more blood and energy to the large muscles needed to fight or run.
- The pupils of our eyes begin to dilate, aiding vision. Other senses such as hearing also become heightened.
- We feel an urge to urinate and move the bowels, to reduce the danger of infection if abdominal injury should occur.
- Arteries in our arms and legs begin to constrict, so that less blood will be lost if we become wounded or injured. (You may notice that your hands get cold during times of stress, which is the principle behind "stress cards" that change color in your hand as you become more relaxed.)
- Our blood clots more quickly, so we'll lose less blood if we become wounded or injured.

These mechanisms have evolved over the centuries to help us survive danger. They work best when the danger is clear, well defined, and short-term. An example of an acute stress graph is shown in Figure 6.1. It illustrates the following situation. You are crossing a street on your way home (point 1), when suddenly, out of the corner of your eye, you notice a car coming at you at high speed. Your muscles tense, you feel a surge of energy, and you lunge backward, smashing into a newspaper vending machine and cutting an artery in your hand, which quickly stops bleeding (point 2). These fight-or-flight mechanisms help to save your life. After the danger has passed, you may experience a compensatory parasympathetic response (point 3): your knees feel shaky, you feel weak, your muscles relax, and your arteries dilate. After a few minutes, you return to baseline (point 4) (Pelletier, 1977).

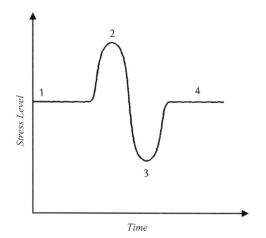

Figure 6.1. Acute Stress Graph

Unfortunately, emotional stress in modern times tends to be chronic rather than acute. The pace of life in the past ten years seems to be increasingly faster—the so-called acceleration syndrome. Like Alice in Wonderland, we go faster and faster while remaining in the same place. FedEx overnight service is no longer quick enough—that letter needs to be sent by fax immediately. Even the traditional places of refuge in the twentieth century—the car and the home—are transformed, with fax machines and computers at home, telephones in the car, even fax machines for the car. With portable telephones and laptop computers, anywhere can be an office.

Of course, the technology is not to blame. These same devices can be used to decrease stress by allowing people more flexibility in choosing their work environments. (I have a fax machine, portable phone, and laptop computer, and these allow me to work out of my home.) It's what we *do* with technology that determines its effects on our lives.

Likewise, our "inner technology" is correct—we're built right—but we are designed to cope with acute stress, not the chronic stress of modern life. We often don't have time to recover from one stressful situation before we get hit with another. An example of a chronic stress graph is shown in Figure 6.2. It illustrates the case of a mythical Mr. Jones.

Mr. Jones is already having a tough day. The alarm clock jars him out of bed, but he's still going to be late for an important morning meeting at work—daylight savings time began last night and he forgot to set the clock ahead. He turns on the radio while shaving and hears that another airplane began losing important pieces of its fuselage while in flight, and he's scheduled to fly across the country the next day. Ouch—suddenly there's blood all over the towel. Damn razor! While reading the newspaper over breakfast, he learns that his stocks are down; now he's not sure how he's going to make the mortgage payment and send his son to college. No time to talk with his family over breakfast—he's late! He gulps down two cups of coffee, bacon, eggs, and toast and rushes out the door.

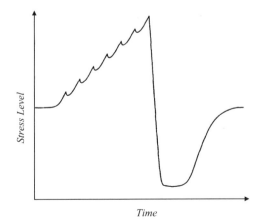

Figure 6.2. Chronic Stress Graph

Trouble ahead: An eighteen-wheeler jackknifed, and traffic is backed up for miles—Why today? He arrives at work over an hour late, just as the important meeting is ending. Both his boss and his main competitor smile at him as they walk by. He goes into his office as his secretary tells him that the IRS called to schedule an audit of his tax returns for the last five years. And his day is just beginning!

When our stress mechanisms are *chronically* activated, the same responses that are designed to protect us can become harmful—even lethal. Arteries constrict not just in our arms and legs but also inside our hearts. Blood clots are more likely to form inside our coronary arteries.

Thus, most of our muscles constrict during times of chronic, intense emotional stress, ranging from the large muscles (causing tension and pain in the neck, back, shoulders, etc.) to the smooth muscle that lines the coronary arteries (leading to spasm) to the fibers of the heart muscle itself (leading to contraction band necrosis, described later in this chapter).

Dr. Andrew Selwyn at Harvard Medical School and Dr. John Deanfield at the Hammersmith Hospital in London used cardiac PET scans to measure blood flow to the heart in patients with heart disease. While patients were being scanned, they asked the patients to do some simple arithmetic problems. Just the emotional stress of doing mental arithmetic caused a measurably reduced blood flow to the heart (Selwyn et al., 1985). Similarly, Dr. Alan Rozanski at the University of California, Los Angeles, School of Medicine found that mental stress caused the heart to beat less effectively in people who had coronary heart disease (Rozanski et al., 1988).

There are a lot of misconceptions about stress and the heart. The ability to respond to stress and the ability to relax are equally important in being able to function effectively while remaining healthy. I'm not saying we should all be laid-back, avoid stress, and never get mentally or physically aroused. Both arousal and relaxation are healthy responses.

The ideal course of action is to respond to challenges or difficult situations fast and efficiently and then to relax. However, many people are better at getting pumped up than at relaxing afterward. During acute stress, the hormones adrenaline and noradrenaline give us more energy and help us to think more clearly to deal with the challenge. It is when we lose the ability to return to baseline—to relax—that the stress response becomes chronic. When this happens, the noradrenaline and adrenaline levels remain high, causing anxiety and insomnia, coronary artery spasm, and increased blood clotting. Also, excessive cortisol and other steroids are produced, causing blockages to build up more rapidly in the arteries, as well as emotional depression, impotence, acne, and immune system impairment. These effects are independent of diet and other factors. (Athletes who have been taking steroids to build up muscles are beginning to find that they can also build up coronary artery blockages.)

Recent research shows that the lining of normal coronary arteries produces a substance called *endothelium-derived relaxation factor* (EDRF) that dilates the coronary arteries, allowing more blood to flow to the heart. When the lining of the coronary arteries is damaged by atherosclerosis, much less EDRF is produced, so the arteries tend to constrict and reduce coronary blood flow. As a result, atherosclerotic coronary arteries tend to be hyperresponsive to stress. In other words, the same amount of stress hormones cause partially blocked coronary arteries to constrict even more than normal ones. The more blocked with plaque an artery is, the less EDRF is produced, so the more likely the artery will go into spasm at the site of the coronary artery blockage.

Normally, exercise causes the arteries to secrete more EDRF, causing the coronary arteries to dilate despite the increase in sympathetic nervous system stimulation. In people who have coronary artery blockages, however, the reduced EDRF production causes the coronary arteries to constrict during exercise, making an already bad situation even worse. Smoking also decreases the production of EDRF from your cells.

Dr. David Harrison and his colleagues (1987) fed monkeys a high-cholesterol diet and found that they developed coronary artery blockages and their production of EDRF decreased. Here's some good news: He then fed these monkeys a very low-fat, low-cholesterol diet similar to our Reversal Diet and found that the monkeys' EDRF levels returned to normal even though the coronary artery blockages only partially reversed.

"You know, it's a real jungle out there. I mean, sometimes my office is a zoo. Just when I think I've finally got it made and get some respect, along comes someone else to challenge my authority. I feel stressed all the time, trying to keep my position and worrying about others trying to get what *I've* got." A typical day in the business world? "Yes, but it's monkey business."

Studies by Dr. Jay Kaplan, Dr. Thomas Clarkson, and their colleagues at the Bowman Gray School of Medicine have given the best scientific evidence to date of the role of emotional stress in causing coronary artery blockages. Dr. Kaplan and his colleagues (1982) studied cynomolgus monkeys, which are very similar to people in how they develop coronary artery blockages. These monkeys, like humans, have a complex social organization; like many people, these monkeys are very aware of their social ranking and social status. The investigators determined social rankings among these monkeys on the basis of fight outcomes or competitions among individual monkeys. Winners of fights or competitions were judged dominant to losers.

In their first experiment, thirty monkeys were divided into two groups. Half were placed in a chronically stressful, socially unstable environment, and the other half were maintained in a nonstressful, socially stable one. Both groups were fed a high-fat, high-cholesterol, typical American diet.

After twenty-two months, the dominant, highly aggressive, and competitive monkeys in the chronically stressed, socially disrupted, unstable groups had developed coronary artery blockages *more than twice as severe* as the dominant monkeys in the unstressed group. The dominant stressed monkeys also had twice as much blockage as the subordinate monkeys (who did not fight to achieve or maintain social status). *These differences in coronary artery blockages occurred even though blood pressure and cholesterol levels were comparable in all groups.*

The investigators then repeated this study, but this time the monkeys were fed a diet that was somewhat lower in fat (the "prudent diet" of the American Heart Association). As expected, the monkeys developed less extensive blockages than in the first study, but once more the dominant, chronically stressed monkeys had significantly more blockages than the other groups of monkeys. Again, both the stressed and unstressed monkeys had comparable blood pressure and cholesterol levels, so the effects of stress on the heart must have been caused by other mechanisms.

Kaplan and his colleagues wrote, "We concluded from this study that psychosocial influences on coronary artery atherosclerosis were not dependent on the presence of large amounts of fat and cholesterol in the diet" (p. 368). In other words, stress caused formation of coronary artery blockages even when monkeys were fed a diet lower in fat and cholesterol. When the diet was high in fat and cholesterol, the influence of stress on causing arterial blockages was magnified thirty times! Therefore, in monkeys, both emotional stress and diet are powerful influences on the development of coronary artery blockages.   .

In other experiments, Kaplan found that chronic stress increased the permeability of the monkeys' arterial walls to cholesterol—that is, stress made the coronary arteries absorb more cholesterol. Also, stress decreased levels of HDL ("good") cholesterol.

The investigators also found that the monkeys whose heart rates and blood pressures showed the largest increases when the monkeys were stressed also had the greatest severity of coronary artery blockages. The dominant, chronically stressed monkeys showed the widest swings in heart rate and blood pressure when they went from a relaxed to a stressed state. Even the presence of the investigators was enough to cause a marked rise in the heart rate of dominant monkeys. (Dr. Robert Eliot [1987] has termed people who react to stress in this way "hot reactors," and his research and the work of others indicate that hot reactors are at higher risk of dying from heart disease.)

The dominant monkeys were chronically stressed by trying to maintain control in a constantly changing social environment. That is, each dominant monkey had to keep fighting to maintain his high-status position when new monkeys were continually introduced to his group—similar to what is often seen in organizations and corporations.

In monkeys and in humans, chronic stress causes overproduction of the stress hormone cortisol, which in turn increases the formation of coronary artery blockages. Chronic stress also decreases estrogen production—one reason that stressed women sometimes have irregular menstrual cycles. This disruption of estrogen production by the ovaries can contribute to coronary heart disease in women.

Dr. Kaplan's experiments also demonstrated that *subordinate* female monkeys developed almost as much coronary atherosclerosis as the *dominant* male monkeys. (In monkeys, at least, perhaps males need to learn to be less dominant and females to be less subordinate.) Almost half of the subordinate female monkeys developed menstrual abnormalities, and most had low estrogen levels, another side effect of chronic stress.

Dominant male monkeys tended to spend significantly more time alone than the other monkeys. In contrast, monkeys who engaged in friendly, positive behaviors such as grooming or passive body contact had lower heart rates (indicating relaxation) than the same monkeys when they were alone. Female monkeys who were isolated in individual cages had twice the atherosclerosis as those who were allowed to live together with other monkeys.

A brutal study by Dr. Boris Lapin and Dr. Genja Cherkovich, published in a Soviet scientific journal, also demonstrated that emotional stress can cause coronary artery blockages to form. In a series of experiments conducted several years ago, a male baboon was taken from his female mate and placed in a separate cage. Then the male was forced to watch his mate copulate with a rival monkey. After four or five months of this, the isolated male monkeys had significant increases in coronary artery blockages, blood pressure, and heart attacks (Lapin, Cherkovich, & Iakovleva, 1966).

In monkeys and baboons, social isolation is a major cause of emotional stress. I think the same is true for humans, as well: when we go far enough back in the causal chain, we find that feeling isolated leads to emotional stress and, in turn, to heart disease.

Chronic emotional stress may cause coronary artery blockages to form in humans as it does in monkeys. A recent study by Dr. Abla Sibai found that people exposed to the stress of fourteen years of war in Beirut had significantly more coronary artery blockages at angiography than visitors who were not under this chronic stress, independent of other risk factors such as blood pressure and cholesterol (Sibai, Armenian, & Alam, 1989).

A recent study by Dr. Peter Schnall at Cornell found that workers who faced high psychological demands without having much control over day-to-day decisions had three times the risk of having high blood pressure. *All* of these chronically stressed workers had thickened or enlarged hearts (Schnall et al., 1990).

SUDDEN CARDIAC DEATH

It's as bad as it sounds. Approximately 40 percent of people who die from heart disease didn't even know they had a heart problem until they died from it—clearly not the best way to find out. So, no matter how good we get at treating heart disease, the major focus needs to be on prevention.

Sudden death due to heart disease occurs in two ways:

- Blood flow to the heart is reduced, causing a heart attack.
- The heart begins to beat erratically.

So far, we have been discussing what causes heart attacks. Not surprisingly, the same lifestyle factors that can lead to heart attacks also can lead to an irregular or erratic heart rhythm, known as an *arrhythmia*.

Irregular heartbeats are of two types: life-threatening and harmless. Almost everyone has an occasional "skipped beat," which is harmless (actually, "skipped beats" are usually extra or premature beats). An electro-cardiogram (EKG) helps a doctor figure out if a person is having irregular heartbeats that may be dangerous. The most dangerous type is called *ventricular fibrillation*.

Ventricular fibrillation is caused when blood flow to the heart is suddenly reduced by any of the mechanisms already discussed (coronary artery blockages, blood clots, spasm, and so on), even if a heart attack does not occur. It can also occur when the electrical conduction system of the heart is disrupted, usually by emotional stress or stimulants.

Studies by Dr. Bernard Lown at Harvard Medical School and by others have shown that emotional stress—even just the sight of the experimenters—can cause ventricular fibrillation to occur in dogs (Lown, 1980a, 1980b, 1987; Lown, DeSilva, Reich, & Murawski, 1980). Similar work by Drs. Mark Entman and James Skinner at Baylor College of Medicine showed that emotional stress caused ventricular fibrillation to occur in pigs when coronary blood flow was reduced, whereas putting pigs in a familiar and relaxed environment helped to prevent sudden cardiac death even when coronary blood flow was reduced (Skinner, Beder, & Entman, 1983; Skinner, Lie, & Entman, 1975).

A study by Dr. Michael Brodsky, reported in the *Journal of the American Medical Association*, examined six patients who had life-threatening irregular heartbeats and no coronary artery blockages. Five of these six patients reported marked psychological stress. For example, one patient was a Cambodian refugee who had been separated from her husband and six children for years during the Khmer Rouge takeover. She later found her children in a refugee camp, where she began having fainting spells and palpitations (Brodsky, Sato, Iseri, Wolff, & Allen, 1987). Closer to home, Dr. Thomas Graboys (1981) of Harvard Medical School reported that one of his patients began to have life-threatening irregular heartbeats while watching the closing minutes of a close Boston Celtics basketball game. And the Japanese government recently began funding a $2 million study of *karōshi*, or "sudden cardiac death from overwork."

In humans, unfortunately, all of the drugs used to *treat* irregular heartbeats can also *cause* irregular heartbeats and sudden cardiac death in some people—and there is no way to predict whether these drugs will make a patient better or worse. Recently, a large-scale clinical trial of two new anti-arrhythmia drugs sponsored by the National Institutes of Health was discontinued when the researchers realized that sudden cardiac deaths were much *higher* in the patients who were receiving these drugs.

CONTRACTION BAND NECROSIS

Recently, another mechanism was discovered that can cause damage to the heart muscle independent of coronary blood flow. It, too, is dependent on lifestyle. Stress hormones such as adrenaline and steroids open calcium channels at the cellular level in the heart, causing the coronary arteries to constrict (spasm). (This is why calcium-channel-blocking drugs like Cardizem and Procardia are often prescribed.) Under conditions of intense chronic stress, even the muscle fibers inside the heart itself can begin to contract so vigorously that the normal architecture of these fibers is disrupted, damaging the heart muscle. This mechanism is known as *contraction band necrosis, myofibrillar degeneration,* or *coagulative myocytolysis,* and it can lead to a condition called *cardiomyopathy,* in which the heart doesn't pump blood very well. This, in turn, can cause heart failure.

Although obscured by these medical terms, what we are really seeing is, to me, an amazing metaphor: the inability of the heart to relax causes the heart's muscle fibers to constrict to the point that it damages itself—like clenching your fist so hard and for so long that the bones and knuckles in your hand begin to break. This inability to relax and the resulting chronic constriction manifest themselves throughout the body, from the large muscles in the back down to the smallest fibers in the heart.

In summary, when we go far enough back in the causal chain, we can see that heart disease is usually due to excess: too much fat and cholesterol, too much stress, too many cigarettes, and so on. What this means is that we have the power to change our lifestyles to begin healing ourselves.

The body has a great capacity to heal itself when given a chance to—unfortunately, most people eat more fat and cholesterol than the body can metabolize, so it builds up in the arteries. People often feel chronically stressed, so the body never has a chance to recover from one stress before getting hit with another one. And many people compound the problem by smoking a pack or two of cigarettes every day and leading sedentary lives. When we identify and remove the excess, then the heart can begin to heal itself. Best of all, this healing process can begin to take effect sooner than we had thought possible.

REFERENCES

Brodsky, M. A., Sato, D. A., Iseri, L. T., Wolff, L. J., & Allen, B. J. (1987). Ventricular tachyarrhythmia associated with psychological stress: The role of the sympathetic nervous system. *Journal of the American Medical Association, 257*(15), 2064–2067.

Eliot, R. S. (1987). Stress and cardiovascular disease: Mechanisms and measurement. *Annals of Clinical Research, 19*(2), 88–95.

Graboys, T. B. (1981). Celtics fever: Playoff-induced ventricular arrhythmia [letter]. *New England Journal of Medicine, 305*(8), 467–468.

Harrison, D. G., Armstrong, M. L., Freiman, P. C., & Heistad, D. D. (1987). Restoration of endothelium-dependent relaxation by dietary treatment of atherosclerosis. *Journal of Clinical Investigation, 80*(6), 1808–1811.

Kaplan, J. R., Manuck, S. B., Clarkson, T. B., Lusso, F. M., & Taub, D. M. (1982). Social status, environment, and atherosclerosis in cynomolgus monkeys. *Arteriosclerosis, 2*(5), 359–368.

Lapin, B. A., Cherkovich, G. M., & Iakovleva, L. A. (1966). Eksperimental'noe vosproizvedenie na obez'ianakh zabolevanii serdechno-sosudistoi sistemy [The experimental production of cardiovascular diseases in monkeys]. *Vestnik Akademii meditsinskikh nauk SSSR, 21*(4), 73–81.

Lown, B. (1980a). Higher nervous activity and sudden cardiac death. *Bulletin et mémoires de l'Académie Royale de Médecine de Belgique, 135*(8), 487–505.

Lown, B. (1980b). Neural and psychologic factors in sudden death. *Verhandlungen der Deutschen Gesellschaft fur Herz- und Kreislaufforschung, 46,* 28–37.

Lown, B. (1987). Sudden cardiac death: Biobehavioral perspective. *Circulation, 76*(1, Pt. 2), I186–196.

Lown, B., DeSilva, R. A., Reich, P., & Murawski, B. J. (1980). Psychophysiologic factors in sudden cardiac death. *American Journal of Psychiatry, 137*(11), 1325–1335.

Pelletier, K. R. (1977). *Mind as healer, mind as slayer: A holistic approach to preventing stress disorders.* New York: Delacorte Press.

Rozanski, A., Bairey, C. N., Krautz, D. S., Friedman, J., Resser, K. J., Morell, M., et al. (1988). Mental stress and the induction of silent myocardial ischemia in patients with coronary artery disease. *New England Journal of Medicine, 318*(16), 1005–1012.

Schnall, P. L., Pieper, C., Schwartz, J. E., Karasek, R. A., Schlussel, Y., Devereux, R. B., et al. (1990). The relationship between "job strain," workplace diastolic blood pressure, and left ventricular mass index: Results of a case-control study. *Journal of the American Medical Association, 263*(14), 1929–1935.

Selwyn, A. P., Shea, M. J., Deanfield, J. E., Wilson, R. A., deLandsheere, C., & Jones, T. (1985). Clinical problems in coronary disease are caused by the wide variety of ischemic episodes that affect patients out of hospital. *American Journal of Medicine, 79*(Suppl. 3A), 12–17.

Sibai, A. M., Armenian, H. K., & Alam, S. (1989). Wartime determinants of arteriographically confirmed coronary artery disease in Beirut. *American Journal of Epidemiology, 130*(4), 623–631.

Skinner, J. E., Beder, S. D., & Entman, M. L. (1983). Psychological stress activates phosphorylase in the heart of the conscious pig without increasing heart rate and blood pressure. *Proceedings of the National Academy of Sciences of the United States of America, 80*(14), 4513–4517.

Skinner, J. E., Lie, J. T., & Entman, M. L. (1975). Modification of ventricular fibrillation latency following coronary artery occlusion in the conscious pig. *Circulation, 51*(4), 656–667.

CHAPTER 7

Racial Differences in Attitudes Regarding Cardiovascular Disease Prevention and Treatment

LeChauncy D. Woodard, Marie T. Hernandez, Emily Lees, and Laura A. Petersen

While mortality due to coronary heart disease (CHD) impacts Americans of all ethnicities, African Americans aged 35 to 64 have a much higher risk for death due to CHD than their white counterparts (Centers for Disease Control, 1998). To eliminate this disparity, the underlying causes for it must be elucidated.

Potential contributors to the excess CHD mortality among African Americans include a lower likelihood of undergoing invasive cardiac procedures (Chen, Rathore, Radford, Wang, & Krumholz, 2001; Kressin & Petersen, 2001; Petersen, Wright, Peterson, & Daley, 2002; Peterson et al., 1997), a greater prevalence of cardiovascular disease risk factors (Clark & Emerole, 1995; Cooper et al., 2000; Giles, Kittner, Hebel, Losonczy, & Sherwin, 1995; Lewis, Raczynski, Oberman, & Cutter, 1991), and a greater likelihood that those risk factors are poorly controlled (Qureshi, Suri, Guterman, & Hopkins, 2001). Some studies also indicate that African Americans are less likely to be aware of, and have lower rates of treatments for, these conditions than whites (Nieto et al., 1995; Schneider, Zaslavsky, & Epstein, 2002; Sprafka, Burke, Folsom, & Hahn, 1989). Additionally, differences in health care access and health care–seeking behavior between African Americans and whites may result in diagnostic and treatment delays as well as increased disease severity at the time of diagnosis (Lewis et al., 1991; Syed et al., 2000). Lastly, variation in the physician–patient relationship, including mistrust of physicians among African Americans, may be a source of disparate CHD outcomes (Collins, Clark, Petersen, & Kressin, 2002; Corbie-Smith, Thomas, Williams, & Moody-Ayers, 1999; Petersen, 2002).

While numerous studies have documented disparities in process of care and outcomes for CHD, few have examined these differences from the perspective of patients. Using focus groups, we explored the cardiovascular health care experiences and beliefs of African American and white patients to further elicit causes of the disparity in CHD mortality and to identify barriers to the treatment and prevention of CHD. As a qualitative research technique, focus groups offer insight into the diverse types of communication that people use in daily interactions that may not be recognized in more traditional data collection methods (Kitzinger, 1995). They also provide an inductive approach for generating themes and hypotheses from the perspective of the participants (Ludescher et al., 1993).

METHODS

Participants

Four focus groups were conducted at the Veterans Administration Medical Center (VAMC) in Houston, Texas. Participants were identified from a list of 354 patients at the Houston VAMC who had previously participated in a study assessing health beliefs and use of invasive cardiac procedures (Kressin et al., 2002). All potential subjects underwent a cardiac stress test graded as positive for ischemia within two years of the current study. Of the 354 potential participants, 244 (68.9%) were white and 110 (31.1%) were African American. There were no differences between white and African American patients in mean age (63.3 years versus 61.3 years, respectively) or mean education level (12.1 years versus 11.9 years, respectively).

Patients were contacted by telephone and invited to participate in the study. We successfully contacted a convenience sample of sixty-six (thirty-nine white, twenty-seven African American) patients. Thirty-three (sixteen white, seventeen African American) of them agreed to participate in the study. Reasons for nonparticipation included illness, lack of transportation, scheduling conflicts, and disinterest in involvement. Patients who agreed to participate received a reminder phone call prior to their scheduled focus group session. Of those recruited to participate, nine (two white, seven African American) did not attend their assigned session. When compared to all CHD patients receiving care in the Houston VAMC during fiscal year 2003, focus group participants were similar in terms of age and gender.

Design

Because racial variations in experiences were central to the study, the focus groups were stratified by race and comprised the following patients:

- Group 1: Eight white males, 56 to 75 years old
- Group 2: Six white males, 57 to 68 years old
- Group 3: Four African American males, 48 to 83 years old
- Group 4: Six African American males, 52 to 80 years old

Focus groups of this size are standard in qualitative research (Kitzinger, 1995). Larger group sizes do not facilitate open discussion (Denzin & Lincoln, 2000).

Written informed consent was obtained from participants at the commencement of each session. The study protocol was approved by the Institutional Review Board for Human Subject Research at Baylor College of Medicine and by the Department of Veterans Affairs Research and Development Committee at the Houston VAMC.

Data Collection

Focus groups, lasting approximately ninety minutes, were conducted jointly by a white moderator (EL) and an African American general internist (LW). The investigators were blinded to treatment that ensued after the diagnosis of CHD was established. Patients were encouraged to speak without reservation and assured that all comments would remain confidential. Using a written discussion guide consisting of open-ended questions, the moderator asked participants to share experiences regarding care received for their heart disease, perceptions about physicians providing their care, and beliefs about treatments used to manage their disease. The moderator followed patient responses with probes to facilitate disclosure of additional information and clarify topics arising from the discussion. The sessions were audiotaped, and notes were taken to record events, such as nonverbal cues, that could not be captured by audiotape. Focus group data were transcribed verbatim from audiotapes of each session and rendered anonymous to ensure patient confidentiality.

Data Analysis

A thematic analysis of verbatim transcripts was conducted by a team of four investigators consisting of an anthropologist (MH), qualitative researcher (EL), and two general internists (LW, LP). Researchers listened to audiotapes of the focus group sessions and read the transcripts multiple times. Two investigators independently reviewed each transcript to identify passages relating to patient perceptions of their CHD health care experiences and interactions with health care providers. We generated codes from key words and phrases in each passage. Similar codes were aggregated into emergent categories, and thematic elements of participants' health care experiences were developed. Throughout this process, investigators met to discuss content, compare findings, present alternative explanations, and resolve differences in data interpretation. When there were discrepancies in coding, the team met to discuss and reach consensus on the meaning of the passage and the codes to be assigned to the passage. There were no instances of disagreement in coding where consensus could not be reached. After reaching consensus as to the meaning of the passages, representative quotations were selected to exemplify each theme.

RESULTS

As shown in Table 7.1, four themes were delineated from our analysis of the data:

1. Risk factor knowledge
2. Physician–patient relationship
3. Medical system access
4. Treatment beliefs

Each will be presented in turn.

Risk Factor Knowledge

Both African American and white participants displayed similar general knowledge of cardiovascular disease risk factors, particularly the need for diet modification and smoking cessation. Members of all groups acknowledged high cholesterol as a risk factor. However, African American

Table 7.1. Focus Group Participant Responses Stratified by Race and Theme

Theme	African American	White
Risk factor knowledge	• "First of all, I would like to know, how did I contract heart disease?" • In reference to physician explanations of cholesterol: "They will tell you the high and the low or the good and the bad, and to tell you the truth, the average patient doesn't even know the difference, and that's kind of confusing." • In reference to racism as a stressor: "How would you feel if somebody was on your back for no apparent reason? . . . That's got something to do with my heart disease." • "It's a shame that we're still going through this racial thing, you know." • "I don't think you can prevent heart disease. When the good Lord is ready for it to stop, it's going to do just like that."	• "I'm trying to keep my weight down . . . and I don't smoke." • "Is my good cholesterol high enough, or is it still low and the bad's too high? Because you could be below 200 points and still be in trouble." • "There's a lot of ways you can take care of yourself, but I do feel everything is predestined."

Table 7.1. (*Continued*)

Theme	African American	White
Physician–patient relationship	• "I have only seen him twice. . . . I really can't say if his opinion means anything or not right now." • "If they would just listen [to patients] . . . it would be a much better relationship between doctor and patient." • "You don't know, but I had them try to explain it to me, and I still didn't know. So, what can you do?" • In reference to obtaining test results: "I said, 'Well, can you explain it to me?' and they said, 'Well you know everything is okay. We'll get back to you. Just pick up your medication.' It's just not worth it for me to sit up there and argue back and forth about what the deal is, but you know, I need to find out."	• In reference to his physician: "He takes a personal interest . . . he knows my family. . . . I have extreme confidence in his decision-making ability." • "One of the things a doctor can't do, he can't tell each of us what we're going through. . . . Some of these doctors, they don't listen to what you tell 'em." • "You tell a doctor, you know, inform them what's going on so they best know how to treat the symptom." • In reference to medications: "If it doesn't work, I come back, and tell him."
Medical system access	• "I go in there and see him for ten minutes, but I've been here all day."	• "I believe they need to make the appointments a little closer together."
Treatment beliefs	• In reference to medications: "From what I can understand, generic is not quite as strong." • "I believe, in a lot of instances, it will work better if we could afford the real one. I'm just saying . . . if you were to have a heart attack and you're taking the medicine that I'm taking now, I don't think it would act as fast."	• "Anytime you're paying money, you're going to get a better hospital than when you're not paying money." • Referring to physicians: "When they come to an environment like this, I don't believe that they have as much incentive to be caring about the people, because we kind of look downtrodden sometimes and so they look at us and say, 'These are throwaway people.'"

participants demonstrated less specific knowledge, as shown by the comment: "They will tell you the high and the low or the good and the bad and to tell you the truth, the average patient do not even know the difference, and that's kind of confusing" [group 4]. Another African American participant questioned, "How did I contract heart disease?" [group 3], possibly indicating poorer understanding of how risk factors are linked to the development of CHD.

Both African American and white participants stated that they felt heart disease is "predestined." One white patient expressed this sentiment with the comment: "There's a lot of ways you can take care of yourself, but I do feel that everything is predestined. No matter what measures you take to stay in good health, things are going to catch up with you" [group 2]. Similarly, an African American participant stated, "I don't think you can prevent heart disease. When the good Lord is ready for it to stop, it's going to do just like that" [group 3].

Participants also identified stress as a contributor to heart disease. Two African American group members highlighted stress due to racism, stating, "How would you feel if somebody was on your back for no apparent reason? ... That's got something to do with my heart disease," and, "It's a shame that we're still going through this racial thing, you know" [group 3]. The participants went on to describe experiences with racism in their daily life as well as in their interactions with the health care system. For example, one of the participants described a visit with his physician in which the physician focused on issues that he felt were important, rather than addressing the concerns that the patient felt were important. While several participants in both groups described similar difficulties in communicating with their physicians, this participant viewed his physician's dismissal of his concerns as an example of racism.

Unique to one of the African American groups was the expression of fear associated with physical activity after being diagnosed with heart disease. With regard to exercise, patients either expressed skepticism about its benefit or stated that, while they understood the importance of physical activity, they felt it was important to limit the amount of exertion or risk an adverse outcome. Comments illustrative of these findings include: "I've been kind of skeptical about this exercising" [group 4], and, "Exercise is good for you, but always watch your limits" [group 4].

Physician–Patient Relationship

African American and white participants identified similar characteristics of the physician–patient relationship as important to them. The length of relationship between the patient and provider appeared to influence willingness of the patient to accept physician recommendations. One white patient stated: "He takes a personal interest ... he knows my family.... I have extreme confidence in his decision-making ability" [group 2]. An African American participant's comment demonstrated that limited interaction with a provider can negatively impact patients' trust in their physician: "I have only seen him twice.... I really can't say if his opinion really means anything or not" [group 3]. The consensus of both African American and white participants was best expressed by a member of group 2, who stated, "With a doctor, you have to build a doctor–patient relationship and it's all based on integrity.... You've got to see your doctor before you build any kind of a relationship" [group 2].

Both African American and white participants wanted physicians to effectively communicate information to them and indicated that poor communication presents a significant barrier to understanding their conditions and being satisfied with their treatment: "One of the things a doctor can't do, he can't tell each of us what we're going through.... Some of these doctors, they don't listen to what you tell 'em" [group 2]; "If they would just listen [to patients] ... it would be a much better relationship between doctor and patient" [group 3]. Another presented a comparable view: "If I've got a question, I would like to have an answer to it, and a lot of times, you get part of an answer. You don't get a complete answer" [group 1]. One participant recalled prior experiences with physicians this way: "They're suppose to be checking you for this and for that. Most of them are sitting on the computer and after about five minutes, they say, 'Well, everything checks out today.' ... They're writing all this stuff on this computer; the computer is getting it, but I'm not getting it" [group 3]. Finally, use of medical terms by physicians was emphasized as an obstacle to successful communication during medical encounters, "I keep asking questions, he's talking real fast in very technical terms like it was none of my business" [group 1].

Both white and African American participants asserted a preference for nonforeign physicians, with some highlighting their war experiences to justify this position: "I think they should never hire a doctor that cannot speak clear English" [group 1]. "I don't trust him [in reference to a Vietnamese physician].... I didn't trust them when I was in the military, so why am I going to trust them with my medical help?" [group 3].

While the groups did not vary in what they considered integral to good physician–patient communication, comments by white participants indicated more assertiveness in their encounters with their physicians. For example, one patient stressed: "You tell a doctor, you know, inform them what's going on so they best know how to treat the symptom" [group 2]. In reference to side effects experienced with new medications, another participant stated: "If it don't work, I come back, and tell him" [group 1]. Alternatively, an African American participant described asking his physician about cholesterol with the statement: "You don't know, but I had them try to explain it to me, and I still didn't know. So, what can you do?" [group 4]. Similarly, another African American participant described an instance when he was unable to get an explanation of his test results from his physician, stating, "I said, 'Well, can you explain it to me?' and they said, 'Well, you know everything is okay. We'll get back to you. Just pick up your medication.' It's just not worth it for me to sit up there and argue back and forth about what the deal is, but you know, I need to find out" [group 4].

Medical System Access

Participants in both groups conveyed comparable difficulties accessing care. Complaints were similar in both groups and centered on the excessive time spent waiting to be seen by physicians, short duration of the physician visit, and length of time until follow-up. As one participant noted, "I go in there and see him for ten minutes, but I've been here all day" [group 3]. Referring to the interval between visits, another patient stated, "I believe they need to make the appointments a little closer together" [group 2].

Treatment Beliefs

Several white participants in the same group expressed concern that their limited financial resources were correlated with poor quality of care. Comments emblematic of this perception include: "Anytime you're paying money, you're going to get a better hospital than when you're not paying money" [group 1], and, referring to physicians, "When they come to an environment like this, I don't believe that they have as much incentive to be caring about the people, 'cause we kind of look downtrodden sometimes and so they look at us and say, 'These are throwaway people.'" [group 1].

While African Americans did not relate financial resources to treatment by health care providers, they worried that generic medications received within the Veterans Administration (VA) were less effective than brand-name medications. As one stated, "From what I can understand, generic is not quite as strong" [group 4]. Similarly, another participant commented: "I believe, in a lot of instances, it will work better if we could afford the real one. I'm just saying ... if you were to have a heart attack and you're taking the medicine that I'm taking now, I don't think it would act as fast" [group 4].

DISCUSSION

We convened four focus groups of African American and white male patients with coronary heart disease to explore racial differences in cardiovascular health care experiences that may contribute to poorer CHD outcomes among African Americans. Four major themes were identified: risk factor knowledge, physician–patient communication, access to care, and treatment beliefs.

African American participants displayed less specific knowledge of cardiovascular disease risk factors and the impact of these on the development of CHD. For example, comments by African Americans demonstrated less clarity about the etiology of CHD and less knowledge about hypercholesterolemia, particularly the implications of "good" and "bad" cholesterol. African American patients also diverged from white patients by expressing skepticism about the benefit of exercise. These findings suggest lower cardiovascular disease health literacy among African American patients and are consistent with prior research demonstrating that African Americans are less likely to be aware of and receive treatment for their conditions despite having a greater prevalence of CHD risk factors (Nieto et al., 1995; Sprafka et al., 1989). Diminished recognition of how CHD risk factors impact the development of heart disease may contribute to treatment delays, increased disease severity at the time of diagnosis, and poorer outcomes (Lewis et al., 1991).

Some African American participants indicated that the experience of racism contributed to their heart disease. While not directly linked to CHD, prior research suggests an association between racism and hypertension, a known CHD risk factor (Krieger & Sidney, 1996; Williams & Neighbors, 2001). In addition, racial discrimination is often perceived as stressful, and self-perceived stress is associated with a higher incidence of CHD and greater risk of recurrent ischemia (Gullette et al., 1997; Kubzansky et al., 1997; Rozanski et al., 1988). These findings imply that racism may play a role in the heightened CHD risk experienced by African Americans.

A significant amount of discussion centered on the physician–patient interaction, with participants agreeing on characteristics of a successful physician–patient relationship. Participants emphasized the need for physicians to listen to and acknowledge their concerns as well as effectively convey information about their medical conditions. Participants also indicated that the duration of the physician–patient relationship was related to their readiness to comply with physician recommendations. These results suggest that a more enduring relationship with a physician fosters trust between the patient and physician, perhaps facilitating treatment adherence. Given the extensive body of literature documenting African American distrust of the health care system (Collins et al., 2002; Corbie-Smith et al., 1999; Gamble, 1993; Petersen, 2002), the implications of this finding may have a more significant impact on this population. This hypothesis would need to be tested in further work.

Racial differences were apparent in the examples of communication during the medical encounter, with African American patients displaying less assertiveness in their interactions with physicians. Because patient assertiveness reflects a higher level of participation during the medical encounter (Street, 2001), this finding suggests that African Americans may be less active health care consumers and adds to growing literature showing that African Americans are less likely to have participatory visits with their physicians (Cooper-Patrick et al., 1999; Kaplan, Gandek, Greenfield, Roger, & Ware, 1995). Numerous studies demonstrate that shared decision making between physicians and patients is associated with higher patient satisfaction, improved health outcomes, and better self-perceived health status (Cooper-Patrick et al., 1999; Greenfield, Kaplan, Ware, Yano, & Frank, 1988; Kaplan et al., 1995).

In contrast to prior studies demonstrating that African Americans have poorer access to health care than whites (Bach, Cramer, Warren, & Begg, 1999; Chen et al., 2001; Fiscella, Franks, Doescher, & Saver, 2002; Kressin & Petersen, 2001; Petersen et al., 2002; Peterson et al., 1997; Shi, 1999), we found that both groups in our study experienced similar difficulties in accessing care. This finding may reflect that all study participants received care at a single VAMC. The groups were also comparable in that both attributed some of the problems they experienced in their encounters with the health care system to having lower levels of socioeconomic status. While both groups perceived barriers related to their social status, it is possible that lower levels of health literacy and perceptions of racism may have exacerbated these problems for African American patients.

CONCLUSIONS AND PRACTICE IMPLICATIONS

What are the implications of these findings for health care providers and their patients? One approach to reducing disparities in CHD outcomes is through interventions that enable minority patients to assume a more active role in their health care. Prior health promotion programs have invoked community-wide and individual-level educational programs to effect change in cardiovascular disease outcomes (Fortmann & Varady, 2000; Goodman, Wheeler, & Lee, 1995; Luepker et al., 1996). While these programs have produced some favorable changes in cardiovascular risk factor levels, such as cholesterol, tobacco use, and hypertension (Fortmann & Varady, 2000; Goodman et al., 1995), they have been largely ineffective at accomplishing their larger goal of reducing cardiovascular disease morbidity and mortality (Fortmann & Varady, 2000; Luepker et al., 1996).

More recently, medical researchers have employed innovative strategies to reach high-risk populations such as African Americans. For example, numerous programs aimed at reducing cardiovascular disease risk factors through lifestyle modification have been implemented in church settings and have shown promising results (Oexmann et al., 2000; Wiist & Flack, 1990; Yanek, Becker, Moy, Gittelsohn, & Koffman, 2001). Health promotion efforts have also been successfully tied to locations such as beauty salons and barber shops, providing valuable health information in a culturally familiar setting (Forte, 1995; Weinrich, Boyd, Bradford, Mossa, & Weinrich, 1998). While these strategies provide encouraging results, our study suggests that a more comprehensive approach to patient education may improve patient outcomes. In addition to providing culturally sensitive education that increases CHD knowledge, interventions should empower African American patients to become active partners in their medical care by providing skills necessary to successfully negotiate treatment decisions with their physicians. This approach may encourage more proficient health care utilization by African American patients, leading to better CHD health outcomes. However, these are speculative conclusions that need to be confirmed in future work.

We must acknowledge important limitations of our study. As with all qualitative studies, generalizability is limited. Additionally, our groups consisted of male patients from one VA hospital and therefore results cannot be generalized to females and non-VA patients. However, the purpose of our study was not to test a given hypothesis, but rather to explore patient attitudes about their cardiovascular health care experiences to generate hypotheses for further study. Finally, among those recruited to participate, African American patients were less likely than white patients to attend their scheduled focus group session. This finding is consistent with numerous studies documenting low rates of African American participation in research studies and may reflect African American mistrust of the medical community and of medical researchers (Corbie-Smith et al., 1999; Freimuth et al., 2001; Shavers, Lynch, & Burmeister, 2001).

In summary, we identified four themes: risk factor knowledge, physician–patient relationship, medical system access, and treatment beliefs. Racial differences were evident in the experience of racism as a stress, knowledge of the specifics of CHD risk factors, and assertiveness in the physician–patient relationship. These findings highlight an area where culturally competent interventions to increase patient knowledge and strengthen patient participation in the medical encounter may prove fruitful in decreasing disparities in CHD outcomes. The efficacy of such interventions would need to be tested in further work.

REFERENCES

Bach, P. B., Cramer, L. D., Warren, J. L., & Begg, C. B. (1999). Racial differences in the treatment of early-stage lung cancer. *New England Journal of Medicine, 341,* 1198–1205.

Centers for Disease Control (1998). Trends in ischemic heart disease rates for blacks and whites—United States, 1981–1995. *Morbidity & Mortality Weekly Report, 47*(44), 945–949.

Chen, J., Rathore, S. S., Radford, M. J., Wang, Y., & Krumholz, H. M. (2001). Racial differences in the use of cardiac catheterization after acute myocardial infarction. *New England Journal of Medicine, 344,* 1443–1449.

Clark, L. T., & Emerole, O. (1995). Coronary heart disease in African Americans: Primary and secondary prevention. *Cleveland Clinic Journal of Medicine, 62,* 285–292.

Collins, T. C., Clark, J. A., Petersen, L. A., & Kressin, N. R. (2002). Racial differences in how patients perceive physician communication regarding cardiac testing. *Medical Care, 40*(Suppl. 1), I27–I34.

Cooper, R., Cutler, J., Desvigne-Nickens, P., Fortmann, S. P., Friedman, L., Havlik, R., et al. (2000). Trends and disparities in coronary heart disease, stroke, and other cardiovascular disease in the United States: Findings of the National Conference on Cardiovascular Disease Prevention. *Circulation, 102*(25), 3137–3147.

Cooper-Patrick, L., Gallo, J. J., Gonzales, J. J., Vu, H. T., Powe, N. R., Nelson, C., et al. (1999). Race, gender, and partnership in the physician–patient relationship. *Journal of the American Medical Association, 282,* 583–589.

Corbie-Smith, S., Thomas, B., Williams, M. V., & Moody-Ayers, S. (1999). Attitudes and beliefs of African Americans toward participation in medical research. *Journal of General Internal Medicine, 14,* 537–546.

Denzin, N. K., & Lincoln, Y. S. (2000). *Handbook of qualitative research.* Thousand Oaks, CA: Sage.

Fiscella, K., Franks, P., Doescher, M. P., & Saver, B. G. (2002). Disparities in health care by race, ethnicity, and language among the insured: Findings from a national sample. *Medical Care, 40,* 52–59.

Forte, D. A. (1995). Community-based breast cancer intervention program for older African American women in beauty salons. *Public Health Reports, 110,* 179–183.

Fortmann, S. P., & Varady, A. N. (2000). Effects of a community-wide health education program on cardiovascular disease morbidity and mortality: The Stanford Five-City Project. *American Journal of Epidemiology, 152,* 316–323.

Freimuth, V. S., Quinn, S. C., Thomas, S. B., Cole, G., Zook, E., & Duncan, T. (2001). African Americans' views on research and the Tuskegee Syphilis Study. *Social Science & Medicine, 52,* 797–808.

Gamble, V. N. (1993). A legacy of distrust: African Americans and medical research. *American Journal of Preventive Medicine, 9,* 35–38.

Giles, W. H., Kittner, S. J., Hebel, J. R., Losonczy, K. G., & Sherwin, R. W. (1995). Determinants of black–white differences in the risk of cerebral infarction. *Archives of Internal Medicine, 155,* 1319–1324.

Goodman, R. M., Wheeler, F. C., & Lee, P. R. (1995). Evaluation of the Heart to Heart Project: Lessons from a community-based chronic disease prevention project. *American Journal of Health Promotion, 9,* 443–455.

Greenfield, S., Kaplan, H., Ware, J. E., Yano, E. M., & Frank, H. J. L. (1988). Patients' participation in medical care: Effects on blood sugar control and quality of life in diabetes. *Journal of General Internal Medicine, 3,* 448–457.

Gullette, E. C., Blumenthal, J. A., Babyak, M., Jiang, W., Waugh, R. A., Frid, D. J., et al. (1997). Effects of mental stress on myocardial ischemia during daily life. *Journal of the American Medical Association, 277*(19), 1521–1526.

Kaplan, S. H., Gandek, B., Greenfield, S., Roger, W., & Ware, J. E. (1995). Patient and visit characteristics related to physicians' participatory decision-making style. *Medical Care, 33,* 1176–1187.

Kitzinger, J. (1995). Introducing focus groups. *BMJ (Clinical Research Ed.), 311,* 299–302.

Kressin, N. R., Clark, J. A., Whittle, J., East, M., Peterson, E. D., Chang, B. H., et al. (2002). Racial differences in health-related beliefs, attitudes, and experiences of VA cardiac patients: Scale development and application. *Medical Care, 40*(Suppl. 1), 172–185.

Kressin, N. R., & Petersen, L. A. (2001). Racial differences in use of invasive cardiovascular procedures: Review of the literature and prescription for future research. *Annals of Internal Medicine, 135,* 352–366.

Krieger, N., & Sidney, S. (1996). Racial discrimination and blood pressure: The CARDIA Study of young black and white adults. *American Journal of Public Health, 86,* 1370–1378.

Kubzansky, L. D., Kawachi, I., Spiro, A., Weiss, S. T., Vokonas, P. S., & Sparrow, D. (1997). Is worrying bad for your heart? A prospective study of worry and coronary heart disease in the Normative Aging Study. *Circulation, 95,* 818–824.

Lewis, C. E., Raczynski, J. M., Oberman, A., & Cutter, G. R. (1991). Risk factors and the natural history of coronary heart disease in blacks. *Cardiovascular Clinics, 21,* 29–45.

Ludescher, G., Nishiwaki, R., Lewis, D., Brown, E., Glacken, D., & Jenkins, E. (1993). Black male college students and hypertension: A qualitative investigation. *Health Education Research, 8,* 271–282.

Luepker, R. V., Rastam, L., Hannan, P. J., Murray, D. M., Gray, C., Baker, W. L., et al. (1996). Community education for cardiovascular disease prevention: Morbidity and mortality results from the Minnesota Heart Health Program. *American Journal of Epidemiology, 144,* 351–362.

Nieto, F. J., Alonso, J., Chambless, L. E., Zhong, M., Ceraso, M., Romm, F. J., et al. (1995). Population awareness and control of hypertension and hypercholesterolemia: The Atherosclerosis Risk in Communities Study. *Archives of Internal Medicine, 155*(7), 677–684.

Oexmann, M. J., Thomas, J. C., Taylor, K. B., O'Neil, P. M., Garvey, W. T., Lackland, D. T., et al. (2000). Short-term impact of a church-based approach to lifestyle change on cardiovascular risk in African Americans. *Ethnicity & Disease, 10,* 17–23.

Petersen, L. A. (2002). Racial differences in trust: Reaping what we have sown? *Medical Care, 40,* 79–82.

Petersen, L. A., Wright, S. M., Peterson, E. D., & Daley, J. (2002). Impact of race on cardiac care and outcomes in veterans with acute myocardial infarction. *Medical Care, 40*(Suppl. 1), I86–I96.

Peterson, E. D., Shaw, L. K., DeLong, E. R., Pryor, D. B., Califf, R. M., & Mark, D. B. (1997). Racial variation in the use of coronary-revascularization procedures. *New England Journal of Medicine, 336,* 480–486.

Qureshi, A. I., Suri, F. K., Guterman, L. R., & Hopkins, L. N. (2001). Ineffective secondary prevention in survivors of cardiovascular events in the US population. *Archives of Internal Medicine, 161,* 1621–1628.

Rozanski, A., Bairey, C. N., Krantz, D. S., Friedman, J., Resser, K. J., Morell, M., et al. (1988). Mental stress and the induction of silent myocardial ischemia in patients with coronary artery disease. *New England Journal of Medicine, 318,* 1005–1012.

Schneider, E. C., Zaslavsky, A. M., & Epstein, A. M. (2002). Racial disparities in quality of care for enrollees in Medicare managed care. *Journal of the American Medical Association, 287,* 1288–1294.

Shavers, V. L., Lynch, C. F., & Burmeister, L. F. (2001). Factors that influence African-Americans' willingness to participate in medical research studies. *Cancer, 91,* 233–236.

Shi, L. (1999). Experience of primary care by racial and ethnic groups in the United States. *Medical Care, 37,* 1068–1077.

Sprafka, J. M., Burke, G. L., Folsom, A. R., & Hahn, L. P. (1989). Hypercholesterolemia prevalence, awareness, and treatment in blacks and whites: The Minnesota Heart Survey. *Preventative Medicine, 18,* 423–432.

Street, R. L., Jr. Active patients as powerful communicators. In W. P. Robinson & H. Giles (Eds.) *The new handbook of language and social psychology* (pp. 541–555). New York: John Wiley & Sons.

Syed, M., Khaja, F., Rybicki, B. A., Wulbrecht, N., Alam, M., Sabbah, H. N., Goldstein, S., & Borzak, S. (2000). Effect of delay on racial differences in thrombolysis for acute myocardial infarction. *American Heart Journal, 140*(4), 643–650.

Weinrich, S. P., Boyd, M. D., Bradford, D., Mossa, M. S., & Weinrich, M. (1998). Recruitment of African Americans into prostate cancer screening. *Cancer Practice, 6,* 23–30.

Wiist, W. H., & Flack, J. M. (1990). A church-based cholesterol education program. *Public Health Reports, 105,* 381–388.

Williams, D. R., & Neighbors, H. (2001). Racism, discrimination and hypertension: Evidence and needed research. *Ethnicity & Disease, 11,* 800–816.

Yanek, L. R., Becker, D. M., Moy, T. F., Gittelsohn, J., & Koffman, D. M. (2001). Project Joy: Faith based cardiovascular health promotion for African American women. *Public Health Reports, 116,* 68–81.

CHAPTER 8

Stress: Health and Illness

Fiona Jones and Jim Bright

The view that stress leads to illness is fundamental to much that we read or hear about stress, so much so that it is often assumed that conclusive evidence exists. For example, Pollock (1988), in an interview study of 114 people in the United Kingdom, found that there was a general belief that stress could be a direct cause of illness. Two specific conditions were thought to be most strongly associated with stress, heart attacks and "nervous breakdowns." Situations (e.g., in the workplace) were typically thought to cause heart attacks, whereas people were thought to cause nervous breakdowns. An archetypal heart attack victim was seen as an executive or businessman under pressure. More minor symptoms such as headaches or stomachaches were also thought to be related to stressors or worries. Since Pollock's study, it is unlikely that these beliefs have changed greatly. Statements about the contribution of stress to disease appear regularly in the press, as well as in the academic literature, serving to confirm the belief that stress causes disease.

In fact, given the vagueness and generality of the term *stress*, it would appear that the question "Does stress lead to illness?" is problematic. Indeed, Briner and Reynolds (1993) go so far as to suggest the question is "naive and trivial." To even begin to consider the issues underpinning the question, we need to consider a large number of different questions. Some of the more obvious are:

- Does exposure to a range of demanding stimuli (stressors) lead to psychiatric and/or physical illness?
- If so, what *kind* of stressors (major life events, chronic stressors, hassles)?
- Are stressors related to all illnesses or just some?

- Is it the existence of stressors or the *feeling* of being "stressed," anxious, or depressed that leads to illness?
- Why do only some people seem to be affected?
- What are the mechanisms?

Despite the volume of research addressing these questions, it has nevertheless been surprisingly difficult to establish a link between psychosocial factors and disease. Evidence comes from a wide range of sources and different types of studies published in both the medical and psychological literature. For many years, the focus of this research was on major *life events*. Many studies have been conducted into the relationships between life events and both physical and psychiatric disorders, with often conflicting conclusions (e.g., Dohrenwend, 1998; Miller, 1989). Studies now often also look at *daily hassles* and *chronic stressors*. All three approaches can be seen in studies discussed in this chapter.

Before considering the links between psychosocial factors and specific illnesses, we look briefly at why research in this area might be difficult.

WHAT DIFFICULTIES ARE THERE IN ESTABLISHING RELATIONSHIPS BETWEEN PSYCHOSOCIAL FACTORS AND DISEASE?

The reaction to stressors has been associated with a variety of different physiological changes, for example, in immune functioning. Frequently psychophysiologists look at relatively short-term changes in physiological indicators such as sIgA or cortisol. However, it cannot necessarily be assumed that these changes are of significance in causing disease. To confirm this, we need to look at effects of stressors and diseases such as cancer in the real world. There is then, however, the complication that many other potential confounding factors cannot easily be controlled. Furthermore, the possible short- and long-term links between different stressors and different diseases that can be investigated are almost unlimited. In many cases, the evidence, as we shall see, is ambiguous. Lazarus (1992) suggests that there are a number of reasons why a relationship between psychosocial factors and health (and by implication, illness) might be difficult to establish:

- Health is affected by a great many factors, including genetic influences and accidents. There may be little variance left to be accounted for by factors such as stress.
- Health is generally fairly stable and slow to change, making it difficult to demonstrate that psychosocial factors lead to changes in health.
- To demonstrate that stress affects long-term health, it is necessary to measure what is happening consistently over time. This may require repeated sampling and is likely to be costly, although it can and has been done over relatively short periods of time (months rather than years) examining illness symptoms or colds (e.g., DeLongis, Folkman, & Lazarus, 1988; Evans & Edgerton, 1991).

- The criterion of health is unclear; for example, a criterion of longevity would exclude some quite debilitating diseases, whereas a criterion based on social functioning would lead to a conclusion that the person with high blood pressure is healthy.

These factors make it very difficult to establish the relationship between psychosocial factors and health. As we shall see in the following sections, some researchers feel that we cannot claim to have established with any degree of certainty the extent and nature, or even the existence, of the relationship.

STRESS AND PHYSICAL ILLNESS

It would be a vast undertaking to review the large number of studies that exist in both medical and psychological literature on the role of life events, hassles, and chronic stressors in a huge range of illnesses. This chapter will focus on three different aspects that serve to illustrate the diversity of approaches.

Early researchers focused predominantly on the effect of major life events. One area considered below, which has attracted a great deal of attention, is the relationship between stress and breast cancer. Here the debate for and against the influence of psychosocial factors has been particularly fierce. A second aspect that will be considered here is the influence of the chronic stressors of job control and job demands. The relationship between this factor and cardiovascular disease has been a particular focus of attention. The third aspect of physical illness highlighted in this chapter is the common cold. Because of its prevalence and the fact that it is a minor illness, it is more amenable to research than other diseases.

Life Events and Breast Cancer

There is widespread belief among both the general public and the medical profession in an association between stressful experiences and the onset of breast cancer. For example, a study by Baghurst, Baghurst, and Record (1992) reports that 40 percent of South Australian women hold this belief, while Steptoe and Wardle (1994) found that almost half of a sample of medical experts were either undecided or confident of the role of stress in the causation of breast cancer.

The belief that emotionally distressing events are implicated in all types of cancer can be traced back to medical literature from the nineteenth century. There were numerous anecdotal reports in the literature commenting on the frequency with which negative events, grief, and depression were associated with the onset of all kinds of cancer (see LeShan, 1959). The first statistical study of this association is attributed to Snow (1893), who studied 250 cancer patients in London and reported that in 156 of them there was some "immediately antecedent trouble," frequently the loss of a close relative. LeShan suggests that the idea disappeared in the literature in the early part of the twentieth century, as the developments in surgery and radiation offered the most promising hope for an answer to the problem of cancer. The notion of the importance of loss in cancer causation emerged again in the second quarter of the century. Again, most studies were based on clinical observations. Nevertheless LeShan remarks on the consistency with which, "in different countries and at different times," physicians independently described their patients using descriptions such as "despair," "hopelessness," "loss of a child," "loss of a spouse," or "afflictions that appear insurmountable." In his own work, LeShan also found that cancer frequencies and age-adjusted mortality rates were higher among groups who had experienced loss; for example, the highest incidence was found in the widowed, followed by divorced, married, then single people (LeShan & Worthington, 1956).

More recent work focusing specifically on breast cancer, rather than cancer in general, has also produced many studies that show associations (e.g., Chen et al., 1995; Cooper, Cooper, & Faragher, 1989; Geyer, 1991). For example, Cooper and colleagues studied 1,596 women attending breast screening clinics with symptoms of breast lumpiness or tenderness, as well as 567 controls. Prior to being examined and diagnosed, they completed a questionnaire, which asked about life events in the previous two years. This design is known as a limited prospective study. They found that some life events, including the death of a husband or close friend, were associated with breast disease and its severity. More recently, Chen and colleagues investigated 119 women who were referred for biopsies. They were interviewed using Brown and Harris's (1989) life events and difficulties schedule before they received a definitive diagnosis. Chen and colleagues found that nineteen out of forty-one women with cancer had "greatly threatening life events" during the five years before diagnosis, compared with fifteen out of the seventy-eight controls. There was also increased risk associated with moderately threatening events, but none with minor events.

However, persuasive as these results are, there are many studies that have used similar approaches and failed to confirm these findings (e.g., Greer & Morris, 1975; Muslin, Gyarfas, & Pieper, 1966; Protheroe et al., 1999). Over the years, while isolated studies have continued to find links, reviews of the literature (e.g., Stolbach & Brandt, 1988) have tended to conclude that there is little evidence for an association. Genuine prospective studies (which follow people from before the appearance of symptoms) are rare, but one was conducted by Jones, Goldblatt, and Leon (1984), who investigated the notion that widows, having experienced loss, should be more prone to breast cancer than others. They followed up a 1 percent sample of the UK population and found that, although there was a slight increase in breast cancer mortality among widows, it was not statistically significant.

More recently, meta-analyses (research reviews in which higher quality studies are given more weight) have been conducted to try to reach conclusions from this conflicting evidence. Petticrew, Fraser, and Regan (1999) considered twenty-nine studies of the association of life events and breast cancer. The studies are described as being of "variable design," but all included controls. Assessment of events was typically based on checklists (e.g., the Social Readjustment Rating Scale, SRRS) or interviews (e.g., Life Events and Difficulties Schedule, LEDS). Overall, Petticrew and colleagues concluded that there was "no good evidence for a relationship" between negative life events and cancer on the basis of analysis of better quality studies. However, the meta-analysis did suggest that breast cancer patients were more than twice as likely than controls to report negative life events, though there was no greater likelihood of them reporting bereavement. The reviewers suggest, however, that this result may be due to methodological flaws. When only the five highest quality studies are considered, they found no significantly increased cancer risk.

Petticrew et al. (1999) further suggest that there is some evidence of publication bias in this area and that nonsignificant studies are less likely to be published. Published studies that have found a relationship (e.g., Chen et al., 1995) are also more likely to get media coverage, thus fueling public beliefs.

A further meta-analysis was conducted by McKenna, Zevon, Corn, and Rounds (1999). They considered a smaller and largely overlapping sample of studies and found a significant relationship between the development of breast cancer and both severe life events and loss experiences. However, they, too, go on to criticize the methodological approaches used and to argue that the associations found are "draped with much qualification." They conclude that "results overall support only a modest association between specific psychosocial factors and breast cancer," but also, somewhat ambivalently, that "results speak against the conventional wisdom that ... stress factors influence the development of breast cancer" (p. 528).

Reviewers frequently identify methodological flaws, and these may certainly account for the relationships that have been found in many studies. Methods that rely on retrospective recall (e.g., case-control studies) may be biased, as those who are diagnosed with cancer may be inclined to search hard for life events to explain their illness. The use of limited prospective studies (such as that of Chen et al., 1995), assessing life events just before diagnosis, is a methodological improvement on the early retrospective studies. Nevertheless, these are still open to the criticism that people with symptoms that are later confirmed to be cancer may already have a strong suspicion of their diagnosis. Hence they can be subject to the same biasing factors as retrospective studies.

Overall, given the contradictory findings in the literature and the somewhat marginal and confusing findings from the meta-analyses, it is difficult to avoid concluding that, as yet, we simply do not know for sure whether or not life events cause breast cancer. However, it also seems likely that, if there is an effect, it is likely to be very small compared to the influence of biological factors. Methodological flaws are often blamed for inconclusive results, but this is because it is extraordinarily difficult to control all possible confounding variables. What seems to be required is a large-scale and long-term prospective study assessing (objectively) a range of events or stressors prior to the occurrence of symptoms. However, a study of this sort would be extremely costly and may still not settle the issue conclusively. For example, McGee (1999) points out that causative factors may be operating years before diagnosis, and thus it is difficult to rule out the possibility that life events accelerate development of cancer or influence the likelihood of diagnosis.

Similar debates have raged concerning whether life events influence not just the initiation but also the development and recurrence of breast cancer. Here again the results are inconclusive (Jensen, 1991).

In addition to the effects of life events, much interest has also focused on the related topic of the importance of affective states (e.g., depression) or personality characteristics such as the repression of emotion in the causation and recurrence of breast cancer. Detailed review of this research is beyond the scope of this chapter, but the meta-analysis by McKenna et al. (1999) found no support for the hypotheses that breast cancer patients experienced heightened anxiety or depression or had difficulty expressing anger. The reviewers did find a significant effect size suggesting that those with breast cancer tended to cope by denial or repressive coping, but they also highlighted the methodological flaws and said that more research is needed. Mixed findings also exist concerning the success of psychosocial interventions in reducing mortality.

One difficulty researchers have in assessing the effect of life events is (as McGee, 1999, points out) the very vagueness of the hypothesis. Life events and even the single event of bereavement encompass a very broad range of experiences. The next section looks at some rather more focused research on two chronic work stressors.

Chronic Work Stressors and Cardiovascular Disease

There is a great deal of research looking at the relationships between two particular aspects of work stress (job demands and control) and health. This largely stems from the popularity of Karasek's job strain model, which suggests that these two aspects are particularly important for predicting strain. According to Karasek, a job that is high in demands (workload and pace of work) and in which employees have little control (e.g., over what they do and when they do it) will be a high strain job. Early epidemiological studies by Karasek and colleagues (e.g., Alfredsson, Karasek, & Theorell, 1982; Karasek, Baker, Marxer, Ahlbom, & Theorell, 1981) suggested that the combination of these two variables did indeed predict heart disease. These variables are now frequently used in studies in both the medical and psychological literature generating a large and complex body of research. This includes work on psychological well-being, musculoskeletal disorders (Krause, Ragland, Geiner, Syme, & Fisher, 1997; Skov, Borg, & Orhede, 1996), adverse outcome of pregnancy (Brandt & Nielsen, 1992), cancer of the colon (Courtney, Longnecker, & Peters, 1996), periodontal disease (Marcenes & Sheiham, 1992), and drug use (Storr, Trinkoff, & Anthony, 1999).

However, the largest number of studies has considered the relationship between these work stressors and cardiovascular disease (CVD) and its associated risk factors (e.g., raised blood pressure). A number of large epidemiological studies have now related the incidence of heart disease and mortality from CVD to type of employment. Frequently these studies assess people's work stressors using a methodology that classifies individuals on the job strain dimensions (in terms of level of demand and control) according to their job title. Thus, for example, all waiters might be classified as having low-control, high-demand jobs. Alternatively, some studies have assessed job stressors using the more subjective method of asking individuals to rate their levels of demand and control. Using the former method, Alfredsson et al. (1982) found that hectic work combined with low control was associated with higher incidence of heart disease. Using the latter method, Johnson, Hall, and Theorell (1989) found the greatest risk was in high-demand, low-control isolated jobs.

There is also a large number of studies relating job features to risk factors that are implicated in cardiovascular disease such as high blood pressure (e.g., Brisson et al., 1999; Fletcher & Jones, 1993; Fox, Dwyer, & Ganster, 1993) or measures of adrenaline and cortisol (e.g., Fox et al., 1993; Pollard, Ungpakorn, Harrison, & Parkes, 1996). Fox, Dwyer, and Ganster, in their study of nurses, found that the combination of high demands and low control predicted both blood pressure and high cortisol levels. However, Fletcher and Jones, in a sample from heterogeneous occupations, found no relationships between control and blood pressure, and where demands showed relationships, these were in the opposite direction to that predicted (i.e., those with lower demands had higher blood pressure).

In addition, there is a small number of experimental studies that have manipulated levels of job strain in the laboratory and examined the relationship to short-term physiological indicators that are implicated in CVD development. These include heart rate levels and cortisol (Perrewe & Ganster, 1989; Steptoe, Fieldman, Evans, & Perry, 1993). For example, Steptoe et al. found that middle-aged men showed greater changes in blood pressure when they could not control the pace at which they performed laboratory tasks involving problem solving and mirror drawing. However, pacing had little effect on cortisol, suggesting work pace has a specific effect on cardiovascular functioning.

A comprehensive meta-analysis or systematic review is perhaps overdue, but given the different measures and lack of comparability between studies, it would be very difficult to achieve (Kristensen, 1995). However, the literature in relation to CVD has been reviewed by Schnall, Landsbergis, and Baker (1994), who state that the literature "strongly suggests a causal association between job strain and CVD" (p. 405). However, when the main effects are examined, seventeen out of twenty-five studies found significant associations between job decision latitude and outcome, whereas only eight out of twenty-three studies showed significant relationships between demand and outcome. Since this review, a further large study by Alterman, Shekelle, Vernon, and Burau (1994) also suggests the greater importance of control in coronary heart disease mortality. A few recent studies have also found an effect for demands opposite to that predicted (e.g., Alterman et al., 1994; Hlatky et al., 1995; Steenland, Johnson, & Nowlin, 1997).

Until recently, most studies used male samples, and it has been suggested that the model is less applicable for women, but here again there are conflicting results. For example, Weidner, Boughal, Pieper, Connor, and Mendell (1997) found that having a high-demand, low-control job was unrelated to standard coronary risk factors in both sexes, but that it was related to increased medical symptoms and health-damaging behavior in a sample of men but not women. However, a more recent study by Amick et al. (1998) did find that high demand and low control, together with low support, predicted poorer health status in women. Furthermore, Brisson et al. (1999) found a combination of large family responsibilities and high-strain jobs was related to raised blood pressure in well-educated women in white-collar jobs.

There have inevitably been numerous criticisms of this literature. For example, the accusation is often made that the research fails to adequately take into account the influence of social class (Muntaner & O'Campo, 1993). Others have criticized the ways in which the core constructs of demand and control are operationalized (measured in the research), suggesting that they are too vague and all-encompassing (e.g., Jones, Bright, Searle, & Cooper, 1998). In addition, Kristensen (1996) points out that the two methods of assessing job strain classify the same people very differently.

Thus, overall, deriving a clear message from this literature is difficult. However, a review by Van der Doef and Maes (1998), which does not separate the effects of demand and control, concludes that across different populations, measurement methods, and job designs, there is substantial support for the hypothesis that high-demand, low-control jobs lead to increased CVD. Our view is that where evidence exists, this primarily seems to point to the importance of job control rather than demands. While evidence here is mounting, further work is needed (including more laboratory studies) to find out what specific aspects of control may be important; for example, is it control over pace of work that is important, or does more general involvement in decisions about work have an impact?

Psychosocial Factors and the Common Cold

The mounting evidence for the influence of stressors on immune functioning has resulted in an increased interest in the effects of factors such as life events, hassles, and perceptions of stress on infectious diseases. Cohen and Williamson (1991) point out that in order to successfully predict the occurrence of a disease from these variables, it is necessary to have a reasonably high incidence of the disease in the sample studied. This has led to an emphasis in the research literature on the study of common diseases such as colds, influenza, and herpes.

It should be noted that in the study of infection, there is a distinction between the presence of infection and the presence of actual symptoms. In the case of the common cold, a clinical cold develops only in a proportion of those infected. Evidence of infection can be found by analyzing blood samples. Evidence of the presence of clinical colds is dependent on the assessment of external symptoms, either reported by the participant or detected by, for example, measuring mucus weight (by weighing used tissues).

A large number of studies using different types of methodology have demonstrated a relationship between stressors and colds. Prospective studies using measures of family stressors (such as life events) and family functioning have shown these predict the frequency of occurrence of verified colds and influenza in family members (e.g., Clover, Abell, Becker, Crawford, & Ramsey, 1989; Graham, Douglas, & Ryan, 1986). Daily stressors have also been studied by Evans and Edgerton (1991), who got one hundred people to fill in daily questionnaires for ten weeks, during which time seventeen developed a cold. They found that desirable events decreased in frequency in the week just before the onset of a cold (referred to as the "four-day desirability dip") and there was an increase in hassles or negative events. Specifically, there was lack in social support and intimacy, and the most important hassles related to interpersonal problems.

An alternative interpretation for the reported relationships between stressors and colds could be simply that people who are exposed to a lot of stressful events may be more likely to come into contact with a cold virus. One way in which researchers have attempted to gain greater control over possible confounding variables in this area is to use a quasi-experimental approach. Typically, in such studies, healthy individuals complete retrospective measures of psychosocial factors before being exposed to a controlled amount of a cold virus. Such quasi-experimental studies are referred to as "viral-challenge" studies by Cohen and Williamson (1991) in their review. These have provided mixed and generally rather limited evidence for the influence of stress on susceptibility to colds, perhaps because of methodological limitations. However, some more recent reports provide stronger evidence.

In the United Kingdom, such studies were conducted at the Medical Research Council's now-defunct Common Cold Unit in Salisbury. In studies by Cohen and his colleagues (e.g., Cohen, Tyrell, & Smith, 1991, 1993), healthy volunteers were recruited to stay at the unit for a period of weeks. On arrival, they completed retrospective questionnaires about major life events, perceptions of stress, and negative affect, as well as measures of health practices. Blood tests were also taken for immune assessment. One group of volunteers was then given nasal drops containing a low dose of one of five types of cold virus. The doses were designed to be similar to those experienced in normal person-to-person transmission. A small number in a control condition were given saline drops instead of the virus. Neither the investigators nor volunteers knew who had been given the virus and who had received the saline drops. The participants remained in quarantine, either alone or with one or two others, for two days before and seven days after the viral challenge. During this time, they were examined daily for signs and symptoms. Twenty-eight days later, further blood tests were taken.

Cohen, Tyrell, and Smith (1991) reported that of the 394 participants exposed to the viruses, 82 percent were infected and 38 percent
got clinical colds. In the twenty-six people in the control group, only 19
percent were infected and none got clinical colds. The reporting of psychological stress before exposure to the virus (using a combined index
based on life events, perceived stress, and negative affect) was associated
with an increase in respiratory infection in a dose-response manner; that
is, for each increase in stress score, there was a corresponding increase in
the proportion with colds. Stress scores were more strongly associated
with infection than with clinical illness. The overall results remained the
same when levels of immunity, health practices, and personality variables
(self-esteem, personal control, and introversion/extroversion) were taken
into account.

Using the same sample, Cohen et al. (1993) looked at the separate
effects of stressful life events, perceived stress, and negative affect. They
suggested that different processes mediated the relationships between life
events and colds and between perceived stress and colds:

> Negative life events were associated with greater rates of clinical illness, and
> this association was primarily mediated by increased symptoms among
> infected persons. Perceived stress and negative affect were also related to
> clinical illness, but their associations were primarily due to increased infec-
> tion. (p. 138)

Cohen and his colleagues found that life events predicted illness even
when perceptions of stress and negative affect, as well as health behaviors,
were controlled for. This casts doubt on the common assumption that life
events influence health via their effect on feelings and emotions. Instead,
it suggests that life events might lead to colds even though we are not
aware of feelings of stress, such as anxiety or unhappiness. Whether we
need to feel stressed for it to have an impact on our health is an issue that
is discussed further in Box 8.1.

Moving on to even more specific examination of the stressors implicated in the common cold, Cohen et al. (1998), in research conducted in
the United States, found that particular types of stressors were associated
with developing colds. In this study, both acute and chronic stressors were
assessed. In addition, personality factors, as well as social networks, were
assessed. As in the previous studies, participants were then exposed to the
virus, with similar numbers showing signs of infection and clinical colds.
The researchers found that acute stressors (lasting less than a month) did
not increase the risk of colds, but that more enduring, chronic stressors
were associated with greater susceptibility. This was primarily due to a
greater number of colds developing among infected people. The strongest
associations were found for interpersonal conflicts and work stressors (particularly unemployment or underemployment). However, Leventhal,
Patrick-Miller, and Leventhal (1998) point out that the high level of payment for participation for this study may mean it attracted people with
these problems. There was also some indication that, for those with

---

Box 8.1. Do We Need to Feel "Stressed" or Anxious for Life Events and Other Stressors to Be Harmful for Health?

Yet another problem with the construct of "stress" is that it is not entirely clear whether we need to *feel* stressed to *be* stressed. Implicit in popular notions of stress is the idea that it is a feeling we can report on. This assumption also underlies the use of self-report questionnaires such as the General Health Questionnaire (GHQ). However, many researchers also look at relationships between stressors and health (e.g., whether life events are related to health) without considering appraisals of distress or anxiety. This seems to contradict Lazarus's transactional approach to stress, for which appraisal is the central component.

A snag with the notion of appraisal and its assessment by self-report measures is that it requires conscious awareness of appraisal, yet Lazarus suggests that "an individual may be unaware of any or all of the elements of an appraisal." He suggests that this may operate via a defense mechanism. If stressors need not be *consciously* appraised, then it makes sense to measure the relationship between stressors and strains without necessarily looking at the impact of perceptions of stress or anxiety. Thus the questions "Do stressors such as life events lead to illness?" and "Does feeling stressed and anxious lead to illness?" are two different, though related, questions. Unfortunately the vague nature of the stress concept means that this distinction is often not made clear. Self-reports of anxiety and stress are likely to be only one of the pathways by which stressors lead to ill health.

Researchers such as Kasl (1978) consider that stressors should be measured independently of appraisals. The value of this approach is demonstrated by Cohen et al. (1993), as discussed in this chapter.

---

chronic stressors, having an acute event actually offered some protection, perhaps distracting from the chronic problem. While the study did find that introverts and those with few social networks were more likely to be infected, this did not effect the stressor–strain relationship (i.e., these factors have a direct effect only).

The conclusion drawn by Cohen, Tyrell, and Smith—that chronic stressors are the most important type of stressor implicated in the development of colds—contradicts the work of Evans and Edgerton (1991) discussed above, which emphasizes the importance of minor hassles in the days preceding development of colds. Cohen and colleagues suggest this may be because of the different kinds of events studied, the acute events measured by the LEDS being much more serious than the minor day-to-day perceptions of hassles.

Some recent studies also suggest that positive life events may be even more important than negative events. Stone et al. (1992), for example, have found that positive events, rather than negative ones, predict colds, while Evans, Doyle, Hucklebridge, and Clow (1996) found that only positive events predicted the subsequent occurrence of colds. Like Cohen et al. (1993), they found that self-reports of perceptions of stress were not related to colds, and that the effect was not explained by health behaviors. Furthermore, they consider that the link cannot be fully explained by the people with positive events being more socially active and exposing themselves to more pathogens. The mechanisms for this relationship are therefore unclear. Nevertheless, this study adds further support to the view that the perception of "stress" may not be a key issue.

Overall, Cohen et al. (1998) suggest that studies using sophisticated methodologies provide strong evidence for a dose–response relationship between psychological stress (defined in terms of negative events and the affective states they cause) and risk of developing a cold. Perceptions of stress may not always be crucial. Emotional distress seems to be associated with a greater risk of infection, while life events—including positive events—seem to be associated with actually *getting* a cold.

What Might Be the Mechanisms Underpinning a Relationship between Stressors and Physical Health and Disease?

Steptoe (1991) identifies two major links whereby stress responses may be linked to health:

- *The cognitive-behavioral pathway.* Steptoe suggests that cognitive, affective, and behavioral aspects of the stress response can have an impact on health that is independent of any direct physiological effects. For example, work stressors may lead to a person feeling anxious (affective element), thinking that having a cigarette would help them relax and cope better (cognition), and therefore smoking more (behavioral). Developing a smoking-related disorder is thus an indirect effect of smoking, rather than a direct effect of the reaction to work stressors. In the literature, this kind of relationship is often described as *mediation*—that is, smoking *mediates* the relationship between stressors and health.
- *The psychophysiological pathway.* These pathways are complex, and Steptoe has identified three types of physiological processes involved. For example, under stress, there may be a hyperreactive response, that is, an exaggerated physiological response, which may be implicated in disease causation (for example, exaggerated blood pressure responses to stress may predict future blood pressure). Second, hyperreactivity may destabilize existing disease processes to exacerbate a disease (such as diabetes). Third, stressors may have an effect on the immune response, for example, via their influence on endocrine responses. Here, stressors are related to illness by lowering resistance.

Many of the studies discussed above have considered the possible mechanisms to explain relationships. Thus, studies such as that by Cohen, Tyrell, and Smith (1991) control for the effects of health behaviors when they look at the relationship between life events and illness. Many studies also take physiological measures such as blood pressure or measures of immune functioning to explore the mechanisms (e.g., Cohen, Tyrell,

& Smith, 1991, 1993; Cohen et al., 1998; Steptoe et al., 1993). The next sections consider some possible mechanisms in more depth. First, cognitive-behavioral pathways are discussed. This is followed by an introduction to the psychophysiological pathway associated with immune functioning, which has received a great deal of attention as a possible link between psychosocial factors and disease.

WHAT EVIDENCE IS THERE FOR STRESSORS LEADING TO CHANGES IN HEALTH BEHAVIORS?

Research looking at the cognitive-behavioral pathways has focused predominantly on whether stressors are linked to the negative health behaviors of smoking and drinking alcohol. Positive health behaviors such as eating healthily and exercising have received relatively little attention, though it is also likely that such behaviors can be disrupted by stressful events. Existing research is typically built on an assumption that the negative effects on health of smoking, drinking, and not exercising are firmly established. This assumption is reasonably well founded. Certainly the evidence that smoking damages health is now overwhelming (e.g., Dunn et al., 1999), and the value of exercise seems clear (e.g., Blair et al., 1989). Extreme alcohol consumption also has an established damaging health effect, although the evidence in relation to moderate levels of alcohol consumption is far less clear (see Box 8.2). This factor further complicates the interpretation of evidence in relation to this "risk factor."

Generally, studies of the effects of stressors on substance use suggest relationships between high levels of life stress and various aspects of substance use such as the initiation of smoking, drinking, and drug use (Wills, 1990). Wills also suggests that stressors are linked with an increased amount of substances used by regular users and reduced success in cessation.

One study that supports the notion of a cognitive-behavioral pathway between such substance use and physical health is that of DeFrank, Jenkins, and Rose (1987). This study looked at the links between work stressors, social supports, alcohol consumption, and blood pressure in a study of air traffic controllers. Their evidence suggested that high levels of work stressors and good social supports were primarily related to greater alcohol use and that this in turn predicted raised blood pressure.

However, the links between stressors and health behaviors are not straightforward. For example, Cohen, Schwartz, Bromet, and Parkinson (1991) found gender differences in the pattern of relationships with smoking, showing relationships with full-time employment, depression, increased marital conflict, and higher numbers of negative life events for women. Depression and marital conflict and the interaction between full-time employment and marital conflict were also related to increased alcohol consumption for women. However, for men only, smoking was related to psychosocial factors, specifically to depression and to job demands and job control.

Box 8.2. The Relationship between Alcohol and Health

Alcohol consumption is probably one of the most ubiquitous methods that we use to cope with stressors. Some of the effects of alcohol are well known, including mild elation, depression, lack of judgment, temporary and chronic cognitive impairment, and loss of coordination. We also know that it is addictive.

Excessive consumption of alcohol is widely agreed to be injurious, though it is not at all clear what *excessive* means in this context. There are those who argue that *any* alcohol consumption is bad for you, others who suggest that moderate amounts of alcohol such as two to three glasses of wine per day is harmless, and still others who argue that even much greater quantities (e.g., one liter of wine per day) may be harmless. Furthermore, there are some groups that suggest that ingestion of alcohol has positive health benefits. Some examples of the complex findings are given below.

Boffetta and Garfinkel (1990) studied 276,802 U.S. men to see whether moderate alcohol drinkers have a lower total mortality and coronary heart disease (CHD) mortality than nondrinkers. The data suggested that alcohol has a protective effect for mortality generally for those drinking one or two drinks a day and a protective effect more specifically for CHD for those drinking considerably more.

However, not all studies have concluded that alcohol has a positive health benefit. A twenty-one-year follow-up study of more than five thousand men found no relationship between alcohol and CHD once potentially confounding factors were ruled out. However, overall risk of mortality was higher for men drinking twenty-two units per week, and there was a particularly strong association with mortality from strokes (Hart, Smith, Hole, & Hawthorne, 1999).

Alcohol has also been linked to greater risk of cancer. Merletti, Boffetta, Ciccone, Mashberg, and Terracini (1989) compared 122 cancer sufferers with 606 controls and found that heavy consumers of alcohol and tobacco had very high risks of both oral and throat cancer. Hiatt (1990) conducted a meta-analysis of twenty-one studies investigating the link between alcohol consumption and breast cancer in women. He found that there was a 50 percent increase in breast cancer risk for women who average between one and two drinks per day.

Other studies that have investigated job demands and control support the finding that work features affect the health behaviors of men and women in different ways (e.g., Weidner et al., 1997; Hellerstedt and Jeffrey, 1997). For example, Weidner et al. found that demand and decision latitude were related to health-damaging behavior (a combined measure of smoking, drinking alcohol and coffee, and lack of exercise) in men but not women. They suggest that these behaviors may in part mediate the relationships between work factors and coronary risk factors. Other job demands, such as shift work, piecework, hazardous exposure, and physical load, were associated with increased smoking in both sexes (Johansson, Johnson, & Hall, 1991).

Not surprisingly the health behaviors of students preparing for exams has also come under scrutiny. The fact that students are a readily accessible sample that are experiencing a common stressor at the same time means that they have been a popular focus of research. For example, Steptoe, Wardle, Pollard, and Canaan (1996) compared a group of university students undergoing exams to a group with no exams. Those taking exams were assessed at baseline and then within the two weeks before exams, and the control group was assessed at an equivalent interval. As expected, measures of perceived stress and distress increased when students were closer to exams. Physical activity decreased nearer to the exams. However, changes in alcohol consumption were dependent on level of support; specifically, there was a reduction in alcohol consumption in students with high social support, while those with low social support increased their alcohol intake. In other words, the relationship between stressors and alcohol was moderated by social support. When smoking was considered, both gender and social support moderated the relationship such that, in the exam group, women who had few social supports showed increased smoking between the two assessments whereas men did not. Controls showed no systematic changes in health behaviors between the two assessments. Ogden and Mtandabari (1997) found similar results and in particular report reductions in alcohol use, less exercise, and greater numbers smoking.

Thus we see that the relationship between stressors and health behavior is not a simple one, with exam stress often improving one health behavior (alcohol use) while having negative impact on another. This reduction in alcohol in the face of exam stress is perhaps surprising but makes sense when health behaviors are viewed as coping strategies, as has been suggested by Ingledew, Hardy, and Cooper (1996). Reducing exercise, increasing smoking, and reducing alcohol consumption can all be viewed as coping strategies that help by freeing up time and increasing concentration.

One possibility seldom considered is that, where perceptions of stress are related to health behavior, it is the poor health behavior that actually causes an increase in the perception of stress. However, Wills (1990), in his review of substance use, suggests that evidence converging from a number of different types of study indicates that the predominant direction of causation is from perceptions of life stress to substance use rather than vice versa. He suggests two possible models of this effect that could be used to guide future research:

- *Affect regulation model.* Under conditions of stress, substance use serves a coping function in that it reduces anxiety.
- *Self-control model.* Stress reduces self-control because it increases cognitive load and reduces feelings of efficacy, both of which may impact on maintenance of self-control and resisting temptation.

Of course, these models are not mutually exclusive, and both may play a part. They may also apply to other health behaviors.

Overall, evidence suggests that stressors do sometimes impact on health behaviors, but the relationships are complex. The extent to which observed relationships between stressors and illness can be attributed to health behaviors is inadequately understood. However, a number of studies suggest that, where there is a relationship between stressors and health, it is only partially explained by health behaviors (e.g., Cohen et al., 1993; Evans et al., 1996).

What Evidence Is There for Stressors Leading to Changes in Immune Functioning?

The relationship between stress and immune functioning has been a major focus of research in the specialism of psychoneuroimmunology. Acute stressors have been the focus of many such studies (for a review, see O'Leary, 1990). This has included the study of dramatic events such as the effects of splashdown on Apollo astronauts (Fischer et al., 1972). However, O'Leary suggests such extreme stressors may confound physiological and psychological effects on immune functioning.

A more everyday, but still relatively acute, stressor is that of college examinations. Longitudinal studies assess immune functioning typically over a few weeks before, during, and after the exam period. Kiecolt-Glaser, Glaser, and colleagues have conducted a series of such studies on medical students and have found immunosuppressive effects such as reduction in the percentages of T-cells and in the numbers of natural killer cells (Kennedy, Kiecolt-Glaser, & Glaser, 1988). Exam-related immune changes have also been shown to have a dramatic effect on the length of time it takes for wounds to heal. For example, Marucha, Kiecolt-Glaser, and Favegehi (1998) inflicted standardized wounds consisting of a punch biopsy on the hard palate of dental students both during the summer vacation and three days before an exam. They found that the wounds took three days (40 percent) longer to heal in the approach to exams than during vacation.

It may be, however, that such acute events are less important than the chronic stressors of daily life, including such aspects as marital discord or caring for elderly relatives. The work of Kiecolt-Glaser, Glaser, and colleagues has been particularly influential in establishing a link between such stressors and immune functioning. In a study comparing women who had separated from their partners with matched married controls, they found poorer immune functioning in women who had separated in the last year (Kiecolt-Glaser, Ogrocki, Stout, Speicher, & Glaser, 1987). Of course, it may be the case that separated people have unhealthier lifestyles; however, they found no evidence to suggest that this was the case. Furthermore, even among the married women, poorer quality marriages were associated with some reductions in immunocompetence.

The processes involved have been examined further by Malarkey, Kiecolt-Glaser, Pearl, and Glaser (1994) in a study in which ninety newlywed couples were admitted to a research unit for twenty-four hours. Couples were asked to discuss and resolve marital issues likely to produce conflict (e.g., relating to in-laws or finances) in a thirty-minute discussion. This was recorded and later analyzed. Blood samples were taken before, during, and after the discussion, and levels of hormones were analyzed (including adrenaline, noradrenaline, and cortisol). The researchers found that marital conflict and hostility were related to changes in levels of all the hormones assessed, with the exception of cortisol. They suggest these changes could lead to poorer immune functioning. Women demonstrated greater impacts than men in response to marital conflict. Similar results have also been reported in older couples (Kiecolt-Glaser, Glaser, Cacioppo, & Malarkey, 1998).

In a further group of studies, this time focusing on the caregivers of Alzheimer's patients, Kiecolt-Glaser and colleagues found that caregivers report higher perceived stress levels and have poorer immune functioning than controls (Kiecolt-Glaser, Dura, Speicher, Trask, & Glaser, 1991). This effect was still present in the two years following bereavement (Esterling, Kiecolt-Glaser, Bodnar, & Glaser, 1994). Caregivers also show slower healing of wounds than controls (Kiecolt-Glaser, Marucha, Malarkey, Mercado, & Glaser, 1995).

Herbert and Cohen (1993) conducted a meta-analysis of thirty-eight studies looking at the relationship between stressors and immune outcomes in healthy people. They included studies of short-term laboratory stressors (lasting less than half an hour), short-term naturalistic stressors (lasting between several days and a month, e.g., college examinations), and long-term naturalistic stressors (lasting longer than a month, e.g., bereavement or unemployment). Overall, they found substantial evidence for relationships between stressors and a range of immune parameters and observed that objective stressors were related to larger changes in immune functioning than self-reports of stress. They also found that acute laboratory stressors and long-term real-life stressors showed different immune changes, reflecting different processes. Furthermore, interpersonal stressors led to different immune effects than nonsocial stressors.

Overall, this area of research is uncovering potentially important links between psychosocial factors and immune functioning. In this section, we have only been able to give a very brief introduction to this complex and expanding area of research, providing a flavor of the complicated relationships between different types of stressors and different immune parameters. What we do not yet know is how important these demonstrated immune changes are in causing disease. However, studies have shown that caregivers and stressed/anxious students show poorer antibody responses to the influenza virus and hence are likely to be more vulnerable to infection (Glaser, Kiecolt-Glaser, Malarkey, & Sheridan, 1998; Vedhara et al., 1999). This provides evidence of a link between immune parameters and disease. However, whether stress-related immune changes can be linked to more severe illness is unclear.

Stein, Miller, and Trestman (1991) argue that there is a lack of evidence for a link between depression and stressful events and any increase in mortality or morbidity from disorders associated with the immune system. As we have seen above, for example, there is little evidence that life events or depression are implicated in breast cancer causation. Stein also points out that mortality following the stressful event of bereavement has been linked to cardiovascular disease and not immune disorders (Osterweis, Solomon, & Green, 1984). Stein et al. suggest that it is important to establish links between psychiatric disorders and/or stressful experiences and specific immune-related disorders *before* seeking mechanisms.

Why Do Some People Seem to Be More Susceptible to the Effects of Stressors than Others?

Insofar as there is evidence for a relationship between stressors and disease, it is very clear that not everyone who is subject to a particular stressor becomes ill. The diathesis-stress approach suggests that whether an individual is affected by stressors will depend on their individual physiological predisposition (a type of "diathesis"). However, psychological and social factors may also predispose the individual to be adversely affected by, or conversely protected from, the effects of stressors. These may include individual personality factors or factors in the environment, for example, the availability of resources such as social supports. In researching stress and disease, certain personality factors have been researched more than others. The predominant focus has been on those factors that are regarded as being related to dysfunctional coping styles and strategies.

Box 8.3. Pessimistic Explanatory Style and Disease

One personality variable, clearly related to negative affectivity, that has been useful in predicting disease is that of pessimistic explanatory style. Work in this area is associated with Peterson, Seligman, and colleagues. Peterson, Seligman, and Vaillant (1988), drawing conclusions from a study that spanned thirty-five years, suggest that a person with a pessimistic explanatory style tends to explain negative events by making stable, global, internal attributions. For example, such a person might explain a serious conflict with a friend as something "which is never going to go away" (stable), "is going to ruin everything" (global), and "is my fault" (internal). By contrast, a more optimistic person may interpret the event as less long-lasting, with much more restricted implications, and blame it on the other person or the circumstances.

In their study, Peterson et al. classified the explanatory style of ninety-nine graduates who were at Harvard in the years 1942 to 1945 when they were age 25. To assess explanatory style, they used a method whereby written accounts of difficult wartime experiences were content-analyzed for stable, global, internal explanations. They then measured a range of health outcomes (based on scores from medical examinations) every five years until the subjects were age 60. Peterson et al. found that pessimistic explanatory style was related to overall health from ages 45 to 60 even when initial health at the age of 25 was controlled for. They proposed a number of potential mechanisms. For example, pessimism may result in passivity in the face of illness and failure to seek medical advice. Alternatively, because they tend to be poor at problem solving, this group may fail to "nip a crisis in the bud" and thus may experience more or worse life events. They may neglect health behaviors because they may feel they are not worthwhile, or they may be socially withdrawn and lack the buffer of social support.

More recent research has also linked pessimistic explanatory style to immune functioning (Kamen-Siegel, Rodin, Seligman, & Dwyer, 1991), and catastrophizing (that is, attributing bad events to global causes) has been shown to predict accidental or violent deaths (Peterson, Seligman, Yurko, Martin, & Friedman, 1998).

A cluster of characteristics associated with negative emotions has been particularly related to disease. These include Type A personality (characterized by impatience, irritability, hostility, competitiveness, job involvement, and achievement striving) and negative affectivity (the dispositional tendency to experience negative emotions and a negative self-concept). Box 8.3 introduces one specific type of approach to examining personality that seems to be related to higher incidence of disease generally.

One further way in which individual differences may be important in some studies of illness outcomes is that some people may be more inclined to report illness than others. For example, Feldman and Cohen (1999) have found that personality symptoms such as neuroticism and conscientiousness increased reporting of cold symptoms that had no physiological basis. This effect may influence results in studies that are based purely on self-reports or on physician diagnosis, which may be heavily dependent on patient reports.

Summary

The findings from the studies discussed so far in this chapter are complex. While many interesting links between psychosocial factors and health have been found, the overall evidence for relationships between psychosocial factors and disease is far from unambiguous. At best, it seems that public belief in the relationship has raced ahead of scientific evidence. Some researchers have suggested that currently there is still only limited evidence for relationships (e.g., Briner & Reynolds, 1993; Cohen & Williamson, 1991). The evidence we have suggests the relationship may vary dependent on which stressors, diseases, and individuals are considered.

For example, evidence seems to support the influence of stressors on the development of colds (e.g., Cohen et al., 1998). This does not, of course, mean that the findings can be generalized to other kinds of disease such as cancer or heart disease (Leventhal et al., 1998). In considering the broad range of diseases, Cohen and Manuck (1995) have concluded that "convincing evidence that stress contributes to the pathophysiology of human disease is sparse and, even where evidence exists, relatively small proportions of variance are explained."

While the link between psychosocial factors and physical illness has proved difficult to establish, it might be expected that it would be easier to prove connections between stressors such as life events and psychiatric illness. However, this area has similar difficulties.

STRESS AND PSYCHIATRIC ILLNESS

Psychiatric symptoms are frequently measured by stress researchers. This is not just because they are of interest in their own right but also because they are presumed to be the precursors of both physical and psychiatric disorders. While definitions of stress are vague, some kind of manifestation in the form of symptoms, such as anxiety, tension, or "feeling stressed," seems central to the notion (but see Box 8.1). Thus researchers typically use measures of anxiety and depression as a reliable and valid way of assessing these factors. A large amount of literature now exists looking at the influence of various stressors on psychiatric symptoms, although many of these studies are limited by cross-sectional designs and may suffer common method problems (e.g., Parkes, 1991; Fletcher & Jones, 1993). Typically these do show relationships between stressors and levels of anxiety and depression that are comparable with levels experienced by psychiatric outpatients. For example, studies have shown high levels of psychiatric "caseness" in employed samples. The relationship is so commonly found that it may seem logical to assume that more extreme stressors lead to more serious incidents of verifiable psychiatric illness.

Certainly, it is a commonly held belief that psychosocial factors are related to psychiatric disorders. From analyzing the lay beliefs of more than two thousand adults, Ridder (1995) found psychosocial stress to be the second most popular explanation of the cause of mental disorders.

To confirm this view, however, evidence is needed linking psychosocial factors with independently diagnosed clinical illnesses (such as depression and schizophrenia) using designs that can show the direction of causation. Rabkin (1993) reviews this literature and, echoing the kind of statements we have heard throughout this chapter, states:

> In view of this nearly universal conceptualization of stress as a relevant consideration in illness onset, it is all the more surprising that the large majority of studies of stress and psychiatric disorder have failed to demonstrate a clinically significant association, although small, statistically significant relationships repeatedly have been found. (p. 477)

Where studies exist, Rabkin suggests that much of the research has been flawed because stress researchers pay regrettably little attention to the systematic diagnosis of psychiatric disorders, many just assessing the presence or absence of illness on the basis of interviews or global ratings.

In the case of psychiatric illness, Rabkin suggests there is also a particular problem with the assessment of stressors. Frequently it is not possible to tell the extent to which stressful events and experiences in the period before diagnosis have been triggered by the patient's deteriorating state. Thus the direction of causation is frequently unclear. There is also the familiar problem of potentially biased retrospective recall in many studies. As is common in the study of physical illness, many studies use retrospective methodology in which recall of events is likely to be unreliable. However, this is all the more likely to be a problem if the patient is seriously depressed or suffering schizophrenia. Nevertheless, it is a fact that the most common approach to research has been the retrospective study, which assesses the frequency of stressful events in people who are already diagnosed with a disorder. Genuine prospective studies, which follow a cohort of people over time and see who becomes ill, are rare.

Depression

There is much more research relating to depression than to other psychiatric disorders. One particularly well-known prospective study by Brown and Harris (1978) found that women who both suffered life events and lacked the support of a confiding relationship were more likely to develop depression. Brown and Harris considered in detail the difficulty of distinguishing between clinical depression and depressed mood, and they based diagnosis of depression on a standardized clinical interview, including ratings of severity. They established clear criteria for defining cases of clinical depression and borderline cases.

Gruen reviews research in this area and concludes that "the results of a large number of studies suggest that life stress is significantly but moderately related to depression" (1993, p. 554). However, Rabkin (1993), in her review, takes a slightly more cautious view, stating that the effects are small, at best accounting for 10 percent of the variance. Stress researchers seldom find that psychosocial factors account for much of the variance in any measure of well-being. Given the number of other possible contributing factors (e.g., age, gender, genetic, or developmental influences, as well as unmeasured psychological factors), even small amounts of variance being explained by a limited number of psychosocial events may be seen as impressive. Frese (1985) argues that such small effects can still be clinically significant. For example, it may mean that over a large population exposed to a major stressor, a considerable number will become depressed who would not otherwise have done so.

However, it is also clear that, in the face of the same stressful event, most people will not become depressed. As is suggested by Brown and Harris's research (1978), stressful experiences alone seldom explain the onset of depression. Many factors are likely to contribute. For example, some people may be more vulnerable to the effects of stressful events due to genetic predisposition or childhood experiences. A lack of interpersonal resources may also have an impact on resistance to stressors. These resources are both external (such as degree of control, social support, and income) and internal (personality, coping style, interpersonal skills, etc.).

Other Psychiatric Disorders

The evidence relating stressors such as life events to other psychiatric disorders is less strong. For example, the onset of phobic disorders (such as agoraphobia) is often thought to be related to stressful events. According to Rabkin (1993), a number of studies indicate that around two-thirds of patients report a precipitating stressor. However, we do not have sufficient good quality studies in this area to establish a clear link.

In the case of schizophrenia, an etiological role for stress is less often proposed, and more research has focused on the role of stressors in precipitating a relapse. Rabkin here suggests that there is no positive evidence for any association between stressful life events and the onset of schizophrenia. Evidence arguing against the role of life events is produced by a case-control study by Stueve, Dohrenwend, and Skodol (1998), who compared the role of life events in depression, schizophrenia, and other nonaffective disorders as well as community controls. This found that stressful events were associated with the onset of depression, but not with the other disorders.

There is more evidence that life events may be related to the onset of a relapse (e.g., Birley & Brown, 1970). However, these are likely to interact with many other factors, such as social support (Hultman, Wieselgren, & Oehman, 1997).

CONCLUSIONS

Overall, it appears that there is some evidence for stressful events predicting depressive illness, but not schizophrenia or other psychotic disorders. Difficulties and lack of clarity about objective diagnosis, coupled with further difficulties relating to self-reports, make this area of research perhaps even more problematic than that of physical illness. However, in both areas it is clear that research is complicated by a range of dispositional and individual differences that may impact the relationships between stressors and strains. These may include psychological predispositions and protective factors, as well as physiological factors (including genetic influences). The latter is beyond the scope of this chapter; however, the rapid progress in the study of genetics opens up new possibilities for stress research. Individuals now can be easily tested for genetic markers for an ever-increasing number of diseases. This gives the possibility of controlling for such factors in studies examining psychosocial factors and offers exciting future possibilities for separating genetic and environmental influences such as that of life events.

REFERENCES

Alfredsson, L., Karasek, R., & Theorell, T. (1982). Myocardial infarction risk and psychosocial work environment: An analysis of the male Swedish working force. *Social Science & Medicine, 16,* 463–467.

Alterman, T., Shekelle, R. B., Vernon, S. W., & Burau, K. D. (1994). Decision latitude, psychologic demand, job strain, and coronary heart disease in the Western Electric Study. *American Journal of Epidemiology, 139,* 620–627.

Amick, B. C., Kawachi, I., Coakley, E. H., Lerner, S., Levine, S., & Colditz, G. A. (1998). Relationship of job strain and isostrain to health status in a cohort of women in the United States. *Scandinavian Journal of Work and Environmental Health, 24,* 54–61.

Baghurst, K. I., Baghurst, P. A., & Record, S. J. (1992). Public perceptions of the role of dietary and other environmental factors in cancer causation and prevention. *Journal of Epidemiology and Community Health, 46,* 120–126.

Birley, J. L., & Brown, G. W. (1970). Crises and life changes preceding the onset or relapse of acute schizophrenia: Clinical aspects. *British Journal of Psychiatry, 116,* 327–333.

Blair, S. N., Kohl, H. W., Paffenbarger, R. S., Clark, D. G., Cooper, K. H., & Gibbons, L. W. (1989). Physical fitness and all-cause mortality: A prospective study of healthy men and women. *Journal of the American Medical Association, 262,* 2395–2401.

Boffetta, P., & Garfinkel, L. (1990). Alcohol drinking and mortality among men enrolled in an American Cancer Society prospective study. *Epidemiology, 1*, 342–348.

Brandt, L. P., & Nielsen, C. V. (1992). Job stress and adverse outcome of pregnancy: A causal link or recall bias? *American Journal of Epidemiology, 135*, 302–311.

Briner, R. B., & Reynolds, S. (1993). Bad theory and bad practice in occupational stress. Social and Applied Psychology Unit memo 1405. Sheffield, England: Sheffield University.

Brisson, C., Laflamme, N., Moisan, J., Milot, A., Masse, B., & Vezina, M. (1999). Effect of family responsibilities and job strain on ambulatory blood pressure among white collar women. *Psychosomatic Medicine, 61*, 205–131.

Brown, G. W., & Harris, T. O. (1978). *Social origins of depression: A study of psychiatric disorder in women.* London: Tavistock.

Brown, G. W., & Harris, T. O. (1989). *Life events and illness.* New York: Guilford.

Chen, C. C., David, A. S., Nunnerley, H., Mitchell, M., Dawson, J. L., Berry, H., et al. (1995). Adverse life events and breast cancer: Case-control study. *British Medical Journal, 311*, 1527–1530.

Clover, R. D., Abell, T., Becker, L. A., Crawford, S., & Ramsey, C. N., Jr. (1989). Family functioning and stress as predictors of influenza B infection. *Journal of Family Practice, 28*, 535–539.

Cohen, S., Frank, E., Doyle, W. J., Skoner, D. P., Rabin, B. S., & Gwaltney, J. M. (1998). Types of stressors that increase susceptibility to the common cold in healthy adults. *Health Psychology, 17*, 214–223.

Cohen, S., & Manuck, S. B. (1995). Stress, reactivity and disease. *Psychosomatic Medicine, 57*, 427–435.

Cohen, S., Schwartz, J. E., Bromet, E. J., & Parkinson, D. K. (1991). Mental health, stress and poor health behaviors in two community samples. *Preventive Medicine, 20*, 306–315.

Cohen, S., Tyrell, D. A., & Smith, A. P. (1991). Psychological stress and susceptibility to the common cold. *New England Journal of Medicine, 325*, 606–612.

Cohen, S., Tyrell, D. A., & Smith, A. P. (1993). Negative life events, perceived stress, negative affect and susceptibility to the common cold. *Journal of Personality and Social Psychology, 64*, 131–140.

Cohen, S., & Williamson, G. M. (1991). Stress and infectious diseases in humans. *Psychological Bulletin, 109*, 5–24.

Cooper, C. L., Cooper, R., & Faragher, E. B. (1989). Incidence and perception of psychosocial stress: The relationship with breast cancer. *Psychological Medicine, 19*, 315–318.

Courtney, J. G., Longnecker, M. P., & Peters, R. K. (1996). Psychosocial aspects of work and the risk of colon cancer. *Epidemiology, 7*, 175–181.

DeFrank, R. S., Jenkins, C. D., & Rose, R. M. (1987). A longitudinal investigation of the relationships among alcohol consumption, psychosocial factors, and blood pressure. *Journal of Psychosomatic Medicine, 49*, 236–249.

DeLongis, A., Folkman, S., & Lazarus, R. S. (1988). The impact of daily stress on health and mood: Psychological and social resources as mediators. *Journal of Personality and Social Psychology, 54*, 486–495.

Dohrenwend, B. P. (Ed.). (1998). *Adversity, stress and psychopathology.* New York: Oxford University Press.

Dunn, N. R., Faragher, B., Thorogood, M., de Caestecker, L., MacDonald, T. M., McCollum, C., et al. (1999). Risk of myocardial infarction in young female smokers. *Heart, 82*, 581–583.

Esterling, B. A., Kiecolt-Glaser, J. K., Bodnar, J. C., & Glaser, R. (1994). Chronic stress, social support, and persistent alterations in the natural killer cell response to cytokines in older adults. *Health Psychology, 13*, 291–298.

Evans, P. D., Doyle, F., Hucklebridge, F., & Clow, A. (1996). Positive but not negative life-events predict vulnerability to upper respiratory illness. *British Journal of Health Psychology, 1*, 339–348.

Evans, P. D., & Edgerton, N. (1991). Life-events and mood as predictors of the common cold. *British Journal of Medical Psychology, 64*, 35–44.

Feldman, P. J., & Cohen, S. (1999). The impact of personality on the reporting of unfounded symptoms and illness. *Journal of Personality and Social Psychology, 77*, 370–378.

Fischer, C. L., Gill, C., Daniels, J. C., Cobb, E. K., Berry, C. A., & Ritzmann, S. E. (1972). Effects of the space flight environment on man's immune system. I. Serum proteins and immunoglobins. *Aerospace Medicine, 43*, 856–891.

Fletcher, B. C., & Jones, F. (1993). A refutation of Karasek's demand-discretion model of occupational stress with a range of dependent measures. *Journal of Organizational Behaviour, 14*, 319–330.

Fox, M. L., Dwyer, D. J., & Ganster, D. C. (1993). Effects of stressful job demands and control on physiological and attitudinal outcomes in a hospital setting. *Academy of Management Journal, 36*, 289–318.

Frese, M. (1985). Stress at work and psychosomatic complaints: A causal interpretation. *Journal of Applied Psychology, 70*, 314–328.

Geyer, S. (1991). Life events prior to the manifestation of breast cancer: A limited prospective study covering eight years before diagnosis. *Journal of Psychosomatic Research, 35*, 355–363.

Glaser, R., Kiecolt-Glaser, J. K., Malarkey, W. B., & Sheridan, J. F. (1998). The influence of psychological stress on the immune response to vaccines. *Annals of the New York Academy of Science, 840*, 649–651.

Graham, N. M., Douglas, R. M., & Ryan, P. (1986). Stress and acute respiratory infection. *American Journal of Epidemiology, 124*, 340.

Greer, S., & Morris, T. (1975). Psychological attributes of women who develop breast cancer: A controlled study. *Journal of Psychosomatic Research, 19*, 147–153.

Gruen, R. J. (1993). Stress and depression: Toward the development of integrative models. In L. Goldberger & S. Breznitz (Eds.), *Handbook of stress: Theoretical and clinical aspects* (pp. 550–569). New York: Free Press.

Hart, C. L., Smith, G. D., Hole, D. J., & Hawthorne, V. M. (1999). Alcohol consumption and mortality from all causes, coronary heart disease, and stroke: Results from a prospective cohort study of Scottish men with twenty-one years of follow up. *BMJ (Clinical Research Ed.), 318*, 1725–1729.

Hellerstedt, W. L., & Jeffrey, R. W. (1997). The association of job strain and health behaviours in men and women. *International Journal of Epidemiology, 26*, 575–583.

Herbert, T. B., & Cohen, S. (1993). Stress and immunity in humans: A meta-analytic review. *Psychosomatic Medicine, 55*, 364–379.

Hiatt, R. A. (1990). Alcohol consumption and breast cancer. *Medical Oncology and Tumor Pharmacotherapy, 7*(2–3), 143–151.

Hlatky, M. A., Lam, L. C., Lee, K. L., Clapp-Channing, N. E., Williams, R. B., Pryor, D. B., et al. (1995). Job strain and the prevalence and outcome of coronary artery disease. *Circulation, 92*, 327–333.

Hultman, C. M., Wieselgren, I. M., & Oehman, A. (1997). Relationships between social support, social coping and life events in the relapse of schizophrenic patients. *Scandinavian Journal of Psychology, 38*, 3–13.

Ingledew, D. K., Hardy, L., & Cooper, C. L. (1996). Health behaviors reported as coping strategies: A factor analytic study. *British Journal of Health Psychology, 1,* 263–281.

Jensen, A. B. (1991). Psychological factors in breast cancer and their possible impact upon prognosis. *Cancer Treatment Reviews, 18,* 191–210.

Johansson, G., Johnson, J. V., & Hall, E. M. (1991). Smoking and sedentary behavior as related to work organization. *Social Science & Medicine, 32,* 837–846.

Johnson, J. V., Hall, E. M., & Theorell, T. (1989). Combined effects of job strain and social isolation on cardiovascular disease morbidity and mortality in a random sample of the Swedish male working population. *Scandinavian Journal of Work and Environmental Health, 15,* 271–279.

Jones, D. R., Goldblatt, P. O., & Leon, D. A. (1984). Bereavement and cancer: Some data on deaths of spouses from the longitudinal study of the OPCS. *British Medical Journal, 289,* 461–464.

Jones, F., Bright, J. E. H., Searle, B., & Cooper, L. (1998). Modelling occupational stress and health: The impact of the demand-control model on academic research and on workplace practice. *Stress and Health, 14,* 231–236.

Kamen-Siegel, L., Rodin, J., Seligman, M. E., & Dwyer, J. (1991). Explanatory style and cell-mediated immunity in elderly men and women. *Health Psychology, 10,* 229–235.

Karasek, R. A., Baker, D., Marxer, F., Ahlbom, A., & Theorell, T. (1981). Job decision latitude, job demands and cardiovascular disease: A prospective study of Swedish men. *American Journal of Public Health, 71,* 694–705.

Kasl, S. V. (1978). Epidemiological contributions to the study of work stress. In C. L. Cooper & R. L. Payne (Eds.), *Stress at work* (pp. 3–48). Chichester, England: John Wiley & Sons.

Kennedy, S., Kiecolt-Glaser, J. K., & Glaser, R. (1988). Immunological consequences of acute and chronic stressors: Mediating role of interpersonal relationships. *British Journal of Medical Psychology, 61,* 77–85.

Kiecolt-Glaser, J. K., Dura, J. R., Speicher, C. E., Trask, O. J., & Glaser, R. (1991). Spousal caregivers of dementia victims: Longitudinal changes in immunity and health. *Psychosomatic Medicine, 53,* 345–362.

Kiecolt-Glaser, J. K., Glaser, R., Cacioppo, J. T., & Malarkey, W. B. (1998). Marital stress: Immunologic, neuroendocrine, and autonomic correlates. *Annals of the New York Academy of Science, 1,* 656–663.

Kiecolt-Glaser, J. K., Marucha, P. T., Malarkey, W. B., Mercado, A. M., & Glaser, R. (1995). Slowing of wound healing by psychological stress. *Lancet, 346,* 1194–1196.

Kiecolt-Glaser, J. K., Ogrocki, P., Stout, J. C., Speicher, C. E., & Glaser, R. (1987). Marital quality, marital disruption and immune function. *Psychosomatic Medicine, 49,* 13–34.

Krause, N., Ragland, D. R., Geiner, B. A., Syme, L., & Fisher, J. M. (1997). Psychosocial job factors associated with back and neck pain in public transit operators. *Scandinavian Journal of Environmental Health, 23,* 179–186.

Kristensen, T. S. (1995). The demand-control-support model: Methodological challenges for future research. *Stress Medicine, 11,* 17–26.

Kristensen, T. S. (1996). Job stress and cardiovascular disease: A theoretical critical review. *Journal of Occupational Health Psychology, 1*(3), 246–260.

Lazarus, R. S. (1992). Four reasons why it is difficult to demonstrate psychosocial influences on health. *Advances, 8,* 6–7.

LeShan, L. (1959). Psychological states as factors in the development of malignant disease. *Journal of the National Cancer Institute, 22,* 1–18.

LeShan, L., & Worthington, R. E. (1956). Loss of cathexes as a common psycho-dynamic characteristic of cancer patients: An attempt at clinical validation of a clinical hypothesis. *Psychological Reports, 2*, 183–193.

Leventhal, H., Patrick-Miller, L., & Leventhal, E. (1998). It's long-term stressors that take a toll: Comment on Cohen et al. (1998). *Health Psychology, 17*, 211–213.

Malarkey, W. B., Kiecolt-Glaser, J. K., Pearl, D., & Glaser, R. (1994). Hostile behavior during marital conflict alters pituitary and adrenal hormones. *Psychosomatic Medicine, 56*, 41–51.

Marcenes, W. S., & Sheiham, A. (1992). The relationship between work stress and oral health status. *Social Science & Medicine, 12*, 1511–1520.

Marucha, P. T., Kiecolt-Glaser, J. K., & Favegehi, M. (1998). Mucosal wound healing is impaired by examination stress. *Psychosomatic Medicine, 60*, 362–365.

McGee, R. (1999). Does stress cause cancer? *British Medical Journal, 319*, 1015–1016.

McKenna, M. C., Zevon, M. A., Corn, B., & Rounds, J. (1999). Psychosocial factors and the development of breast cancer: A meta-analysis. *Health Psychology, 18*, 520–531.

Merletti, F., Boffetta, P., Ciccone, G., Mashberg, A., & Terracini, B. (1989). Role of tobacco and alcoholic beverages in the etiology of cancer of the oral cavity/oropharynx in Torino, Italy. *Cancer Research, 49*, 4919–4924.

Miller, T. W. (Ed.). (1989). *Stressful life events.* Madison, CT: International Universities Press.

Muntaner, C., & O'Campo, P. J. (1993). A critical appraisal of the demand/control model of the psychosocial work environment: Epistemological, social and class considerations. *Social Science & Medicine, 36*, 1509–1517.

Muslin, H. L., Gyarfas, K., & Pieper, W. J. (1966). Separation experience and cancer of the breast. *Annals of the New York Academy of Science, 125*, 802–806.

O'Leary, A. (1990). Stress, emotion and human immune function. *Psychological Bulletin, 108*, 363–382.

Ogden, J., & Mtandabari, T. (1997). Examination stress and changes in mood and health related behaviours. *Psychology & Health, 12*, 289–299.

Osterweis, M., Solomon, F., & Green M. (Eds.). (1984). *Bereavement: Reactions, consequences and care.* Washington, DC: National Academy Press.

Parkes, K. R. (1991). Locus of control as a moderator: An explanation for additive versus interactive findings in the demand-discretion model of work stress? *British Journal of Psychology, 82*(Pt. 3), 291–312.

Perrewe, P. L., & Ganster, D. C. (1989). The impact of job demands and behavioural control on experienced job stress. *Journal of Organizational Behaviour, 10*, 213–229.

Peterson, C., Seligman, M. E. P., & Vaillant, G. E. (1988). Pessimistic explanatory style is a risk factor for physical illness: A thirty-five-year longitudinal study. *Journal of Personality and Social Psychology, 55*, 23–27.

Peterson, C., Seligman, M. E., Yurko, K. H., Martin, L. R., & Friedman, H. S. (1998). Catastrophizing and untimely death. *Psychological Science, 9*, 127–130.

Petticrew, M., Fraser, J. M., & Regan, M. F. (1999). Adverse life events and risk of breast cancer: A meta-analysis. *British Journal of Health Psychology, 4*, 1–17.

Pollard, T., Ungpakorn, G., Harrison, G. A., & Parkes, K. R. (1996). Epinephrine and cortisol responses to work: A test of the models of Frankenhaueuser and Karasek. *Annals of Behavioral Medicine, 18*, 229–237.

Pollock, K. (1988). On the nature of social stress: Production of a modern mythology. *Social Science & Medicine, 26*, 381–392.

Protheroe, D., Turvey, K., Horgan, K., Benson, E., Bowers, D., & House, A. (1999). Stressful life events and difficulties and onset of breast cancer: Case-control study. *British Medical Journal, 319*, 1027–1030.

Rabkin, J. G. (1993). Stress and psychiatric disorders. In L. Goldberger & S. Breznitz (Eds.), *Handbook of stress: Theoretical and clinical aspects* (pp. 477–495). New York: Free Press.

Ridder, D. T. D. (1995). Social status and coping: An exploration of the mediating role of beliefs. *Anxiety, Stress, and Coping, 8*(4), 311–324.

Schnall, P. L., Landsbergis, P. A., & Baker, D. (1994). Job strain and cardiovascular health. *Annual Review of Public Health, 15*, 381–411.

Skov, T., Borg, V., & Orhede, E. (1996). Psychosocial and physical risk factors for musculoskeletal disorders of the neck, shoulders, and lower back in salespeople. *Occupational and Environmental Medicine, 53*, 351–356.

Snow, H. (1893). *Cancer and the cancer process.* London: J. and A. Churchill.

Steenland, K., Johnson, J., & Nowlin, S. (1997). A follow-up study of job strain and heart disease among males in the NHANES1 population. *American Journal of Industrial Medicine, 31*, 256–260.

Stein, M., Miller, A. H., & Trestman, R. L. (1991). Depression, the immune system, and illness. *Archives of General Psychiatry, 48*, 171–177.

Steptoe, A. (1991). The links between stress and illness. *Journal of Psychosomatic Research, 35*, 633–644.

Steptoe, A., Fieldman, G., Evans, O., & Perry, L. (1993). Control over work pace, job strain and cardiovascular responses in middle aged men. *Journal of Hypertension, 11*, 751–759.

Steptoe, A., & Wardle, J. (1994). What the experts think: A European survey of expert opinion about the influence of lifestyle on health. *European Journal of Epidemiology, 10*, 195–203.

Steptoe, A., Wardle, J., Pollard, T. M., & Canaan, L. (1996). Stress, social support and health related behavior: A study of smoking, alcohol consumption and physical exercise. *Journal of Psychosomatic Research, 41*, 171–180.

Stolbach, L. L., & Brandt, U. C. (1988). Psychosocial factors in the development and progression of breast cancer. In C. L. Cooper (Ed.), *Stress and breast cancer* (pp. 3–24). Chichester, England: John Wiley & Sons.

Stone, A. A., Bovbjerg, D. H., Neale, J. M., Napoli, A., Valdimarsdottir, H., Cox, D., et al. (1992). Development of common cold symptoms following experimental rhinovirus infection related to prior stressful events. *Behavioral Medicine, 18*, 115–120.

Storr, C. J., Trinkoff, A. M., & Anthony, J. C. (1999). Job strain and non-medical drug use. *Drug and Alcohol Dependence, 55*(1–2), 45–51.

Stueve, A., Dohrenwend, B. P., & Skodol, A. E. (1998). Relationships between stressful life events and episodes of major depression and non-affective disorders: Selected results from a New York risk factors study. In Dohrenwend 1998, 341–357.

Van der Doef, M., & Maes, S. (1998). The job demand-control-support model and physical outcomes: A review of the strain and buffer hypotheses. *Psychology & Health, 13*, 909–936.

Vedhara, K., Cox, N. K., Wilcock, G. K., Perks, P., Hunt, M., Anderson, S., et al. (1999). Chronic stress in elderly carers of dementia patients and antibody response to influenza vaccine. *Lancet, 353*, 627–631.

Weidner, G., Boughal, T., Pieper, C., Connor, S. L., & Mendell, N. R. (1997). Relationship of job strain to standard coronary risk factors and psychological characteristics in women and men of the Family Heart Study. *Health Psychology*, *16*(3), 239–247.

Wills, T. A. (1990). Stress and coping factors in the epidemiology of substance use. In L. T. Kozlowski, H. M. Annis, H. D. Capell, F. B. Glaser, M. S. Goodstadt, Y. Israel, H. Kalant, E. M. Sellers & E. R. Vingilis (Eds.), *Research advances in alcohol and drug problems* (pp. 215–250). New York: Plenum Press.

CHAPTER 9

The Noonday Demon: An Atlas of Depression

Andrew Solomon

The birth and death that constitute depression occur at once. I returned, not long ago, to a wood in which I had played as a child and saw an oak, a hundred years dignified, in whose shade I used to play with my brother. In twenty years, a huge vine had attached itself to this confident tree and had nearly smothered it. It was hard to say where the tree left off and the vine began. The vine had twisted itself so entirely around the scaffolding of tree branches that its leaves seemed from a distance to be the leaves of the tree; only up close could you see how few living oak branches were left, and how a few desperate little budding sticks of oak stuck like a row of thumbs up the massive trunk, their leaves continuing to photosynthesize in the ignorant way of mechanical biology.

Fresh from a major depression in which I had hardly been able to take on board the idea of other people's problems, I empathized with that tree. My depression had grown on me as that vine had conquered the oak; it had been a sucking thing that had wrapped itself around me, ugly and more alive than I. It had had a life of its own that bit by bit asphyxiated all of my life out of me. At the worst stage of major depression, I had moods that I knew were not my moods: they belonged to the depression, as surely as the leaves on that tree's high branches belonged to the vine. When I tried to think clearly about this, I felt that my mind was immured, that it couldn't expand in any direction. I knew that the sun was rising and setting, but little of its light reached me. I felt myself sagging under what was much stronger than I; first I could not use my ankles, and then I could not control my knees, and then my waist began to break under the strain, and then my shoulders turned in, and in the end I was compacted and fetal, depleted by this thing that was crushing me without holding me. Its tendrils threatened to pulverize my mind and my courage and my stomach, and crack my bones and desiccate my body. It went on glutting itself on me when there seemed nothing left to feed it.

I was not strong enough to stop breathing. I knew then that I could never kill this vine of depression, and so all I wanted was for it to let me die. But it had taken from me the energy I would have needed to kill myself, and it would not kill me. If my trunk was rotting, this thing that fed on it was now too strong to let it fall; it had become an alternative support to what it had destroyed. In the tightest corner of my bed, split and racked by this thing no one else seemed to be able to see, I prayed to a God I had never entirely believed in, and I asked for deliverance. I would have been happy to die the most painful death, though I was too dumbly lethargic even to conceptualize suicide. Every second of being alive hurt me. Because this thing had drained all fluid from me, I could not even cry. My mouth was parched as well. I had thought that when you feel your worst, your tears flood, but the very worst pain is the arid pain of total violation that comes after the tears are all used up, the pain that stops up every space through which you once metered the world, or the world, you. This is the presence of major depression.

I have said that depression is both a birth and a death. The vine is what is born. The death is one's own decay, the cracking of the branches that support this misery. The first thing that goes is happiness. You cannot gain pleasure from anything.[1] That's famously the cardinal symptom of major depression. But soon other emotions follow happiness into oblivion: sadness as you had known it, the sadness that seemed to have led you here; your sense of humor; your belief in and capacity for love. Your mind is leached until you seem dim-witted even to yourself. If your hair has always been thin, it seems thinner; if you have always had bad skin, it gets worse. You smell sour even to yourself. You lose the ability to trust anyone, to be touched, to grieve. Eventually, you are simply absent from yourself.

Maybe what is present usurps what becomes absent, and maybe the absence of obfuscatory things reveals what is present. Either way, you are less than yourself and in the clutches of something alien. Too often, treatments address only half the problem: they focus only on the presence or only on the absence. It is necessary both to cut away that extra thousand pounds of vines and to relearn a root system and the techniques of photosynthesis. Drug therapy hacks through the vines. You can feel it happening, how the medication seems to be poisoning the parasite so that bit by bit it withers away. You feel the weight going, feel the way that the branches recover much of their natural bent. Until you have got rid of the vine, you cannot think about what has been lost. But even with the vine gone, you may still have few leaves and shallow roots, and the rebuilding of your self cannot be achieved with any drugs that now exist. With the weight of the vine gone, little leaves scattered along the tree skeleton become viable for essential nourishment. But this is not a good way to be. It is not a strong way to be. Rebuilding of the self in and after depression requires love, insight, work, and, most of all, time.

Diagnosis is as complex as the illness. Patients ask doctors all the time, "Am I depressed?" as though the result were in a definitive blood test.

The only way to find out whether you're depressed is to listen to and watch yourself, to feel your feelings and then think about them. If you feel bad without reason most of the time, you're depressed. If you feel bad most of the time *with* reason, you're also depressed, though changing the reasons may be a better way forward than leaving circumstance alone and attacking the depression. If the depression is disabling to you, then it's major. If it's only mildly distracting, it's not major.

Psychiatry's bible—the *Diagnostic and Statistical Manual* (currently in its fourth edition, *DSM-IV*; American Psychiatric Association, 1994)—ineptly defines depression as the presence of five or more on a list of nine symptoms. The problem with the definition is that it's entirely arbitrary. There's no particular reason to qualify five symptoms as constituting depression; four symptoms are still more or less depression, and five symptoms are less severe than six. Even one symptom is unpleasant. Having slight versions of all the symptoms may be less of a problem than having severe versions of just two of them. After enduring diagnosis, most people seek causation, despite the fact that knowing why you are sick has no immediate bearing on treating the sickness.

Illness of the mind is real illness. It can have severe effects on the body. People who show up at the offices of their doctors complaining about stomach cramps are frequently told, "Why, there's nothing wrong with you except that you're depressed!" Depression, if it is sufficiently severe to cause stomach cramps, is actually a really bad thing to have wrong with you, and it requires treatment. If you show up complaining that your breathing is troubled, no one says to you, "Why, there's nothing wrong with you except that you have emphysema!" To the person who is experiencing them, psychosomatic complaints are as real as the stomach cramps of someone with food poisoning. They exist in the unconscious brain, and often enough the brain is sending inappropriate messages to the stomach, so they exist there as well. The diagnosis—whether something is rotten in your stomach or your appendix or your brain—matters in determining treatment and is not trivial. As organs go, the brain is quite an important one, and its malfunctions should be addressed accordingly.

Chemistry is often called on to heal the rift between body and soul. The relief people express when a doctor says their depression is "chemical" is predicated on a belief that there is an integral self that exists across time, and on a fictional divide between the fully occasioned sorrow and the utterly random one. The word *chemical* seems to assuage the feelings of responsibility people have for the stressed-out discontent of not liking their jobs, worrying about getting old, failing at love, hating their families. There is a pleasant freedom from guilt that has been attached to *chemical*. If your brain is predisposed to depression, you need not blame yourself for it. Well, blame yourself or evolution, but remember that blame itself can be understood as a chemical process and that happiness, too, is chemical. Chemistry and biology are not matters that impinge on the "real" self; depression cannot be separated from the person it affects. Treatment does not alleviate a disruption of identity, bringing you back to some kind of normality; it readjusts a multifarious identity, changing in some small degree who you are.

Anyone who has taken high school science classes knows that human beings are made of chemicals and that the study of those chemicals and the structures in which they are configured is called biology. Everything that happens in the brain has chemical manifestations and sources. If you close your eyes and think hard about polar bears, that has a chemical effect on your brain. If you stick to a policy of opposing tax breaks for capital gains, that has a chemical effect on your brain. When you remember some episode from your past, you do so through the complex chemistry of memory. Childhood trauma and subsequent difficulty can alter brain chemistry. Thousands of chemical reactions are involved in deciding to read this book, picking it up with your hands, looking at the shapes and the letters on the page, extracting meaning from those shapes, and having intellectual and emotional responses to what they convey.

If time lets you cycle out of a depression and feel better, the chemical changes are no less particular and complex than the ones that are brought about by taking antidepressants. The external determines the internal as much as the internal invents the external. What is so unattractive is the idea that in addition to all other lines being blurred, the boundaries of what makes us ourselves are blurry. There is no essential self that lies pure as a vein of gold under the chaos of experience and chemistry. Anything can be changed, and we must understand the human organism as a sequence of selves that succumb to or choose one another. And yet the language of science, used in training doctors and, increasingly, in nonacademic writing and conversation, is strangely perverse.

The cumulative results of the brain's chemical effects are not well understood. In the 1989 edition of the standard *Comprehensive Textbook of Psychiatry*, for example, one finds this helpful formula (Kaplan & Sadock, 1989, p. 870):

$$\text{D-type score} = C_1 (\text{MHPG}) - C_2 (\text{VMA}) + C_3 (\text{NE}) - C_4 (\text{NMN} + \text{MN})/\text{NMA} + C_0$$

In words, this defines a depression score as equivalent to the level of 3-methoxy-4-hydroxyphenylglycol (a compound found in the urine of all people and not apparently affected by depression), minus the level of 3-methoxy-4-hydroxymandelic acid, plus the level of norepinephrine, minus the combined levels of normetanephrine and metanepherine divided by the level of 3-methoxy-4-hydroxymandelic acid, plus an unspecified conversion variable. The score should come out between 1 for unipolar and 0 for bipolar patients, so if you come up with something else—you're doing it wrong. How much insight can such formulas offer? How can they *possibly* apply to something as nebulous as mood? To what extent specific experience has conduced to a particular depression is hard to determine, nor can we explain through what chemistry a person comes to respond to external circumstance with depression, nor can we work out what makes someone essentially depressive.

Although depression is described by the popular press and the pharmaceutical industry as though it were a single-effect illness such as diabetes, it is not. Indeed, it is strikingly dissimilar to diabetes. Diabetics produce insufficient insulin, and diabetes is treated by increasing and stabilizing insulin in the bloodstream. Depression is *not* the consequence of a reduced level of anything we can now measure. Raising levels of serotonin in the brain triggers a process that eventually helps many depressed people to feel better, but that is *not* because they have abnormally low levels of serotonin. Furthermore, serotonin does *not* have immediate salutary effects. You could pump a gallon of serotonin into the brain of a depressed person and it would not in the instant make him feel one iota better, though a long-term sustained raise in serotonin level has some effects that ameliorate depressive symptoms.

"I'm depressed but it's just chemical" is a sentence equivalent to "I'm murderous but it's just chemical" or "I'm intelligent but it's just chemical." *Everything* about a person is just chemical, if one wants to think in those terms. "You can say it's 'just chemistry,'" says Maggie Robbins, who suffers from manic–depressive illness. "I say there's nothing 'just' about chemistry." The sun shines brightly and that's just chemical, too. And it's chemical that rocks are hard, and that the sea is salty, and that certain springtime afternoons carry in their gentle breezes a quality of nostalgia that stirs the heart to longings and imaginings kept dormant by the snows of a long winter. "This serotonin thing," says David McDowell of Columbia University, "is part of modern neuromythology." It's a potent set of stories.

Internal and external reality exist on a continuum. What happens and how you understand it to have happened and how you respond to its happening are usually linked, but none of those is predictive of the others. If reality itself is often a relative thing, and the self is in a state of permanent flux, then the passage from slight mood to extreme mood is a glissando. Illness is an extreme state of emotion, and one might reasonably describe emotion as a mild form of illness. If we all felt up and great (but not delusionally manic) all the time, we could get more done and might have a happier time on earth, but that idea is creepy and terrifying (though, of course, if we felt up and great all the time, we might forget all about creepiness and terror).

Influenza is straightforward: one day you do not have the responsible virus in your system, and another day you do. HIV passes from one person to another in a definable, isolated split second. But depression? It's like trying to come up with clinical parameters for hunger, which affects us all several times a day, yet in its extreme version is a tragedy that kills its victims. Some people need more food than others; some can function under circumstances of dire malnutrition, while others grow weak rapidly and collapse in the streets. Similarly, depression hits different people in different ways: some are predisposed to resist or battle through it, while others are helpless in its grip. Willfulness and pride may allow one person to get through a depression that would fell another whose personality is more gentle and acquiescent.

Depression interacts with personality. Some people are brave in the face of depression (during it and afterward), and some are weak. Since personality, too, has a random edge and a bewildering chemistry, one can write everything off to genetics, but that is too easy. "There is no such thing as a mood gene," says Steven Hyman, director of the National Institute of Mental Health. "It's just shorthand for very complex gene–environment interactions."

If everyone has the capacity for some measure of depression under some circumstances, everyone also has the capacity to fight depression to some degree under some circumstances. Often, the fight takes the form of seeking out the treatments that will be most effective in the battle. It involves finding help while you are still strong enough to do so. It involves making the most of the life you have between your most severe episodes. Some horrendously symptom-ridden people are able to achieve real success in life, and yet other people are utterly destroyed by the mildest forms of the illness.

Working through a mild depression without medications has certain advantages. It gives you the sense that you can correct your own chemical imbalances through the exercise of your own chemical will. Learning to walk across hot coals is also a triumph of the brain over what appears to be the inevitable physical chemistry of pain, and it is a thrilling way to discover the sheer power of mind. Getting through a depression "on your own" allows you to avoid the social discomfort associated with psychiatric medications. It suggests that we are accepting ourselves as we were made, reconstructing ourselves with only our own interior mechanics and without help from the outside. Returning from distress by gradual degrees gives sense to affliction itself.

Interior mechanics, however, are difficult to commission and are frequently inadequate. Depression frequently destroys the power of mind over mood. Sometimes the complex chemistry of sorrow kicks in because you've lost someone you love, and the chemistry of loss and love may lead to the chemistry of depression. The chemistry of falling in love can kick in for obvious external reasons, or along lines that the heart can never tell the mind. If we wanted to treat this madness of emotion, we could perhaps do so. It is mad for adolescents to rage at parents who have done their best, but it is a conventional madness, uniform enough so that we tolerate it relatively unquestioningly. Sometimes, however, that same chemistry kicks in for external reasons that are not sufficient, by mainstream standards, to explain the despair: someone bumps into you in a crowded bus and you want to cry, or you read about world overpopulation and find your own life intolerable. Everyone has on occasion felt disproportionate emotion over a small matter or has felt emotions whose origin is obscure or that may have no origin at all. There are times when the chemistry kicks in for no apparent external reason. Most people have had moments of inexplicable despair, often in the middle of the night or in the early morning before the alarm clock sounds. If such feelings last ten minutes, they're a strange, quick mood. If they last ten hours, they're a disturbing febrility, and if they last ten years, they're a crippling illness.

It is too often the quality of happiness that you feel at every moment its fragility, while depression, when you are in it, seems to be a state that will never pass. Even if you accept that moods change, that whatever you feel today will be different tomorrow, you cannot relax into happiness as you can into sadness. For me, sadness always has been and still is a more powerful feeling; and if that is not a universal experience, perhaps it is the base from which depression grows. I hated being depressed, but it was also in depression that I learned my own acreage, the full extent of my soul. When I am happy, I feel slightly distracted by happiness, as though it fails to use some part of my mind and brain that wants the exercise. Depression is something to do. My grasp tightens and becomes acute in moments of loss: I can see the beauty of glass objects fully at the moment when they slip from my hand toward the floor. "We find pleasure much less pleasurable, pain much more painful than we had anticipated," Schopenhauer wrote (1970, pp. 42–43). "We require at all times a certain quantity of care or sorrow or want, as a ship requires ballast, to keep on a straight course."

There is a Russian expression: if you wake up feeling no pain, you know you're dead. While life is not only about pain, the experience of pain, which is particular in its intensity, is one of the surest signs of the life force. To quote Schopenhauer again:

> Imagine this race transported to a Utopia where everything grows of its own accord and turkeys fly around ready-roasted, where lovers find one another without any delay and keep one another without any difficulty: in such a place some men would die of boredom or hang themselves, some would fight and kill one another, and thus they would create for themselves more suffering than nature inflicts on them as it is ... the polar opposite of suffering [is] boredom. (1970, p. 43)

I believe that pain needs to be transformed but not forgotten, gainsaid but not obliterated.

Three separate events—a decrease in serotonin receptors, a rise in the stress hormone cortisol, and depression—are coincident. Their sequence is unknown: it's a sort of chicken-and-chick-and-egg mystery. If you lesion the serotonin system in an animal brain, the levels of cortisol go up (López, Vazquez, Chalmers, & Watson, 1997). If you raise levels of cortisol, serotonin seems to go down. If you stress a person, corticotrophin-releasing factor (CRF) goes up and causes the level of cortisol to go up. If you depress a person, levels of serotonin go down (López, Akil, & Watson, 1999).

What does this mean? One of the hottest substances of recent years has been serotonin, and the treatments most frequently used for depression in the United States are ones that raise the functional level of serotonin in the brain. Every time you affect serotonin, you also modify the stress systems and change the level of cortisol in the brain.[2] "I wouldn't say that cortisol is depression," says Elizabeth Young, who works in this field at the University of Michigan, "but it may well exacerbate a minor condition and create a real syndrome." Cortisol, once it is produced, binds to glucocorticoid receptors in the brain. Antidepressants increase the number of these glucocorticoid receptors—which then absorb the excess cortisol that is floating around up there. This is extremely important for overall body regulation. The glucocorticoid receptors actually turn on and off some genes, and when you have relatively few receptors being swamped with a lot of cortisol, the system goes into overdrive. "It's like having a heating system," Young says. "If the temperature sensor for the thermostat it is in a spot that's become drafty, the heat will never turn off even though the room is scalding. If you add a few more sensors located around the room, you can get the system back under control."

Under ordinary circumstances, cortisol levels stick to fairly straightforward rules. Cortisol's circadian pattern is to be high in the morning (it's what gets you out of bed) and then to go down during the day. In depressed patients, cortisol tends to remain elevated throughout the day. Something's wrong with the inhibitory circuits that should be turning off the production of cortisol as the day wears on, and this may be part of why the jolted feeling that is usual first thing in the morning continues so far into the day for depressed people.

It may be possible to regulate depression by addressing the cortisol system directly, instead of working through the serotonin system. Building on basic research done at Michigan, investigators elsewhere have treated treatment-resistant depression patients with ketoconazole (e.g., Wolkowitz et al., 1999), a cortisol-reducing medication, and almost 70 percent of these patients showed marked improvement. At the moment, ketoconazole causes too many side effects to be attractive as an antidepressant, but several major pharmaceutical companies are investigating related medications that may not have these negative side effects. Such treatment must be carefully regulated, however, since cortisol is necessary for fight-or-flight responses, for that adrenal energy that helps one to struggle on in the face of difficulty, for anti-inflammatory action, for decision making and resolution, and most importantly, for knocking the immune system into action in the face of an infectious disease.

Cortisol patterning studies have recently been done on baboons and air traffic controllers. The baboons who had long-term high levels of cortisol tended to be paranoid, unable to distinguish between a real threat and a mildly uncomfortable situation, likely to fight as desperately over a banana next to a tree heavy with ripe fruit as over their own lives.[3] Among air traffic controllers, those who were psychologically healthy had an exact correlation between the extent to which they were overworked and their level of cortisol, while those who were in poor condition had their cortisol skyrocketing and peaking all over the place (Rose, Jenkins, Hurst, Herd, & Hall, 1982). Once the cortisol–stress correlation gets distorted, you can get hysterical about bananas; you will find that everything that happens to you is stressful. "And that is a form of depression, and then of course being depressed is itself stressful," observes Young. "A downward spiral."

Once you've had a stress sufficient to cause a protracted increase of your cortisol levels, your cortisol system is damaged, and in the future it will not readily turn off once it has been activated. Thereafter, the elevation of cortisol after a small trauma may not normalize as it would under ordinary circumstances. Like anything that has been broken once, the cortisol system is prone to break again and again, with less and less external pressure. People who have had a myocardial infarction (heart attack) after great physical strain are subject to relapse even while sitting in an armchair—the heart is now a bit worn-out, and sometimes it just gives up without much strain.[4] The same thing can happen to the mind.

The fact that something is medical doesn't contravene its having psychosocial origins. "My wife is an endocrinologist," says Juan López, who works with Young, "and she sees kids with diabetes. Well, diabetes is clearly a disease of the pancreas, but external factors influence it. Not only what you eat, but also how stressed you are—kids in really bad homes get frantic and their blood sugar goes haywire. The fact that this happens doesn't make diabetes a psychological disease." In the field of depression, psychological stress transduces to biological change, and vice versa. If a person subjects herself to extreme stress, CRF is released and often helps bring about the biological reality of depression. The psychological techniques for preventing yourself from getting too stressed can keep down your levels of CRF, and so of cortisol. "You've got your genes," López says, "and there's nothing you can do about them. But you can sometimes control how they express themselves."

In his research work, López went back to the most straightforward animal models (López, Chalmers, Little, & Watson, 1998). "If you stress the hell out of a rat," López says, "that rat will have high levels of stress hormones. If you look at his serotonin receptors, they're clearly screwed up by stress. The brain of a highly stressed rat looks very much like the brain of a very depressed rat. If you give him serotonin-altering antidepressants, his cortisol eventually normalizes. It is likely that some depression is more seratonergic and some is more tightly linked to cortisol, and most mixes these two sensitivities in some way. The cross-talk between these two systems is part of the same pathophysiology."

The rat experiments have been revealing, but the prefrontal cortex, that area of the brain that humans have and that makes us more developed than rats, also contains many cortisol receptors, and those are probably implicated in the complexities of human depression. The brains of human suicides show extremely high levels of CRF—"It's hyper, like they've been pumping this stuff," López says. Their adrenal glands are larger than those of people who die from other causes because the high level of CRF has actually caused the expansion of the adrenal system (López et al. 1997). López has found that suicide victims actually show significant decrease in cortisol receptors in the prefrontal cortex (which means that the cortisol in that area is not mopped up as quickly as it should be). The next step, he says, is to look at the brains of people who, when subjected to huge amounts of stress, can keep going despite it. "What is the biochemistry of their coping mechanism?" López asks. "How do they sustain such resilience? What are the patterns of CRF release in their brains? What do their receptors look like?"

John Greden, López and Young's department chair at the University of Michigan, focused on the long-term effects of sustained stress and sustained depressive episodes.[5] If you have too much stress and too high a level of cortisol for too long, you start destroying the very neurons that should regulate the feedback loop and turn down the cortisol level after the stress is resolved. Ultimately, this results in lesions to the hippocampus and the amygdala, a loss of neuronal networking tissue. The longer you remain in a depressed state, the more likely you are to have significant lesioning, which can lead to peripheral neuropathy: your vision starts to fade and all kinds of other things can go wrong. "This reflects the obvious fact that we need not only to treat depression when it occurs," says Greden, "but also to prevent it from recurring. Our public health approach at the moment is just wrong. People with recurrent depression must stay on medication permanently, not cycle on and off it, because beyond the unpleasantness of having to survive multiple painful depressive episodes, such people are actually ravaging their own neuronal tissue." Greden looks to a future in which our understanding of the physical consequences of depression may lead us to strategies to reverse them. "Maybe we'll be trying selective injection of neurotropic growth factors into certain regions of the brain to make some kind of tissue proliferate and grow. Maybe we'll be able to use other kinds of stimulation, magnetic or electric, to encourage growth in certain areas."

I hope so. Taking the pills is costly—not only financially but also psychically. It is humiliating to be reliant on them. It is inconvenient to have to keep track of them and to stock up on prescriptions. And it is toxic to know that without these perpetual interventions, you are not yourself as you have understood yourself. I'm not sure why I feel this way—I wear contact lenses and without them am virtually blind, and I do not feel shamed by my lenses or by my need for them (though given my druthers, I'd choose perfect vision). The constant presence of the medications is for me a reminder of frailty and imperfection, and I am a perfectionist and would prefer to have things inviolate out of the hand of God.

NOTES

1. *Anhedonia* is "the inability to experience pleasure," as defined by Francis Mondimore (1995, p. 22).

2. This explanation of stress responses in depression is based on the work of Juan López and Elizabeth Young at the University of Michigan and Ken Kendler at the Medical College of Virginia in Richmond. There are as many explanations of depression as there are stars in the night sky, but I think the Michigan scientists' stress-based model is particularly convincing.

3. The studies on baboons were done by Robert Sapolsky and described to me in an oral interview with Elizabeth Young.

4. That the heart is weakened after a myocardial infarction is a well-established idea. However, the severity of damage done to the heart depends upon the size of the area of dead tissue within the heart. While the data indicate that isolation lesions don't necessarily put one at a higher rate of relapse than controls, diffuse coronary disease almost certainly does. Nonetheless, close attention must be paid to the heart condition of anyone who has experienced a heart attack, and therapies to prevent relapse are in order for such a person. I thank Dr. Joseph Hayes of Cornell University for his assistance with this matter.

5. Work on the effects of continued stress on the brain may be found in a number of articles, a large majority of them headed by Robert Sapolsky. For information on the brain's response to stress, see Sapolsky, Uno, Rebert, & Finch (1990). For studies concerning the interaction of biological stress and social status, see Sapolsky (1990, 1995). Greden's discussion of the epidemiology of major depression is in Burns, Ryan, Gaynes, Wells, & Schulberg (2000).

REFERENCES

American Psychiatric Association. (1994). *Diagnostic and statistical manual of mental disorders* (4th ed.). Washington, DC: American Psychiatric Association.

Burns, B. J., Ryan, W. H., Gaynes, B. N., Wells, K. B., & Schulberg, H. C. (2000). General medical and specialty mental health service use for major depression. *International Journal of Psychiatry in Medicine, 30*(2), 127–143.

Kaplan, H. I., & Sadock, B. J. (Eds.). (1989). *Comprehensive textbook of psychiatry* (5th ed.). Baltimore, MD: Williams & Wilkins.

López, J. F., Akil, H., & Watson, S. J. (1999). Neural circuits mediating stress. *Biological Psychiatry, 46*(11), 1461–1471.

López, J. F., Chalmers, D. T., Little, K. Y., & Watson, S. J. (1998). Regulation of serotonin1A, glucocorticoid, and mineralocorticoid receptor in rat and human hippocampus: Implications for the neurobiology of depression. *Biological Psychiatry, 43*(8), 547–573.

López, J. F., Vazquez, D. M., Chalmers, D. T., & Watson, S. J. (1997). Regulation of 5-HT receptors and the hypothalamic-pituitary-adrenal axis: Implications for the neurobiology of suicide. *Annals of the New York Academy of Sciences, 836*, 106–134.

Mondimore, F. M. (1995). *Depression: The mood disease.* Baltimore, MD: Johns Hopkins University Press.

Rose, R. M., Jenkins, C. D., Hurst, M., Herd, J. A., & Hall, R. P. (1982). Endocrine activity in air traffic controllers at work. II. Biological, psychological and work correlates. *Psychoneuroendocrinology, 7*, 113–123.

Sapolsky, R. M. (1990). Stress in the wild. *Scientific American, 262*(1), 116–123.

Sapolsky, R. M. (1995). Social subordinance as a marker of hypercortisolism: Some unexpected subtleties. *Annals of the New York Academy of Sciences, 771*, 626–639.

Sapolsky, R. M., Uno, H., Rebert, C. S., & Finch, C. E. (1990). Hippocampal damage associated with prolonged glucocorticoid exposure in primates. *Journal of Neuroscience, 10*(9), 2897–2902.

Schopenhauer, A. (1970). *Essays and aphorisms* (R. J. Hollingdale, ed./trans.). London: Penguin Books.

Wolkowitz, O. M., Reus, V. I., Chan, T., Manfredi, F., Raum, W., Johnson, R., et al. (1999). Antiglucocorticoid treatment of depression: Double-blind ketoconazole. *Biological Psychiatry, 45*(8), 1070–1074.

CHAPTER 10

Why Zebras Don't Get Ulcers: Stress, Metabolism, and Liquidating Your Assets

Robert M. Sapolsky

So you're sprinting down the street with a lion after you. Things were looking grim for a moment there, but—your good luck—your cardiovascular system kicked into gear, and now it is delivering oxygen and energy to your exercising muscles. But what energy? There's not enough time to consume a candy bar and derive its benefits as you sprint along; there's not even enough time to digest food already in the gut. Your body must get energy from its places of storage—fat or liver or nonexercising muscle. To understand how you mobilize energy in this circumstance, and how that mobilization can make you sick at times, we need to learn how the body stores energy in the first place.[1]

PUTTING ENERGY IN THE BANK

The basic process of digestion consists of breaking down chunks of animals and vegetables so that they can then be transformed into chunks of human. We can't make use of the chunks exactly as they are, though; we can't, for example, make our leg muscles stronger by grafting on the piece of chicken muscle we ate. Instead, complex food matter is broken down into its simplest parts (molecules): amino acids (the building blocks of protein), simple sugars like glucose (the building blocks of more complex sugars and of starches [carbohydrates]), and free fatty acids and glycerol (the constituents of fat). This is accomplished in the gastrointestinal tract by enzymes, chemicals that can degrade more complex molecules. The simple building blocks thus produced are absorbed into the bloodstream for delivery to whichever cells in the body need them. Once you've done that, the cells have the ability to use those building blocks to construct the proteins, fats, and carbohydrates needed to stay in business. And just as important, those simple building blocks (especially the fatty acids and sugars) can also be burned by the body to provide the energy to do all that construction and to operate those new structures afterward.

It's Thanksgiving, and you've eaten with porcine abandon. Your bloodstream is teeming with amino acids, fatty acids, and glucose. It's far more than you need to power you over to the couch in a postprandial daze. What does your body do with the excess? This is crucial to understand because, basically, the process gets reversed when you're later sprinting for your life.

To answer this question, it's time we talked finances, the works—savings accounts, change for a dollar, stocks and bonds, negative amortization of interest rates, shaking coins out of piggy banks—because the process of transporting energy through the body bears some striking similarities to the movement of money. It is rare today for the grotesquely wealthy to walk around with their fortunes in their pockets or to hoard their wealth as cash stuffed inside mattresses. Instead, surplus wealth is stored elsewhere, in forms more complex than cash: mutual funds, tax-free government bonds, Swiss bank accounts. In the same way, surplus energy is not kept in the body's form of cash—circulating amino acids, glucose, and fatty acids—but is stored in more complex forms. Enzymes in fat cells can combine fatty acids and glycerol to form *triglycerides* (see Table 10.1). Accumulate enough of these in the fat cells and you grow plump. Meanwhile, your cells can stick series of glucose molecules together. These long chains, sometimes thousands of glucose molecules long, are called *glycogen*. Most glycogen formation occurs in your muscles and liver. Similarly, enzymes in cells throughout the body can combine long strings of amino acids, forming them into proteins.

The hormone that stimulates the transport and storage of these building blocks into target cells is *insulin*. Insulin is this optimistic hormone that plans for your metabolic future. Eat a huge meal and insulin pours out of the pancreas into the bloodstream, stimulating the transport of fatty acids into fat cells and stimulating glycogen and protein synthesis. It's insulin that's filling out the deposit slips at your fat banks. We even secrete insulin when we are about to fill our bloodstream with all those nutritive building blocks: if you eat dinner each day at six o'clock, by 5:45 you're already secreting insulin in anticipation of the rising glucose levels in your

Table 10.1. How the Body Processes Food Components

What you stick in your mouth	How it winds up in your bloodstream	How it gets stored if you have a surplus	How it gets mobilized in a stressful emergency
Protein	Amino acids	Protein	Amino acids
Starch, sugar, carbohydrates	Glucose	Glycogen	Glucose
Fat	Fatty acids and glycerol	Triglycerides	Fatty acids, glycerol, ketone bodies

bloodstream (Schwartz, Woods, Porte, Seeley, & Baskin, 2000). Logically, it is the parasympathetic nervous system that stimulates the anticipatory secretion, and this ability to secrete insulin in preparation for the glucose levels that are about to rise is a great example of the anticipatory quality of allostatic balance.

EMPTYING THE BANK ACCOUNT: ENERGY MOBILIZATION DURING A STRESSOR

This grand strategy of breaking your food down into its simplest parts and reconverting it into complex storage forms is precisely what your body should do when you've eaten plenty. And it is precisely what your body should *not* do in the face of an immediate physical emergency. Then, you want to stop energy storage. Turn up the activity of the sympathetic nervous system, turn down the parasympathetic, and down goes insulin secretion: step one in meeting an emergency accomplished.

The body makes sure that energy storage is stopped in a second way as well. With the onset of the stressful emergency, you secrete glucocorticoids, which block the transport of nutrients into fat cells. This counteracts the effects of any insulin still floating around.

So you've made sure you don't do anything as irrational as store away new energy at this time. But in addition, you want your body to gain access to the energy *already* stored. You want to dip into your bank account, liquidate some of your assets, turn stored nutrients into your body's equivalent of cash to get you through this crisis. Your body reverses all of the storage steps through the release of the stress hormones glucocorticoids, glucagon, epinephrine, and norepinephrine. These cause triglycerides to be broken down in the fat cells and, as a result, free fatty acids and glycerol pour into the circulatory system. The same hormones also trigger the degradation of glycogen to glucose in cells throughout the body, and the glucose is then flushed into the bloodstream. Furthermore, these hormones cause protein in nonexercising muscle to be converted back to individual amino acids. The stored nutrients have now been reconverted into simpler forms.

Your body makes another simplifying move. Amino acids are not a very good source of energy, but glucose is. So, your body shunts the circulating amino acids to the liver, where they are converted to glucose. The liver can also generate new glucose, through a process called *gluconeogenesis,* and this glucose now becomes readily available for energy during the disaster.[2]

As a result of these processes, lots of energy is available to your leg muscles. There's a burst of activity; you leave the lion in the dust and arrive at the restaurant only a smidgen late for your 5:45 anticipatory insulin secretion.

The scenario I've been outlining is basically a strategy to shunt energy from storage sites like fat to muscle during an emergency. But it doesn't make adaptive sense to automatically fuel, say, your arm muscles while you're running away from a predator if you happen to be an upright human. It turns out that the body has solved this problem. Glucocorticoids and the other hormones of the stress response also act to block energy uptake into muscles and into fat tissue. But somehow the individual muscles that are exercising during the emergency have a means to override this blockade and to grab all the nutrients floating around in the circulation. The net result is that you shunt energy from fat and from *nonexercising* muscle to the exercising ones.

What if you *can't* mobilize energy during a crisis? This is what occurs in Addison's disease, where people cannot secrete adequate amounts of glucocorticoids, or in Shy-Drager syndrome, where it is epinephrine and norepinephrine that are inadequate and unable to mobilize the body during energetic demands. Obviously, the lion is more likely to feast. And in a more subtle scenario, what if you live in a Westernized society and tend to have a somewhat underactive stress response? Just as obviously, you'll have trouble mobilizing energy in response to the demands of daily life. And that is precisely what is seen in individuals with *chronic fatigue syndrome*, which is characterized by, among other things, too low levels of glucocorticoids in the bloodstream (Raison & Miller, 2003).

SO WHY DO WE GET SICK?

You most definitely want to have a metabolic stress response if you're evading a lion, and even if you are doing anything as taxing as walking up a flight of stairs (or getting up in the morning, the time of day when our glucocorticoid levels normally peak). But what about the more typical scenario for us, one of turning on the stress response too often, for months on end? We get into metabolic trouble for many of the same reasons that constantly running to the bank and drawing on your account is a foolish way to handle your finances.

On the most basic level, it's inefficient. Another financial metaphor may help. Suppose you have some extra money and decide to put it away for a while in a high-interest account. If you agree not to touch the money for a certain period (six months, two years, whatever), the bank agrees to give you a higher-than-normal rate of interest. And, typically, if you request the money earlier, you will pay a penalty for the early withdrawal. Suppose, then, that you happily deposit your money on these terms. The next day you develop the financial jitters, withdraw your money, and pay the penalty. The day after, you change your mind again, put the money back in, and sign a new agreement, only to change your mind again that afternoon, withdraw the money, and pay another penalty. Soon you've squandered half your money on penalties.

In the same way, every time you store energy away from the circulation and then return it, you lose a fair chunk of the potential energy.[3] It takes energy to shuttle those nutrients in and out of the bloodstream, to power the enzymes that glue them together (into proteins, triglycerides, and glycogen) and the other enzymes that then break them apart, and to fuel the liver during that gluconeogenesis trick. In effect, you are penalized if you activate the stress response too often: you wind up expending so much energy that, as a first consequence, you tire more readily—just plain old everyday fatigue.

As a second consequence, your muscles can waste away, although this rarely happens to a significant degree. Muscle is chock-full of proteins. If you are chronically stressed, constantly triggering the breakdown of proteins, your muscles never get the chance to rebuild. Fortunately, while they atrophy ever so slightly each time your body activates this component of the stress response, it requires a really extraordinary amount of stress for this to happen to a serious extent. Sometimes clinicians give patients massive doses of synthetic glucocorticoids. In this scenario, significant amounts of *myopathy*—atrophy of muscle—can occur, of a type similar to that seen in people who are bedridden for long periods.[4]

Finally, another problem with constantly mobilizing the metabolic stress response is that you don't want to have tons of fat and glucose perpetually circulating in your bloodstream. That increases the chances of the stuff glomming on to some damaged blood vessel and worsening atherosclerosis. Cholesterol also plays into this. As is well understood, there is "bad" cholesterol, also known as low-density lipoprotein-associated cholesterol (LDL) and "good" cholesterol (high-density lipoprotein-associated cholesterol, HDL). LDL cholesterol is the type that gets added to an atherosclerotic plaque, whereas HDL is cholesterol that has been removed from plaques and is on its way to be degraded in the liver. As a result of this distinction, your total level of cholesterol in the bloodstream is not actually a meaningful number. You want to know how much of each type you have, and lots of LDL and minimal HDL are independently bad news. The amount of vascular inflammation, as measured by C-reactive protein levels, is the best predictor out there of cardiovascular disease risk. Nonetheless, you don't want to have tons of LDL cholesterol floating around and not enough HDL to counteract it.

During stress, you increase LDL cholesterol levels and decrease HDL (Stoney & West, 1997).[5] Therefore, if you are stressed too often, the metabolic features of the stress response can increase your risks of cardiovascular disease. This becomes particularly relevant with diabetes.

JUVENILE DIABETES

There are multiple forms of diabetes, and two are relevant to this chapter.[6] The first is known as juvenile diabetes (or Type 1, insulin-dependent diabetes). For reasons that are just being sorted out, in some people the immune system decides that the cells in the pancreas that secrete insulin are, in fact, foreign invaders and attacks them. This destroys those cells, leaving the person with little ability to secrete insulin. For equally mysterious reasons, this tends to hit people relatively early in life (hence the "juvenile" part of the name), although, to add to the mystery, in recent decades the rate at which adults—even middle-aged adults—are getting diagnosed with juvenile diabetes is climbing.

Because the person can no longer secrete adequate amounts of insulin (if any), there is little ability to promote the uptake of glucose (and, indirectly, fatty acids) into target cells. Cells starve, which is big trouble—not enough energy, organs don't function right, and so on. In addition, there's now all that glucose and fatty acid circulating in the bloodstream—oleaginous hoodlums with no place to go, and soon there's atherosclerotic trouble there as well. The circulating stuff gums up the blood vessels in the kidneys, causing them to fail. The same can occur in the eyes, causing blindness.[7] Blood vessels elsewhere in the body are clogged, causing little strokes in those tissues and, often, chronic pain. With enough glucose in the circulation, it begins to stick to proteins, Velcroing proteins together that have no business being connected and knocking them out of business. None of this is good.

What is the best way to manage insulin-dependent diabetes? As we all know, by accommodating that dependency with insulin injections. If you're diabetic, you never want your insulin levels to get too low—cells are deprived of energy, circulating glucose levels get too high. But you also don't want to take too much insulin. For complex reasons, this deprives the brain of energy, potentially putting you into shock or a coma and damaging neurons. The better the metabolic control in a diabetic, the fewer the complications and the longer the life expectancy. Thus, it's a major task for this type of diabetic to keep things just right—to keep food intake and insulin dosages balanced with respect to activity, fatigue, and so on. And this is an area where there has been extraordinary technological progress enabling diabetics to monitor blood glucose levels minute by minute and make minuscule changes in insulin dosages accordingly.

How does chronic stress affect this process? First, the hormones of the stress response cause even more glucose and fatty acids to be mobilized into the bloodstream. For a juvenile diabetic, this increases the likelihood of the now familiar pathologies of glucose and fatty acids gumming up in the wrong places.

Another, more subtle problem occurs with chronic stress as well. When something stressful happens, you don't just block insulin secretion. Basically, the brain doesn't quite trust the pancreas not to keep secreting a little insulin, so a second step occurs. As noted earlier, during stress, glucocorticoids act on fat cells throughout the body to make them less *sensitive* to insulin, just in case there's some still floating around (Rizza, Mandarino, & Gerich, 1982). Fat cells then release some newly discovered hormones that get other tissues, like muscle and liver, to stop responding to insulin as well (Saltiel & Kahn, 2001; Steppan et al., 2001; Abel et al., 2001). Stress promotes insulin resistance (Brandi et al., 1993). (And when people get into this diabetic state because they are taking large amounts of synthetic glucocorticoid to control any of a variety of diseases, they have succumbed to "steroid diabetes.")

Why is this stress-induced insulin resistance bad for someone with juvenile diabetes? They have everything nice and balanced, with a healthy diet, a good sensitivity to their body's signals as to when a little insulin needs to be injected, and so on. But throw in some chronic stress, and suddenly insulin doesn't work quite as well, causing people to feel terrible until they figure out that they need to inject more of the stuff—which can make cells even more resistant to insulin, spiraling the insulin requirements upward until the period of stress is over with, at which point it's not clear when to start getting the insulin dose down because different parts of the body regain their insulin sensitivity at different rates. The perfectly balanced system is completely upended.

Stress, including psychological stress, can wreak havoc with metabolic control in a juvenile diabetic (Moberg, Kollind, Lins, & Adamson, 1994). In one demonstration of this, diabetics were exposed to an experimental stressor (speaking in public) and their glucocorticoid secretion was monitored. Those who tended to have the largest stress response under those circumstances were the ones least likely to have their diabetes well controlled (Dutour et al., 1996). Moreover, in related studies, those who had the strongest emotional reactions to an experimental stressor tended to have the highest blood glucose levels (Stabler, Morris, Litton, Feinglos, & Surwit, 1986).

Stress may sneak in another way. Some careful studies have shown higher rates of major stressors suffered by people during the three years before the onset of their juvenile diabetes than would be expected by chance (e.g., Robinson & Fuller, 1985). Does this mean that stress can make the immune system more likely to attack the pancreas? There is a little bit of evidence for this. A more likely explanation is built around the fact that once the immune system begins to attack the pancreas (that is, once the diabetes has started), it takes a while before the symptoms become apparent. By having all the adverse effects just talked about, stress can speed up the whole process, making the person notice sooner that he or she is just not feeling right.

Thus, frequent stress and/or big stress responses might increase the odds of getting juvenile diabetes, accelerate the development of the diabetes, and, once it is established, cause major complications in this life-shortening disease. Clearly, this is a population in which successful stress management is critical.[8]

ADULT-ONSET DIABETES

In adult-onset diabetes (type 2, non–insulin-dependent diabetes), the trouble is not too little insulin, but the failure of the cells to *respond* to insulin. Another name for the disorder is thus insulin-*resistant* diabetes. The problem here arises with the tendency of many people to put on weight as they age (Andres, 1971; Davidson, 1979).[9] With enough fat stored away, the fat cells essentially get full (see Figure 10.1); by the time you are an adolescent, the number of fat cells you have is fixed, so if you put on weight, the individual fat cells are distended. Yet another heavy meal, a burst of insulin trying to promote more fat storage by the fat cells, and the fat cells eventually refuse—"Tough luck. I don't care if you are insulin; we're completely full." No room at the inn. The fat cells become less responsive to insulin trying to promote more fat storage (Hirosumi et al., 2002; Ukkola & Santaniemi, 2002; Alper, 2000), and less glucose is taken up by these cells.[10] The overstuffed fat cells even release hormones that trigger other fat cells and muscle into becoming insulin resistant.

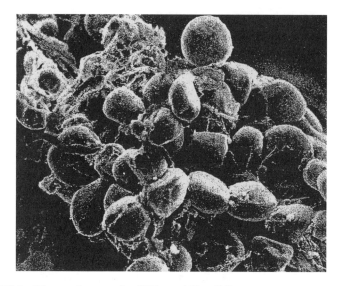

Figure 10.1. Photomicrograph of Bloated Fat Cells

Do the cells now starve? Of course not, the abundant amounts of fat stored in them was the source of the trouble in the first place. The body gets into trouble because of all that circulating glucose and fatty acid damaging blood vessels. Same old problem. And if the adult-onset diabetes goes on for a while, an additional, miserable development can occur. Your body has become insulin resistant, and your pancreas responds by secreting even more insulin than usual. You're still resistant, so the pancreas secretes even more. Back and forth, your pancreas pumping out ever higher levels of insulin, trying to be heard. Eventually, this burns out the insulin-secreting cells in the pancreas, actually destroying them. So you finally get your adult-onset diabetes under control, thanks to losing weight and exercising, and you discover you've now got juvenile diabetes, thanks to that damage to your pancreas (Bell & Polonsky, 2001; Mathis, Vence, & Benoist, 2001).

How does chronic stress affect adult-onset diabetes? Once again, constantly mobilizing glucose and fatty acids into the bloodstream adds to the atherosclerotic glomming. And there's that problem of the stress response instructing your fat cells to become less responsive to insulin. Suppose that you're in your sixties, overweight, and just on the edge of insulin resistance. Along comes a period of chronic stress with those stress hormones repeatedly telling your cells what a great idea it is to be insulin resistant. Enough of this and you pass the threshold for becoming overtly diabetic.[11]

Why is any of this worth paying attention to? Because there is a worldwide epidemic of adult-onset diabetes going on, especially in the United States (Wickelgren, 1998; Friedman, 2003; Kluger, 2000). As of 1990, about 15 percent of Americans over age 65 had adult-onset diabetes. That was considered a health disaster then. As of a decade later, there's been a

33 percent increase above that, and among middle-aged adults as well. And this disease of aging is suddenly hitting far younger people as well—in the last decade, there's been a 70 percent increase in its incidence among thirty-year-olds. In addition, something like 20 million Americans are "pre-diabetic"—barreling toward a formal diagnosis. Adult-onset diabetes has even become more prevalent among kids than juvenile diabetes, which is pretty horrifying. Moreover, as people in the developing world are first being exposed to Westernized diets, not only do they develop diabetes but they develop it at a faster rate than do Westerners, for reasons that are probably both cultural and genetic.[12] This once-nonexistent disease afflicts an estimated 300 million people worldwide and killed 200,000 Americans in 2003.

What's this about? It's obvious. Despite the impression that everyone spends their days eating low-fat, low-carb, low-cholesterol, cardboard diets and power walking uphill while loudly reciting the writings of Atkins or Ornish, with each passing year we are eating more food—more junk food—and exercising less. Twenty percent of Americans are now technically "obese" (versus 12 percent in 1990), and 54 percent are "overweight" (versus 44 percent then). To paraphrase allostasis theorist Joseph Eyer, prosperity has become a cause of death.[13]

METABOLIC SYNDROME/SYNDROME X

In the well-entrenched tradition of medical compartmentalizing, there's a whole set of things that can go wrong in you that would get you sent to a cardiologist, whereas a bunch of different problems would get you turfed to an internal medicine doc who specializes in diabetes. With any luck, they'd even confer with each other now and then. Your metabolic and cardiovascular systems are intimately interconnected. "Metabolic syndrome" (also known as "Syndrome X") is a new term recognizing this interconnection.[14] It's actually not so new, having been formalized in the late 1980s by Gerald Reaven of Stanford University. It's just become tremendously trendy in the past few years (so trendy that it's even been described in a population of wild baboons who forage through the desserts in a garbage dump at a tourist lodge in East Africa; see Banks, Altmann, Sapolsky, Phillips-Conroy, & Morley, 2003).

Make a list of some of the things that can go wrong with the metabolic or cardiovascular systems: Elevated insulin levels in the blood. Elevated glucose levels. Elevated systolic and diastolic blood pressure. Insulin resistance. Too much LDL cholesterol. Too little HDL. Too much fat or cholesterol in the blood. Suffer from a subset of these, and you've got Metabolic syndrome (the formal diagnosis involves "one or more" from a list of some of these problems, and "two or more" from a list of the others).[15] The syndrome-ness is a way of stating that if you have a subset of those symptoms, you're probably heading toward the rest of them, since they're all one or two steps away from each other. Have elevated insulin levels, low HDL, and abdominal obesity and the chances are pretty good you're going to get insulin resistance. Have elevated LDL cholesterol, high blood pressure, and insulin resistance, and you're likely to be obese soon. Another bunch and they predict hypertension (Vitaliano et al., 2002).

Subsets of these clusters of traits not only predict each other but also collectively predict major disease outcomes, such as heart attacks or stroke, and mortality rates. This was shown with particular subtlety in an impressive study carried out by a team headed by Teresa Seeman of UCLA (Seeman, McEwen, Rowe, & Singer, 2001). Medicine normally works in diagnostic categories: have glucose levels above X, and it's official you have hyperglycemia. Have blood pressure levels above Z, you're hypertensive. But how about if your glucose levels, blood pressure, HDL cholesterol, and so on are all in the normal range, but all of them are getting near the edge of where you have to start worrying? In other words, what if no measure is abnormal, but there's an abnormally large number of measures that are *almost* abnormal? Technically, nothing is wrong, but it is obvious that things are not right. What Seeman and her colleagues did was to take more than a thousand study subjects, all over age 70, none of whom was certifiably sick—that is to say, none of those measures were technically abnormal—and to see how they were doing on all those Metabolic syndrome measures. They threw in some other measures as well, including resting levels of glucocorticoids, epinephrine, and norepinephrine, combining the insights into these measures mathematically. Collectively, this information was significantly predictive of who was going to have heart disease, a decline in cognitive or physical functioning, and mortality—far more predictive than subsets of those variables alone.

This is the essence of that "allostasis" concept, of keeping things in balance through interactions among different, far-flung systems in the body. This is also the essence of the wear-and-tear concept of "allostatic load," a formal demonstration that, even if there's no single measure that's certifiably wrong, if there are enough things that are not quite right, you're still in trouble. And, as the final, obvious point, this is also the essence of what stress does. No single disastrous effect, no lone gunman. Instead, kicking and poking and impeding, here and there, make this a bit worse, that a bit less effective. Thus making it more likely for the roof to cave in at some point.

NOTES

1. The basics of this vastly complicated subject—involving storage tissues throughout the body, a variety of different hormonal messengers, and the liver as Grand Central Station for various nutrients coming and going—are covered in any physiology textbook. A fairly lucid presentation of the subject on an introductory college level can be found in Vander, Sherman, & Luciano (1994). For a discussion of how stress causes energy mobilization, see Mizock (1995). Note that this discusses big-time stressors in humans (sepsis, burns, and trauma); the same principles hold for the more subtle ones that dominate this book.

2. Recent findings about the workings of gluconeogenesis can be found in Herzig et al. (2003) and Yoon et al. (2001).

3. The inefficiency of the repeated activation of the metabolic stress-response is horrendously complicated. Vander et al. (1994) will teach the general principle that it is inefficient to repeatedly store away energy and then reverse the process by mobilizing it. However, in order to gain a detailed, quantitative understanding of it, one must become something of an accountant—learning what the currency of energy in the body is and how much it costs to make all those deposits and withdrawals in the body's metabolic banks. For this, one must consult biochemistry texts (typically, of the early graduate school level of difficulty); among the best is Stryer (1995).

4. For a classic demonstration of this, see Kaplan & Shimizu's "Effects of Cortisol on Amino Acids in Skeletal Muscle and Plasma" (1963) (cortisol is the glucocorticoid found in humans and primates). For some more recent findings, see Hong & Forsberg (1995).

5. It can be bad news to frequently boost LDL levels because of frequent stressors. But, independent from that, it is also not a good sign if, for any given stressor, you have a particularly large LDL increase. Studies have shown that the offspring of people with heart disease tend to have atypically large LDL responses to stress, suggesting a vulnerability factor that has been passed on to them.

6. The workings of the two types of diabetes mellitus dominate chapters of every endocrinology textbook. For a review of the autoimmune features of insulin-dependent diabetes, see Andre et al. (1996). For a classic demonstration that type 2 (adult-onset) diabetes involves impaired sensitivity to insulin, rather than impaired secretion of insulin, see Reaven, Bernstein, Davis, & Olefsky (1976). For demonstrations that the insulin resistance arises from a loss of insulin receptors, see Gavin, Roth, Neville, de Meyts, & Buell (1974). For a discussion of how the insulin resistance also arises from the remaining insulin receptors not working properly (what is called a "post-receptor" defect), see Flier (1983). Finally, despite the primary defect of target tissue resistance to insulin's actions, a subset of patients also has a defect in the secretion of insulin. The mechanisms underlying this are reviewed by Unger (1991).

7. One of the puzzles of how diabetes affects your health has been solved. It is relatively easy to understand how extra glucose in the bloodstream can clog blood vessels and cause damage. One of the mysteries, however, is why high levels of circulating glucose damage the eye (diabetes is the leading cause of blindness in this country). It turns out that glucose can stick to all sorts of proteins, causing them to form aggregates; indeed, because of its structure, glucose can stick onto proteins without the aid of enzymes to mediate the process, something called *nonenzymatic modification*. Once glucose fuses onto these proteins, they have to be broken apart and replaced. However, in some tissues—such as the lens of the eye—proteins are not recycled very frequently, and those cells are stuck with the fused mess. For a discussion of the nonenzymatic chemistry of sugars, focusing on its implications for aging and adult-onset diabetes, see Lee & Cerami (1990). Hyperglycemia can cause vascular damage even in nondiabetics: this is because of the nonenzymatic modification of glucose just discussed; see Schmidt et al. (1994). For more mechanisms by which hyperglycemia can be damaging, see Brownlee (2001).

8. A major challenge for diabetologists in their attempt to keep the disease under control in their patients is that juvenile diabetes is often occurring in juveniles who stress their system by behaving in ways that are, well, juvenile—eating the wrong things, skipping meals, not getting enough sleep. A major management headache. See Davidson, Boland, & Grey (1997).

9. Insulin-resistant diabetes seems not to be an obligatory part of aging. If people do not put on weight as they age, as is usually the case among people in

non-Westernized populations, they show no increased risk of this disease. Aging rats and aging humans in our own society do not become more glucose-intolerant with age, so long as they remain active and lean (Reaven & Reaven, 1985). The disease is not, therefore, a normal feature of aging; instead, it is a disease of inactivity and fat surplus (Goldberg & Coon, 1987), conditions that just happen to be more common with age in some societies.

10. The careful reader may be confused at this point—if insulin regulates glucose uptake, why does it influence the amount of fat being stored in fat cells? For immensely complex reasons that I once understood for a few hours for a final exam, the storage of fat as triglycerides requires glucose uptake.

11. Glucocorticoids and stress can exacerbate the symptoms of insulin-resistant diabetes (Surwit, Ross, & Feinglos, 1991; Surwit & Williams, 1996). (For a study that does not show an association between stress and worsening of symptoms, see Pibernik-Okanovic, Roglic, Prasek, & Metelko, 1993.) Stress causes insulin resistance and metabolic imbalances even in nondiabetics (Raikkonen, Keltikangas-Jarvinen, Adlercreutz, & Hautanen, 1996; Nilsson, Moller, & Solstad, 1995) and worsens metabolic control in nondiabetics who are at genetic risk for diabetes (Esposito-Del Puente et al., 1994).

12. For cultural reasons for the onset of diabetes with a Westernized diet, see Sterling (2003). For genetic reasons—and a demonstration of extremely low rates of insulin-resistant diabetes in non-Westernized populations, for example, the Inuit and other Native Americans, New Guinea islanders, inhabitants of rural India, and North African nomads—see Table 5 in Eaton, Konner, & Shostak (1988).

The low rates of insulin-resistant diabetes in non-Westernized populations pose a fascinating mystery. If these people begin eating Westernized diets, they get astonishingly high rates of insulin-resistant diabetes. Part of this has an obvious explanation: once these various groups gain entrée into our world of packaged food and processed sugars, they tend to eat themselves into obesity (and, thus, high rates of this diabetes). However, the mystery is that, given the same diet and degree of obesity, most people in the developing world are at greater risk for such diabetes than people in Western societies. Diabetes rates soar among Mexicans and Japanese after they emigrate to the United States, among Asian Indians moving to Britain, and among Yemenite Jews moving to Israel. In the most striking cases, about half the adult residents of the Pacific island of Nauru have diabetes (fifteen times the rate in the United States), while more than 70 percent of the Pima people of Arizona over age 55 have diabetes. In the absence of a Western diet, there is virtually no diabetes—as a striking correlate of this, Pima in Arizona weigh an average of 60 pounds more than Pima living in Mexico, who eat a more traditional diet (Kopelman, 2000).

Why should those in the developing world be at such risk for diabetes once they start consuming a Western diet? One fascinating theory is that the gene for a propensity to diabetes is adaptive in non-Westernized settings. Normally, Westerners are inefficient at handling dietary sugar; not all of it is absorbed from the circulation, getting lost in the urine. The notion is that people of the developing world are more efficient at utilizing sugar; the second they get any in their circulation, they have a burst of insulin secretion and every bit of the sugar gets stored, instead of urinated away. This makes sense, given their tough environments with intermittent food sources, where every little bit must be exploited. And it is easy to imagine this as a genetic trait—for example, genes might alter the sensitivity with which the pancreas senses circulating glucose concentrations and releases insulin, or the sensitivity with which target tissues respond to insulin. These have been termed "thrifty genes," and at least one such candidate in fat cells has been found to have a mutation among Pima Indians (reviewed in Ezzell, 1995). Another has been related to cholesterol transport in populations in northern India (Holden, 2003).

With traditional diets in the developing world, this trigger-happy insulin secretion keeps the body from wasting any sugar. But once people begin eating a Westernized, high-sugar diet, this tendency leads to constant bursts of insulin secretion, which is more likely to cause storage tissues to become insulin resistant, leading to insulin-resistant diabetes. People in Western countries, in contrast, are theorized to have more sluggish insulin responses to sugar; the net result is less efficient storing of sugar from the circulation, but lower risk of diabetes. And why are people in Westernized societies theorized to be genetically less efficient in handling blood sugar? Because a few centuries back, as we first began eating typical Westernized diets, those people with the greatest tendency toward insulin secretion failed to survive and pass on their genes. This predicts that populations like the Nauru islanders and Pima are undergoing the same process now; in a few centuries, most of their descendents will be the offspring of the rare individuals now with the lower diabetes risk. In support of this prediction, the rate of diabetes is already beginning to decline among the Nauru islanders (Diamond, 1992a, 2003).

But at present, the existence of thrifty genes, and their differential presence in different human populations, is mostly speculative. For a nontechnical discussion of these ideas, see Diamond (1992b). For technical discussions from the originator of the idea, see Neel (1962, 1982). For some technical discussions of the change in the incidence of diabetes with Westernization, see Bennett, Rushforth, Miller, & LeCompte (1976); O'Dea, Spargo, & Nestel (1982); and Cohen, Fidel, Cohen, Furst, & Eisenberg (1979). For a discussion of other cases of thrifty genes, see Sapolsky (1997). And for evidence of the "thriftiness" of metabolism among people such as Nauru islanders, see Robinson & Johnston (1995).

13. If you learned your physiology sitting on the knee of Walter Cannon, none of this makes sense: "What's the deal with our bodies gaining all *this* weight, what happened to that 'wisdom of the body' business?" you would ask. Sterling (2003) points out that if the body worked by classical homeostatic principles of low-level, local feedback control, then adult-onset diabetes shouldn't exist. It would be avoided with a simple regulatory issue—put on a certain amount of weight, and the fat cells would tell appetite centers in the brain to stop being hungry. But it doesn't work that way. As we collectively keep putting on more weight, we collectively keep getting hungrier. Sterling points out the allostatic fact that there is a lot more to regulating appetite than simply how much fat you have stored; all sorts of higher-level factors, including numerous societal ones, tend to override the efforts of fat cells to decrease appetite.

14. For a general review of Metabolic syndrome, see Zimmet, Alberti, & Shaw (2001).

15. I'm being a bit vague here because there doesn't seem to be a consensus, as far as I can tell, as to which are the exact set of symptoms to choose from to diagnose Metabolic syndrome.

REFERENCES

Abel, E. D., Peroni, O., Kim, J. K., Kim, Y. B., Boss, O., Hadro, E., et al. (2001). Adipose-selective targeting of the GLUT4 gene impairs insulin action in muscle and liver. *Nature, 409*(6821), 729–733.

Alper, J. (2000). Biomedicine: New insights into type 2 diabetes. *Science, 289*(5476), 37–39.

Andre, I., Gonzalez, A., Wang, B., Katz, J., Benoist, C., & Mathis, D. (1996). Checkpoints in the progression of autoimmune disease: Lessons from diabetes models. *Proceedings of the National Academy of Sciences of the United States of America, 93*(6), 2260–2263.

Andres, R. (1971). Aging and diabetes. *Medical Clinics of North America, 55*(4), 835–846.

Banks, W. A., Altmann, J., Sapolsky, R. M., Phillips-Conroy, J. E., & Morley, J. E. (2003). Serum leptin levels as a marker for a Syndrome X–like condition in wild baboons. *Journal of Clinical Endocrinology and Metabolism, 88*(3), 1234–1240.

Bell, G. I., & Polonsky, K. S. (2001). Diabetes mellitus and genetically programmed defects in beta-cell function. *Nature, 414*(6865), 788–791.

Bennett, P. H., Rushforth, N. B., Miller, M., & LeCompte, P. M. (1976). Epidemiologic studies of diabetes in the Pima Indians. *Recent Progress in Hormone Research, 32*, 333–376.

Brandi, L. S., Santoro, D., Natali, A., Altomonte, F., Baldi, S., Frascerra, S., et al. (1993). Insulin resistance of stress: Sites and mechanisms. *Clinical Science, 85*(5), 525–535.

Brownlee, M. (2001). Biochemistry and molecular cell biology of diabetic complications. *Nature, 414*(6865), 813–820.

Cohen, A. M., Fidel, J., Cohen, B., Furst, A., & Eisenberg, S. (1979). Diabetes, blood lipids, lipoproteins, and change of environment: Restudy of the "new immigrant Yemenites" in Israel. *Metabolism: Clinical and Experimental, 28*(7), 716–728.

Davidson, M. (1979). The effect of aging on carbohydrate metabolism: A review of the English literature and a practical approach to the diagnosis of diabetes mellitus in the elderly. *Metabolism: Clinical and Experimental, 28*(6), 688–705.

Davidson, M., Boland, E. A., & Grey, M. (1997). Teaching teens to cope: Coping skills training for adolescents with insulin-dependent diabetes mellitus. *Journal of the Society of Pediatric Nurses, 2*, 65–72.

Diamond, J. (1992a). Human evolution: Diabetes running wild. *Nature, 357*(6377), 362–363.

Diamond, J. (1992b). Sweet death. *Natural History, 9*, 2–6.

Diamond, J. (2003). The double puzzle of diabetes. *Nature, 423*(6940), 599–602.

Dutour, A., Boiteau, V., Dadoun, F., Feissel, A., Atlan, C., & Oliver, C. (1996). Hormonal response to stress in brittle diabetes. *Psychoneuroendocrinology, 21*(6), 525–543.

Eaton, S. B., Konner, M., & Shostak, M. (1988). Stone agers in the fast lane: Chronic degenerative diseases in evolutionary perspective. *American Journal of Medicine, 84*(4), 739–749.

Esposito-Del Puente, A., Lillioja, S., Bogardus, C., McCubbin, J. A., Feinglos, M. N., Kuhn, C. M., et al. (1994). Glycemic response to stress is altered in euglycemic Pima Indians. *International Journal of Obesity and Related Metabolic Disorders, 18*(11), 766–770.

Ezzell, C. (1995). Fat times for obesity research: Tons of new information, but how does it all fit together? *Journal of NIH Research, 7*, 39–43.

Flier, J. S. (1983). Insulin receptors and insulin resistance. *Annual Review of Medicine, 34*, 145–160.

Friedman, J. M. (2003). A war on obesity, not the obese. *Science, 299*(5608), 856–858.

Gavin, J. R., 3rd, Roth, J., Neville, D. M., Jr., de Meyts, P., & Buell, D. (1974). Insulin-dependant regulation of insulin receptor concentrations: A direct demonstration in cell culture. *Proceedings of the National Academy of Sciences of the United States of America, 71*, 84–88.

Goldberg, A. P., & Coon, P. J. (1987). Non–insulin-dependant diabetes mellitus in the elderly: Influence of obesity and physical inactivity. *Endocrinology and Metabolism Clinics, 16*(4), 843–865.

Herzig, S., Hedrick, S., Morantte, I., Koo, S. H., Galimi, F., & Montminy, M. (2003). CREB controls hepatic lipid metabolism through nuclear hormone receptor PPAR-gamma. *Nature, 426*(6963), 190–193.

Hirosumi, J., Tuncman, G., Chang, L., Gorgun, C. Z., Uysal, K. T., Maeda, K., et al. (2002). A central role for JNK in obesity and insulin resistance. *Nature, 420*(6913), 333–336.

Holden, C. (2003). Race and medicine. *Science, 302*(5645), 594–596.

Hong, D. H., & Forsberg, N. E. (1995). Effect of dexamethasone on protein degradation and protease gene expression in rat L8 myotube cultures. *Molecular and Cellular Endocrinology, 108*(1–2), 199–209.

Kaplan, S. A., & Shimizu, C. S. (1963). Effects of cortisol on amino acids in skeletal muscle and plasma. *Endocrinology, 72*, 267–272.

Kluger, J. (2000). The diabetes explosion. *Time*, September 4, 58.

Kopelman, P. G. (2000). Obesity as a medical problem. *Nature, 404*(6778), 635–643.

Lee, A. T., & Cerami, A. (1990). Modifications of proteins and nucleic acids by reducing sugars: Possible role in aging. In E. Schneider & J. Rowe (Eds.), *Handbook of the Biology of Aging* (3rd ed.). New York: Academic Press.

Mathis, D., Vence, L., & Benoist, C. (2001). Beta-cell death during progression to diabetes. *Nature, 414*(6865), 792–798.

Mizock, B. (1995). Alterations in carbohydrate metabolism during stress: A review of the literature. *American Journal of Medicine, 98*, 75–84.

Moberg, E., Kollind, M., Lins, P. E., & Adamson, U. (1994). Acute mental stress impairs insulin sensitivity in IDDM patients. *Diabetologia, 37*(3), 247–251.

Neel, J. V. (1962). Diabetes mellitus: A "thrifty" genotype rendered detrimental by "progress"? *American Journal of Human Genetics, 14*, 353–362.

Neel, J. V. (1982). The thrifty gene revisited. In J. Kobberling & R. Tattersall (Eds.), *The genetics of diabetes mellitus, proceedings of the Serono Symposia*, (Vol. 47, pp. 283–293). New York: Academic Press.

Nilsson, P. M., Moller, L, & Solstad, K. (1995). Adverse effects of psychosocial stress on gonadal function and insulin levels in middle-aged males. *Journal of Internal Medicine, 237*(5), 479–486.

O'Dea, K., Spargo, R. M., & Nestel, P. J. (1982). Impact of westernization on carbohydrate and lipid metabolism in Australian Aborigines. *Diabetologia, 22*, 148–153.

Pibernik-Okanovic, M., Roglic, G., Prasek, M., & Metelko, Z. (1993). War-induced prolonged stress and metabolic control in type 2 diabetic patients. *Psychological Medicine, 23*(3), 645–651.

Raikkonen, K., Keltikangas-Jarvinen, L., Adlercreutz, H., & Hautanen, A. (1996). Psychosocial stress and the insulin resistance syndrome. *Metabolism: Clinical and Experimental, 45*(12), 1533–1538.

Raison, C. L., & Miller, A. H. (2003). When not enough is too much: The role of insufficient glucocorticoid signaling in the pathophysiology of stress-related disorders. *American Journal of Psychiatry, 160*(9), 1554–1565.

Reaven, G. M., & Bernstein, R., Davis, B., & Olefsky, J. M. (1976). Nonketotic diabetes mellitus: Insulin deficiency or insulin resistance? *American Journal of Medicine, 60,* 80–88.

Reaven, G. M., & Reaven, E. P. (1985). Age, glucose intolerance, and non–insulin-dependant diabetes mellitus. *Journal of the American Geriatrics Society, 33*(4), 286–290.

Rizza, R. A., Mandarino, L. J., & Gerich, J. E. (1982). Cortisol-induced insulin resistance in man: Impaired suppression of glucose production and stimulation of glucose utilization due to a postreceptor defect of insulin action. *Journal of Clinical Endocrinology and Metabolism, 54,* 131–138.

Robinson, N., & Fuller, J. H. (1985). Role of life events and difficulties in the onset of diabetes mellitus. *Journal of Psychosomatic Research, 29*(6), 583–591.

Robinson, S., & Johnston, D. G. (1995). Advantage of diabetes? *Nature, 375*(6533), 640.

Saltiel, A. R., & Kahn, C. R. (2001). Insulin signaling and the regulation of glucose and lipid metabolism. *Nature, 414*(6865), 799–806.

Sapolsky, R. M. (1997). The dangers of fallen soufflés in the developing world. In *"The Trouble with Testosterone" and Other Essays on the Biology of the Human Predicament* (pp. 197–210). New York: Scribner.

Schmidt, A. M., Hori, O., Brett, J., Yan, S. D., Wautier, J. L., & Stern, D. (1994). Cellular receptors for advanced glycation end products: Implications for induction of oxidant stress and cellular dysfunction in the pathogenesis of vascular lesions. *Arteriosclerosis and Thrombosis, 14*(10), 1521–1528.

Schwartz, M. W., Woods, S. C., Porte, D., Jr., Seeley, R. J., & Baskin, D. G. (2000). Central nervous system control of food intake. *Nature, 404*(6778), 661–671.

Seeman, T. E., McEwen, B. S., Rowe, J. W., & Singer, B. H. (2001). Allostatic load as a marker of cumulative biological risk: MacArthur studies of successful aging. *Proceedings of the National Academy of Sciences of the United States of America, 98*(8), 4770–4775.

Stabler, B., Morris, M., Litton, J., Feinglos, M., & Surwit, R. (1986). Differential glycemic response to stress in type A and type B individuals with IDDM. *Diabetes Care, 9*(5), 550–552.

Steppan, C. M., Bailey, S. T., Bhat, S., Brown, E. J., Banerjee, R. R., Wright, C. M., et al. (2001). The hormone resistin links obesity to diabetes. *Nature, 409*(6818), 307–312.

Sterling, P. (2003). Principles of allostasis: Optimal design, predictive regulation, pathophysiology and rational therapeutics. In J. Schulkin (Ed.), *Allostasis, homeostasis, and the costs of adaptation* (pp. 17–64). Cambridge, MA: MIT Press.

Stoney, C. M., & West, S. G. (1997). Lipids, personality, and stress: Mechanisms and modulators. In M. Hillbrand & R. T. Spitz (Eds.), *Lipids and human behavior* (pp. 47–66). Washington, DC: APA Books.

Stryer, L. (1995). *Biochemistry* (4th ed.). New York: W. H. Freeman.

Surwit, R. S., Ross, S. L., & Feinglos, M. N. (1991). Stress, behavior, and glucose control in diabetes mellitus. In P. M. McCabe, N. Schneiderman, T. M. Field, & J. S. Skyler (Eds.), *Stress, coping and disease* (pp. 97–117). Hillsdale, NJ: Erlbaum.

Surwit, R. S., & Williams, P. G. (1996). Animal models provide insight into psychosomatic factors in diabetes. *Psychosomatic Medicine, 58*(6), 582–589.

Ukkola, O., & Santaniemi, M. (2002). Adiponectin: A link between excess adiposity and associated comorbidities? *Journal of Molecular Medicine* (Berlin), *80*(11), 696–702.

Unger, R. (1991). Role of impaired glucose transport by cells in the pathogenesis of diabetes. *Journal of NIH Research, 3,* 77–80.

Vander, A., Sherman, J., and Luciano, D. (1994), *Human physiology: The mechanisms of body function* (6th ed.). New York: McGraw-Hill.

Vitaliano, P. P., Scanlan, J. M., Zhang, J., Savage, M. V., Hirsch, I. B., & Siegler, I. C. (2002). A path model of chronic stress, the metabolic syndrome, and coronary heart disease. *Psychosomatic Medicine, 64*(3), 418–435.

Wickelgren, I. (1998). Obesity: How big a problem? *Science, 280*(5368), 1364–1367.

Yoon, J., Puigserver, P., Chen, G., Donovan, J., Wu, Z., Rhee, J., et al. (2001). Control of hepatic gluconeogenesis through the transcriptional coactivator PGC-1. *Nature, 413*(6852), 131–138.

Zimmet, P., Alberti, K., & Shaw, J. (2001). Global and societal implications of the diabetes epidemic. *Nature, 414*(6865), 782–787.

CHAPTER 11

Psychological Factors and Immunity in HIV Infection: Stress, Coping, Social Support, and Intervention Outcomes

Susan Kennedy

The relationships among psychological variables, changes in immune and endocrine function, and possible health outcomes have long been of interest to researchers and practitioners. It has been only recently, however, that these complex relationships have begun to be more clearly understood. There is now substantial evidence that cells of the immune system interact with the nervous and endocrine systems (e.g., Ader, Felten, & Cohen, 1991). For example, lymphocytes possess receptor sites for a number of neurotransmitters and neuroendocrine substances, respond to signals from the brain, and relay information back to the nervous and endocrine systems (Ader et al., 1991; Blalock, 1989; Blalock, Bost, & Smith, 1985; Carr & Blalock, 1989; Felten, Felten, Carlson, Olschowka, & Livnat, 1985). It is believed that psychological factors may have effects on immune function through these neuroimmune-endocrine pathways.

To explore the possible immune effects of psychological factors in humans, early work in psychoneuroimmunology examined changes in immune responses in healthy individuals experiencing stressful life events. A number of stressful events, including marital disruption, bereavement, and caregiving, were shown to have negative effects on several immune measures (Bartrop, Lazarus, Luckhurst, Kiloh, & Penny, 1977; Kiecolt-Glaser, Fisher et al., 1987; Kiecolt-Glaser, Glaser et al., 1987; Kiecolt-Glaser et al., 1988; Schleifer, Keller, Camerino, Thornton, & Stein, 1983).

In more recent studies investigating possible health consequences of stressful experiences, healthy medical students who reported higher stress levels during academic examinations were slower to produce antibody to a hepatitis-B vaccine (Glaser et al., 1992). In addition, elderly adults providing care for a spouse with Alzheimer's disease were impaired in their antibody response to an influenza virus vaccine relative to a well-matched

From David I. Mostofsky, David H. Barlow, eds., *The Management of Stress and Anxiety in Medical Disorders*. Published by Allyn and Bacon, Boston, MA. Copyright 2000 by Pearson Education. Reprinted by permission of the publisher.

group of comparison subjects (Kiecolt-Glaser, Glaser, Gravenstein, Malarkey, & Sheridan, 1996). Moreover, the stress associated with caregiving has been found to significantly impair the healing of an experimentally induced wound in a group of thirteen elderly women (Kiecolt-Glaser, Marucha, Malarkey, Mercado, & Glaser, 1995). Collectively these studies suggest that in otherwise healthy individuals, stressful life events may have health-related outcomes, including increased susceptibility to infectious disease or more prolonged recovery times from injury or surgical procedures (Glaser et al., 1992; Kiecolt-Glaser et al., 1995; Kiecolt-Glaser et al., 1996).

Further support for possible stress-associated health effects was shown in a series of studies by Cohen and colleagues. Subjects in these studies who reported higher levels of stress or who were experiencing more stressful events were more likely to develop cold symptoms than individuals reporting lower stress levels (Cohen, Tyrrell, & Smith, 1991, 1993). In a later study (Cohen, Doyle, Skoner, Rabin, & Gwaltney, 1997), persons with more social ties (including ties to family and friends, job, and community) were most resistant to developing colds.

The importance of healthy social relationships to immune competence and disease progression has been widely studied, with social support generally found to be associated with better prognosis of disease outcome in cancer patients (e.g., Levy, Herberman, Maluish, Schlien, & Lippman, 1985), healthier immune outcomes in divorced or separated women (Kiecolt-Glaser, Fisher, et al., 1987), and stronger immune responses in a group of current and former elderly caregivers (Esterling, Kiecolt-Glaser, & Glaser, 1996).

The growing evidence that stress might impact on immune function has raised the important question of whether behavioral interventions might be effective in strengthening immune responses in populations with chronic illness. Work with cancer patients by Fawzy and colleagues (Fawzy et al., 1990, 1993) found enhanced immune function in a group of malignant melanoma patients randomly assigned to an intervention program consisting of stress management techniques and coping strategies. The benefits of the intervention were apparent at a six-year follow-up, which indicated lower mortality and lower disease recurrence in the intervention subjects (Fawzy et al., 1993).

Spiegel and colleagues also found beneficial effects of intervention in a group of breast cancer patients. Women in this study, who were randomly assigned to yearlong weekly intervention sessions, had significantly longer survival times than women in the no-intervention group, and at a ten-year follow-up, the only survivors from the study were women who had been members of the intervention group (Spiegel, Bloom, Kraemer, & Gottheil, 1989).

Acquired immune deficiency syndrome (AIDS) was first brought to the attention of the public in the early 1980s, as descriptions of rare and debilitating infections and cancers surfaced in a sample of homosexual men. Since that time, the human immunodeficiency virus (HIV) has been identified as the etiologic agent of AIDS, and a constellation of symptoms has been described that characterize the illness, including neuronal damage and subsequent dementia, significant weight loss ("wasting"), opportunistic infections, lymphoma, and Kaposi's sarcoma. These symptoms are the result of the profound immunosuppression associated with HIV infection.

Importantly, however, many individuals infected with HIV often remain asymptomatic for a number of years, while others develop symptoms of AIDS more quickly following initial infection (Curran et al., 1988; Kaplan, Wofsky, & Volberding, 1987; Munoz et al., 1988). The variability in disease progression has prompted a number of researchers to examine the relationships between psychological factors, subsequent immune changes, and health status in HIV-infected individuals. This question is of utmost importance as psychological variables may have the most significant health outcomes in individuals whose immune systems are already compromised, such as HIV-infected persons or persons with AIDS (Kiecolt-Glaser & Glaser, 1992).

This chapter will begin with a brief overview of the immunology of HIV and AIDS. Studies will then be presented that examine the impact of stressful events and coping on immune changes and health status in HIV-infected individuals. The importance of social relationships will then be discussed, followed by a discussion of studies that examine the outcomes of behavioral or cognitive interventions in HIV-infected individuals.

IMMUNOPATHOLOGY OF HIV INFECTION/AIDS

The distinguishing immunological parameter associated with the time course of HIV infection is a progressive decline in the number of helper/inducer T-lymphocytes (CD4 cells) (Detels et al., 1987; Fahey et al., 1990). CD4 lymphocytes are critical for a number of important immune functions, including assisting in antibody production from B-lymphocytes and stimulating replication of cytotoxic T-lymphocytes and helper/inducer T-lymphocytes by the production of interleukin 2. In addition, CD4 lymphocytes release interferon-gamma, a glycoprotein that facilitates the ability of natural killer (NK) cells to destroy cancer cells and cells that have become infected with a virus (Herberman et al., 1982; Whiteside & Herberman, 1994). Significant loss of these cells by HIV infection, therefore, renders the immune system ineffective in protecting against infectious agents and viruses.

In the laboratory, numbers of CD4 cells in a blood sample can be quantified by the use of monoclonal antibodies, which bind to particular molecules on the cell surface, thereby identifying a cell from a population of lymphocytes as a helper/inducer T-lymphocyte, an NK cell, and so on. Numbers of helper/inducer T-lymphocytes in a blood sample are often compared to numbers of suppressor/cytotoxic T-lymphocytes (CD8 cells), cells that regulate the function of helper/inducers and B-lymphocytes when their activity is no longer necessary. The ratio of helper to suppressor lymphocytes is sometimes used as an index of overall immune competence (e.g., Herbert & Cohen, 1993; Kennedy, Kiecolt-Glaser, & Glaser,

1988), with low ratios observed in AIDS patients, chemotherapy patients, and others who are immunocompromised and high ratios typical in patients with certain autoimmune diseases.

In addition to quantification of T-lymphocytes, it is also possible to assess the function of these cells by stimulating their proliferation with mitogens, substances thought to stimulate bacteria and viruses found in the environment. Decreased proliferative responses may indicate poorer lymphocyte function (Kennedy et al., 1988).

Although there are other immune changes that accompany the progression of HIV, the loss of CD4 lymphocytes is generally used as the primary marker of disease status in infected individuals. In fact, the relationship between CD4 cell loss and the appearance of AIDS-related symptoms is well established (e.g., Detels et al., 1987; Fahey et al., 1987; Patarca et al., 1996).

PSYCHOLOGICAL AND PSYCHOSOCIAL INFLUENCES ON HIV PROGRESSION

Stressful Events and Coping Style

The relationships between stressful life events, coping style, immune responses, and HIV progression have been explored by a number of investigators. Although there is some suggestion that psychological factors might have an impact on HIV progression, other studies find little evidence of these relationships.

Learning that one is positive for HIV is likely to be a significant stressor for any individual, and how one copes with HIV infection and the probable subsequent development of AIDS may be critical for the rate of progression of the infection. Ironson et al. (1990) found increased anxiety and intrusive thoughts in a sample of homosexual men following notification of their HIV-positive serostatus. However, no differences were found in lymphocyte proliferative responses to mitogens relative to prenotification baseline, suggesting a "dissociation" between psychological and immune events.

In a subsequent study, plasma cortisol levels were measured in addition to mitogen responses in a larger sample of homosexual men learning of their HIV serostatus (Antoni et al., 1991). Cortisol is an adrenal hormone that is typically elevated in times of distress, emergency, or threat. As expected, seronegative men were less distressed and anxious, and had decreased cortisol levels and increased mitogen responses, following notification of their antibody status. However, men who learned that they had tested positive for HIV also had decreased cortisol levels after notification and showed no changes in mitogen responses from baseline, despite increases in anxiety and distress.

Because HIV-positive individuals show smaller catecholamine responses to stressors relative to HIV-negative individuals (e.g., Kumar, Morgan, Szapocznik, & Eisdorfer, 1991), these paradoxical findings may be attributed to an impaired feedback loop from the adrenal gland to the pituitary and hypothalamus that results in lower pituitary-adrenal activity and lower levels of cortisol (Kumar et al., 1991).

The relationship between cognitive processing style and immune function in asymptomatic homosexual men awaiting notification of HIV serostatus was examined by Lutgendorf and colleagues (Lutgendorf, Antoni, Ironson, Klimas, Kumar, et al., 1997). Higher scores on the avoidance scale of Impact of Events Scale were associated with poorer mitogen responses as well as lower percentages of CD4 lymphocytes. In addition, higher intrusion subscale scores were also predictive of lower CD4 counts. These data suggest that one's particular style of cognitive processing may be an important predictor of subsequent immune changes in individuals with a recent diagnosis of HIV and suggest the need for future efforts aimed at cognitive interventions with these individuals.

One aspect of cognitive processing that has received considerable attention in the literature is attributional style, which refers to how one perceives and designates the causes of events in his or her environment. To explore the possibility that attributional style might be related to immune function and the onset of AIDS in HIV-positive individuals, Segerstrom, Taylor, Kemeny, Reed, and Visscher (1996) obtained CD4 counts from a group of gay men at an initial interview and eighteen months later. Men who engaged in more internal negative attributions (i.e., those who attributed more negative events to themselves) had a faster decline of CD4 lymphocytes at the eighteen-month follow-up; there was no effect, however, of attributional style on the subsequent diagnosis of AIDS.

A number of studies have examined the importance of coping style to immune changes in HIV-positive individuals. Goodkin and colleagues (Goodkin, Fuchs, Feaster, Leeka, & Rishel, 1992) found that passive coping style was associated with lower total lymphocyte counts and lower CD4 counts. Recognizing the limitations of this study due to the small sample size $(n = 11)$, the investigators performed a subsequent study using a larger sample of sixty-two asymptomatic HIV-positive gay men (Goodkin, Blaney, et al., 1992). Coping strategies were assessed using the Coping Orientations to Problems Experienced (COPE) scale, and blood samples were obtained for quantification of HIV antibody and NK cell function. Greater NK cell cytotoxicity was associated with more active styles of coping. Thus, how one adapts to the stress of a life-threatening illness may be critical for certain aspects of immune function.

Taylor, Kemeny, and colleagues have conducted a series of well-designed studies with large sample sizes examining coping style and adaptation in HIV-positive men and individuals with AIDS (e.g., Reed, Kemeny, Taylor, Wang, & Visscher, 1994; Taylor et al., 1992). In one study, 550 homosexual men who were aware of their HIV serostatus were given a series of psychological questionnaires that assessed optimism about AIDS, coping, distress levels, and perceived control over AIDS (Taylor et al., 1992). Seropositive men had more AIDS-related optimism than seronegative men; in addition, this optimism was related to an active coping style and higher levels of perceived control over AIDS in the HIV-positive group. Although it is surprising that men with a positive serostatus would be more optimistic about AIDS and perceive themselves as having control over AIDS, the researchers note that the "illusion" of optimism in HIV-positive men may serve as a way of coping (Taylor et al., 1992). Although immune measures were not taken in this study, previous work has supported a relationship between active coping style and better NK cell function in HIV-positive men (Goodkin, Fuchs, et al., 1992), and between self-esteem instability and avoidance coping in gay men (Martin & Knox, 1997).

A critical question is the extent to which coping style and adaptation might predict survival time in individuals who have developed full-blown AIDS. This question was explored in a study by Reed et al. (1994). In persons with life-threatening illnesses such as AIDS, the process of accepting one's illness and likely death is typically viewed as both adaptive and necessary (e.g., Kubler-Ross, 1987, cited in Reed et al., 1994). Curiously, however, realistic acceptance in this study was related to *shorter* survival times and could not be accounted for by other factors, such as CD4 cell count, age, distress level, or drug use. Although speculative, the authors suggest that the effect of realistic acceptance on decreased survival time in this sample may have immunologic correlates involving virus progression. In contrast to these findings, however, Ironson et al. (1994) found that denial of HIV infection was associated with lower mitogenic responses of lymphocytes and greater loss of CD4 cells, as well as increased reports of symptoms at a one-year follow-up.

Not all studies have found associations between psychological factors and immune system changes, however. Kessler et al. (1991) obtained self-reports of stressful events from a sample of HIV-positive gay men and found no relationship between these events and the onset of AIDS-related symptoms nor to numbers of CD4 lymphocytes in the six months previous to the time that initial data were obtained.

Similarly, a longitudinal study conducted by Perry, Fishman, Jacobsberg, and Frances (1992) examined the relationships between CD4 cell counts and a number of psychological variables, including anxiety, stressful events, and avoidant/intrusive thoughts about AIDS, in a sample of HIV-seropositive individuals. No relationships were obtained between psychological variables and CD4 counts at the initial time point nor at six- and twelve-month follow-ups. Finally, Vassend, Eskild, and Halvorsen (1997) found no association between passive coping, anxiety, and CD4 counts in HIV-infected persons.

Interpersonal Relationships: Social Support, Bereavement, and Depression

The importance of interpersonal relationships to health is well recognized. Social support has been found to be predictive of mortality in a group of elderly individuals (Blazer, 1982), as well as being linked to self-reports of physical symptoms in elderly persons (Cohen, Teresi, & Holmes, 1985). Cohen and Wills (1985) describe the effects of social support in terms of providing a "buffer" that might protect an individual from the potentially harmful effects of stress.

Recently the relationship between social support and immune function has been examined. Men and women who were recently divorced or separated and students who reported that they were lonely showed decreased NK cell function, lower percentages of helper T-lymphocytes, decreased mitogen responses of lymphocytes, and a greater incidence of upper respiratory tract infections that limited their daily activities (Kiecolt-Glaser, Fisher et al., 1987; Kiecolt-Glaser, Garner, Speicher, Penn, & Glaser, 1984; Kiecolt-Glaser et al., 1988).

However, the mere presence of an individual is not sufficient; rather, the quality of one's relationship with others has been found to be critical. For example, social relationships that are positive are correlated with attenuated endocrine and autonomic indices of stress (Kamarck, Manuck, & Jennings, 1990), while hostile or unstable social relationships are associated with physiological disturbances, including endocrine and immune changes (e.g., Kiecolt-Glaser et al., 1993). Moreover, in a study of divorced and married women, poorer-quality marriages were associated with more impaired immune measures (Kiecolt-Glaser, Fisher et al., 1987).

Individuals with HIV infection are faced with a number of illness-related stressors that involve coping with the likelihood of their impending death, as well as losing close friends or partners to AIDS. In fact, it is not uncommon for individuals in the gay community to experience numerous losses over time (Dean, Hall, & Martin, 1988). Thus, the question of the relationship of social relationships to immune status, HIV progression, and possible disease outcome is an important one that has been investigated by a number of researchers. Specifically, these studies have focused on the effects of social support, loss, and intimacy.

Evidence of the importance of social support in HIV-infected individuals was provided by Hays, Turner, and Coates (1992). A sample of gay men was studied longitudinally for depression levels and symptoms related to HIV infection. Higher social support satisfaction levels were found to be predictive of lower depression scores a year later. Furthermore, a specific type of social support—informational support—was the best predictor of lower depression scores at the one-year time point. Informational support may provide the individual with a realistic perspective on the nature of the illness, as well as with more practical information, including available medical and personal resources.

Straits-Tröster et al. (1994) gathered psychological data from a sample of HIV-positive homosexual men and a group of healthy controls. Blood samples were also obtained for quantification of CD4 lymphocytes. Seropositive men who described themselves as lonely perceived themselves as less competent in initiating social interaction and less competent in providing support to others. In addition, there were differences in CD4 counts between "low lonely" and "high lonely" individuals, with the lonelier HIV-infected men having significantly fewer numbers of CD4 lymphocytes, an effect that was independent of the stage of HIV infection.

Similarly, the beneficial immune consequences of social support were studied in a longitudinal investigation of HIV-infected hemophilic men (Theorell et al., 1995). Subjects in this study were given "availability of attachment" (AVAT; Theorell et al., 1995) scores based on completed questionnaires that assessed sources of emotional support. It was found that subjects with low AVAT scores had faster CD4 cell count declines, but only at the five-year time point. At earlier sample points, no differences in CD4 counts between low- and high-AVAT subjects were found.

Social support may therefore be an important mediator of immunity in individuals with HIV. In further support of this, the effects of bereavement in HIV-infected individuals who have lost a friend or partner to AIDS have been studied by a number of investigators. Losing a loved one is described as one of the most stressful events that an individual can experience (Holmes & Rahe, 1967). In early studies of immune consequences associated with bereavement, bereaved men whose wives died of an extended bout with breast cancer had significant decreases in mitogen responses of lymphocytes after her death, as compared with prebereavement levels, even though the wife's death was anticipated (Bartrop et al., 1977). Similarly, NK cell activity was found to be impaired in a sample of men during bereavement, relative to prebereavement levels (Irwin, Daniels, Bloom, Smith, & Weiner, 1987).

Kemeny et al. (1994) examined the immune correlates in a group of HIV-seropositive and HIV-seronegative homosexual men who had recently lost a close friend to AIDS. No immune differences between the bereaved and nonbereaved men were reported; however, there was a relationship between depressed mood, lower CD4 numbers, and decreased mitogen responses of lymphocytes in the nonbereaved group, suggesting that depressed mood and grief may be manifested differently in terms of the immune response.

Subsequently, Kemeny and Dean (1995) assessed CD4 cell loss and symptom onset over the course of three to four years in a group of asymptomatic HIV-positive men who had recently lost a friend to AIDS. Compared to a nonbereaved group of seropositive men, the bereaved individuals were more depressed and had significantly more somatic complaints and cognitive disturbances than nonbereaved men. In addition, bereaved individuals showed a faster decline of CD4 cell numbers, even when a number of potential confounding variables were controlled for (age, drug use, health status at the start of the study). Thus, as previously reported by Kemeny et al. (1994), a distinction was found between grief and depression, with depression related to the loss of CD4 lymphocytes but grief unrelated to cell loss. Importantly, the differences in GD4 cell decline were not apparent until two years following bereavement and remained significantly different between the groups at the three- to four-year follow-up.

A number of researchers have suggested that the level of intimacy within a social relationship may be critical for an individual's psychological well-being (e.g., Gove, Hughes, & Style, 1983; Hobfoll & Lerman, 1988). For instance, spousal relationships characterized by high intimacy levels have been associated with less psychological distress during a period of time when a son or daughter was experiencing a medical problem (Hobfoll & Lerman, 1988), possibly by offering protection against stressor effects (Cohen & Wills, 1985; Miller & Lefcourt, 1983).

The immune effects of losing an intimate partner to AIDS were examined in a group of HIV-positive men by Kemeny et al. (1995). Compared to nonbereaved men, bereaved men were found to have significantly higher levels of neopterin in serum samples (an indicator of subsequent AIDS development) as well as lower mitogen responses of lymphocytes. Contrary to what was hypothesized, there was no relationship between neopterin levels or decreased mitogenesis and depressed mood. Depressed mood was related to lower CD4 number, however, but only in the nonbereaved group.

Collectively the studies on interpersonal relationships and immune function in HIV-infected individuals are important for several reasons. First, they provide further evidence for the effect of bereavement on immune function found in previous work (Bartrop et al., 1977; Irwin et al., 1987; Schleifer et al., 1983). Second, they underscore the importance of obtaining longitudinal data from HIV-infected individuals over relatively long periods of time and at multiple sample points to provide a clearer understanding of time-sensitive immune changes related to bereavement (e.g., Kennedy, Glaser, & Kiecolt-Glaser, 1990; Theorell et al., 1995). Finally, they suggest the need for studies that further investigate the immune correlates and possible health consequences of depression versus grief (Kemeny et al., 1994, 1995).

The reports of relationships between social support, bereavement, and immune function in HIV-infected individuals have not been consistent, however. For example, Kessler et al. (1991) examined symptom onset in HIV-positive men who had been bereaved and found no relationship of bereavement to CD4 count or onset of symptoms. Work by Goodkin and colleagues (Goodkin, Blaney, et al., 1992; Goodkin, Fuchs, et al., 1992) suggested only possible relationships between social support and NK cell activity in an HIV-positive sample, but stronger associations between coping style and NK cell function.

INTERVENTION AND STRESS MANAGEMENT IN HIV INFECTION

One of the most exciting and potentially useful areas of psychoneuroimmunology research is that of the immune outcomes associated with behavioral interventions (e.g., Kiecolt-Glaser & Glaser, 1992).

For individuals with chronic illness such as HIV, interventions that might modify immune function with possible outcomes related to the progression of HIV or to symptom onset are of monumental importance. Two interventions that have been investigated in this regard are cognitive-behavioral stress management (CBSM) and aerobic exercise training.

Antoni et al. (1991) randomly assigned asymptomatic gay men to either a CBSM group or a control group. All men in the study were initially unaware of their HIV serostatus but were notified of their serostatus five weeks after the intervention began. Two blood samples, as well as psychological data, were obtained 72 hours prior to notification and a week following notification. Men who were in the CBSM group and who were found to be HIV positive had significantly higher numbers of CD4 lymphocytes and NK cells, as well as higher mitogen responses of lymphocytes;

no increases in depression scores were found for these men from the first to second sample points. In contrast, men in the control group who were HIV positive were more depressed following serostatus notification, but only slightly impaired in terms of mitogenesis and CD4 cell counts.

More recently, Lutgendorf et al. (1998) randomly assigned symptomatic HIV-positive men to either a ten-week CBSM condition or a no-intervention condition. Men in the CBSM group showed increases in coping strategies and in a number of social support measures after intervention. Of particular importance was the finding that members of the intervention group learned coping strategies that facilitated acceptance of their HIV infection. A previous study by this group (Lutgendorf, Antoni, Ironson, Klimas, Kumar, et al., 1997) found that CBSM was effective in reducing levels of distress and anxiety and in decreasing antibody titers to a human herpes virus, herpes simplex virus 2 (HSV-2). No effect of CBSM on number of CD4 lymphocytes or on other immune measures was found in this study, however.

Thus, CBSM appears to be beneficial in modulating a number of psychological and immune parameters in HIV-infected individuals. Not all studies have reported positive effects of stress management, however. Coates, McKusick, Kuno, and Stites (1989) assessed lymphocyte subset numbers, NK cell activity, and mitogen responsiveness in a sample of HIV-positive men randomly assigned to either eight weeks of stress reduction training or a control group. Pre- and posttreatment assessments were made with no significant differences found between intervention members and controls on any immune measures.

In addition to CBSM, aerobic exercise training has been investigated as a useful intervention in HIV-infected individuals. LaPerriere et al. (1990) randomly assigned a group of fifty asymptomatic gay men to either an aerobic exercise training group or a control group for five weeks prior to notification of HIV serostatus. Immune measures, as well as self-reports of distress and anxiety, were gathered 72 hours prior and one week following notification. Men who were HIV positive and who had been given aerobic exercise training were indistinguishable from seronegative men, both on measures of depression and anxiety and in terms of numbers of NK cells at the postnotification sample point. Seropositive men in the control condition, however, were more depressed and anxious and had significant decreases in NK cell numbers following notification of serostatus.

As reviewed by LaPerriere and colleagues (1997), however, studies on the effects of exercise intervention and immune changes in HIV infection must be carefully examined in terms of the stage of infection of participants, because studies that report beneficial effects of exercise have typically used subjects in the earlier stages of the infection.

CONCLUDING COMMENTS

Individuals with HIV infection are faced with a number of potentially stressful events that might influence immunity and, ultimately, disease progression. These include learning of one's seropositive status (e.g., Ironson et al., 1990) and losing friends or partners to AIDS (Kemeny et al., 1994,

1995; Kemeny & Dean, 1995). This chapter has presented findings from a number of studies suggesting that coping style and social relationships may be important modulators of stress-associated immune changes in HIV-positive individuals (e.g., Goodkin, Blaney, et al., 1992; Goodkin, Fuchs, et al., 1992; Hays et al., 1992; Lutgendorf, Antoni, Ironson, Klimas, Fletcher, et al., 1997; Straits-Tröster et al., 1994).

However, evidence for these relationships has not been consistently reported in the literature (e.g., Kessler et al., 1991; Perry et al., 1992; Vassend et al., 1997). These discrepant findings may be due, at least in part, to important differences in methodology between the studies, including differences in stage of infection at the time of study and the length of time subjects are studied, as well as differences in subject populations used (Kemeny, 1994; Uchino, Cacioppo, & Kiecolt-Glaser, 1996).

The stage of HIV infection must be considered in studies of psychosocial modulation of HIV. This may be most critical when evaluating the effects of interventions (LaPerriere et al., 1997). For example, many studies that have reported beneficial intervention effects in HIV-positive persons have been done during the asymptomatic stage of the illness (e.g., Antoni et al., 1991; LaPerriere et al., 1990). Clearly there is a need for studies similar to that of Lutgendorf et al. (1998) that examine cognitive and behavioral interventions at later stages of HIV infection, particularly once symptoms have begun to appear (Schneiderman et al., 1994).

Not unrelated to this is the inherent value of longitudinal studies. Prospective research designs that follow a cohort of HIV-positive individuals over relatively long time periods may be particularly important in studies of progressive illnesses, including HIV/AIDS (Kemeny, 1994; Theorell et al., 1995; Uchino et al., 1996), especially when one considers that meaningful changes in immunity may occur only over long periods of time in HIV-infected individuals (Kemeny, 1994). The value of longitudinal studies is seen in the study by Theorell et al. (1995), in which immune correlates of social support in HIV-positive men were seen only during the fourth and fifth years of the study, and not in the first two years. Studies such as this, therefore, underscore the need to follow subjects with HIV for extended time periods.

Although this chapter has focused primarily on studies that use homosexual men as subjects, HIV infection is certainly not limited to this population. Studies that include a diverse representation of age groups (including children with HIV) and ethnic backgrounds and that examine gender differences are crucial in investigations of psychological influences on HIV, as these factors may be related to differences in rates of HIV progression (e.g., Kemeny, 1994; Schneiderman et al., 1994).

Finally, an important methodological concern in any psychoimmunology study using human subjects is the importance of gathering data from subjects on a number of health-related behaviors, including nutritional status, sleep patterns, and drug use, as any of these may affect immunity and therefore might confound the effects of stress (e.g., Ironson et al., 1994; Kiecolt-Glaser & Glaser, 1988).

The research examining psychological contributions to HIV progression is important and promises to aid in our understanding of the ways in which coping strategies and social support might alter immune function and disease outcome. Future work in this exciting area will continue to elucidate the complex interactions among psychological variables and neuroimmune-endocrine systems, with possible outcomes to pathogenesis and health.

REFERENCES

Ader, R., Felten, D. L., & Cohen, N. (Eds.). (1991). *Psychoneuroimmunology* (2nd ed.). San Diego: Academic Press.

Antoni, M. H., Baggett, L., Ironson, G., LaPerriere, A., August, S., Klimas, N., et al. (1991). Cognitive-behavioral stress management intervention buffers distress responses and immunologic changes following notification of HIV-1 seropositivity. *Journal of Consulting and Clinical Psychology, 59*, 906–915.

Bartrop, R. W., Lazarus, L., Luckhurst, E., Kiloh, L. G., & Penny, R. (1977). Depressed lymphocyte function after bereavement. *Lancet, 1*, 834–836.

Blalock, J. E. (1989). A molecular basis for bidirectional communication between the immune and neuroendocrine systems. *Physiological Reviews, 69*, 1–32.

Blalock, J. E., Bost, K. L., & Smith, E. M. (1985). Neuroendocrine peptide hormones and their receptors in the immune system: Production, processing and action. *Journal of Neuroimmunology, 10*, 31–40.

Blazer, D. (1982). Social support and mortality in an elderly community population. *American Journal of Epidemiology, 115*, 684–694.

Carr, D. J., & Blalock, J. E. (1989). From the neuroendocrinology of lymphocytes toward a molecular basis of the network theory. *Hormone Research, 31*, 76–80.

Coates, T., McKusick, L., Kuno, R., & Stites, D. P. (1989). Stress reduction training changed number of sexual partners but not immune function in men infected with HIV. *American Journal of Public Health, 79*, 885–887.

Cohen, S., Doyle, W. J., Skoner, D. P., Rabin, B. S., & Gwaltney, J. M. (1997). Social ties and susceptibility to the common cold. *Journal of the American Medical Association, 277*, 1940–1944.

Cohen, S., Teresi, J., & Holmes, D. (1985). Social networks, stress, and physical health: A longitudinal study of an inner-city elderly population. *Journal of Gerontology, 40*, 418–486.

Cohen, S., Tyrrell, D. A., & Smith, A. P. (1991). Psychological stress and susceptibility to the common cold. *New England Journal of Medicine, 325*, 606–612.

Cohen, S., Tyrrell, D. A., & Smith, A. P. (1993). Negative life events, perceived stress, negative affect, and susceptibility to the common cold. *Journal of Personality and Social Psychology, 64*, 131–140.

Cohen, S., & Wills, T. A. (1985). Stress, social support, and the buffering hypothesis. *Psychological Bulletin, 109*, 5–24.

Curran, J. W., Jaffe, H. W., Hardy, A. M., Morgan, W. M., Selk, R. M., & Dondero, T. J. (1988). Epidemiology of HIV infection and AIDS in the United States. *Science, 239*, 610–616.

Dean, L., Hall, W. E., & Martin, J. L. (1988). Chronic and intermittent AIDS related bereavement in a panel of homosexual men in New York City. *Journal of Palliative Care, 4*, 54–57.

Detels, R., Visscher, B. R., Fahey, J. L., Sever, J. L., Gravell, M., Madden, D. L., et al. (1987). Predictors of clinical AIDS in young homosexual men in a high risk area. *International Journal of Epidemiology, 16*, 271–276.

Esterling, B. A., Kiecolt-Glaser, J. K., & Glaser, R. (1996). Psychosocial modulation of cytokine-induced natural killer cell activity in older adults. *Psychosomatic Medicine, 58,* 264–272.

Fahey, J. L., Giorgi, J. V., Martinez-Maza, O., Detels, R., Mitsuyasu, R., & Taylor, J. (1987). Immune pathogenesis of AIDS and related syndromes. *Annales de l'Institut Pasteur. Immunologie, 138,* 245–252.

Fahey, J. L., Taylor, J. M., Detels, R., Hofmann, B., Melmed, R., Nishanian, P., et al. (1990). The prognostic value of cellular and serologic markers in infection with human immunodeficiency virus type 1. *New England Journal of Medicine, 322,* 166–172.

Fawzy, F. I., Fawzy, N. W., Hyun, C. S., Elashoff, R., Guthrie, D., Fahey, J., et al. (1993). Malignant melanoma: Effects of an early structured psychiatric intervention, coping, and affective state on recurrence and survival six years later. *Archives of General Psychiatry, 50,* 681–689.

Fawzy, F. I., Kemeny, M. E., Fawzy, N. W., Elashoff, R., Morton, D., Cousins, N., et al. (1990). A structured psychiatric intervention for cancer patients. II. Changes over time in immunological measures. *Archives of General Psychiatry, 47,* 729–735.

Felten, D. L., Felten, S. Y., Carlson, S. L., Olschowka, J. A., & Livnat, S. (1985). Noradrenergic and peptidergic innervation of lymphoid tissue. *Journal of Immunology, 135*(Suppl. 2), 755s–765s.

Glaser, R., Kiecolt-Glaser, J. K., Bonneau, R. H., Malarkey, W., Kennedy, S., & Hughes, J. (1992). Stress-induced modulation of the immune response to recombinant hepatitis B vaccine. *Psychosomatic Medicine, 54,* 22–29.

Goodkin, K., Blaney, N. T., Feaster, D., Fletcher, M. A., Baum, M. K., Mantero-Atienza, E., et al. (1992). Active coping style is associated with natural killer cell cytotoxicity in asymptomatic HIV-1 seropositive homosexual men. *Journal of Psychosomatic Research, 36,* 635–650.

Goodkin, K., Fuchs, I., Feaster, D., Leeka, J., & Rishel, D. D. (1992). Life stressors and coping style are associated with immune measures in HIV-1 infection: A preliminary report. *International Journal of Psychiatry in Medicine, 22,* 155–172.

Gove, W., Hughes, M., & Style, C. B. (1983). Does marriage have positive effects on the psychological well-being of the individual? *Journal of Health and Social Behavior, 24,* 122–131.

Hays, R. B., Turner, H., & Coates, T. J. (1992). Social support, AIDS-related symptoms, and depression among gay men. *Journal of Consulting and Clinical Psychology, 60,* 463–469.

Herberman, R. B., Ortaldo, J. R., Riccardi, C., Timonen, T., Schmidt, A., Maluish, A., et al. (1982). Interferon and NK cells. In T. C. Merigan & R. M. Friedman (Eds.), *Interferons* (pp. 287–294). London: Academic Press.

Herbert, T. B., & Cohen, S. (1993). Stress and immunity in humans: A meta-analytic review. *Psychosomatic Medicine, 55,* 364–379.

Hobfoll, S. E., & Lerman, M. (1988). Personal relationships, personal attitudes, and stress resistance: Mothers' reactions to their child's illness. *American Journal of Community Psychology, 16,* 565–589.

Holmes, T., & Rahe, R. (1967). The Social Readjustment Rating Scale. *Journal of Psychosomatic Research, 11,* 213–218.

Ironson, G., Friedman, A., Klimas, N., Antoni, M., Fletcher, M. A., LaPerriere, A., et al. (1994). Distress, denial, and low adherence to behavioral interventions predict faster disease progression in gay men infected with human immunodeficiency virus. *International Journal of Behavioral Medicine, 1,* 90–105.

Ironson, G., LaPerriere, A. R., Antoni, M. H., O'Hearn, P., Schneiderman, N., Klimas, N., et al. (1990). Changes in immune and psychosocial measures as a function of anticipation and reaction to news of HIV-1 antibody status. *Psychosomatic Medicine, 52*, 247–270.

Irwin, M., Daniels, M., Bloom, E., Smith, T. L., & Weiner, H. (1987). Impaired natural killer cell activity during bereavement. *Brain, Behavior and Immunity, 1*, 98–104.

Kamarck, T. W., Manuck, S. B., & Jennings, J. R. (1990). Social support reduces cardiovascular reactivity to psychological challenge: A laboratory model. *Psychosomatic Medicine, 52*, 42–58.

Kaplan, L. D., Wofsky, C. B., & Volberding, P. A. (1987). Treatment of patients with acquired immunodeficiency syndrome and associated manifestations. *Journal of the American Medical Association, 257*, 1367–1376.

Kemeny, M. E. (1994). Stressful events, psychological responses, and progression of HIV infection. In R. Glaser & J. K. Kiecolt-Glaser (Eds.), *Handbook of human stress and immunity* (pp. 245–266). San Diego: Academic Press.

Kemeny, M. E., & Dean, L. (1995). Effects of AIDS-related bereavement on HIV progression among New York City gay men. *AIDS Education and Prevention, 7*, 36–47.

Kemeny, M. E., Weiner, H., Duran, R., Taylor, S. E., Visscher, B., & Fahey, J. L. (1995). Immune system changes after the death of a partner in HIV-positive gay men. *Psychosomatic Medicine, 57*, 547–554.

Kemeny, M. E., Weiner, H., Taylor, S. E., Schneider, S., Visscher, B., & Fahey, J. L. (1994). Repeated bereavement, depressed mood, and immune parameters in HIV seropositive and seronegative gay men. *Health Psychology, 13*, 14–24.

Kennedy, S., Glaser, R., & Kiecolt-Glaser, J. K. (1990). Psychoneuroimmunology. In J. T. Cacioppo & L. G. Tassinary (Eds.), *Principles of psychophysiology: Physical, social and inferential elements* (pp. 177–190). New York: Cambridge University Press.

Kennedy, S., Kiecolt-Glaser, J. K., & Glaser, R. (1988). Social support, stress, and the immune system. In B. R. Sarason, I. G. Sarason, & G. R. Pierce (Eds.), *Social support: An interactional view* (pp. 253–266). New York: John Wiley & Sons.

Kessler, R. C., Foster, C., Joseph, J., Ostrow, D., Wortman, C., Phair, J., et al. (1991). Stressful life events and symptom onset in HIV infection. *American Journal of Psychiatry, 148*, 733–738.

Kiecolt-Glaser, J. K., Fisher, L., Ogrocki, P., Stout, J. C., Speicher, C. E., & Glaser, R. (1987). Marital quality, marital disruption, and immune function. *Psychosomatic Medicine, 49*, 13–34.

Kiecolt-Glaser, J. K., Garner, W., Speicher, C. E., Penn, G., & Glaser, R. (1984). Psychosocial modifiers of immunocompetence in medical students. *Psychosomatic Medicine, 46*, 7–14.

Kiecolt-Glaser, J. K., & Glaser, R. (1988). Methodological issues in behavioral immunology research with humans. *Brain, Behavior and Immunity, 2*, 67–78.

Kiecolt-Glaser, J. K., & Glaser, R. (1992). Psychoneuroimmunology: Can psychological interventions modulate immunity? *Journal of Consulting and Clinical Psychology, 60*, 569–575.

Kiecolt-Glaser, J. K., Glaser, R., Gravenstein, S., Malarkey, W. B., & Sheridan, J. (1996). Chronic stress alters the immune response to influenza virus vaccine in older adults. *Proceedings of the National Academy of Sciences, 93*, 3043–3047.

Kiecolt-Glaser, J. K., Glaser, R., Shuttleworth, E. C., Dyer, C. S., Ogrocki, P., & Speicher, C. E. (1987). Chronic stress and immunity in family caregivers of Alzheimer's disease victims. *Psychosomatic Medicine, 49*, 523–535.

Kiecolt-Glaser, J. K., Kennedy, S., Malkoff, S., Fisher, L., Speicher, C. E., & Glaser, R. (1988). Marital discord and immunity in males. *Psychosomatic Medicine, 50,* 213–229.

Kiecolt-Glaser, J. K., Malarkey, W. B., Chee, M., Newton, T., Cacioppo, J. T., Mao, H. Y., et al. (1993). Negative behavior during marital conflict is associated with immunological down-regulation. *Psychosomatic Medicine, 55,* 395–409.

Kiecolt-Glaser, J. K., Marucha, P. T., Malarkey, W. B., Mercado, A. M., & Glaser, R. (1995). Slowing of wound healing by psychological stress. *Lancet, 346,* 1194–1196.

Kubler-Ross, E. (1987). *AIDS: The ultimate challenge.* New York: Collier Books.

Kumar, M., Morgan, R., Szapocznik, J., & Eisdorfer, C. (1991). Norepinephrine response in early HIV infection. *Journal of Acquired Immune Deficiency Syndromes, 4,* 782–786.

LaPerriere, A., Antoni, M. H., Schneiderman, N., Ironson, G., Klimas, N., Caralis, P., et al. (1990). Exercise intervention attenuates emotional distress and natural killer cell decrements following notification of positive serologic status for HIV-1. *Biofeedback and Self-Regulation, 15,* 229–242.

LaPerriere, A., Klimas, N., Fletcher, M. A., Perry, A., Ironson, G., Perna, F., et al. (1997). Changes in CD4+ cell enumeration following aerobic exercise training in HIV-1 disease: Possible mechanisms and practical applications. *International Journal of Sports Medicine, 18*(Suppl. 1), s56–s61.

Levy, S. M., Herberman, R. B., Maluish, A. M., Schlien, B., & Lippman, M. (1985). Prognostic risk assessment in primary breast cancer by behavioral and immunological parameters. *Health Psychology, 4,* 99–113.

Lutgendorf, S. K., Antoni, M. H., Ironson, G., Klimas, N., Fletcher, M. A., & Schneiderman, N. (1997). Cognitive processing style, mood, and immune function following HIV seropositivity notification. *Cognitive Therapy and Research, 21,* 157–184.

Lutgendorf, S. K., Antoni, M. H., Ironson, G., Klimas, N., Kumar, M., Starr, K., et al. (1997). Cognitive-behavioral stress management decreases dysphoric mood and herpes simplex virus–type 2 antibody titers in symptomatic HIV-seropositive gay men. *Journal of Consulting and Clinical Psychology, 65,* 31–43.

Lutgendorf, S. K., Antoni, M. H., Ironson, G., Starr, K., Costello, N., Zuckerman, M., et al. (1998). Changes in cognitive coping skills and social support during cognitive behavioral stress management intervention and distress outcomes in symptomatic human immunodeficiency virus (HIV) seropositive gay men. *Psychosomatic Medicine, 60,* 204–214.

Martin, J. I., & Knox, J. (1997). Self-esteem instability and its implications for HIV prevention among gay men. *Health and Social Work, 22,* 264–273.

Miller, L. C., & Lefcourt, H. M. (1983). The stress buffering function of social intimacy. *American Journal of Community Psychology, 11,* 127–139.

Munoz, A., Carey, V., Saah, A. J., Phair, J. P., Kingsley, L. A., Fahey, J. L., et al. (1988). Predictors of decline in CD4 lymphocytes in a cohort of homosexual men infected with human immunodeficiency virus. *Journal of Acquired Immune Deficiency Syndromes, 1,* 396–404.

Patarca, R., Friedlander, A., Harrington, W. J., Cabral, L., Byrnes, J. J., & Fletcher, M. A. (1996). Peripheral blood T cell subsets as prognostic indicators of chemotherapy outcome in AIDS patients with large cell lymphoma. *AIDS Research and Human Retroviruses, 12,* 645–649.

Perry, S., Fishman, B., Jacobsberg, L., & Frances, A. (1992). Relationships over 1 year between lymphocyte subsets and psychosocial variables among adults with infection by human immunodeficiency virus. *Archives of General Psychiatry, 49*, 396–401.

Reed, G. M., Kemeny, M. E., Taylor, S. E., Wang, H. Y., & Visscher, B. R. (1994). Realistic acceptance as a predictor of decreased survival time in gay men with AIDS. *Health Psychology, 13*, 299–307.

Schleifer, S. J., Keller, S. E., Camerino, M., Thornton, J. C., & Stein, M. (1983). Suppression of lymphocyte stimulation following bereavement. *Journal of the American Medical Association, 250*, 374–377.

Schneiderman, N., Antoni, M., Ironson, G., Klimas, N., LaPerriere, A., Kumar, M., et al. (1994). HIV-1, immunity, and behavior. In R. Glaser & J. K. Kiecolt-Glaser (Eds.), *Handbook of human stress and immunity*, 267–300. San Diego: Academic Press.

Segerstrom, S. C., Taylor, S. E., Kemeny, M. E., Reed, G. M., & Visscher, B. R. (1996). Causal attributions predict rate of immune decline in HIV-1 seropositive gay men. *Health Psychology, 15*, 485–493.

Spiegel, D., Bloom, J., Kraemer, H., & Gottheil, E. (1989). Effect of psychosocial treatment on survival of patients with metastatic breast cancer. *Lancet, 2*, 888–901.

Straits-Tröster, K. A., Patterson, T. L., Semple, S. J., Temoshok, L., Roth, P. G., McCutchan, J. A., et al., and the HIV Neurobehavioral Research Center Group. (1994). The relationship between loneliness, interpersonal competence, and immunologic status in HIV-infected men. *Psychology & Health, 9*, 205–219.

Taylor, S. E., Kemeny, M. E., Aspinwall, L. G., Schneider, S. G., Rodriguez, R., & Herbert, M. (1992). Optimism, coping, psychological distress, and high-risk sexual behavior among men at risk for acquired immunodeficiency syndrome (AIDS). *Journal of Personality and Social Psychology, 63*, 460–473.

Theorell, T., Blomkvist, V., Jonsson, H., Schulman, S., Berntorp, E., & Stigendal, L. (1995). Social support and the development of immune function in human immunodeficiency virus infection. *Psychosomatic Medicine, 57*, 32–36.

Uchino, B. N., Cacioppo, J. T., & Kiecolt-Glaser, J. K. (1996). The relationship between social support and physiological processes: A review with emphasis on underlying mechanisms and implications for health. *Psychological Bulletin, 119*, 488–531.

Vassend, O., Eskild, A., & Halvorsen, R. (1997). Negative affectivity, coping, immune status, and disease progression in HIV infected individuals. *Psychology & Health, 12*, 375–388.

Whiteside, T. L., & Herberman, R. B. (1994). Role of human natural killer cells in health and disease. *Clinical and Diagnostic Laboratory Immunology, 1*, 125–133.

Part III

Posttraumatic Stress

Introduction to
"Posttraumatic Stress"

This third part of our book focuses on a special type of stress reaction—posttraumatic stress disorder (PTSD), introduced by Lazarus in Chapter 2. According to the *Diagnostic and Statistical Manual*, fourth edition (*DSM-IV*; American Psychiatric Association, 1994), PTSD manifests following exposure to an extreme traumatic stressor and is characterized by the following symptoms: persistent anxiety (arousal); reexperiencing of the traumatic event, for example, through nightmares or flashbacks; and an emotional or psychological "numbing" that was not present before the trauma occurred. PTSD can be associated with extreme suffering. Over the past few years, researchers have made some progress in understanding mechanisms that are related to the development of PTSD.

In the first chapter, "Epidemiologic Studies of Trauma, Posttraumatic Stress Disorder, and Other Psychiatric Disorders," Breslau (2002) begins by describing symptoms of PTSD and stressors that may cause it. She contrasts the current diagnostic criteria for PTSD, which are delineated in *DSM-IV*, with the criteria of the prior edition of the manual *(DSM-III-R)*. With *DSM-IV*, the number of potentially traumatic events has increased. For example, with *DSM-IV*, but not with *DSM-III-R*, "sudden and unexpected" death of a loved one qualifies as a stressor that may lead to PTSD. Another addition to *DSM-IV* is that, to be diagnosed with PTSD, the individual's response must have "involved intense fear, helplessness, or horror." This reference to an individual's response acknowledges that individuals may vary in their responses to the same stressor. Notice that this evolution in the PTSD concept parallels the evolution of the general stress concept. That is, as discussed in Part I of our book, early stress researchers such as Holmes and Rahe identified major life events as stressors but failed to acknowledge individual differences in appraisal. Later, Lazarus and colleagues began to speak about individual differences in appraisal of potentially stressful life events. Breslau continues by discussing estimates of prevalence of exposure to traumatic events. She then reviews the research on risk factors for PTSD and concludes the chapter by discussing connections between PTSD and other psychiatric conditions—depression, anxiety disorders, and substance use disorders in particular.

Chapter 13, "Posttraumatic Stress Disorder and Terrorism" (Lee, Isaac, & Janca, 2002), reviews research on the psychological effects of terrorism. Based on the literature reviewed, the authors estimate that 28 to 35 percent of people who experience a terrorist attack, and possibly more, may develop PTSD. Following the attacks of September 11, 2001, 44 percent of adults in the United States experienced at least one serious stress symptom. The authors also provide some description of drug and alcohol use as a reaction to terrorism-induced stress, particular types of stress reactions in children, and the high incidence of PTSD in countries experiencing "low-intensity" wars and other forms of violence. The authors close with a discussion of prevention and treatment of PTSD.

In the third chapter in this part, "Neuropsychological Processes in Posttraumatic Stress Disorder" (Golier & Yehuda, 2002), the authors review studies about neuropsychological processes, especially memory, in PTSD patients. The authors explain that PTSD is characterized by vivid, even intrusive and unpleasant, memories of some aspects of the traumatic event. This hypermemory stands in contrast to amnesia for other aspects of the event, and possibly other memory deficits. Golier and Yehuda, through exploring the literature, seek to determine which types of memory deficits may exist with PTSD patients and whether these deficits may be part of a broader cognitive disturbance characteristic of PTSD sufferers. They describe the possibility that stress hormones such as cortisol may cause damage to the brain, especially the hippocampus, and that this is the mechanism through which memory deficits may occur (see also McEwen & Lasley, 2002, and Vasterling & Brewin, 2005, for discussions of the neuropsychology of PTSD). In conclusion, the authors state that the studies they reviewed suggest both memory and attention deficits in PTSD patients and that, at this point, it is unclear whether these differences are specifically related to damage to the hippocampus or other regions of the brain. Also, at present, we cannot conclude that trauma causes PTSD, which in turn causes brain damage; another possibility is that some individuals may have preexisting conditions, such as abnormalities in the brain or in cognitive processes, that may make them vulnerable to PTSD symptoms. Determining the causal mechanisms involved in the development of PTSD symptoms is an area of ongoing research.

The final chapter in this part of our book focuses on children. In "Growing Up under the Gun: Children and Adolescents Coping with Violent Neighborhoods," Duncan (1996) begins by describing the prevalence of children's exposure to violence and their fears about violence, in both urban and rural areas. He follows with a discussion of children's symptomatic responses to extreme stressors, including PTSD as a response. Duncan explains how children cope with trauma and identifies internal locus of control, self-efficacy, optimistic and planful attitudes, and cognitive reappraisal as helpful coping mechanisms for children (these mechanisms are all discussed more thoroughly in Part IV). He also describes the importance of parental support when a child is faced with potential threats of violence, while acknowledging the complexity involved in providing appropriate support (for example, support must be provided at an appropriate developmental level for the child, and parents may have their own difficulties providing support—they may feel unsafe themselves). Duncan concludes with a brief review of some family intervention and school intervention models. With its emphasis on coping and interventions, this chapter forms a good transition to the next part of our book, "The Coping Concept," in Volume 2.

TERMS

The readings in Part III of our book include a number of technical terms. Can you define these terms? Definitions are included in the glossary in the back of the book.

General Stress and General Psychology Terms

- Affect
- Antereograde amnesia
- Appraisal
- Declarative (explicit) memory
- *Diagnostic and Statistical Manual of Mental Disorders (DSM)*
- Diathesis
- Dissociative symptoms
- Locus of control
- Priming effect
- Procedural memory
- Psychogenic amnesia
- Self-efficacy

Physiological Terms

- Cortisol
- Glucocorticoid
- Hippocampus
- Hypothalamic-pituitary-adrenal (HPA) axis

Statistical or Research Methods Terms

- Cross-sectional study
- Longitudinal study
- Mediation
- Meta-analysis
- Prospective study
- Retrospective study
- Standard deviation

REFERENCES

American Psychiatric Association. (1994). *Diagnostic and statistical manual of mental disorders* (4th ed.). Washington, DC: American Psychiatric Association.

Breslau, N. (2002). Epidemiologic studies of trauma, posttraumatic stress disorder, and other psychiatric disorders. *Canadian Journal of Psychiatry, 47*(10), 923–929.

Duncan, D. F. (1996). Growing up under the gun: Children and adolescents coping with violent neighborhoods. *Journal of Primary Prevention, 16*(4), 343–354.

Golier, J., & Yehuda, R. (2002). Neuropsychological processes in post-traumatic stress disorder. *Psychiatric Clinics of North America, 25,* 295–315.

Lee, A., Isaac, M., & Janca, A. (2002). Post-traumatic stress disorder and terrorism. *Current Opinions in Psychiatry, 15,* 633–637.

McEwen, B., & Lasley, E. (2002). *The end of stress as we know it.* Washington, DC: Joseph Henry Press.

Vasterling, J. J., & Brewin, C. R. (2005). *Neuropsychology of PTSD: Biological, cognitive, and clinical perspectives.* New York: Guilford Press.

CHAPTER 12

Epidemiologic Studies of Trauma, Posttraumatic Stress Disorder, and Other Psychiatric Disorders

Naomi Breslau

In 1980, posttraumatic stress disorder (PTSD) was introduced into the official classification of psychiatric disorders, the *Diagnostic and Statistical Manual of Mental Disorders*, in its third edition (*DSM-III*; American Psychiatric Association, 1980). This marked the beginning of contemporary research on the psychiatric response of traumatic event victims. The *DSM-III* and subsequent *DSM* definitions of PTSD (*DSM-III-R*, American Psychiatric Association, 1987; *DSM-IV*, American Psychiatric Association, 1994) are based on a conceptual model that distinguishes traumatic events from other stressful experiences, and PTSD from other responses to stress. In contrast to "ordinary" stressful experiences, traumatic or catastrophic events are linked etiologically in the *DSM* to a specific syndrome—PTSD. The disorder's criterion symptoms are defined in terms of their connection, in time and in content, with a distinct traumatic event. They include reexperiencing the event through intrusive thoughts and dreams, avoidance of stimuli that symbolize the event, numbing of general responsiveness, and increased arousal not present before the event. Many of these symptoms are among the characteristic features of other psychiatric disorders; however, it is the connection with a distinct event that renders the list of PTSD symptoms a specific syndrome.

Since 1980, research on PTSD has focused primarily on Vietnam War veterans and, to a lesser extent, on victims of specific traumatic events such as disaster or rape. In recent years, several epidemiologic studies have been conducted in the general population (Breslau, Davis, Andreski, & Peterson, 1991; Breslau, Davis, Peterson, & Schultz, 1997; Breslau et al., 1998; Creamer, Burgess, & McFarlane, 2001; Kessler, Sonnega, Bromet, Hughes, & Nelson, 1995; Norris, 1992; Resnick, Kilpatrick, Dansky, Saunders, & Best, 1993; Stein, Walker, Hazen, & Forde, 1997). These studies describe the prevalence of traumatic events and PTSD and their distribution across population subgroups. They identify risk factors for trauma exposure and PTSD and describe aspects of the course of PTSD, including duration of symptoms and comorbidity with other psychiatric disorders.

This chapter reviews results from these studies. It focuses also on core methodologic issues for research in this growing field. It addresses changes in the definition of the stressor criterion in the *DSM-IV* and presents data on the implications of the *DSM-IV* shift toward an emphasis on the subjective experience of trauma victims and a more inclusive variety of stressors. Approaches to measuring exposure to traumatic events and PTSD are discussed. This review also provides a summary of findings on the prevalence of trauma exposure and PTSD and a brief summary of findings on risk factors. Research on other psychiatric disorders that might be attributed to traumatic events, the logic of the approach to this inquiry, and the implications of recent findings are discussed in more detail.

THE DEFINITION OF TRAUMA AND PTSD

According to the current nosology expressed in the *DSM-IV*, the core features of posttraumatic stress disorder comprise a stressor criterion that defines the etiologic event and a configuration of symptoms, drawn from three groups, that define the characteristic PTSD syndrome. The three symptom groups that constitute the PTSD syndrome are as follows:

- Reexperiencing the trauma in nightmares, intrusive memories, or "flashbacks" (Criterion B)
- Numbing of affect and avoidance of thoughts, acts, and situations that symbolize the trauma (Criterion C)
- Symptoms of excessive arousal (Criterion D)

The diagnosis requires the persistence of symptoms for at least a month (Criterion E) and clinically significant distress or impairment (Criterion F).

The *DSM-IV* definition of the PTSD syndrome is little changed from earlier *DSM* editions. However, the stressor criterion in *DSM-IV* clearly departs from earlier editions. *Traumatic experience* was originally defined as an overwhelming experience outside the usual range. The *DSM-IV* redefined traumatic experiences in subjective terms. The current definition has two parts: the first (Criterion A1) defines the range of qualifying stressors, and the second (Criterion A2) requires that "the person's response involved intense fear, helplessness, or horror." Criterion A1 broadens the variety of qualifying traumatic events. In addition to the original core category of traumas used to define PTSD (military combat, disaster, and criminal violence), the expanded *DSM-IV* definition attempts to cover all possible events that clinicians might regard as potentially culminating in PTSD symptoms. Although stressors classified as less extreme are explicitly excluded (for example, one's spouse leaving, or being fired), the *DSM-IV* list of examples (p. 427) is clearly more inclusive than those of earlier *DSM* editions. For the first time, death of a loved one from any cause (including natural causes) qualifies as a stressor, as long as it was "sudden and unexpected." Being diagnosed with a life-threatening illness is another example of the wider range of traumatic events included in the new definition. The *DSM-IV* revision—the broader range of qualifying traumatic events and the added criterion of a specific emotional response—deemphasizes the objective features of the stressors and highlights the clinical principle that people may perceive and respond differently to outwardly similar events.

A recent report from a general population study that used the *DSM-IV* suggests that the net effect of the wider variety of events and the added subjective component has been to increase by more than 20 percent the total number of qualifying events, compared with previous *DSM* definitions (Breslau & Kessler, 2001). The subjective component of the *DSM-IV* stressor criterion did little to offset the effect of the broadened range of qualifying stressors: approximately 90 percent of those who have ever been exposed to one or more stressors have responded with "intense fear, helplessness or horror" to one (the worst) of their stressors. There has also been a considerable increase in PTSD cases, with most of the added cases attributable to a single type of trauma, namely, "learning about unexpected death of a close relative/friend" (Breslau & Kessler, 2001). The *DSM-IV* definition requires, for the first time, that the syndrome cause significant distress or impairment—an addition that renders the diagnostic definition of PTSD more stringent. This is particularly true in epidemiologic surveys of the general population, as opposed to clinical practice, where impairment or distress are generally the reasons for seeking treatment. In the study described above (Breslau et al., 1998; Breslau & Kessler, 2001), the requirement that the syndrome cause significant distress or impairment led to a reduction by approximately 25 percent in the number of PTSD cases identified.

ASSESSING EXPOSURE TO TRAUMATIC EVENTS AND PTSD IN COMMUNITY STUDIES

The standard measurement procedure in contemporary epidemiologic studies of psychiatric disorders (including PTSD) has been the National Institute of Mental Health–Diagnostic Interview Schedule (NIMH-DIS) and the World Health Organization–Composite International Diagnostic Interview (WHO-CIDI), which is based on the NIMH-DIS (Robins, Helzer, Cottler, & Golding, 1989; World Health Organization, 1997). These structured interviews are designed to be administered by experienced interviewers without clinical training. The PTSD section inquires about lifetime history of traumatic events and asks respondents to nominate the worst event ever experienced. It then elicits information about PTSD symptoms connected with that event. Some epidemiologic studies have introduced modifications to the NIMH-DIS—chiefly, in the approach to eliciting information about exposure to traumatic events (Norris, 1992; Resnick et al., 1993).

Estimates of the prevalence of exposure to traumatic events vary according to the inclusiveness of the stressor criterion and the methods used to measure exposure to qualifying stressors. In the *DSM-III* and *DSM-III-R*, qualifying stressors were defined as events that would be "distressing to almost everyone" and as "generally outside the range of usual human experience." Typical PTSD traumas were military combat, rape, physical assault, natural disaster, witnessing violence, and learning about the violent injury or violent death of a loved one. *DSM-IV* has broadened the stressor criterion beyond the earlier definition, as described above. According to one study, the impact of the revision on the lifetime prevalence has been an increase from 68.1 percent to 89.6 percent (Breslau & Kessler, 2001).

Differences in estimates of the prevalence of exposure to traumatic events across epidemiologic studies that predate the 1994 publication of the *DSM-IV* reflect differences in measurement approaches. The key difference is between studies that used the revised NIMH-DIS, which elicits history of exposure to traumatic events with a single question incorporating examples of typical PTSD events (Robins et al., 1989), and studies that used a list of events and inquired about each event separately (Norris, 1992; Resnick et al., 1993). The use of a list of events and the number of events included in the list have important implications for estimating the prevalence of traumatic events. Using a list, compared with using a single question, and using a long versus a short list, yields higher prevalence estimates of trauma exposure and higher estimates of the average number of traumas per exposed person. A list of events has become the standard measurement procedure, incorporated into current versions of the major structured interviews—the WHO-CIDI and the NIMH-DIS for *DSM-IV* (Robins, Cottler, Bucholz, & Compton, 1995; World Health Organization, 1997).

Estimates of the conditional probability of PTSD are derived from information on the prevalence of exposure to one or more qualifying events (the denominator) and the proportion of those exposed who meet criteria for PTSD in connection with one of their events (the numerator). Estimates of the overall conditional risk for PTSD depend in part on the stressor definition. A definition that includes only rare and highly traumatic events will yield a lower prevalence of exposure and a higher conditional risk for PTSD, compared with an inclusive definition that encompasses a wide range of events. In addition, a measurement procedure such as a single question, which yields a lower prevalence of exposure, yields a higher conditional risk for PTSD, compared with procedures that yield a higher prevalence of exposure, such as a list of events. It appears that using a list versus a single item (or a long versus a short list) enhances recall of events that are less memorable but also less likely to have led to PTSD.

Kessler and others identified a methodological issue in community studies of PTSD (Kessler et al., 1995, 1999). When two or more qualifying traumas were reported, previous studies focused on traumatic events selected by the respondent as the worst or the most upsetting ever experienced. This approach is an efficient way to identify persons with PTSD and estimate the prevalence of the disorder. Only a few respondents who fail to meet PTSD diagnostic criteria for their worst trauma are likely to meet criteria for other traumas they experienced (Breslau et al., 1997). The worst-event method has also been used to estimate the conditional risk for PTSD. The worst events yield estimates of the probability of PTSD in persons who have experienced one or more traumas in their lifetime and allow the investigation of risk factors and consequences of PTSD among this group. However, the approach has been suspected of overstating the conditional risk for PTSD associated with the class of *DSM*-qualifying events as a whole (that is, typical trauma) (Kessler et al., 1995, 1999).

An alternative to inquiring about PTSD symptoms in relation to all reported events, which would impose too great a respondent's bias, involves selecting a random event from the complete list of traumatic events reported by each respondent. Such an approach, together with a weighting procedure to adjust for differences in the selection probabilities of events across respondents, provides a representative sample of qualifying, or typical, traumatic events. This method was used in a recent survey of the general population, and several reports have been published based on it (for example, Breslau, Chilcoat, Kessler, & Davis, 1999; Breslau, Chilcoat, Kessler, Peterson, & Lucia, 1999; Breslau et al., 1998; Breslau & Kessler, 2001). A comparison of the estimates based on the two methods—the randomly selected events and the worst events—suggests that the worst events moderately overstate the conditional risk for representative (typical) traumas. Specifically, the conditional probability of PTSD based on the sample of the worst events was 13.6 percent; based on the representative sample of events, it was 9.2 percent (Breslau et al., 1998). This new method provides an estimate of the conditional probability of PTSD following typical traumas. However, it is incapable of identifying all (or nearly all) those who met criteria for PTSD following exposure to traumatic events, either in a lifetime or during a specified time period. In other words, the randomly selected events cannot replace the worst events as a shortcut when an inquiry about all traumatic events is not feasible.

Prevalence of Exposure to Traumatic Events and Conditional Risk for PTSD

As summarized above, the lifetime prevalence of exposure to traumatic events varies across epidemiologic studies as a function of the combined effects of differences in the stressor definitions and ascertainment methods. Earlier studies (Breslau et al., 1991, 1997; Creamer et al., 2001; Kessler et al., 1995; Norris, 1992; Resnick et al., 1993) reported estimates of exposure ranging from 40 to 60 percent, whereas a recent study that used the *DSM-IV*'s enlarged definition approached 90 percent (Breslau et al., 1998). Despite the differences across studies, all studies reported a higher prevalence of exposure in men than in women. Although consistent across studies, the sex difference in exposure is modest, with a prevalence ratio in men versus women of less than 1.2 to 1. The average number of traumatic events reported by exposed men exceeds the corresponding average in women. Several surveys reported that the prevalence estimates of rape or sexual assault other than rape were higher in women than in men; the lifetime occurrences of other events involving assaultive violence, accidents, and witnessing violence were higher in men than in women (e.g., Breslau et al., 1998; Kessler et al., 1995; Norris, 1992; Stein et al., 1997).

Despite large differences in the prevalence of exposure to traumatic events across studies, the lifetime prevalence of *DSM-III-R* PTSD varied within a narrow range: 5 to 6 percent in men and 10 to 14 percent in women. The lifetime prevalence of *DSM-IV* PTSD was higher, reflecting the enlarged stressor criterion that includes relatively common traumatic events (Breslau, 1998; Breslau et al., 1998).

The higher prevalence of PTSD in women is a function of the sex difference in the conditional probability of PTSD. Women are approximately twice as likely as men to succumb to PTSD following traumatic events. Even when cases with rape are excluded or when event type is controlled, women have a higher rate of PTSD following traumatic experiences than do men (Breslau et al., 1998; Kessler et al., 1995; Stein et al., 1997; Stein, Walker, & Forde, 2000). There is evidence to suggest that women's greater PTSD risk may not be a generalized vulnerability but, rather, a specific vulnerability to the PTSD-inducing effects of assaultive violence (Breslau, Chilcoat, Kessler, Peterson, et al., 1999; Kessler et al., 1995; Stein et al., 2000). The sex difference in the risk for PTSD is not attributable to sex differences in the history of previous exposure to trauma nor sex differences in preexisting psychiatric disorders (Breslau, 1998; Breslau, Chilcoat, Kessler, & Davis, 1999).

Risk Factors for Exposure to Traumatic Events

Traumatic events are not random. The prevalence of exposure varies across subgroups of the population classified by sociodemographic characteristics. Men, the young, and members of minority groups residing in inner cities have higher lifetime risk for exposure to assaultive violence, compared with women, older persons, and residents of middle-class suburbs (Breslau et al., 1998). Men are also at higher risk than women for exposure to serious accidents and to witnessing violence perpetrated on others. With respect to other event types—events grouped under learning about trauma to others or learning about the unexpected death of a loved one—differences by sociodemographic characteristics are trivial (Breslau, 1998; Breslau et al., 1998). There is evidence that a history of exposure to trauma predicts new exposure (Breslau, Davis, & Andreski, 1995).

Personality traits of neuroticism and extroversion, early conduct problems, family history of psychiatric disorders, and preexisting psychiatric disorders are associated with increased risk for exposure to traumatic events defined according to *DSM-III-R* (Breslau, Davis, Peterson, & Schultz, 2000; Breslau et al., 1991, 1995; Bromet, Sonnega, & Kessler, 1998;

Kessler et al., 1995). The applicability of these findings to the enlarged definition of stressors in *DSM-IV* is uncertain.

Risk Factors for PTSD following Exposure to Traumatic Events

A recent meta-analysis identified three risk factors for PTSD that are reported consistently across studies: psychiatric history, history of childhood trauma, and family history of psychiatric disorders (Brewin, Andrews, & Valentine, 2000). With respect to other risk factors investigated in that analysis, effects varied across studies. For example, sex differences in the risk for PTSD following exposure that were observed across studies of civilian samples were nonexistent among Vietnam veterans. Studies of military samples found that younger age at trauma was a risk factor for PTSD, whereas studies of the general population failed to find age-at-trauma effects (Breslau, Chilcoat, Kessler, & Davis, 1999). The meta-analysis did not examine the suspected risk factors of neuroticism and prior exposure to traumatic events (other than childhood abuse) (Breslau et al., 1991, 1995).

Other Posttrauma Disorders

Epidemiologic studies of general population samples have confirmed earlier observations, from clinical samples and samples of Vietnam veterans, that persons diagnosed with PTSD have high rates of other psychiatric disorders (Breslau et al., 1991, 1995). These include major depression, anxiety disorders (other than PTSD), and substance use disorders. Alternative explanations have been proposed for the association of PTSD and these disorders.

First, preexisting psychiatric disorders may increase the likelihood of PTSD by increasing the risk for exposure to traumatic events of the type that lead to PTSD or increase victims' susceptibility to the PTSD-inducing effects of trauma. For example, drug use disorder has been suspected of increasing the likelihood of PTSD because it is associated with lifestyles that involve an elevated risk for exposure to violence. Similarly, there is evidence that a history of major depression increases the risk for exposure to traumatic events (Breslau et al., 1997), as it does for exposure to ordinary stressful life events (Kendler, Kessler, Neale, Heath, & Eaves, 1993).

Second, PTSD may be a causal risk factor for other psychiatric disorders. Use of alcohol or drugs to relieve the distressing symptoms of PTSD may increase the likelihood of dependence; major depression may develop as a complication of PTSD and its associated impairment.

Third, the associations may be noncausal, reflecting shared genetic or environmental factors. Genetic factors common to PTSD and substance use disorders have been reported (McLeod et al., 2001; Xian et al., 2000). Also, personality traits (primarily, neuroticism) and family history of major depression have been implicated separately in the development of PTSD, as well as in the development of major depression (Breslau et al., 1991, 1997; Connor & Davidson, 1997).

A suspected shared environmental risk factor for PTSD comorbid with other psychiatric disorders is exposure to trauma (Jordan et al., 1991; Kulka et al., 1990). It has been suggested that traumatic events leading to PTSD also induce diatheses for other disorders (Friedman & Yehuda, 1995). Although PTSD has been defined as the signature disorder in victims of traumatic events, stressors—both those that qualify for the diagnosis of PTSD and those that do not—may also precipitate other disorders. According to this hypothesis, some trauma victims develop PTSD, whereas others develop major depression or substance use disorder, depending on their preexisting vulnerabilities. Comorbidity of PTSD with other disorders would thus reflect the co-occurrence of distinct diatheses (Friedman & Yehuda, 1995; Yehuda, McFarlane, & Shalev, 1998).

The notion that traumatic events cause various disorders apart from PTSD and that there may be distinct diatheses determining the specific psychiatric sequelae of trauma originated in observations of high rates of various disorders among trauma victims. For example, rates of depression and anxiety disorders (other than PTSD) appeared elevated in trauma patients admitted to the emergency room (Shalev et al., 1998). Similarly, an elevated rate of major depression that was equal to the rate of PTSD was found in a survey of New York City residents several months after the attacks on the World Trade Center of September 11, 2001 (Galea et al., 2002). However, these data, in themselves, do not indicate that exposure to traumatic events was the cause.

To test whether exposure to traumatic events increases the risk for a psychiatric disorder other than PTSD (for example, major depression), it is necessary to compare the disorder's incidence in persons exposed to trauma who did not develop PTSD with the incidence in persons not exposed to trauma (Breslau, Chase, & Anthony, 2002). That is, with respect to psychiatric disorders other than PTSD, evaluating the potential causal role of exposure to trauma requires a different approach from that used to estimate the risk for PTSD. By definition, PTSD requires a link to an identifiable qualifying stressor, and the symptoms of PTSD are closely connected with that stressor. In consequence, the risk for PTSD in trauma victims is measured by a conditional probability or conditional risk (that is, risk for those exposed to the stressor). By contrast, the definition of major depression, anxiety, or substance use disorder does not require a link to a stressor, and these disorders can occur without a stressor. As a result, the association between trauma exposure and subsequent occurrence of major depression (or other disorders) is measured by a ratio of risks or by a relative risk estimate (that is, risk for depression among those exposed divided by risk among those not exposed). Without such a comparison of risks, we could not test whether the risk among exposed persons is in fact higher than it would have been if they were not exposed to trauma. By definition, PTSD has no such an alternative. A relative risk for PTSD with respect to the presence or absence of a stressor cannot be estimated.

The *DSM*'s essential linking of PTSD with a traumatic experience is difficult to challenge, given the way in which PTSD has been understood and described from its early origins: without exposure to trauma, what is posttraumatic about the ensuing syndrome of traumatic memories and associated distressing symptoms? Such is clearly not the case with major depression or substance use disorders.

Further, to evaluate the role of trauma exposure in the onset of another disorder, it is not sufficient to show that the disorder's rate is higher in exposed than in nonexposed persons. Support for the hypothesis that trauma is associated with an increased risk for major depression (or another disorder), independent of its PTSD-inducing effects, requires evidence of a higher incidence of the disorder in exposed persons who did not succumb to PTSD, compared with nonexposed persons. Evidence of an increased risk for the disorder in trauma victims with PTSD but not in trauma victims without PTSD would not support the hypothesis. It would suggest instead that PTSD might cause the disorder or that shared antecedent factors other than trauma exposure account for the PTSD–other disorder link.

Reports based on prospective and retrospective data show a markedly increased risk for major depression in trauma-exposed persons with PTSD (Breslau et al., 2000). Elevated risk for major depression was not reported in trauma-exposed persons without PTSD, compared with nonexposed persons (Breslau et al., 1997, 2000). This pattern of a markedly higher rate of major depression in victims with PTSD can also be observed in reports from other studies that did not explicitly address this question, including postdisaster studies (Galea et al., 2002; North et al., 1999). For example, although the New York City survey conducted after the attacks on the World Trade Center found similar rates of PTSD and major depression (Galea et al., 2002), hand calculations of reported numbers reveal that the prevalence of major depression in persons with PTSD was 49 percent, and in those without PTSD, it was only 6.5 percent. The latter figure is not far from what could be expected for past-thirty-day major depression in the general population (Blazer, Kessler, McGonagle, & Swartz, 1994).

With respect to the relation of substance use disorders to trauma exposure and PTSD, a recent report shows an increased risk for the subsequent onset of nicotine dependence and drug abuse or dependence in trauma victims with PTSD but not in those without PTSD, compared with unexposed persons (Breslau, Davis, & Schultz, 2003; Chilcoat & Breslau, 1998). (The results on nicotine dependence are equivocal, and a modestly elevated risk in trauma victims in the absence of PTSD has not been safely ruled out.)

The findings regarding elevated rates of subsequent major depression, nicotine dependence, and drug use disorder in trauma victims with PTSD but not in those without PTSD, compared with nonexposed persons, narrow the potential explanations of the relation between PTSD and the subsequent onset of these disorders. PTSD may be a determinant of these disorders, or PTSD and each of these disorders may have a shared diathesis or shared environmental causes other than trauma exposure. The extent to which a diathesis shared with PTSD accounts for the elevated risk for other disorders may vary across disorders. The PTSD–major depression association may primarily reflect a shared diathesis (Breslau et al., 2000). Evidence that preexisting major depression and family history of major depression are associated with increased risk for PTSD following trauma exposure support this interpretation (Breslau et al., 1997, 2000; Bromet et al., 1998; Connor & Davidson, 1997). The PTSD–drug use disorder association may reflect primarily a causal effect of PTSD (Chilcoat & Breslau, 1998), although a common genetic contribution to the association has also been reported (McLeod et al., 2001; Xian et al., 2000).

Recent results on the relation between PTSD and the risk for alcohol use disorders in exposed persons suggest the possibility that female, but not male, trauma victims who did not succumb to PTSD may be at increased risk for alcohol use disorder (Breslau et al., 1997, 2003). Previous research in Vietnam combat veterans and civilian victims of traumatic events generally found considerably stronger associations between trauma exposure and alcohol use disorder when PTSD was present rather than absent (Kulka et al., 1991; Stewart, 1996). Some studies found weak or no association between trauma exposure and drinking or alcohol use disorder (Green, Lindy, Grace, & Gleser, 1989; North et al., 1999). Notably, there is little support for the notion that male trauma victims (whose risk for PTSD is generally lower than that of female trauma victims) respond to traumatic experiences by abusing alcohol or drugs. Such a susceptibility would result in an increased risk for alcohol and drug use disorders in trauma-exposed men without PTSD, relative to unexposed men.

Epidemiologic studies have consistently reported that only a small subset of trauma victims succumb to PTSD; most do not. Recent studies indicate that trauma victims who do not succumb to PTSD (that is, most victims) are not at a markedly elevated risk for the subsequent first onset of other psychiatric disorders, compared with unexposed persons. The excess incidence of the first onset of other disorders following trauma exposure is concentrated primarily in the small subset of trauma victims with PTSD. These observations suggest that PTSD identifies a subset of trauma victims at considerable risk for a range of disorders. The extent to which the increased risk for these other disorders represents shared diatheses versus complications of PTSD may vary across disorders. Studies designed to test genetic and environmental factors in PTSD and comorbid disorders are needed.

REFERENCES

American Psychiatric Association (1980). *Diagnostic and statistical manual of mental disorders* (3rd ed.). Washington, DC: American Psychiatric Association.
American Psychiatric Association (1987). *Diagnostic and statistical manual of mental disorders* (3rd ed., rev.). Washington, DC: American Psychiatric Association.
American Psychiatric Association (1994). *Diagnostic and statistical manual of mental disorders* (4th ed.). Washington, DC: American Psychiatric Association.
Blazer, D. G., Kessler, R. C., McGonagle, K. A., & Swartz, M. S. (1994). The prevalence and distribution of major depression in a national community

sample: The National Comorbidity Survey. *American Journal of Psychiatry, 151,* 979–986.

Breslau, N. (1998). Epidemiology of trauma and post-traumatic stress disorder. In R. Yehuda (Ed.), *Psychological trauma,* vol. 17 of J. M. Oldham & M. B. Riba (Eds.), *Review of psychiatry* (pp. 1–29). Washington, DC: American Psychiatric Press.

Breslau, N., Chase, G. A., & Anthony, J. C. (2002). The uniqueness of the DSM definition of posttraumatic stress disorder: Implications for research. *Psychological Medicine, 32,* 573–576.

Breslau, N., Chilcoat, H. D., Kessler, R. C., & Davis, G. C. (1999). Previous exposure to trauma and PTSD effects of subsequent trauma: Results from the Detroit Area Survey of Trauma. *American Journal of Psychiatry, 156,* 902–907.

Breslau, N., Chilcoat, H. D., Kessler, R. C., Peterson, E. L., & Lucia, V. C. (1999). Vulnerability to assaultive violence: Further specification of the sex difference in post-traumatic stress disorder. *Psychological Medicine, 29,* 813–821.

Breslau, N., Davis, G. C., & Andreski, P. (1995). Risk factors for PTSD-related traumatic events: A prospective analysis. *American Journal of Psychiatry, 152,* 529–535.

Breslau, N., Davis, G. C., Andreski, P., & Peterson, E. (1991). Traumatic events and posttraumatic stress disorder in an urban population of young adults. *Archives of General Psychiatry, 48,* 216–222.

Breslau, N., Davis, G. C., Peterson, E. L., & Schultz, L. (1997). Psychiatric sequelae of posttraumatic stress disorder in women. *Archives of General Psychiatry, 54,* 81–87.

Breslau, N., Davis, G. C., Peterson, E. L., & Schultz, L. R. (2000). A second look at comorbidity in victims of trauma: The posttraumatic stress disorder–major depression connection. *Biological Psychiatry, 48,* 902–909.

Breslau, N., Davis, G. C., & Schultz, L. R. (2003). Posttraumatic stress disorder and the incidence of nicotine, alcohol, and other drug disorders in persons who have experienced trauma. *Archives of General Psychiatry, 60,* 289–294.

Breslau, N., & Kessler, R. C. (2001). The stressor criterion in *DSM-IV* posttraumatic stress disorder: An empirical investigation. *Biological Psychiatry, 50,* 699–704.

Breslau, N., Kessler, R. C., Chilcoat, H. D., Schultz, L. R., Davis, G. C., & Andreski, P. (1998). Trauma and posttraumatic stress disorder in the community: The 1996 Detroit Area Survey of Trauma. *Archives of General Psychiatry, 55,* 626–632.

Brewin, C. R., Andrews, B., & Valentine, J. D. (2000). Meta-analysis of risk factors for posttraumatic stress disorder in trauma-exposed adults. *Journal of Consulting and Clinical Psychology, 68,* 748–766.

Bromet, E., Sonnega, A., & Kessler, R. C. (1998). Risk factors for *DSM-III-R* posttraumatic stress disorder: Findings from the National Comorbidity Survey. *American Journal of Epidemiology, 147,* 353–361.

Chilcoat, H. D., & Breslau, N. (1998). Posttraumatic stress disorder and drug use disorders: Testing causal pathways. *Archives of General Psychiatry, 55,* 913–917.

Connor, K. M., & Davidson, J. R. (1997). Familial risk factors in posttraumatic stress disorder. *Annals of the New York Academy of Science, 821,* 32–51.

Creamer, M., Burgess, P., & McFarlane, A. C. (2001). Post-traumatic disorder: Findings from the Australian National Survey of Mental Health and Well-Being. *Psychological Medicine, 31,* 1237–1247.

Friedman, M. J., & Yehuda, R. (1995). Post-traumatic stress disorder and comorbidity: Psychobiological approaches to differential diagnosis. In M. J. Friedman, D. S. Charney, & A. Y. Deutch (Eds.), *Neurobiological and clinical consequences of stress: From normal adaptation to post-traumatic stress disorder* (pp. 429–445). New York: LippincottRaven.

Galea, S., Ahern, J., Resnick, H., Kilpatrick, D., Bucuvalas, M., Gold, J., et al. (2002). Psychological sequelae of the September 11 terrorist attacks in New York City. *New England Journal of Medicine, 346,* 982–987.

Green, B. L., Lindy, J. D., Grace, M. C., & Gleser, G. C. (1989). Multiple diagnosis in posttraumatic stress disorder: The role of war stressors. *Journal of Nervous and Mental Disease, 177,* 329–335.

Jordan, B. K., Schlenger, W. E., Hough, R., Kulka, R. A., Weiss, D., Fairbank, J. A., et al. (1991). Lifetime and current prevalence of specific psychiatric disorders among Vietnam veterans and controls. *Archives of General Psychiatry, 48,* 207–215.

Kendler, K. S., Kessler, R. C., Neale, M. C., Heath, A. C., & Eaves, L. J. (1993). The prediction of major depression in women: Toward an integrated etiologic model. *American Journal of Psychiatry, 150,* 1139–1148.

Kessler, R. C., Sonnega, A., Bromet, E., Hughes, M., & Nelson, C. B. (1995). Posttraumatic stress disorder in the National Comorbidity Survey. *Archives of General Psychiatry, 52,* 1048–1060.

Kessler, R. C., Sonnega, A., Bromet, E., Hughes, M., Nelson, C. B., & Breslau, N. (1999). Epidemiologic risk factors for trauma and PTSD. In R. Yehuda (Ed.), *Risk factors for posttraumatic stress disorder* (pp. 23–59). Washington, DC: American Psychiatric Press.

Kulka, R. A., Schlenger, W. E., Fairbank, J. A., Hough, R. L., Jordan, B. K., Marmar, C. R., et al. (1990). *Trauma and the Vietnam War generation: Report of findings from the National Vietnam Veterans Readjustment Study.* New York: Brunner/Mazel.

McLeod, D. S., Koenen, K. C., Meyer, J. M., Lyons, M. J., Eisen, S., True, W., et al. (2001). Genetic and environmental influences on the relationship among combat exposure, posttraumatic stress disorder symptoms, and alcohol use. *Journal of Traumatic Stress, 14,* 259–275.

Norris, F. H. (1992). Epidemiology of trauma: Frequency and impact of different potentially traumatic events on different demographic groups. *Journal of Consulting and Clinical Psychology, 60,* 409–418.

North, C. S., Nixon, S. J., Shariat, S., Mallonee, S., McMillen, J. C., Spitznagel, E. L., et al. (1999). Psychiatric disorders among survivors of the Oklahoma City bombing. *Journal of the American Medical Association, 282,* 755–762.

Resnick, H. S., Kilpatrick, D. G., Dansky, B. S., Saunders, B. E., & Best, C. L. (1993). Prevalence of civilian trauma and posttraumatic stress disorder in a representative national sample of women. *Journal of Consulting and Clinical Psychology, 61,* 984–991.

Robins, L., Cottler, L., Bucholz, K., & Compton, W. (1995). *Diagnostic interview schedule for* DSM-IV. St. Louis: Washington University.

Robins, L. N., Helzer, J. E., Cottler, L., & Golding, E. (1989). *NIMH Diagnostic Interview Schedule, version III revised.* St. Louis: Washington University.

Shalev, A. Y., Freedman, S., Peri, T., Brandes, D., Sahar, T., Orr, S. P., et al. (1998). Prospective study of posttraumatic stress disorder and depression following trauma. *American Journal of Psychiatry, 155,* 630–637.

Stein, M. B., Walker, J. R., & Forde, D. R. (2000). Gender differences in susceptibility to posttraumatic stress disorder. *Behaviour Research and Therapy, 38,* 619–628.

Stein, M. B., Walker, J. R., Hazen, A. L., & Forde, D. R. (1997). Full and partial posttraumatic stress disorder: Findings from a community survey. *American Journal of Psychiatry, 154,* 1114–1119.

Stewart, S. H. (1996). Alcohol abuse in individuals exposed to trauma: A critical review. *Psychological Bulletin, 120,* 83–112.

World Health Organization (1997). *Composite International Diagnostic Interview (CIDI, version 2.1.).* Geneva: World Health Organization.

Xian, H., Chantarujikapong, S. I., Scherrer, J. F., Eisen, S. A., Lyons, M. J., Goldberg, J., et al. (2000). Genetic and environmental influences on posttraumatic stress disorder, alcohol and drug dependence in twin pairs. *Drug and Alcohol Dependence, 61,* 95–102.

Yehuda, R., McFarlane, A. C., & Shalev, A. Y. (1998). Predicting the development of posttraumatic stress disorder from the acute response to a traumatic event. *Biological Psychiatry, 44,* 1305–1313.

CHAPTER 13

Posttraumatic Stress Disorder and Terrorism

Alyssa Lee, Mohan Isaac, and Aleksandar Janca

More than twenty years after its initial appearance in the third edition of the *Diagnostic and Statistical Manual of Mental Disorders* (*DSM*) in 1980 (American Psychiatric Association, 1980), posttraumatic stress disorder (PTSD) continues to be a controversial diagnostic category. As recently as 2001, Summerfield (2001) argued that PTSD as a psychiatric diagnosis was constructed largely from sociopolitical ideas that were a legacy of the American war in Vietnam. Although the disorder has a secure place in the current editions of international classification systems such as the fourth edition of *DSM* (American Psychiatric Association, 1994) and the tenth revision of the *International Classification of Diseases* (World Health Organization, 1992), its nosological status is continually being questioned. Nevertheless, the diagnosis of PTSD is used widely across the globe, and its international recognition is perhaps an indication of its usefulness and perceived diagnostic validity (Mezey & Robbins, 2001).

Recent terrorist attacks—in particular, the attacks on the World Trade Center and the Pentagon on September 11, 2001—have focused renewed attention on PTSD. PTSD has been the main topic of several editorials and review articles in leading medical and psychiatric journals (LeDoux & Gorman, 2001; Gidron, 2002; Ursano, 2002; Yehuda, 2002). Numerous research and clinical reports on the rates and characteristics of PTSD after recent terrorist attacks have also been published. The results of these studies are summarized below.

POSTTRAUMATIC STRESS DISORDER AFTER TERRORIST ATTACKS

The fourth edition of *DSM* (American Psychiatric Association, 1994) defined PTSD as a set of typical symptoms that develop after an individual sees, is involved in, or hears of an extreme traumatic stressor. Such a stressor is overwhelming enough to affect almost anyone. It can arise from experiences in war, torture, natural catastrophe, rape, assault, and other forms of criminal victimization and serious accidents. Terrorism, which is increasingly becoming a worldwide problem, can be added to this list of traumatic stressors.

The primary aim of terrorism is to spread fear, panic, confusion, and grief among large groups of people. Although trauma caused by various types of stressors and their psychiatric consequences have been studied extensively, only a few studies have investigated the consequences of terrorist attacks. Gidron (2002) reviewed studies on the prevalence of PTSD after terrorist attacks published in English between 1980 and 2001. He identified studies that included only subjects who were strictly victims of terrorist attacks, defined as deliberate human-made violent events with a political motive; the assessment of subjects with reliable PTSD instruments or measures based on *DSM* criteria was another inclusion criterion for the review. Based on the review of six such studies, which were carried out in France, Northern Ireland, Israel, and the United States, the prevalence rate of PTSD after terrorist attacks was estimated to be 28 percent (range 18–50%). Laypersons appeared to have a considerably higher prevalence than security forces. However, Gidron cautioned that the variability in the forms of subject sampling, type, and timing of assessment and types of subjects (laypersons or police/security personnel) could have contributed to variations in the prevalence rates. The review noted that the literature is inconsistent in relation to the risk factors of PTSD after terrorist attacks.

A prospective study of victims of a terrorist attack in a Paris subway in December 1996 (Jehel, Duchet, Paterniti, Consoli, & Guelfi, 2001) showed that 41 percent of the participants met PTSD criteria at six months and 34.4 percent still had PTSD at eighteen months. Women and younger people presented significantly higher PTSD scores. Individuals with PTSD had increased health care utilization and medication use.

A study by Japan's National Police Agency (Kawana, Ishimatsu, & Kanda, 2001) reportedly showed that more than half the survivors of the sarin gas terrorist attack on Tokyo's underground system in 1995 had symptoms consistent with PTSD four years after the attack. The respondents complained of nightmares and flashbacks and had panic attacks when they boarded trains. The most common complaint of the victims was weakened vision. A lack of knowledge about the long-term effects of the gas was a major anxiety for the victims.

A number of studies (North et al., 1999; Pfefferbaum et al., 2000) after the 1995 bombing of the Alfred P. Murrah Federal Building in Oklahoma City, which was until 2001 the deadliest act of terrorism in the United

States, showed that approximately 35 percent of those who were exposed developed psychiatric disorders, including PTSD.

PSYCHOLOGICAL SEQUELAE OF THE SEPTEMBER 11, 2001, ATTACKS

The terrorist attacks of September 11, 2001, considered to be the largest human-made disaster in the United States in recent history, represented a national catastrophe. The attacks were immediately followed by exhaustive and vivid television coverage of the aftermath of the attacks. There was a continued threat of further terrorist attacks against the United States.

The immediate mental health effects of the terrorist attacks were studied by Schuster et al. (2001) by interviewing a nationally representative sample of 560 adults in the United States within five days after the attack. Random-digit dialing was used to obtain the nationally representative sample, and trained interviewers conducted computer-assisted telephone interviews in English, using a questionnaire developed by the investigators. A total of 44 percent of the U.S. adults who were surveyed reported having had at least one of five substantial stress symptoms since the terrorist attacks. The rates of stress reactions were highest among women, nonwhites, and people with preexisting psychological problems. Distance from the World Trade Center, region of the country, and the extent of television viewing were also associated with the level of stress. Respondents coped with the stress in a variety of ways, such as talking with others, turning to religion, participation in group activities, and making donations. The study highlighted the prevalence of trauma-related symptoms of stress in people who do not necessarily meet the criteria for a psychiatric disorder, and even in people who are far from the scene of trauma (terrorist attack).

The prevalence and correlates of acute PTSD and depression among residents of Manhattan five to eight weeks after the 9/11 terrorist attacks were studied by Galea et al. (2002). Data were collected using random-digit dialing and telephone interviews with 1,008 adults living in households south of 110th Street, the part of Manhattan that included the World Trade Center. Approximately 7 percent of the respondents reported symptoms consistent with the diagnosis of current PTSD, and 9.7 percent reported symptoms consistent with the diagnosis of current depression. These rates are approximately twice the baseline rates of PTSD (3.6%) and depression (4.9%). The prevalence of PTSD was higher among individuals who were most directly exposed to the terrorist attacks or their consequences than among individuals with less direct exposure. Among respondents who lived near the World Trade Center, the prevalence of PTSD was 20 percent. Hispanic ethnicity, female sex, two or more preexisting stressors, and a low level of social support were associated with both PTSD and depression. A panic attack during or shortly after the traumatic event predicted subsequent psychopathology. Losses as a result of the terrorist attack, such as the death of a friend or relative during the attacks or the loss of a job, were predictors of depression. The study suggested that in the area of Manhattan below 110th Street approximately 67,000 individuals had PTSD and approximately 87,000 had depression during the period between October 16 and November 15, 2001.

Vlahov et al. (2002) used the data from the above random-digit dial telephone survey of Manhattan residents below 110th Street to estimate the prevalence and correlates of cigarette smoking, alcohol consumption, and marijuana use after the terrorist attacks. After 9/11, the overall increase in substance use was 9.7 percent for cigarette smoking, 24.6 percent for alcohol consumption, and 3.2 percent for marijuana smoking. Current PTSD was more frequent in those who increased use of cigarettes or marijuana than in those who did not. Current depression was more frequent for those who increased use of any of the three substances than for those who did not.

Studies of Oklahoma City bombing victims also showed that increased alcohol consumption may present a problem months after exposure to the traumatic event (Pfefferbaum & Doughty, 2001). Such studies highlight the need to assess the use of alcohol routinely in disaster victims.

REACTIONS IN CHILDREN AND ADOLESCENTS

The psychological sequelae of terrorist attacks on children have not been adequately studied. Schuster et al. (2001), in their national survey of stress reactions after the 9/11 terrorist attacks, asked respondents questions about children's reactions using five modified items from the Diagnostic Interview Schedule for Children Version IV (parents' version) (Shaffer, Fisher, Lucas, Dulcan, & Schwab-Stone, 2000). Thirty-five percent of parents reported that their children had at least one or more stress symptoms, and 47 percent of children were worried about their own safety or the safety of loved ones. Approximately one-third of the parents reported that they restricted their children's television viewing.

Children exposed to television and other media coverage of disasters and violence are known to develop posttraumatic stress symptoms (Nader, Pynoos, Fairbanks, al-Ajeel, & al-Asfour, 1993; Najarian, Goenjian, Pelcovitz, Mandel, & Najarian, 1996). After the Oklahoma City bombing in 1995, for example, children and adolescents who were exposed to the attack through television viewing were affected, and the posttraumatic stress symptoms persisted for as long as two years (Pfefferbaum et al., 1999; Pfefferbaum et al., 2000). Pfefferbaum et al. (2001) recommended that because the development of posttraumatic stress symptoms in children is significantly related to disaster-related television viewing, such viewing by children should be monitored, and parents or other adults should be available to address their emotional reactions, to answer questions, and to correct misperceptions.

POSTTRAUMATIC STRESS DISORDER
IN POSTCONFLICT SETTINGS

Low-intensity wars and armed conflict, mass violence, and human rights violations (such as torture) of varying intensity have been occurring with increasing frequency in different parts of the world. Terrorism is an integral component of many of these conflicts. Such conflicts affect the lives of large numbers of people in various countries and regions, including Algeria, Israel, Palestine, Spain, Ireland, Sri Lanka, India, Pakistan, and the former Yugoslavia.

To fill the gap in knowledge about the impact of trauma in postconflict settings, particularly in low-income countries, de Jong et al. (2001) reported the prevalence rates and risk factors for PTSD in four such settings. Using similar epidemiological assessment methods among survivors of war or mass violence, the prevalence rates of PTSD were estimated to be 37.4 percent in Algeria, 28.4 percent in Cambodia, 15.8 percent in Ethiopia, and 17.8 percent in Gaza. The patterns of risk factors were diverse and specific to each country. The relatively high rate of PTSD in Algeria may be a result of the continuing and increased terrorist activities by certain armed groups in the country. This study highlights the contextual differences in the occurrence of PTSD in different settings. It is also seen that the rates of PTSD are relatively higher than those reported in Western community samples.

A three-year follow-up study of adult Bosnian refugees in Croatia (Mollica et al., 2001) showed that 45 percent of the original respondents who met the *DSM-IV* criteria for depression, PTSD, or both continued to have these disorders. A total of 16 percent of those who were asymptomatic three years earlier developed one or both disorders.

PREVENTION AND TREATMENT OF POSTTRAUMATIC STRESS DISORDER

LeDoux and Gorman (2001) in an editorial in the *American Journal of Psychiatry* raised the key question: "What can psychiatrists reasonably recommend to those suffering from the emotional disturbances that follow exposure to a life-threatening traumatic event?" They point out that "PTSD is essentially a condition in which emotional learning persists in the form of memories that seize control of mental life and behavior." Therefore, simple but active coping strategies, such as the use of distractions, that is, getting rid of dysphoric thoughts by "thinking or doing something" that leads to pleasure or prevents displeasure, may be an effective initial intervention for posttraumatic stress symptoms. Although they believed that psychological interventions should be the mainstay of treatment for trauma victims, medications such as selective serotonin re-uptake inhibitors (sertraline) are known to alleviate the symptoms of PTSD as well as to improve the overall functioning of sufferers (Ballenger et al., 2000; Davidson, Rothbaum, van der Kolk, Sikes, & Farfel, 2001). The need to actively involve primary care physicians in the management of PTSD has been emphasized by a number of authors (e.g., Davidson, 2001; LeDoux & Gorman, 2001; Mezey & Robbins, 2001).

The role of early psychological interventions, such as psychological debriefing, in preventing the occurrence of PTSD has been controversial. Although the use of such interventions has become widespread and popular, a recent review of the effectiveness of such interventions found that single-session, individual debriefing did not reduce psychological distress nor prevent the onset of PTSD (Rose, Bisson, Churchill, & Wessely, 2001). There was also no evidence that debriefing reduced general psychological morbidity, depression, or anxiety. Some studies have found that debriefing may actually *increase* the risk of PTSD and lead to other negative outcomes in other trauma victims. Gidron (2002); Mayou, Ehlers, and Hobbs (2000); and Rose et al. (2001) recommended that the compulsory debriefing of victims of trauma should stop. Gidron et al. (2001) developed a "memory structuring intervention" aimed at preventing PTSD, which they have used successfully with individuals who met with traffic accidents. However, this intervention has not been tested with victims of terrorist attacks. To assess the effectiveness of any new preventative intervention, it is necessary to incorporate standardized and objective assessments both before and after the intervention (Gidron, 2002).

CONCLUSION

Knowledge of the psychiatric effects of terrorist attacks is steadily accumulating. Numerous studies indicate that at least 28 to 35 percent of people exposed to a terrorist attack may develop PTSD. Women and younger people are more prone to develop PTSD. After the 9/11 terrorist attacks, more than 40 percent of people across the United States experienced substantial symptoms of stress. Five to eight weeks after the terrorist attacks, the rates of acute PTSD and depression among residents of southern Manhattan were twice the baseline rates for these disorders. Besides exposure variables, predictors of PTSD included Hispanic ethnicity, female sex, the presence of preexisting stressors, and the level of social support. There was also an overall increase in cigarette smoking, alcohol consumption, and marijuana smoking during the immediate postdisaster period. In children, disaster-related television viewing was significantly related to the development of posttraumatic stress symptoms. Rates of PTSD are particularly high among populations of low-income countries experiencing terrorism as a part of war, conflict, or mass violence. Although psychological interventions continue to be the mainstay of treatment for PTSD, the role of psychological debriefing in the prevention of PTSD is questionable.

For a number of reasons, such as the indiscriminate use of the diagnosis in civil litigation and the potential for malingering for the sake of compensation, the diagnostic category of PTSD continues to draw widespread criticism (Mezey & Robbins, 2001; Summerfield, 2001). However, there is growing phenomenological as well as biochemical and neuroanatomical evidence to support the separate diagnostic status of PTSD (Yehuda, 2002). The socioeconomic consequences and the personal distress associated with PTSD are known to be substantial. There is a need to refine the diagnosis criteria of PTSD further in the *DSM-V* and the eleventh edition of the *International Classification of Diseases* based on the findings of completed and ongoing research.

There is a general consensus that primary care physicians play an important role in identifying and managing most individuals suffering from the mental health effects of trauma and terrorism (Davidson, 2001; Mayou et al., 2000; Ursano, 2002; Yehuda, 2002). Primary care physicians are best suited to educate their patients about the nature of PTSD, to provide support, as well as to teach various coping strategies. Most sufferers are often reluctant to consult mental health professionals. The training of primary care physicians in the assessment and management of the consequences of trauma will have to be undertaken to establish better mental health treatment programs in primary care settings.

REFERENCES

American Psychiatric Association (1980). *Diagnostic and statistical manual of mental disorders* (3rd ed.). Washington, DC: American Psychiatric Association.

American Psychiatric Association (1994). *Diagnostic and statistical manual of mental disorders* (4th ed.). Washington, DC: American Psychiatric Association.

Ballenger, J. C., Davidson, J. R., Lecrubier, Y., Nutt, D. J., Foa, E. B., Kessler, R. C., et al. (2000). Consensus statement on posttraumatic stress disorder from the International Consensus Group on Depression and Anxiety. *Journal of Clinical Psychiatry, 61*(Suppl. 5), 60–66.

Gidron, Y., Gal, R., Freedman, S., Twiser, I., Lauden, A., Snir, Y., et al. (2001). Translating research findings to PTSD prevention: Results of a randomized-controlled pilot study. *Journal of Traumatic Stress, 14*(4), 773–780.

Jehel, L., Duchet, C., Paterniti, S., Consoli, S. M., & Guelfi, J. D. (2001). Prospective study of post-traumatic stress in victims of terrorist attacks. *Encephale, 27*, 393–400. This paper describes a prospective study of the victims of a terrorist attack in a Paris subway six and eighteen months after the attack.

Kawana, N., Ishimatsu, S., & Kanda, K. (2001). Psycho-physiological effects of the terrorist sarin attack on the Tokyo subway system. *Military Medicine, 166*(Suppl. 12), 23–26.

LeDoux, J. E., & Gorman, J. M. (2001). A call to action: Overcoming anxiety through active coping. *American Journal of Psychiatry, 158*, 1953–1955.

Mayou, R. A., Ehlers, A., & Hobbs, M. (2000). Psychological debriefing for road traffic accident victims: Three-year follow-up of a randomised controlled trial. *British Journal of Psychiatry, 176*, 589–593.

Nader, K. O., Pynoos, R. S., Fairbanks, L. A., al-Ajeel, M., & al-Asfour, A. (1993). A preliminary study of PTSD and grief among the children of Kuwait following the Gulf crisis. *British Journal of Clinical Psychology, 32*(4), 407–416.

Najarian, L. M., Goenjian, A. K., Pelcovitz, D., Mandel, F., & Najarian, B. A. (1996). Relocation after a disaster: Posttraumatic stress disorder in Armenia after the earthquake. *Journal of the American Academy of Child and Adolescent Psychiatry, 35*(3), 374–383.

North, C. S., Nixon, S. J., Shariat, S., Mallonee, S., McMillen, J. C., Spitznagel, E. L., et al. (1999). Psychiatric disorders among survivors of the Oklahoma City bombing. *Journal of the American Medical Association, 282*, 755–762.

Pfefferbaum, B., Nixon, S. J., Krug, R. S., Tivis, R. D., Moore, V. L., Brown, J. M., et al. (1999). Clinical needs assessment of middle and high school students following the 1995 Oklahoma City bombing. *American Journal of Psychiatry, 156*(7), 1069–1074.

Pfefferbaum, B., Seale, T. W., McDonald, N. B., Brandt, E. N., Jr., Rainwater, S. M., Maynard, B. T., et al. (2000). Posttraumatic stress two years after the

Oklahoma City bombing in youths geographically distant from the explosion. *Psychiatry, 63,* 358–370.

Shaffer, D., Fisher, P., Lucas, C. P., Dulcan, M. K., & Schwab-Stone, M. E. (2000). NIMH Diagnostic Interview Schedule for Children Version IV (NIMH DISC-IV): Description, differences from previous versions, and reliability of some common diagnoses. *Journal of the American Academy of Child and Adolescent Psychiatry, 39,* 28–38.

Summerfield, D. (2001). The invention of post-traumatic stress disorder and the social usefulness of a psychiatric category. *BMJ (Clinical Research Ed.), 322,* 95–98.

Ursano, R. J. (2002). Post-traumatic stress disorder. *New England Journal of Medicine, 346,* 130–132.

World Health Organization (1992). *International classification of diseases* (10th ed.). Geneva: World Health Organization.

CHAPTER 14

Neuropsychological Processes in Posttraumatic Stress Disorder

Julia Golier and Rachel Yehuda

PHENOMENOLOGY OF POSTTRAUMATIC STRESS DISORDER IN RELATION TO MEMORY FUNCTIONING

Many of the symptoms of posttraumatic stress disorder (PTSD) are directly or indirectly related to memory. The repetitive intrusion of traumatic memories or fragments of such memories into consciousness characterize the most distinctive set of symptoms of PTSD, the reliving and reexperiencing symptoms. During the day, they take the form of recurrent images or flashbacks; at night, they come as terrifying dreams or nightmares. The memories are typically rich in perceptual detail and accompanied by intense affect, adding to the sense that the trauma is being relived rather than remembered. These symptoms are common in the immediate aftermath of trauma or disaster and typically dissipate over time. However, for persons with PTSD, the distressing images do not fade over time, and, as they persist, the trauma survivor may begin to feel that he or she has little control over them.

The avoidance symptoms consist in part of attempts to ward off these distressing memories. By avoiding certain people, places, or discussions, the survivor hopes to avoid or minimize the recall of traumatic memories. Some survivors are simultaneously unable to recall some aspects of the traumatic event, a symptom formerly called *psychogenic amnesia*, which is included among the avoidance symptoms. Psychogenic amnesia can be part of the overall fragmentation of a traumatic memory and differs from classic amnesia in that the survivor is aware of and upset by having lost information. The origin of psychogenic amnesia is unclear, but it could represent a gap; the information may never have been encoded, perhaps because of the effects of extreme stress on memory for the event. It could also result from the active suppression of painful memories or the unconscious repression of such memories. Another possibility is that the psychogenic amnesia simply results from normal forgetting and that this forgetting is especially upsetting in the context of vivid recall of other aspects of the traumatizing experience. Regardless of the precise mechanism underlying the amnesia, its coexistence with reexperiencing symptoms and other avoidance symptoms suggests that PTSD is not about overremembering or underremembering, but rather about the distortion of memory and the distress associated with it.

Poor concentration is among the symptoms in the hyperarousal cluster. Related to this, PTSD patients frequently complain of poor short-term memory. These difficulties in memory for everyday events stand in stark contrast to the readily accessible and vivid memories of distant traumatic events. These symptoms also raise the question of whether PTSD is associated with a more generalized cognitive disturbance, one that extends beyond the processing of traumatic memories and may account for the subjective sense of poor memory and perhaps other phenomenologic features of PTSD. These are among the questions that can be answered by an examination of the neuropsychology of PTSD. In the last decade, there have been many advances in our understanding of the cognitive disturbances in PTSD that allow us to address these questions.

NEUROPSYCHOLOGICAL ALTERATIONS IN PTSD

Processing of Traumatic Stimuli

Given the prominence of trauma-related symptoms in PTSD patients, a central question has been whether subjects with PTSD process trauma-related information differently from neutral information. A series of studies using the Stroop Word-Color Interference task suggests that there are important differences related to PTSD. In the Stroop task, subjects are asked to name the ink color of a series of printed words. In the original studies, it was found that when the printed word was also the name of a color, there were delays in color naming (for example, if subjects were asked to name the ink color of the word "RED" printed in blue ink). Subsequent studies found that words with emotional meaning also caused interference in color naming (MacLeod, 1991). The task was then modified for use in PTSD research to evaluate the effects of emotionally salient information on cognitive processing.

The first of the Stroop studies in PTSD was conducted with rape victims (Foa, Feske, Murdock, Kozak, & McCarthy, 1991). For rape victims with PTSD, the color-naming latency—the time between stimulus presentation and color naming—was greater for words that were specifically related to trauma ("assault," "attack") than for words in other categories, such as general threat and neutral words. In contrast, the latencies did not differ by type of word in rape victims without PTSD or nontraumatized comparison subjects. In a similar study, rape victims with PTSD, but not those without PTSD or nontraumatized control subjects, took longer to color-name highly threatening words compared with moderately threatening, positive, or neutral words (Cassiday, McNally, & Zeitlin, 1992).

Similar Stroop interference effects have been shown in victims of a ferry disaster (Thrasher, Dalgleish, & Yule, 1994) and in Vietnam combat veterans (McNally, Kaspi, Riemann, & Zeitlin, 1990). In all studies, the effect was apparent in those with PTSD as compared with traumatized subjects without PTSD. Among veterans, the interference correlated with severity of PTSD but not combat exposure (McNally et al., 1990). These findings suggest that the selective processing of trauma-relevant information is a feature of the disorder rather than an effect of trauma exposure. Additionally, interference from highly threatening words correlated with intrusive symptoms in rape victims, suggesting a link between this information-processing alteration and characteristic symptoms of PTSD.

Rapid completion of the Stroop task involves ignoring the meaning of the printed word. Thus, the interference from trauma-related words suggests that these stimuli are more difficult to ignore in subjects with PTSD and are more likely to lead to semantic activation (McNally et al., 1990). Indeed, this interference may be related to the difficulty subjects with PTSD have with the frequent intrusion of traumatic material into awareness and its rapid activation in the presence of reminders (Cassiday et al., 1992).

The Stroop experiments rather consistently demonstrate that PTSD subjects selectively process trauma-related information and raise the question of the extent to which there are more general biases in the processing of highly emotionally salient material in PTSD. It is not known whether the selective processing is a result of trauma exposure or is a characteristic of people more likely to develop PTSD. There are no data supporting either possibility; however, the latter possibility would provide a compelling explanation for why trauma exposure alone does not result in this informational bias. The possibility that it is related to risk factors is suggested by studies of the children of traumatized adults, who themselves are at greater risk for PTSD. Children of war veterans showed greater Stroop interference to war-related stimuli (Motta, Joseph, Rose, Suozzi, & Leiderman, 1997) than children of nonveterans, and children of adults with PTSD were more likely than children of control parents to show interference to threat-related information (Moradi, Neshat-Doost, Teghavi, Yule, & Dalgleish, 1999). Thus, these studies provide clues to the intergenerational effects of trauma and PTSD and highlight the importance of evaluating both risk factors and exposure when trying to understand the origins of information-processing abnormalities in PTSD.

Neuropsychological Test Performance Using Neutral Stimuli

It is also of interest to evaluate PTSD subjects' performance on standard neuropsychological tests, in which only neutral stimuli are used, to determine whether there are more generalized neuropsychological deficits associated with this disorder. These studies can help assess whether and to what extent PTSD-related cognitive symptoms reflect "organic" brain damage and whether they are associated with the subjective sense of impaired concentration and short-term memory seen in PTSD. Indeed, it has been proposed that poor memory in PTSD is a consequence of the deleterious effects of extreme stress on memory and, in particular, on aspects of learning and memory that are dependent upon the medial temporal lobe, especially the hippocampus.

The possibility of a direct link between stress and memory impairment is suggested by the stress literature. There is evidence that exposure to extreme and chronic forms of stress or high doses of the stress hormone cortisone results in atrophy of neurons in subregions of the hippocampus in animals, with a resultant decrease in memory performance (Arbel, Kadar, Silbermann, & Levy, 1994; Fuchs, Uno, & Flugge, 1995; Magarinos, McEwen, Flugge, & Fuchs, 1996; Sapolsky, Uno, Rebert, & Finch, 1990). In humans, such a link is supported by the findings of reduced memory performance following social stress or the administration of exogenous glucocorticoids (Kirschbaum, Wolf, May, Wippich, & Hellhammer, 1996; Newcomer, Craft, Hershey, Askins, & Bardgett, 1994; Wolkowitz et al., 1990). From a clinical perspective, a link is also suggested by the association of normal age-related memory decline with hippocampal atrophy and changes in the hypothalamic-pituitary-adrenal axis, the body's primary biological stress response system (Lupien et al., 1994; Lupien et al., 1998). Thus, because PTSD is precipitated by extreme traumatic stress and associated with persistent alterations in the biological response to stress, a connection between symptoms and reduced hippocampal-dependent memory performance has been sought.

Summarized in Table 14.1 are the studies that have examined cognitive functioning in PTSD using standard neuropsychological measures. Each is reviewed below. Included among the measures are tests of declarative memory, which is thought to be particularly dependent on the hippocampus (for a review, see Squire, 1992). *Declarative* or *explicit memory* is memory for facts or events that requires conscious, effortful recollection (Graf & Schacter, 1985) and is typically measured by tests of verbal recall and recognition. It is impaired in amnesia secondary to medial temporal lobe lesions (Cohen & Squire, 1980; Gabrieli, Milberg, Keane, & Corkin, 1990; Shimamura & Squire, 1984) and is sensitive to age-related hippocampal atrophy (Golomb et al., 1993; Golomb et al., 1996). This is in contrast to implicit forms of memory, such as *procedural memory* (memory of how to do something, such as ride a bike) and *priming effects*, which are not dependent on conscious recollection and are unaffected in classic forms of amnesia (Cohen & Squire, 1980; Gabrieli et al., 1990; Java & Gardiner, 1991; Shimamura & Squire, 1984).

Studies in Vietnam Combat Veterans with PTSD

The majority of neuropsychological studies in PTSD have been conducted in treatment-seeking Vietnam combat veterans. Because these subjects are exclusively male and most have had symptoms of PTSD and

Table 14.1. Summary of Neuropsychological Findings in Posttraumatic Stress Disorder

	Sample characteristics of PTSD subjects					Comparison groups		
Study	Trauma type	Age (y)	Sex (% male)	Sample size (n)	SA	Nonexposed control subjects	Trauma-exposed subjects	Psychiatric subjects
Dalton et al. (1986)	Vietnam combat	37 (1.7)	100%	22	N/A	Y	N	N
Gil et al. (1990)	Mixed	31.7 (9.1)	100%	12	N	Y	N	Y
Bremner et al. (1993)	Vietnam combat	45.7 (3.8)	100%	26	Y	Y	N	N
Gurvits et al. (1993)	Vietnam combat	43.0 (2.0)	100%	27	Y	N	Y	N
Yehuda et al. (1995)	Combat	44.7 (3.4)	100%	20	Y	Y	N	N
Golier, Yehuda, et al. (1997)	Vietnam combat	44.4 (2.2)	100%	24	Y	Y	N	N
Jenkins et al. (1998)	Rape	27.7 (6.9)	7%	15	N	Y	Y	N
Vasterling et al. (1998)	Persian Gulf combat	36.3 (2.0)	79%	19	Y	N	Y	N
Beckham et al. (1998)	Vietnam combat	49	100%	90	Y	N	Y	N
Golier et al. (2002)	Holocaust	67.8 (5.6)	31%	32	N	Y	Y	Y

(continued)

Table 14.1 (*Continued*)

| | | Group Differences | | | | |
Study	IQ	Education	Attention	Verbal memory	Other domains	Comments
Dalton et al. (1986)	N/A	N/A	N TMT	N Serial digit learning	N Stroop Color Word Test	Consecutive admissions to an inpatient stress disorder unit compared with age-scaled normative data
Gil et al. (1990)	Y	Y	Y CPT	Yes Visual reproduction Verbal paired associates (WMS) Remote memory (FES)	Y Verbal fluency	Attention and memory differences observed only in comparison with healthy comparison subjects, not other psychiatric subjects
Bremner et al. (1993)	N	N	Y WMS (immediate recall)	Y Delayed recall and retention on logical memory WMS and verbal memory in selective reminding test	Y Poorer performance in immediate and delayed visual memory	PTSD subjects less educated and with lower IQ than either healthy or psychiatric control subjects
Gurvits et al. (1993)	N	N	N TMT WMS (immediate recall)	No difference in performance on WMS (mental, figural, and logical subcomponents, paired associates)	No differences on WCST, visual reproduction, or digit span	Inpatient population; Comparison group similar number of years of alcohol use
Yehuda et al. (1995)	N	N	N CVLT (immediate recall)	Yes CVLT Greater retroactive interference and poorer delayed recall		Comparable history of past substance abuse in both groups; PTSD group had more neurological soft signs
Golier, Yehuda, et al. (1997)	N	N	N CPT	N/A		PTSD associated with trend-level differences in errors of commission

(continued)

Table 14.1 (*Continued*)

Study	IQ	Education	Attention	Verbal memory	Other domains	Comments
				Group Differences		
Jenkins et al. (1998)	N	N	Y CVLT (immediate recall)	Y CVLT—poorer delayed recall		PTSD group performed less well than both comparison groups; deficits were mild
Vasterling et al. (1998)	Y	Y	Y CPT WAIS Arithmetic	Y AVLT—poorer total, short, and delayed recall and greater retroactive interference	No significant differences on WCST	
Beckham et al. (1998)	N/A	Y	Y TMT	N/A	N/A	Attentional differences persisted even if subjects with substance abuse histories were excluded
Golier et al. (2002)	Y	Y	N/A	Y Paired associate recall		Memory deficits in PTSD group compared with nonexposed subjects and trauma-exposed subjects without PTSD present after controlling for differences in intelligence and education

Abbreviations: AVLT, Auditory-Verbal Learning Test; CPT, Continuous Performance Test; CVLT, California Verbal Learning Test; FES, Famous Events Questionnaire; N, no; N/A, not assessed; PTSD, posttraumatic stress disorder; SA, substance abuse; TMT, Trails Making Test; WAIS, Wechsler Adult Intelligence Scale; WCST, Wisconsin Card Sorting Test; WMS, Weschler Memory Scale; Y, yes.

other comorbid conditions for decades, the results of these studies may not be widely generalizable to other populations with PTSD. Although psychiatric comorbidity is common in PTSD, a particular concern in Vietnam veterans with PTSD is the high prevalence of comorbid substance abuse. Although veterans with recent substance abuse were typically excluded from these studies, a large majority had a history of lifetime substance abuse, which is itself associated with neuropsychological impairment (Svanum & Schladenhauffen, 1986) that may confound the results.

The earliest study compared the neuropsychological test performance of people with sequential admissions to a stress disorder unit with normative data. The objective was to see whether PTSD-related anxiety would so adversely affect performance that the reference norms would be inapplicable (Dalton, Pederson, Blom, & Besyner, 1986). The veterans (mean age 37 years, full-scale IQ [FSIQ] 97.3) performed within the normal range on the individual subsets on the Wechsler Adult Intelligence Scale–Revised (WAIS-R), a widely used test of general intelligence. They showed no evidence of impairment on tests of attention, memory, or "organicity." (In particular, the group's mean performance corresponded to the 50th percentile of norms for the Trail-Making Test and the 43rd percentile of the Serial Digit Learning Test and was within the normal range on the Stroop color and word test and the Shipley-Hartford test.) Thus, this group of veterans with PTSD did not show clinically significant neuropsychological impairment when tested roughly fifteen years after the war ended.

In contrast, some subsequent studies of Vietnam veterans with PTSD have found differences in test performance, although the nature and magnitude of neuropsychological differences vary considerably from one study to the next. In one, Vietnam veterans with PTSD (mean age 46 years, FSIQ 101) who were inpatients, free of alcohol use for up to two months, were compared with noncombat-exposed subjects matched for age, race, handedness, parental education, and years but not magnitude of alcohol abuse (Bremner et al., 1993). The groups did not differ on measures of intelligence but did differ on memory performance at multiple levels of processing. The PTSD veterans showed poorer performance on the logical memory subtest of the Wechsler Memory Scale (WMS) (immediate recall, delayed recall, percent retention) and on the verbal (total recall, long-term storage, long-term retrieval, delayed recall) and visual (total recall, long-term storage, long-term retrieval, delayed recall) subtests of the Selective Reminding Test (SRT). These performance differences suggest considerable impairment. Indeed, the authors note the PTSD group's retention on the SRT was comparable to subjects with gross brain damage, including subjects who had undergone resection of the temporal lobes and hippocampus for intractable epilepsy. Thus, performance differences were clearly apparent in this group. Indeed, the magnitude of impairment was so considerable that it raises the question of whether these deficits are typical of patients with chronic PTSD or are reflective of a particularly ill subset of patients.

The next published study used the California Verbal Learning Test (CVLT), a test of serial verbal learning. This test involves multiple presentations and tests of recall of one list of words followed by a single presentation of a second list. Outpatients with PTSD (mean age 45) were compared to healthy, nonexposed comparison subjects, from whom they did not differ on measures of intelligence (Yehuda et al., 1995). In contrast to the previous study, the groups did not differ on other measures, including initial attention, immediate memory, total learning, recall after the first and fifth learning trials, or cumulative learning. However, the PTSD subjects showed greater retroactive interference. That is, the learning of new material from the second list interfered with the recall of previously learned information from the first list, with a resultant decrease in recall and retention of the first list. Thus, whereas the two studies mentioned above had similar methodologies, one found diffuse and the other circumscribed memory differences. The discrepancy may be caused by differences in the population (inpatients versus outpatients) or may be attributable to differences in attention. Immediate recall, considered a measure of attention, was impaired in the former study but not the latter and may have had diffuse effects on performance with a resultant decrease in short-term and delayed recall.

Finally, in another study of Vietnam combat veterans, those with PTSD performed less well but not significantly differently from combat veterans without PTSD on multiple measures of the WMS scale, including the mental, figural, and logical subcomponents, and on paired associates, digit span, and visual reproduction (Gurvits et al., 1993). Unlike previous studies, this one compared PTSD veterans with veterans who did not have PTSD but had been exposed to combat. Thus, the lack of significant neuropsychological differences between these two groups of veterans supports the possibility that poorer performance in the previously discussed studies may be related to combat exposure or other characteristics of combat veterans rather than to a diagnosis of PTSD per se. On the other hand, the study may have been underpowered with respect to detecting differences between these two groups of veterans.

The findings with respect to attentional abnormalities are also mixed in this population. Although some discrepancies between studies could be attributable to differences in the types of test used, notable differences have emerged even with the use of the same test. For example, the Trail-Making Test, a test of visual search and attention, mental flexibility, and motor function, has been used in multiple studies with varying results. In the earliest study, veterans with PTSD (mean age 37) took an average of 70 seconds to complete Trail B, scoring just below the 50th percentile (65 seconds) for their age group (slower performance is considered worse performance) (Dalton et al., 1986). In the next study, the PTSD group (mean age 45) performed nonsignificantly more slowly than combat-exposed comparison subjects (83 versus 62 seconds) and also just below the 50th percentile for their age range (Gurvits et al., 1993). However, in the largest study, PTSD subjects (mean age 49) performed significantly worse than veterans without PTSD (101 seconds versus 75 seconds) (Beckham, Crawford, & Feldman, 1998); their mean score corresponded to the 10th to the 25th percentile of normative data. Within this larger group, it was possible to examine the contribution of age, education, medication use, and comorbid psychiatric disorders, which did not appear to explain the group differences. Thus, there is considerable variability in attentional performance, but at least a subset of Vietnam veterans with PTSD appears to have reduced attentional capacity and mental flexibility. Older age was associated with worse performance (Beckham et al., 1998), and among the different studies, the worst performance was found in the oldest sample. This suggests the possibility that even within this narrow age range, poorer performance in PTSD may be associated with aging or chronicity of illness and that attentional impairment may become more pronounced over time.

Studies in Other Groups with PTSD

It is important to study neuropsychological performance in groups other than Vietnam veterans to identify whether alterations are also present in PTSD associated with other types of traumatic events or in less chronic or severe forms of the illness. One such group is veterans of the Persian Gulf War, who are younger and more recently exposed to warzone stress than Vietnam veterans and who appear to have lower rates of comorbid substance abuse.

Like Vietnam veterans with PTSD, Gulf War veterans with PTSD show evidence of poorer performance on tests of both attention and memory. Unlike in the studies of Vietnam veterans, poorer performance was evident in veterans with PTSD compared to veterans without PTSD (Vasterling, Brailey, Constans, and Sutker, 1998). On the Auditory-Verbal Learning Test (AVLT) (a test similar to the CVLT), Gulf War veterans with PTSD performed poorly on multiple measures of learning and memory (e.g., total recall, short-delay recall, and long-delay recall) and showed greater retroactive interference. When initial recall was controlled for, the PTSD group no longer showed poorer delayed recall and retention. The pattern of errors was also examined. The PTSD group made more errors of intrusion on the AVLT. Similarly, on the Continuous Performance Test (CPT), a measure of sustained attention, the PTSD group made more errors of commission but not of omission. That is, they incorrectly responded to nontarget stimuli more often but correctly responded to the target sequence as often.

Vasterling et al. (1998) argue that these findings suggest a pattern of response in PTSD characterized by more intrusive errors and a general tendency toward disinhibition. Further analysis of their data revealed that a general tendency to make intrusive errors on these neutral standardized tests was highly positively correlated with reexperiencing symptoms. It was also inversely correlated with avoidance and not associated with hyperarousal. Thus, these data suggest that the intrusion of trauma-related material may reflect a more general tendency for intrusive cognition that applies to both neutral and trauma-related material.

In Israeli trauma survivors with PTSD secondary to combat, accidents, or terrorist attacks, multiple cognitive deficits were found that were more pronounced and diffuse than those described in Gulf War or Vietnam veterans. Compared with healthy normal subjects, the PTSD subjects performed poorly on tests of general intelligence and on tests of attention, memory, and verbal fluency; they also performed poorly on tests sensitive to "organic" lesions, even though the PTSD subjects were free of substance abuse or head trauma (Gil, Calev, Greenberg, Kuglemass, & Lerer, 1990). The authors argued that the group differences in IQ, with a mean of 88.1 (standard deviation [SD] = 11.4) for the PTSD group versus 108.1 (SD = 8.8) for the control group, stem from a decrease in intellectual functioning in the PTSD group, and that the PTSD group's current IQ was lower than their estimated premorbid IQ. If the lower IQ reflects a change in intellectual functioning, then these results point to diffuse impairments beyond memory and attention that originate at the time of trauma or in tandem with the development of PTSD. On the other hand, the significance of the considerable group differences in attention, memory, and organicity are difficult to interpret in light of the significant group differences in both current IQ and educational level (9.9 years [SD = 2.5] for the PTSD group versus 11.9 [SD = 2.9] years for the controls).

Perhaps even more important, though, is that this is the only study in which PTSD subjects were also compared with other psychiatric patients. The PTSD subjects did not differ from the other psychiatric patients in education, current IQ, or estimated premorbid IQ. No performance differences were found between the PTSD group and these psychiatric outpatients with other anxiety or affective disorders. The psychiatric comparison group also performed less well than the healthy group. This further suggests that the cognitive findings may not be specific to PTSD but rather may reflect psychopathology in general.

Finally, performance differences have also been found in PTSD secondary to sexual assault, a type of trauma especially linked to PTSD in women. On the CVLT, rape victims with PTSD showed nonsignificantly poorer performance in total learning and short-term delay and significantly poorer delayed recall (Jenkins, Langlais, Delis, & Cohen, 1998). Unlike in some of the aforementioned studies, the recall deficits were rather mild and were diminished with cueing. Additionally, no differences were apparent in recognition memory. Poorer performance was evident in comparison to both nonexposed subjects and rape victims without PTSD. These comparison groups in turn did not differ from each other, suggesting that the memory differences in the PTSD subjects are not directly attributable to the trauma of rape. Furthermore, because alcohol abuse was uncommon, the rape victims with and without PTSD had similar histories of other anxiety disorders, and the effects of depressive symptoms were controlled for, the performance differences do not appear to be the result of psychiatric comorbidity.

Studies of Aged Survivors

Most studies in PTSD have been conducted in young or middle-aged adults; very few have been done in older trauma survivors. Although PTSD is more common in younger groups, the rationale for studying older survivors is that for survivors with chronic PTSD, symptoms can persist into later life. Because aging has effects on memory and the biological response to stress, age-related changes may bear directly on the expression of PTSD symptoms and related memory complaints. Of particular interest is whether neuropsychological alterations in older survivors are similar to or different from those of younger survivors and whether the alterations change with age.

In veterans of the Korean conflict, former prisoners of war (POWs) (mean age 56) were found to have greater complaints of poor concentration and poorer immediate and delayed verbal recall than combat veterans who had not been interned (Sutker, Winstead, Galina, & Allain, 1991). Physical trauma likely played a role in these differences. For example, many POWs were malnourished in captivity and substantial weight loss during confinement was associated with worse performance on multiple measures (Sutker, Galina, West, & Allain, 1990). However, it is also notable that the POWs had a substantiality higher rate of PTSD than the comparison group (86% versus 9%), which may have also contributed to performance differences.

Clinical observations in another group of older survivors, Holocaust survivors, have suggested that premature memory loss may be characteristic of survivors with the "Concentration Camp Syndrome" (Eitinger, 1985). The question of whether Holocaust survivors suffer from premature senility prompted neuropathologic studies in these older survivors, which did not reveal neuropathological evidence of classic dementing illnesses (Eitinger, 1985). Nonetheless, the question remains about the nature and severity of the cognitive dysfunction in older survivors and whether stress or PTSD contributes to the deleterious effects of age on memory in trauma survivors.

Preliminary studies of the relationships between age, cognition, and PTSD have been conducted in men and women who survived the Holocaust. Using the paired associates tests, Holocaust survivors with PTSD (mean age 66) showed poorer recall of semantically related and unrelated pairs of words than either Holocaust survivors without PTSD or non-exposed subjects (Golier et al., 2002). In contrast to these differences in explicit memory, there were no differences in implicit memory, as measured by the word-stem completion. The relationship between age and explicit memory performance differed significantly among the groups. Poorer performance was strongly associated with older age in the PTSD group but not in the other two groups. There are several potential explanations for this relationship; among them is the possibility that PTSD is associated with greater age-related decline in cognition. The question can only be fully addressed with longitudinal studies. If it turns out that there is greater age-related decline in PTSD, it would suggest that cognitive impairment may be an additional burden of this illness with age.

Relevance of the Neuropsychological Findings

These neuropsychological studies suggest that there are performance differences in both attention and memory in subjects with chronic PTSD that are not limited to one particular type of trauma survivor. The magnitude and nature of the differences varied considerably among the studies. Whereas aging, comorbid substance abuse, and associated physical trauma contributed to greater deficits, considerable performance differences were also observed in the absence of these features. Thus, the question arises about whether these performance differences are indicative of a specific type of neuropsychological impairment or of dysfunction of a particular neuroanatomical region. The finding of such a neuroanatomical substrate in PTSD would have considerable implications for the diagnosis, pathophysiology, and treatment of this disorder.

Poor verbal recall was found in many, but not all, studies, indicating poorer explicit memory in PTSD—a finding that has been taken as evidence of hippocampal impairment in PTSD. However, it would be premature to conclude that the neuropsychological studies in PTSD to date are necessarily indicative of hippocampal impairment. To begin with, poorer memory performance can result from damage to other brain areas. It is typically a pattern of alterations that are indicative of pathology of a given area, including both the presence and absence of certain findings; one particular abnormality is not usually sufficient for localization. This is illustrated in the classic account of H.M., a patient who underwent bilateral removal of the medial temporal lobe, including the hippocampus, and was unable to acquire new memories (Scoville & Milner, 2000). The antereograde amnesia (an inability to form new long-term memories) was severe, but the overall deficit was circumscribed; H.M. had no difficulty in immediate memory or in the recall of early personal experiences and had no measurable change in intelligence or personality. Similar cases were reported, and over time a profile has emerged of typical cases of organic amnesia caused by medial temporal lobe pathology. In typical cases, short-term memory and intelligence are unaffected, whereas there is poor acquisition and retention of new episodic and semantic information, characterized by deficits in both recall and recognition memory (Manns & Squire, 1999; Reed & Squire, 1997; Zola-Morgan & Squire, 1990).

Support for the notion that the hippocampus is critically involved in delayed recall, as opposed to immediate or short-term recall, has been shown more recently in structural imaging studies in normal aging and in pathological states like Alzheimer's disease (Golomb et al., 1993; Golomb et al., 1994). Thus, delayed memory appears to be particularly dependent on the hippocampus. In nearly all studies in PTSD in which delayed recall was impaired, immediate recall was also impaired. Only one study statistically accounted for the effects of immediate recall; it found that delayed recall was no longer significantly impaired after this adjustment (Vasterling et al., 1998). Additionally, recognition memory was unimpaired in PTSD (Jenkins et al., 1998). Thus, the current literature in PTSD does not provide compelling evidence for a specific impairment of delayed verbal recall and recognition memory, which are characteristic of medial temporal lobe lesions.

Explicit memory is also impaired in frontal lobe lesions, although the precise nature of such deficits has not been fully delineated and depends on the location of the lesion and the extent of the damage. However, frontal lobe damage often results in poor recall of recently learned material without impairment in recognition memory (Mayes, 1988). Subjects with frontal lobe damage are also especially sensitive to interference effects and have difficulty judging the temporal order of past events (Shimamura, Janowsky, & Squire, 1990). Furthermore, frontal lobe lesions are associated with changes in intelligence, executive functioning, and attention and with deficits not related to cognition, such as initiative, mood, and personality, which are areas that can also be affected in PTSD. Indeed, Vasterling et al. (1998) argue that the pattern of intrusive errors in Gulf War veterans with PTSD on the CPT and AVLT indicates a pattern of disinhibition more consistent with frontal than medial-temporal lobe pathology.

A similar pattern of errors on the CPT was observed in Vietnam veterans with PTSD, who showed a trend toward more commission errors with no difference in sustained attention (Golier, Yehuda, et al., 1997). Greater interference effects have also been found in both Vietnam and Gulf War veterans with PTSD (Vasterling et al., 1998; Yehuda et al., 1995). Additionally, the paired associate findings in Holocaust survivors could reflect both hippocampal and frontal lobe impairment (Golier et al., 2002). Indeed, functional imaging studies have provided evidence that the prefrontal cortex is activated during explicit memory tasks (Fletcher, Frith, & Rugg, 1997), and the paired associate test in particular activates regions of the frontal cortex (Buckner et al., 1995; Halsband et al., 1998; Krause et al., 1999; Mottaghy et al., 1999). Furthermore, source monitoring (i.e., identification of the source of memories), which is thought to depend on intact frontal lobe pathology, was found to be poor in Vietnam combat veterans with PTSD compared with normative data (Golier, Harvey, Steiner, & Yehuda, 1997). Finally, the studies of trauma survivors in Israel raised the possibility of intellectual decline in survivors with PTSD. All of these are consistent with the possibility of impairment of the frontal lobes, which might also explain some of the nonspecific features of PTSD, such as depressed mood and social withdrawal.

On the other hand, not all the findings have been consistent with respect to frontal lobe pathology. Most notably, performance on the Wisconsin Card Sorting Test, a test of planning and executive functioning thought to be particularly sensitive to frontal lobe pathology (Janowsky, Shimamura, Kritchevsky, & Squire, 1989), was not significantly impaired in either Gulf War or Vietnam veterans with PTSD.

As the field goes forward, it will be important to consider whether individual findings or collections of findings indicate pathology of a specific brain region. Furthermore, it will be important to examine whether there are subgroups of subjects with PTSD that differ according to the type of associated cognitive impairment and whether there is a link between PTSD symptoms, cognitive symptoms, and neuropsychological functioning. Furthermore, because attention and memory abnormalities have been described in multiple psychiatric disorders, additional work is needed to examine which neuropsychological findings are specific to PTSD and which reflect comorbidity or psychopathology in general.

Risk Factors and the Course of Memory Alterations in PTSD

One of the gaps in our knowledge of the neuropsychology of PTSD is that it is not known when the performance differences first become manifest. The question of when the differences are evident bears on the question of whether there are cognitive risk factors for PTSD. One possibility is that individuals with PTSD had preexisting neuropsychological difficulties that made them more susceptible to developing posttraumatic psychopathology and its associated memory disturbances. Alternatively, impairments may not develop until later exposure, supporting the notion that traumatic stress itself induces memory impairments or that they develop in association with or as a consequence of PTSD. To date, there are no prospective studies that could help discriminate among these different possibilities. Indeed, there are not yet neuropsychological studies of acute stress disorder or even of chronic PTSD of relatively brief duration. Thus, the onset and course of memory and attentional impairments is not yet known. However, there is increasing evidence that risk factors play a role in the development of PTSD and that some of the psychological and biological findings described in chronic PTSD may antedate trauma exposure. Poorer cognitive functioning is among these possible risk factors.

Multiple factors mediate the psychological response to trauma. The severity and type of trauma affect the likelihood of developing PTSD (Breslau, Chilcoat, Kessler, Peterson, & Lucia, 1999; Green, Grace, Lindy, Gleser, & Leonard, 1990; Kessler, Sonnega, Bromet, Hughes, & Nelson, 1995), as do the individual characteristics of the survivor. Commonly identified pretraumatic risk factors for PTSD include female gender (Kessler et al., 1995), previous trauma exposure (Breslau, Chilcoat, Kessler, & Davis, 1999), and a personal or family history of psychiatric disorder (Perkonigg, Kessler, Storz, & Wittchen, 2000).

Lower education and intelligence are among the pretraumatic risk factors for PTSD that could directly affect neuropsychological test performance. Intelligence was found to be associated with PTSD symptoms in Vietnam veterans, with lower full-scale IQ significantly predicting a greater severity of PTSD symptoms, beyond that predicted by the magnitude of combat exposure (McNally & Shin, 1995). Because lower intellectual functioning could reflect either psychopathology or be a risk factor for it, a subsequent study examined premorbid intelligence and its relationship to PTSD (Macklin et al., 1998). By obtaining preexposure military aptitude tests in Vietnam veterans, Macklin and colleagues were able to measure preexposure intellectual functioning, which was found to significantly predict PTSD symptoms. In fact, after controlling for precombat intelligence, current intellectual functioning was no longer associated with PTSD. It should be noted, however, that IQ predicted symptoms among a group of veterans with normal intelligence and that the average performance in the PTSD groups in all such studies of veterans was average; thus, although lower IQ may predict PTSD, the PTSD groups were not characterized by low intelligence.

A greater number of neurological soft signs have also been found both in sexually abused women and in Vietnam combat veterans with PTSD. These soft signs suggest subtle neurological compromise and were associated with a history of neurodevelopmental problems and lower IQ (Gurvits et al., 2000). Lower education and early misconduct, which may be associated with poorer test performance, have also been shown to predict trauma exposure in urban youth, both in retrospective and prospective studies (Breslau, Davis, & Andreski, 1995). These findings suggest that there appear to be risk factors directly or indirectly related to cognitive functioning that increase the risk of both exposure and the subsequent development of PTSD. These factors could certainly affect both neuropsychological test performance and the ability to cope after traumatization, but if not accounted for could lead to the erroneous conclusion that performance differences are the result of trauma or chronic PTSD.

In the study by Gil et al. (1990), the researchers found evidence of intellectual decline, so it is also possible that neuropsychological alterations in PTSD represent decreased performance from baseline. The two possibilities are not mutually exclusive, however. The existence of risk factors related to cognition does not exclude the possibility that there is also a posttraumatic decline in cognitive or intellectual functioning in those who develop PTSD. Indeed, in normal aging, lower education or intelligence may be risk factors for cognitive decline.

Prospective and longitudinal studies examining neuropsychological functioning in PTSD have not been done, but one study has been done examining hippocampal volume longitudinally. Assessing brain morphology over time is especially important, because the idea has been put forth that stress might directly induce neuropsychological alterations by causing damage to the brain and in particular to the hippocampus (Bremner, 1999). Several studies have found that adult subjects with chronic PTSD have smaller hippocampal volumes than either nonexposed or trauma-exposed control subjects (Bremner et al., 1995, 1997; Gurvits et al., 1996; Stein, Koverola, Hanna, Torchia, & McClarty, 1997). Whereas the overall findings were similar, these studies suffer from some of the same limitations as the neuropsychological ones—namely, that they were conducted in subjects with very chronic forms of PTSD who had high rates of comorbid substance abuse and other psychiatric conditions. These limitations are particularly important, because smaller hippocampal volumes have been described in depression (Bremner et al., 2000), schizophrenia, and substance abuse (De Bellis et al., 2000; Laakso et al., 2000) and in association with normal aging. In a prospective study of traumatized adults, structural MRIs were obtained very early after traumatization and again six months later (Bonne et al., 2001). No volumetric differences were found at baseline or at six months between those who did or did not develop PTSD. Thus, this study suggests that reduced hippocampal volume is neither a necessary risk factor for the development of PTSD nor was it present early in the course of PTSD.

To the extent that these morphological brain differences may be associated only with chronic PTSD, we need to consider the possibility that this will be the case for the neuropsychological alterations as well. Therefore, additional work is needed to evaluate whether neuropsychological altera- tions are seen only in those with very chronic and treatment-resistant forms of PTSD or are also present in those with less chronic forms, who are more likely to recover.

FUTURE DIRECTIONS

The challenge ahead is in determining whether there are any particular cognitive or neurodevelopmental risk factors that are specific for the devel- opment of PTSD or other forms of posttraumatic psychopathology and whether and to what extent they account for the neuropsychological dif- ferences observed in patients with PTSD. Such information would further our understanding of how these pre- or peritraumatic cognitive factors might interact with the experience of fear and threat to give rise to post- traumatic psychopathology.

One of the problems with trying to find cognitive risk factors for PTSD is that multiple abnormalities have been described, none of which may be specific to PTSD. Rather, there may be a series of abnormalities suggestive of a generalized deficit. Thus, in the search for cognitive risk factors, spe- cifically for PTSD, it may be helpful to look not only at memory and attention but also for evidence of heightened cognitive abilities or particu- lar cognitive styles (Yehuda & Harvey, 1997). Among the candidates sug- gested is hypnotizability, which is not itself pathological but might predispose trauma survivors to develop dissociative symptoms following trauma exposure (Butler, Duran, Jasiukaitis, Koopman, & Spiegel, 1996). Indeed, intense peritraumatic experience has been shown to predict PTSD in both retrospective and prospective studies, independent of the magni- tude of trauma exposure (Koopman, Classen, & Spiegel, 1994; Marmar et al., 1994; Ursano et al., 1999). Survivors may experience a sense of confu- sion, disorientation, and a distortion of sense of time or place or altera- tions in pain perception, reality, or body image (Marmar et al., 1994). Further work is needed to evaluate whether pretraumatic hypnotizability predicts symptoms following exposure and to examine the relationship of peritraumatic dissociation to neuropsychological functioning and other potential cognitive risk factors for PTSD. This would help clarify the extent to which differences in the cognitive and perceptual response to overwhelming trauma that may predate exposure and contribute to the pathological response to trauma.

In summary, there have been multiple studies over the past decade that have revealed that chronic PTSD is associated not only with heightened sensitivity to trauma-related stimuli but also with more generalized deficits in attention and memory that do not appear to be fully accounted for by trauma exposure or associated features of PTSD, such as comorbid sub- stance abuse. No single neuropsychological profile for PTSD has emerged, but multiple studies have found poorer visual search and attention and short-term verbal memory and greater retroactive interference. Poorer delayed verbal recall has also been found consistently, but it remains unclear to what extent this may reflect poorer attention and short-term recall. To aid localization, further work is needed to examine the extent to which there are patterns of deficits within the same individuals or groups of individuals and how consistent they are with models of dysfunction of the medial-temporal or frontal lobes or other brain areas. Additional work is needed to study individuals across the lifespan, cross-sectionally and longitudinally, to assess the relationship of impairments to age and chronicity of illness.

Prospective and longitudinal studies, though expensive and time-consuming, will be critical in determining whether there is evidence for pretraumatic risk factors and posttraumatic decline. The prospective study of trauma survivors would also provide the opportunity to evaluate the specificity of the findings by examining the extent to which they are limited to survivors with PTSD or are also present in those with other posttraumatic psychiatric disorders, such as depression or panic disorder. The elucidation of cognitive risk factors may improve the assessment and triage of survivors in the acute aftermath of trauma, enhance allocation of services to those most at risk, and improve the longer-term outcome of PTSD. Similarly, studying the effects of treatment intervention on memory function could improve our understanding of the process of therapeutic change and whether symptom improvement is associated with changes in neuropsychological functioning. Studies of PTSD subjects before and after successful treatment would also provide information about whether the neuropsychological alterations are state related, in which case they would not likely be related to risk, or are trait markers. Including cognitive assessments in treatment studies would also allow us to examine a broader range of outcomes and predictors of outcome. Thus, a better understanding of the course, specificity, and localization of the neuropsychological alterations in PTSD could ultimately aid in the assessment and effective treatment of trauma survivors.

REFERENCES

Arbel, I., Kadar, T., Silbermann, M., & Levy, A. (1994). The effects of long-term corticosterone administration on hippocampal morphology and cognitive performance of middle-aged rats. *Brain Research, 657*(1–2), 227–235.

Beckham, J. C., Crawford, A. L., & Feldman, M. E. (1998). Trail making test performance in Vietnam combat veterans with and without posttraumatic stress disorder. *Journal of Traumatic Stress, 11,* 811–819.

Bonne, O., Brandes, D., Gilboa, A., Gomori, J. M., Shenton, M. E., Pitman, R. K., et al. (2001). Longitudinal MRI study of hippocampal volume in trauma survivors with PTSD. *American Journal of Psychiatry, 158,* 1248–1251.

Bremner, J. D. (1999). Does stress damage the brain? *Biological Psychiatry, 45,* 797–805.

Bremner, J. D., Narayan, M., Anderson, E. R., Staib, L. F., Miller, H. L., & Charney, D. S. (2000). Hippocampal volume reduction in major depression. *American Journal of Psychiatry, 157,* 115–118.

Bremner, J. D., Randall, P., Scott, T. M., Bronen, R. A., Seibyl, J. P., Southwick, S. M., et al. (1995). MRI-based measurement of hippocampal volumes in patients with combat-related posttraumatic stress disorder. *American Journal of Psychiatry, 152,* 973–981.

Bremner, J. D., Randall, P., Vermetten, E., Staib, L., Bronen, R. A., Mazure, C., et al. (1997). Magnetic resonance imaging–based measurement of hippocampal volume in posttraumatic stress disorder related to childhood physical and sexual abuse: A preliminary report. *Biological Psychiatry, 41,* 23–32.

Bremner, J. D., Scott, T. M., Delaney, R. C., Southwick, S. M., Mason, J. W., Johnson, D. R., et al. (1993). Deficits in short-term memory in posttraumatic stress disorder. *American Journal of Psychiatry, 150,* 1015–1019.

Breslau, N., Chilcoat, H. D., Kessler, R. C., & Davis, G. C. (1999). Previous exposure to trauma and PTSD effects of subsequent trauma: Results from the Detroit Area Survey of Trauma. *American Journal of Psychiatry, 156,* 902–907.

Breslau, N., Chilcoat, H. D., Kessler, R. C., Peterson, E. L., & Lucia, V. C. (1999). Vulnerability to assaultive violence: Further specification of the sex difference in post-traumatic stress disorder. *Psychological Medicine, 29,* 813–821.

Breslau, N., Davis, G. C., & Andreski, P. (1995). Risk factors for PTSD-related traumatic events: A prospective analysis. *American Journal of Psychiatry, 152,* 529–535.

Buckner, R. L., Petersen, S. E., Ojemann, J. G., Miezin, F. M., Squire, L. R., & Raichle, M. E. (1995). Functional anatomical studies of explicit and implicit memory retrieval tasks. *Journal of Neuroscience, 15,* 12–29.

Butler, L. D., Duran, R. E., Jasiukaitis, P., Koopman, C., & Spiegel, D. (1996). Hypnotizability and traumatic experience: A diathesis-stress model of dissociative symptomatology. *American Journal of Psychiatry, 153*(Suppl. 7), 42–63.

Cassiday, K. L., McNally, R. J., & Zeitlin, S. B. (1992). Cognitive processing of trauma cues in rape victims with post-traumatic stress disorder. *Cognitive Therapy and Research, 16,* 283–295.

Cohen, N. J., & Squire, L. R. (1980). Preserved learning and retention of pattern-analyzing skill in amnesia: Dissociation of knowing how and knowing that. *Science, 210,* 207–210.

Dalton, J. E., Pederson, S. L., Blom, B. E., & Besyner, J. K. (1986). Neuropsychological screening for Vietnam veterans with PTSD. *VA Practitioner, 3,* 37–47.

De Bellis, M. D., Clark, D. B., Beers, S. R., Soloff, P. H., Boring, A. M., Hall, J., et al. (2000). Hippocampal volume in adolescent-onset alcohol use disorders. *American Journal of Psychiatry, 157,* 737–744.

Eitinger, L. (1985). The Concentration Camp syndrome: An organic brain syndrome? *Integrative Psychiatry, 3,* 115–126.

Fletcher, P. C., Frith, C. D., & Rugg, M. D. (1997). The functional neuroanatomy of episodic memory. *Trends in Neurosciences, 20,* 213–218.

Foa, E. B., Feske, U., Murdock, T. B., Kozak, M. J., & McCarthy, P. R. (1991). Processing of threat-related information in rape victims. *Journal of Abnormal Psychology, 100,* 156–162.

Fuchs, E., Uno, H., & Flugge, G. (1995). Chronic psychosocial stress induces morphological alterations in hippocampal pyramidal neurons of the tree shrew. *Brain Research, 673,* 275–282.

Gabrieli, J. D., Milberg, W., Keane, M. M., & Corkin, S. (1990). Intact priming of patterns despite impaired memory. *Neuropsychologia, 28,* 417–427.

Gil, T., Calev, A., Greenberg, D., Kuglemass, S., & Lerer, B. (1990). Cognitive functioning in post-traumatic stress disorder. *Journal of Traumatic Stress, 3,* 29–45.

Golier, J., Harvey, P., Steiner, A., & Yehuda, R. (1997). Source monitoring in PTSD. *Annals of the New York Academy of Science, 821,* 472–475.

Golier, J., Yehuda, R., Cornblatt, B., Harvey, P., Gerber, D., & Levengood, R. (1997). Sustained attention in combat-related posttraumatic stress disorder. *Integrative Physiological and Behavioral Science, 32,* 52–61.

Golier, J., Yehuda, R., Lupien, S. J., Harvey, P. D., Grossman, R., & Elkin, A. (2002). Memory performance in Holocaust survivors with posttraumatic stress disorder. *American Journal of Psychiatry, 159,* 1682–1688.

Golomb, J., de Leon, M., Kluger, A., George, A. E., Tarshish, C., & Ferris, S. H. (1993). Hippocampal atrophy in normal aging: An association with recent memory impairment. *Archives of Neurology, 50,* 967–973.

Golomb, J., Kluger, A., de Leon, M. J., Ferris, S. H., Convit, A., Mittelman, M. S., et al. (1994). Hippocampal formation size in normal human aging: A correlate of delayed secondary memory performance. *Learning & Memory, 1,* 45–54.

Golomb, J., Kluger, A., de Leon, M. J., Ferris, S. H., Mittelman, M., Cohen, J., et al. (1996). Hippocampal formation size predicts declining memory performance in normal aging. *Neurology, 47,* 810–813.

Graf, P., & Schacter, D. L. (1985). Implicit and explicit memory for new associations in normal and amnesic subjects. *Journal of Experimental Psychology: Learning, Memory, and Cognition, 11,* 501–518.

Green, B. L., Grace, M. C., Lindy, J. D., Gleser, G. C., & Leonard, A. (1990). Risk factors for PTSD and other diagnoses in a general sample of Vietnam veterans. *American Journal of Psychiatry, 147,* 729–733.

Gurvits, T. V., Gilbertson, M. W., Lasko, N. M., Tarhan, A. S., Simeon, D., Macklin, M. L., et al. (2000). Neurologic soft signs in chronic posttraumatic stress disorder. *Archives of General Psychiatry, 57,* 181–186.

Gurvits, T. V., Lasko, N. B., Schachter, S. C., Kuhne, A. A., Orr, S. P., & Pitman, R. K. (1993). Neurological status of Vietnam veterans with chronic posttraumatic stress disorder. *Journal of Neuropsychiatry and Clinical Neurosciences, 5,* 183–188.

Gurvits, T. V., Shenton, M. E., Hokama, H., Ohta, H., Lasko, N. B., Gilbertson, M. W., et al. (1996). Magnetic resonance imaging study of hippocampal volume in chronic, combat-related posttraumatic stress disorder. *Biological Psychiatry, 40,* 1091–1099.

Halsband, U., Krause, B. J., Schmidt, D., Herzog, H., Tellmann, L., & Müller-Gärtner, H. W. (1998). Encoding and retrieval in declarative learning: A positron emission tomography study. *Behavioural Brain Research, 97*(1–2), 69–78.

Janowsky, J. S., Shimamura, A. P., Kritchevsky, M., & Squire, L. R. (1989). Cognitive impairment following frontal lobe damage and its relevance to human amnesia. *Behavioral Neuroscience, 103,* 548–560.

Java, R. I., & Gardiner, J. M. (1991). Priming and aging: Further evidence of preserved memory function. *American Journal of Psychology, 104,* 89–100.

Jenkins, M. A., Langlais, P. J., Delis, D., & Cohen, R. (1998). Learning and memory in rape victims with posttraumatic stress disorder. *American Journal of Psychiatry, 155,* 278–279.

Kessler, R. C., Sonnega, A., Bromet, E., Hughes, M., & Nelson, C. B. (1995). Posttraumatic stress disorder in the National Comorbidity Survey. *Archives of General Psychiatry, 52,* 1048–1060.

Kirschbaum, C., Wolf, O. T., May, M., Wippich, W., & Hellhammer, D. H. (1996). Stress- and treatment-induced elevations of cortisol levels associated with impaired declarative memory in healthy adults, *Life Sciences, 58*, 1475–1483.

Koopman, C., Classen, C. C., & Spiegel, D. (1994). Predictors of posttraumatic stress symptoms among survivors of the Oakland/Berkeley, Calif., firestorm. *American Journal of Psychiatry, 141*, 888–894.

Krause, B. J., Schmidt, D., Mottaghy, F. M., Taylor, J., Halsband, U., Herzog, H., et al. (1999). Episodic retrieval activates the precuneus irrespective of the imagery content of word pair associates: A PET study. *Brain, 122*(Pt. 2), 255–263.

Laakso, M. P., Vaurio, O., Savolainen, L., Repo, E., Soininen, H., Aronen, H. J., et al. (2000). A volumetric MRI study of the hippocampus in type 1 and 2 alcoholism. *Behavioural Brain Research, 109*, 177–186.

Lupien, S. J., de Leon, M., de Santi, S., Convit, A., Tarshish, C., Nair, N. P., et al. (1998). Cortisol levels during human aging predict hippocampal atrophy and memory deficits. *Nature Neuroscience, 1*, 69–73.

Lupien, S., Lecours, A. R., Lussier, I., Schwartz, G., Nair, N. P., & Meaney, M. J. (1994). Basal cortisol levels and cognitive deficits in human aging. *Journal of Neuroscience, 14*, 2893–2903.

Macklin, M. L., Metzger, L. J., Litz, B. T., McNally, R. J., Lasko, N. B., Orr, S. P., et al. (1998). Lower precombat intelligence is a risk factor for posttraumatic stress disorder. *Journal of Consulting and Clinical Psychology, 66*, 323–326.

MacLeod, C. M. (1991). Half a century of research on the Stroop effect: An integrative review. *Psychological Bulletin, 109*, 163–203.

Magarinos, A. M., McEwen, B. S., Flugge, G., & Fuchs, E. (1996). Chronic psychosocial stress causes apical dendritic atrophy of hippocampal CA3 pyramidal neurons in subordinate tree shrews. *Journal of Neuroscience, 16*, 3534–3540.

Manns, J. R., & Squire, L. R. (1999). Impaired recognition memory on the Doors and People Test after damage limited to the hippocampal region. *Hippocampus, 9*, 495–499.

Marmar, C. R., Weiss, D. S., Schlenger, W. E., Fairbank, J. A., Jordan, B. K., Kulka, R. A., et al. (1994). Peritraumatic dissociation and posttraumatic stress in male Vietnam theater veterans. *American Journal of Psychiatry, 151*, 902–907.

Mayes, A. R. (1988). The memory problems caused by frontal lobe lesions. In *Human organic memory disorders* (pp. 102–123). Cambridge: Cambridge University Press.

McNally, R. J., Kaspi, S. P., Riemann, B. C., & Zeitlin, S. B. (1990). Selective processing of threat cues in posttraumatic stress disorder. *Journal of Abnormal Psychology, 99*, 398–402.

McNally, R. J., & Shin, L. M. (1995). Association of intelligence with severity of posttraumatic stress disorder symptoms in Vietnam combat veterans. *American Journal of Psychiatry, 152*, 936–938.

Moradi, A. R., Neshat-Doost, H. T., Teghavi, R., Yule, W., & Dalgleish, T. (1999). Performance of children of adults with PTSD on the Stroop color-naming task: A preliminary study. *Journal of Traumatic Stress, 12*, 663–671.

Motta, R. W., Joseph, J. M., Rose, R. D., Suozzi, J. M., & Leiderman, L. J. (1997). Secondary trauma: Assessing inter-generational transmission of war experience with a modified Stroop procedure. *Journal of Clinical Psychology, 53*, 895–903.

Mottaghy, F. M., Shah, N. J., Krause, B. J., Schmidt, D., Halsband, U., Jäncke, L., et al. (1999). Neuronal correlates of encoding and retrieval in episodic memory during a paired-word association learning task: A functional magnetic resonance imaging study. *Experimental Brain Research, 128*, 332–342.

Newcomer, J. W., Craft, S., Hershey, T., Askins, K., & Bardgett, M. E. (1994). Glucocorticoid-induced impairment in declarative memory performance in adult humans. *Journal of Neuroscience, 14*, 2047–2053.

Perkonigg, A., Kessler, R. C., Storz, S., & Wittchen, H. U. (2000). Traumatic events and post-traumatic stress disorder in the community: Prevalence, risk factors and comorbidity. *Acta Psychiatrica Scandinavica, 101*, 46–59.

Reed, J. M., & Squire, L. R. (1997). Impaired recognition memory in patients with lesions limited to the hippocampal formation. *Behavioral Neuroscience, 111*, 667–675.

Sapolsky, R. M., Uno, H., Rebert, C. S., & Finch, C. E. (1990). Hippocampal damage associated with prolonged glucocorticoid exposure in primates. *Journal of Neuroscience, 10*, 2897–2902.

Scoville, W. B., & Milner, B. (2000). Loss of recent memory after bilateral hippocampal lesions. 1957. *Journal of Neuropsychiatry and Clinical Neurosciences, 12*, 103–113.

Shimamura, A. P., Janowsky, J. S., & Squire, L. R. (1990). Memory for the temporal order of events in patients with frontal lobe lesions and amnesic patients. *Neuropsychologia, 28*, 803–813.

Shimamura, A. P., & Squire, L. R. (1984). Paired-associate learning and priming effects in amnesia: A neuropsychological study. *Journal of Experimental Psychology: General, 113*, 556–570.

Squire, L. R. (1992). Memory and the hippocampus: A synthesis from findings with rats, monkeys, and humans. *Psychology Review, 99*, 195–231.

Stein, M. B., Koverola, C., Hanna, C., Torchia, M. G., & McClarty, B. (1997). Hippocampal volume in women victimized by childhood sexual abuse. *Psychological Medicine, 27*, 951–959.

Sutker, P. B., Galina, Z. H., West, J. A., & Allain, A. N. (1990). Trauma-induced weight loss and cognitive deficits among former prisoners of war. *Journal of Consulting and Clinical Psychology, 58*, 323–328.

Sutker, P. B., Winstead, D. K., Galina, Z. H., & Allain, A. N. (1991). Cognitive deficits and psychopathology among former prisoners of war and combat veterans of the Korean conflict. *American Journal of Psychiatry, 148*, 67–72.

Svanum, S., & Schladenhauffen, J. (1986). Lifetime and recent alcohol consumption among male alcoholics: Neuropsychological implications. *Journal of Nervous and Mental Disease, 174*, 214–220.

Thrasher, S. M., Dalgleish, T., & Yule, W. (1994). Information processing in post-traumatic stress disorder. *Behaviour Research and Therapy, 32*, 247–254.

Ursano, R. J., Fullerton, C. S., Epstein, R. S., Crowley, B., Vance, K., Kao, T. C., at al. (1999). Peritraumatic dissociation and posttraumatic stress disorder following motor vehicle accidents. *American Journal of Psychiatry, 156*, 1808–1810.

Vasterling, J. J., Brailey, K., Constans, J. I., & Sutker, P. B. (1998). Attention and memory dysfunction in posttraumatic stress disorder. *Neuropsychology, 12*, 125–133.

Wolkowitz, O. M., Reus, V. I., Weingartner, H., Thompson, K., Breier, A., Doran, A., et al. (1990). Cognitive effects of corticosteroids. *American Journal of Psychiatry, 147*, 1297–1303.

Yehuda, R., & Harvey, P. (1997). Relevance of neuroendocrine alterations in PTSD to memory-related impairments of trauma survivors. In J. D. Read &

D. S. Lindsay (Eds.), *Recollections of trauma: Scientific evidence and clinical practice*. New York: Plenum Press.

Yehuda, R., Keefe, R. S., Harvey, P. D., Levengood, R. A., Gerber, D. K., Geni, J., et al. (1995). Learning and memory in combat veterans with posttraumatic stress disorder. *American Journal of Psychiatry, 152*, 137–139.

Zola-Morgan, S., & Squire, L. R. (1990). The neuropsychology of memory: Parallel findings in humans and nonhuman primates: Presented at the Conference of the National Institute of Mental Health, Philadelphia, PA, 1989. *Annals of the New York Academy of Science, 608*, 434–450.

CHAPTER 15

Growing Up under the Gun: Children and Adolescents Coping with Violent Neighborhoods

David F. Duncan

Fear of violence is robbing our children of their childhood.

—Bill Clinton

In a survey of 467 students attending a small, rural Midwestern high school, Weiler, Sliepcevich, and Sarvela (1994) found that 53 percent of the students worried about being murdered. Sixty-one percent reported that they were concerned about crime, 53 percent about family violence, 42 percent about terrorism, 37 percent about gang violence, and 37 percent about guns in school. And this was in a quiet, rural environment—far from the inner city and its violence.

America is a violent society, with a murder rate ten times higher than that of England and twenty-five times higher than Spain (Wolfgang, 1986). The National Research Council (1993) found that, "compared with 30 other industrialized countries, the United States has the highest rates of sexual assault and assault with force, and is third in homicide." Furthermore, U.S. teenagers are much more likely than adults to be victims of crimes of violence. The National Crime Survey (Whitaker & Bastian, 1991) showed that teenagers experienced 67 violent crimes per 1,000 teens each year, compared to a rate of 26 per 1,000 adults age 20 or older. In other words, teenagers were two and a half times as likely to be victims of violent crimes than were adults.

More than one-third (37%) of the violent crimes experienced by twelve- to fifteen-year-old victims took place at school, and another one-quarter on the street (Whitaker & Bastian, 1991). For victims aged 16 to 19, the most common location was the street (26%) followed by the school (17%) and public transit (13%). Bastian and Taylor (1991) report that nearly one student in ten reported being a victim of in-school crime during the six-month period of a national survey. Two percent reported a violent victimization and 7 percent a property crime.

Nearly four thousand American youths, age 18 and younger, die in a shooting each year (Christoffel, 1983). Another eight thousand are injured annually by firearms, and two thousand of those are left with permanent impairments (Rivara & Stapleton, 1982). Youths who live in the inner city, who are male, or who are black are much more likely to be victims of gunshot injuries and deaths (Abel, 1986; Christoffel, Anziger, & Merrill, 1989; Copeland, 1991).

In addition to being victims of violence, children and youth are frequent witnesses of violence in the community where they reside. Shakoor and Chalmers (1991) propose the term *co-victimization* for the traumatic experience of witnessing a violent assault on another person. A recent survey of a thousand elementary and secondary school students in Chicago found that more than one in four had witnessed a murder, nearly 40 percent had seen a shooting, and more than one-third had seen a stabbing (Garbarino, Dubrow, Kostelny, & Pardo, 1992). Bell and Jenkins (1991), in another study of Chicago children, found that 74 percent had witnessed a murder, a shooting, a stabbing, or a robbery and that 47 percent of these incidents had involved friends, classmates, family members, or neighbors.

Not surprisingly, inner-city children know more victims of violence and witness more assaults, rapes, and killings than do upper-middle-class youths (Gladstein, Rusonis, & Heald, 1992). A survey of inner-city first- and second-graders by Telljohan and Price (1994) found that 10 percent of the black and 1 percent of the white students reported having seen someone shot. Surprisingly, perhaps, that was true for 3 percent of the boys and 8 percent of the girls.

In a study of Boston public school students, 37 percent of the boys and 17 percent of the girls reported that they had carried a weapon to school at some time, with fear for their own safety as the major reason (Boston Committee on Safe Public Schools, 1983). This compares to national survey results showing that 3 percent of boys and 1 percent of girls had done so (Bastian & Taylor, 1991). The national survey showed a 1 percent rate in rural schools, 2 percent in suburban schools, and 3 percent in central city schools.

CHILDREN'S RESPONSES TO STRESS

Traumatic events, such as exposure to violence, may provoke a variety of responses in exposed children such as crying, tremors, withdrawal, and so on. In addition to causing such acute stress reactions, exposure to violence can result in more lasting symptoms, including sleep disturbances, nightmares, anxiety, depression, and recurrent intrusive memories of the traumatic event. If enough of these symptoms occur in combination and persist for at least a month, a diagnosis of posttraumatic stress disorder (PTSD) may be applied.

PTSD is described by the American Psychiatric Association's *Diagnostic and Statistical Manual of Mental Disorders* (1994, p. 424) as being a characteristic set of symptoms following exposure to an extreme traumatic stressor. These characteristic symptoms include persistent reexperiencing of the traumatic experience, persistent avoidance of stimuli associated with the trauma, a paradoxical mixture of numbing of general responsiveness and symptoms of increased arousal, and clinically significant distress or impairment in social, occupational, or other important aspects of life. The reexperiencing of the trauma may include nightmares, intrusive memories of the event, or in some cases, reliving the experience for anywhere from several minutes to several hours. Other symptoms frequently observed in PTSD victims include irritability and outbursts of anger, difficulty falling asleep, and a sense of being alienated from those around one.

Terr (1979) studied the twenty-six Chowchilla, California, school children whose school bus was hijacked and buried by kidnappers in a much-publicized case. Her study revealed that all of the children were suffering from PTSD. A follow-up four years later (Terr, 1983) still showed signs of PTSD and a preoccupation with death and self-preservation in all twenty-six children.

Pynoos et al. (1987) studied 159 children attending a Los Angeles school that had been attacked by a sniper. They found that one month after the attack more than half of the children showed symptoms of PTSD. At a fourteen-month follow-up, those children who were not directly exposed to the shooting showed diminished symptoms, while those children who had been near the shooting or had known one of the victims continued to show severe symptoms. Pynoos and colleagues found that factors which increase the likelihood of PTSD in childhood witnesses of violence include being physically close to the violence, knowing the victim, and previous exposure to violence.

Susceptibility to PTSD is related to age-specific developmental issues (Lyons, 1987). Adolescents are more susceptible to psychological trauma than are young adults (van der Kolk, 1987), and preadolescents are more vulnerable than adolescents (Davidson & Smith, 1990), while for preschool children, the distress and poor functioning in response to trauma often end once the trauma is over (Maccoby, 1983). For these very young children, emotional well-being is so strongly tied to the here and now that in most cases, once the cause of distress is removed, their distress quickly dissipates (Nolen-Hoeksema, 1992).

Pynoos and Nader (1988) have concluded that the effects of repeated exposures to violence are additive, with each exposure tending to exacerbate or renew symptoms caused by earlier exposures. Chronic trauma, such as that associated with living in a violent neighborhood, can produce particularly severe reactions. Even the young child will be likely to develop long-term effects if the trauma causing the distress is a chronic situation (Nolen-Hoeksema, 1992).

In addition to PTSD and similar responses, another common outcome is for the child who has been chronically exposed to violence to later become a violent individual. The literature on victimization leading to violence has been reviewed by Widom (1989a, 1989b). Based on visits to war zones around the world and on observations in the inner city of

Chicago, Garbarino, Kostelny, and Dubrow (1991) identify the common results of children being exposed to chronic violence as being a triad of increased aggressiveness, violent revenge seeking, and apathy and despair about the future.

A cross-sectional study by DuRant, Cadenhead, Pendergrast, Slavens, and Linder (1994) of the use of violence by black adolescents in Atlanta showed that previous exposure to violence and victimization was the strongest predictor of use of violence by those teens. The same study also identified resiliency factors that made some violence-exposed youths less likely to engage in violence themselves. These protective factors were: lower levels of hopelessness, a sense of purpose in life, and a belief that they would still be alive at the age of 25. It might be said that those violence-exposed children who have escaped the third element of Garbarino et al.'s (1991) triad of effects are likely to also escape the other two.

Shakoor and Chalmers (1991) have hypothesized that poor school performance and impaired learning are symptoms of the trauma children suffer from witnessing violence. They suggest that high dropout rates and poor academic performance among inner-city African American youth are, in part, a result of such "co-victimization." In this view, the observation that African American males suffer greater academic difficulties than do females would be attributable to the fact that males both experience and witness more acts of violence than do females.

CHILDREN'S COPING WITH TRAUMA

While witnessing a shooting or stabbing would be highly upsetting to any child, vulnerability to PTSD and its effects varies from one child to another. Children are most likely to cope successfully if they have an internal locus of control (a belief that one is in control of his or her outcome), a strong sense of self-efficacy, and an optimistic and planful attitude toward the future (Bandura, 1986). Children with an external locus of control (a belief that something other than oneself controls one's outcomes), low self-efficacy, and a pessimistic outlook are most vulnerable to trauma. Unfortunately, children who are distressed over a period of time become pessimistic in their expectations for themselves and for the future (Nolen-Hoeksema, 1992), thus making them more vulnerable to the effects of further stress.

In her excellent review, Nolen-Hoeksema (1992) identifies three strategies whereby children can cope with uncontrollable stress:

1. Engaging in a cognitive reappraisal or reconstrual of the situation or of the child's role in that situation
2. Using positive imagery and distraction
3. Developing reasonable short-term goals

According to Horowitz (1973), any successful coping with traumatic stress involves both working through feelings about what has happened and developing a cognitive framework that can incorporate and possibly lend some meaning to the events that have occurred. Garbarino et al.

(1991) also emphasize the importance of the child's "processing" of the traumatic experience and developing a cognitive framework that makes sense of that experience. Each of these children needs to arrive at a personal interpretation of events that sustains and supports the child's sense of competence and trust (Anthony & Cohler, 1987; Wallach, 1993).

Studies of Palestinian children affected by the 1987 uprisings indicated that an ideological explanation of the conflict and a sense of being on the "right side" could buffer children from the negative effects of exposure to the violence (Baker, 1990; Garbarino et al., 1992). There can be a danger, however, of children who believe they are on the "right side" in ethnic or religious conflicts coming to adopt a fanatical ideology that not only contributes to the community violence but also impairs their long-term adjustment to the trauma (Garbarino et al., 1992). This could be a concern in some U.S. communities where violence occurs between gangs that have become virtual primary groups for their members or between rival ethnic groups.

Garbarino et al. (1992) use the term *positive revenge* to describe a commitment to positive change and caring for others that has been observed among some survivors of the "killing fields" of Cambodia. This particular cognitive framework has facilitated the emotional healing of many of the children exposed to the Khmer Rouge atrocities—children who typically have suffered a high prevalence of severe and persistent PTSD.

Another important coping strategy is the use of distraction and positive imagery. Provided that it does not lead to the extreme of complete denial of the stress and resulting emotional distress, temporary escape from the chronic trauma through behavioral distraction or cognitive distraction—doing something else or thinking about something else—can be a very positive strategy. Intense involvement in sports, television, videogames, and the like can help children to dampen the fear arising from life in a violent community.

Children with a rich fantasy life can find escape into fantasy from the violence in their real life, unless that violence is reflected in their fantasies. Even violent fantasies (and violent videogames) have some positive value since the child typically fantasizes being in control of the violence, triumphing over enemies, and thus achieving some sense of mastery and efficacy. Such fantasies may, however, contribute to later violent behavior on the part of some of these children.

Developing realistic plans for dealing with the violence in their lives is another important element in successful coping for children in these communities. These children typically have big, long-term goals. They want to get out of the inner city and live in a big house in the suburbs. They want to become a basketball superstar and buy a better life for themselves and their families. Such goals may be very worthwhile, but they can have no immediate resolution, and efforts to achieve them may have little immediate impact on the child's emotional adjustment.

These children need to learn how to translate their long-term goals of escape from the community into more limited short-term goals leading toward their ultimate objectives. This will not only increase the likelihood that they will achieve their long-term goals but will also build their sense of mastery and self-efficacy as they achieve their short-term ones. The boy who hopes to escape the inner city by becoming a basketball superstar, for instance, should be encouraged to focus on short-term goals such as getting on a local youth club team and improving his jump shot or passing.

Children can learn coping techniques by which they can deal with uncontrollable stresses such as living amid inner-city violence. These are techniques that can be taught and that children may readily learn. Helping children to master the techniques of reconstrual, distraction, and working toward attainable goals can keep them from being overwhelmed by their fear and frustration and can prevent the community violence from permanently affecting children's sense of themselves.

PARENTAL SUPPORT

A stable and safe family—in the sense that the family is not characterized by either violence or drug abuse—appears to be a child's best defense against the harms resulting from exposure to violence (Richters & Martinez, 1993). During the World War II bombing of British cities, for instance, it was observed that British children who stayed with their parents in the target cities were less troubled by the air raids than those children who had been sent to the relative safety of rural areas (Freud & Burlingham, 1943). Likewise, a follow-up study of Cambodian children who had survived the Khmer Rouge terror found that those who did not live with a family member were most apt to have developed PTSD as well as other mental disorders (Kinzie, Sack, Angell, Manson, & Rath, 1986).

Studies of children's coping with disasters have shown that open communication in families allows the parents to sympathize with the children's fears, to reassure them that their fears are normal, and to help them to understand the problems in their environment (Bloch, Perry, & Silber, 1956; Figley, 1983). The same is likely to be true for children faced with urban violence, but Nolen-Hoeksema warns that simply getting children to express their feelings may not be helpful if it does not lead to an appropriate parental response; where the child's parents feel powerless to respond, the child's expression of his or her fears "may not help and could even backfire" (1992, p. 184).

Parents who perceive themselves as being capable of coping with danger are better able to transmit a sense of security and confidence to their children (Baker, 1990). When parents provide a model of coping with danger, their children are likely to develop higher self-esteem and greater confidence in their own ability to cope (Scheinfeld, 1983). Parents who are involved in political or community action to combat violence, such as the low-income mothers observed by Dubrow and Garbarino (1989) who established a neighborhood system of "safe houses" for children, can simultaneously provide models of coping and a cognitive framework for dealing with violence.

Figley (1983) found that open, flexible communication could help families to develop such a cognitive framework, which he called a "healing theory"—a rational explanation of the reasons for the traumatic events that gives meaning to those events. Garbarino et al. (1992), however, warn that if this conceptual framework justifies violence, it may impede the children's moral development. They suggest that parents may facilitate their children's moral development, despite a violent environment, by discussing the moral implications of violent situations, taking into account the maturity of their child, and encouraging the child to move in the direction of such concepts as justice, compassion, and responsibility. Promoting altruism and concern for others can simultaneously promote moral development and provide the "healing theory."

Fostering open discussion of neighborhood dangers also gives parents the opportunity to teach safety practices to their children. At the same time, they can also enhance their children's self-esteem and self-efficacy by expressing confidence and pride in their children's ability to adopt such practices and take care of themselves.

A further important perspective on this subject is provided by the research of Baldwin et al. (1993). Seeking factors related to resiliency in children raised in high-risk environments, they found that the parenting practices which are most effective in advantaged families are not effective in disadvantaged families. They found that African American families tended to be more controlling, more critical, and more inclined to value conformity in their child-rearing practices than were white families. Furthermore, they found that these practices were associated with more positive life outcomes for disadvantaged children.

BARRIERS TO PARENTAL SUPPORT

There are a variety of reasons why parents may fail to provide the emotional support their children need in order to cope with community violence: Poor communications between parent and child may leave them unaware of the degree to which their children are exposed to violence. Some parents may have a general tendency to downplay the seriousness of their children's concerns. In other cases, parents may overlook their child's emotional needs while focusing exclusively on physical safety issues. Grief over the loss of another family member may paralyze some parents' ability to respond effectively to their children's needs.

Parents who lack a religious, philosophical, or political framework for giving meaning to their own experience of urban violence can do little to help their children make sense of the experiences of violence (Dubrow & Garbarino, 1989; Garbarino et al., 1992). Simply put, parents can't share with their children what they lack themselves. If they are still grasping for some means to make sense of the violence in their environment, they are less able to help their children find such meaning.

Parental or family pathology may also keep parents from being supportive of their children (Bloch et al., 1956; Pynoos & Nader, 1988). In these situations, family therapy may be necessary before parents can help their children to cope with violence. Patterns of family violence can only compound the negative effects of community violence.

Parents may attempt to protect their children from community violence by adopting very restrictive child-rearing strategies. Parents who forbid their children to play outdoors for fear of drive-by shootings may keep their children safer, but they also deprive them of normal growth experiences. The result is likely to be both impaired social and emotional growth of the child and evasion of or rebellion against parental authority. In order to maintain this protective restrictiveness, parents often feel compelled to adopt a punitive style of discipline, often including corporal punishment. This unfortunately has the effect of heightening aggression on the child's part and increasing the likelihood that they will be drawn into the community violence of gangs and the like.

FAMILY INTERVENTIONS

The most natural setting for preventive interventions for children is in their own families. Not surprisingly, a variety of family-centered strategies have been developed for these children.

Figley's (1983) approach is typical of family therapy models that treat the whole family. His model initially stresses educating the family about the effects of trauma. He then trains family members to be more effectively supportive of each other.

Lyons (1987) summarizes the elements of child-centered family interventions for children exposed to traumatic events. She notes, however, that systematic research has not yet been conducted that would demonstrate whether these interventions are effective or not. The key elements she identifies are:

1. The child is reexposed in imagination or role play to the traumatic event in a structured and supportive situation.
2. Significant adults in the child's life are taught to discuss the traumatic event openly and honestly with the child.
3. The child is helped to develop strategies for coping with danger and with PTSD symptoms.

Less widely reported are parent group approaches (Dubrow & Garbarino, 1989; Pynoos & Nader, 1988). These involve groups in which parents are taught about the consequences of trauma for their children and can discuss their fears and concerns for them. Effectiveness studies of these groups also are lacking. The effectiveness of such interventions is discussed in the general review of indirect treatment of children via parent training by Wright, Stroud, and Keenan (1993).

INTERVENTIONS IN THE SCHOOLS

Schools are in many ways a natural setting for the provision of interventions to help children to cope with the violence in their communities. Schools provide a setting in which professionals can have access to virtually all of the children of a community. Students can find an important support network in their classmates and school personnel.

Programs in the schools have more commonly addressed the primary prevention of violence by students. These efforts have included both educational interventions and environmental modifications.

Educational interventions have generally implemented all or part of the practice paradigm developed by Wodarski and Hedrick (1987), which consisted of conflict resolution skills, cognitive anger control, communication skills, and drug education. Page, Kitchin-Becker, Solovan, Golec, and Hebert (1992) review the major curricula that have been developed for such interventions. Effectiveness of these programs has not yet been established. A discussion of the most widely known of these curricula and of a wider context for prevention of violence is provided by Prothro-Stith and Weissman (1993).

Environmental modifications, such as metal detectors, visitor sign-ins, teachers monitoring halls, or security guards, have not been found to reduce violent victimizations significantly compared to those schools not taking such precautions (Bastian & Taylor, 1991). The students in schools with such precautions, however, were more likely to be fearful of school crime—increasing their risk of PTSD-type reactions. This is not unlike the finding of Norris and Kaniasty (1992) that widely advocated community crime prevention measures not only fail to reduce crime but may also increase fear of crime among residents affected by the prevention efforts.

Those school-based interventions for children exposed to violence that have been reported in the literature have for the most part been based on the assumption that the exposure to violence was a one-time event. Such interventions typically employ techniques of "debriefing" and "anticipatory guidance." Both techniques are most often conducted in a group setting. In debriefing, the children are encouraged to discuss the traumatic event in a supportive setting so that the feelings involved can be worked through and a cognitive framework for understanding the event and those feelings can be developed. In anticipatory guidance, the children are told what effects they may experience as a result of their traumatic experience and discuss or are advised on means of dealing with those effects.

Developing interventions to address chronic exposure to violence in inner-city communities will be much more difficult. Children who are suffering the cumulative effects of ongoing exposure to violence may experience greater difficulty in identifying or discussing the specific events that have placed them under stress. The use of debriefing techniques with such children may arouse intense feelings that cannot readily be dealt with by classroom teachers who are not trained therapists. Such debriefing may even undercut defenses, such as denial or distraction, that the child is using currently to cope with the violent life situation.

More appropriate interventions for these children might be focused on building the children's self-esteem and sense of self-efficacy. The curriculum described by Cowen, Wyman, Work, and Iker (1995) is an example of such an intervention that has positive preliminary results. Another approach might be to encourage the children to discuss and develop active strategies for protecting themselves from the dangers in their community.

The experience of groups for children of battered mothers may provide a useful model of groups developed for children suffering the trauma of being exposed to chronic violence. A book edited by Peled, Jaffe, and Edleson (1994) surveys innovative interventions in this area. They report that most group interventions for these children provide highly structured sessions with specific goals for relatively small numbers of children. Typical groups consisted of three to six children with one or two therapists. Techniques used in the groups include lectures, discussions, modeling, role-playing, art therapy, and "homework" assignments.

The typical goals of groups for children of battered mothers were to help the child participants to:

1. define violence and assign responsibility for violence
2. express their feelings, including anger
3. improve communication, problem-solving, and coping skills
4. increase their self-esteem
5. develop social support networks
6. develop personal safety plans
7. develop feelings of safety and trust in the group sessions

One of the few systematic evaluations of such a group to be found in the literature is that by Peled and Edleson (1992). They concluded that this sort of group succeeded in providing an environment in which the children felt safe, increasing their self-esteem, and allowing them to talk about their experience of violence—breaking the secret of family violence.

Secondary prevention is also an important approach that can be implemented in the schools. Teachers should be trained to identify children suffering from PTSD and related reactions to community violence, and the schools should have established referrals for such children.

CONCLUSION

Several million of our children are growing up in communities characterized by gang violence, drug wars, and drive-by shootings. Exposure to such violence on a chronic basis can produce serious emotional and behavioral problems in these children. Parents and schools can help children to cope with these conditions, but many parents and most schools are poorly equipped to provide these children with that help. Preparing parents and teachers to provide the necessary support should be one of the major primary prevention tasks for the decades ahead.

REFERENCES

Abel, E. L. (1986). Childhood homicide in Eric County, New York. *Pediatrics,* *77*(5), 709–713.

American Psychiatric Association. (1994). *Diagnostic and statistical manual of mental disorders* (4th ed.). Washington, DC: American Psychiatric Association.

Anthony, E. J., & Cohler, B. J. (Eds.). (1987). *The invulnerable child.* New York: Guilford Press.

Baker, A. M. (1990). The psychological impact of the Intifida on Palestinian children in the occupied West Bank and Gaza: An exploratory study. *American Journal of Orthopsychiatry, 60*(4), 496–505.

Baldwin, A. L., Baldwin, C. P., Kasser, T., Zax, M., Sameroff, A., & Seifer, R. (1993). Contextual risk and resiliency during late adolescence. *Development and Psychopathology, 5*(4), 741–761.

Bandura, A. (1986). *Social foundations of thought and action: A social cognitive theory.* Englewood Cliffs, NJ: Prentice-Hall.

Bastian, L. D., & Taylor, B. M. (1991). *School crime: A National Crime Victimization Survey report.* NCJ-131645. Washington, DC: U.S. Dept. of Justice, Office of Justice Programs, Bureau of Justice Statistics.

Bell, C. C., & Jenkins, E. J. (1991). Traumatic stress and children. *Journal of Health Care for the Poor and Underserved, 2,* 175–188.

Bloch, D. A., Perry, S. E., & Silber, E. (1956). Some factors in the emotional reactions of children to disaster. *American Journal of Psychiatry, 113*(5), 416–422.

Boston Committee on Safe Public Schools (1983). *Making our schools safe for learning.* Boston: Boston Public Schools.

Christoffel, K. K. (1983). American as apple pie: Guns in the lives of U.S. children and youth. *Pediatrician, 12,* 46–51.

Christoffel, K. K., Anzinger, N. K., & Merrill, D. A. (1989). Age-related patterns of violent death, Cook County, Illinois, 1977 through 1982. *American Journal of Diseases of Children, 143*(12), 1403–1409.

Copeland, A. R. (1991). Childhood firearms fatalities: The Metropolitan Dade County experience. *Southern Medical Journal, 84*(2), 175–178.

Cowen, E. L., Wyman, P. A., Work, W. C., & Iker, M. R. (1995). A preventive intervention for enhancing resilience among highly stressed urban children. *Journal of Primary Prevention, 15*(3), 247–260.

Davidson, J., & Smith, R. (1990). Traumatic experiences in psychiatric outpatients. *Journal of Traumatic Stress, 3*(3), 459–475.

Dubrow, N. F., & Garbarino, J. (1989). Living in the war zone: Mothers and young children in a public housing development. *Child Welfare, 68,* 3–20.

DuRant, R. H., Cadenhead, C., Pendergrast, R. A., Slavens, G., & Linder, C. W. (1994). Factors associated with the use of violence among urban black adolescents. *American Journal of Public Health, 84*(4), 612–617.

Figley, C. R. (1983). Catastrophes: An overview of family reactions. In C. R. Figley & H. I. McCubbin (Eds.), *Stress and the family,* Vol. 2, *Coping with catastrophe* (pp. 3–20). New York: Brunner/Mazel.

Freud, A., & Burlingham, D. T. (1943). *War and children.* New York: Medical War Books, Willard.

Garbarino, J., Dubrow, N., Kostelny, K., & Pardo, C. (1992). *Children in danger.* San Francisco: Jossey-Bass.

Garbarino, J., Kostelny, K., & Dubrow, N. (1991). What children can tell us about living in danger. *American Psychologist, 46*(4), 376–383.

Gladstein, J., Rusonis, E. J., & Heald, F. P. (1992). A comparison of inner-city and upper-middle-class youths' exposure to violence. *Journal of Adolescent Health, 13*(4), 275–280.

Horowitz, M. J. (1973). Phase oriented treatment of stress response syndromes. *American Journal of Psychotherapy, 27*(4), 506–515.

Kinzie, J. D., Sack, W. H., Angell, R. H., Manson, S. M., & Rath, R. (1986). The psychiatric effects of massive trauma on Cambodian children. *Journal of the American Academy of Child Psychiatry, 25*(3), 370–376.

Lyons, J. A. (1987). Posttraumatic stress disorder in children and adolescents: A review of the literature. *Journal of Developmental and Behavioral Pediatrics, 8*(6), 349–356.

Maccoby, E. E. (1983). Social-emotional development and response to stressors. In N. Garmezy & M. Rutter (Eds.), *Stress, coping, and development in children* (pp. 217–234). New York: McGraw-Hill.

National Research Council (1993). *Losing generations: Adolescents in high-risk settings.* Washington, DC: National Academy Press.

Nolen-Hoeksema, S. (1992). Children coping with uncontrollable stressors. *Applied & Preventive Psychology, 1*(4), 183–189.

Norris, F. H., & Kaniasty, K. (1992). A longitudinal study of the effects of various crime prevention strategies on criminal victimization, fear of crime, and psychological distress. *American Journal of Community Psychology, 20*(5), 625–648.

Page, R. M., Kitchin-Becker, S., Solovan, D., Golec, T. L., & Hebert, D. L. (1992). Interpersonal violence: A priority issue for health education. *Journal of Health Education, 23*(5), 286–292.

Peled, E., & Edleson, J. L. (1992). Multiple perspectives on groupwork with children of battered women. *Violence and Victims, 7*(4), 327–346.

Peled, E., Jaffe, P. G., Edleson, J. L. (Eds.). (1994). Ending the cycle of violence: Community responses to children of battered women. Thousand Oaks, CA: Sage.

Prothro-Stith, D., & Weissman, M. (1993). *Deadly consequences.* New York: Harper Perennial.

Pynoos, R. S., Frederick, C., Nader, K., Arroyo, W., Steinberg, A., Eth, S., et al. (1987). Life threat and posttraumatic stress in school-age children. *Archives of General Psychiatry, 44*(12), 1057–1063.

Pynoos, R. S., & Nader, K. (1988). Psychological first aid and treatment approach to children exposed to community violence: Research implications. *Journal of Traumatic Stress, 1*(4), 445–473.

Richters, J. E., & Martinez, P. E. (1993). Violent communities, family choices, and children's chances: An algorithm for improving the odds. *Development and Psychopathology, 5*(4), 609–627.

Rivara, F. P., & Stapleton, F. B. (1982). Handguns and children: A dangerous mix. *Journal of Developmental and Behavioral Pediatrics, 3*, 35–38.

Scheinfeld, D. R. (1983). Family relationships and school achievement among boys of lower-income urban black families. *American Journal of Orthopsychiatry, 53*, 127–143.

Shakoor, B. H., & Chalmers, D. (1991). Co-victimization of African-American children who witness violence: Effects on cognitive, emotional, and behavioral development. *Journal of the National Medical Association, 83*(3), 233–238.

Telljohan, S. K., & Price, J. H. (1994). A preliminary investigation of inner city primary grade students' perceptions of guns. *Journal of Health Education, 25*, 41–46.

Terr, L. C. (1979). Children of Chowchilla: A study of psychic trauma. *Psychoanalytic Study of the Child, 34*, 547–623.

Terr, L. C. (1983). Chowchilla revisited: The effects of psychic trauma four years after a school-bus kidnapping. *American Journal of Psychiatry, 140*(12), 1543–1550.

Van der Kolk, B. A. (1987). *Psychological trauma.* Washington, DC: American Psychiatric Press.

Wallach, L. B. (1993). Helping children cope with violence. *Young Children,* May, 4–11.

Weiler, R. M., Sliepcevich, E. M., & Sarvela, P. D. (1994). Adolescents' concerns as reported by adolescents, teachers and parents. *Health Values, 18*(2), 50–62.

Whitaker, C. J., & Bastian, L. D. (1991). *Teenage victims: A National Crime Survey report.* NCJ–128129. Washington, DC: U.S. Department of Justice, Bureau of Justice Statistics.

Widom, C. S. (1989a). The cycle of violence. *Science, 244*(4901), 160–166.

Widom, C. S. (1989b). Does violence beget violence? A critical examination of the literature. *Psychological Bulletin, 106*, 3–28.

Wodarski, J. S., & Hedrick, M. (1987). Violent children: A practice paradigm. *Social Work in Education*, Fall, 24–42.

Wolfgang, M. E. (1986). Homicide in other industrialized countries. *Bulletin of the New York Academy of Medicine, 62*(5), 400–412.

Wright, L., Stroud, R., & Keenan, M. (1993). Indirect treatment of children via parent training: A burgeoning form of secondary prevention. *Applied & Preventive Psychology, 2*, 191–200.